Y0-CAI-893

Professional ASP.NET Performance

Scott Allen

James Avery

James Greenwood

Matt Ohdner

Andrew Reid

Doug Thews

Wrox Press Ltd. ®

Professional ASP.NET Performance

© 2002 Wrox Press

All rights reserved. No part of this book may be reproduced, stored in a retrieval system or transmitted in any form or by any means, without the prior written permission of the publisher, except in the case of brief quotations embodied in critical articles or reviews.

The authors and publisher have made every effort in the preparation of this book to ensure the accuracy of the information. However, the information contained in this book is sold without warranty, either express or implied. Neither the authors, Wrox Press, nor its dealers or distributors, will be held liable for any damages caused or alleged to be caused either directly or indirectly by this book.

First Printed November 2002

Published by Wrox Press Ltd.,
Arden House, 1102 Warwick Road, Acocks Green,
Birmingham, B27 6BH
United Kingdom
Printed in the United States of America
ISBN 1-86100-755-8

Trademark Acknowledgements

Wrox has endeavored to provide trademark information about all the companies and products mentioned in this book by the appropriate use of capitals. However, Wrox cannot guarantee the accuracy of this information.

Credits

Authors
Scott Allen
James Avery
James Greenwood
Matt Ohdner
Andrew Reid
Doug Thews

Technical Reviewers
Paul Churchill
Damien Foggon
Mark Horner
Shefali Kulkarni
Sophie McQueen
David Schultz

Managing Editor
Louay Fatoohi

Commissioning Editor
Daniel Kent

Technical Editors
Helen Callaghan
Devin Lunsford
Douglas Paterson
Julian Skinner

Project Manager
Charlotte Smith

Production Coordinator
Sarah Hall

Cover
Natalie O' Donnell

Indexer
Andrew Criddle

Proofreader
Helena Sharman

About the Authors

Scott Allen

Scott Allen received a Master's degree in computer science from Shippensburg University in Pennsylvania, and began writing real time embedded software, numerical analysis algorithms, and serial communication protocols for a leading manufacturer of near infrared spectroscopy instruments. More recently, Scott has been involved in designing and implementing highly scalable Internet applications. This includes using XML and Web Services to integrate C++ COM components into the J2EE based enterprise application of a Fortune 50 company. Scott currently works with Butterfly.Net, a production studio, online publisher, and technology provider for massively multiplayer games that connect PCs, consoles, and mobile devices.

Scott holds an MCSD certification and regularly serves as an adjunct faculty member at several colleges in the Maryland and Pennsylvania areas. Scott lives in Hagerstown, Maryland with his wife Vicky, and sons Alex and Christopher. You can reach him as bitmask@fred.net.

I'd like to dedicate this work to the engineering team of the former Ultraprise Corporation, the finest and brightest collection of professionals I've had the pleasure of working with.

I consider those three years a fabulous success based on what I learned about software, and about opportunity, but mostly on the friends I made.

James Avery

James Avery works as a web application developer for an international imaging company developing applications using ASP.NET and C#. James got started working with ASP.NET and the .NET Framework early in the beta stages and has since switched all of his development to ASP.NET and C#.

James maintains a column at www.aspalliance.com/jamesavery where you can find helpful articles on many subjects. You can also find him on the AspFriends.com lists where he helps with moderation and development.

You can contact James Avery at jamesavery@aspalliance.com

I would like to dedicate my work in this book to Tammy Glasgow, the love of my life. It is only through her love and support (and patience!) that any of this is possible. I love you!

James Greenwood

James Greenwood is a technical architect and author based in West Yorkshire, England. He spends his days (and most of his nights) designing and implementing .NET solutions from Government knowledge-management systems to mobile integration platforms, all the while waxing lyrical on the latest Microsoft technologies. His professional interests include research into distributed interfaces, the automation of application development, and human-machine convergence.

When not at the keyboard, James can be found out and about, indulging in his other great loves – British sports cars and Egyptology. James can be reached at jsg@altervisitor.com.

Matt Ohdner

Matt Odhner is a Program Manager on the Server Manager team at Microsoft. He joined Microsoft in 1993 and managed the development of the Web Application Stress tool while working as a test lead in Microsoft's IT department. Matt also managed the product group responsible for developing Application Center Test shipped in Visual Studio .NET. In his free time Matt enjoys playing drums in a local Seattle rock band, taking care of his multiple fish tanks, and painting.

Andrew Reid

Andrew studied Software Engineering at The University of Sheffield. Upon finishing, he founded a consultancy providing internet-based solutions focusing on the travel industry. Since then, he has worked as Technical Architect at one of the UK's most successful e-commerce sites as well as a mobile application start-up using .NET technologies.

Doug Thews

Doug Thews is the Director of Software Development for D&D Consulting Services. He has over 18 years of software development experience, ranging from assembly language development for the F-16 fighter aircraft avionics system, to real-time platform management systems written exclusively for .NET.

Currently, Doug focuses 100% of his efforts on the development of client solutions targeted for the .NET Framework. He has written development articles for Visual Studio Magazine, MSDN Online, and presented as part of the VB.NET keynote address at VSLive! and TechEd. Doug now spends the majority of his time evangelizing the .NET platform, and working on developing .NET applications for Win32, web, and mobile clients.

Doug lives in Colleyville, Texas with his beautiful wife of 15 years, Dana, and daughter Stefanie. When not developing or writing, Doug enjoys playing golf, working with all the latest beta technology, watching his beloved Athletics and Dolphins and attempting to "survive" the world of online gaming. You can contact Doug at DougThews@ddconsult.com.

> First, I would like to thank my lovely wife, Dana, who has been with me throughout all of the tough breaks that we've had the fortune to survive over the past 9 years. Without you, I wouldn't be here today to write this book. You are my love, my partner and my best friend. I love you!
>
> I would also like to thank the development team at Divine Managed Services. You guys are the best team I've ever had the pleasure to work with. You all rock!
>
> Lastly, to my Dad, Dr. Robert L. Thews. I want to thank you for setting me on the path to what has been a very exciting and rewarding career. I want you to know how much your guidance has meant to me throughout my life, and that I am very proud to be called your son. I dedicate my contributions to this book to you.

Table of Contents

Table of Contents

Table of Contents

Table of Contents

Professional ASP.NET Performance Professional ASP.NET Perfor
ssional ASP.NET Performance Professional ASP.NET Perfor
ssional ASP.NET Performance Professional ASP.NET Perfor
ssional ASP.NET Performance Professional ASP.NET Perfor
ssional ASP.NET Performance Professional ASP.NET Perfor
ssional ASP.NET Performance Professional ASP.NET Perfor
ssional ASP.NET Performance Professional ASP.NET Perfor
ssional ASP.NET Performance Professional ASP.NET Perfor
ssional ASP.NET Performance Professional ASP.NET Perfor
ssional ASP.NET Performance Professional ASP.NET Perfor
ssional ASP.NET Performance Professional ASP.NET Perfor
ssional ASP.NET Performance Professional ASP.NET Perfor
ssional ASP.NET Performance Professional ASP.NET Perfor
ssional ASP.NET Performance Professional ASP.NET Perfor
ssional ASP.NET Performance Professional ASP.NET Perfor
ssional ASP.NET Performance Professional ASP.NET Perfor
ssional ASP.NET Performance Professional ASP.NET Perfor
ssional ASP.NET Performance Professional ASP.NET Perfor
ssional ASP.NET Performance Professional ASP.NET Perfor
ssional ASP.NET Performance Professional ASP.NET Perfor
ssional ASP.NET Performance Professional ASP.NET Perfor
ssional ASP.NET Performance Professional ASP.NET Perfor
ssional ASP.NET Performance Professional ASP.NET Perfor
ssional ASP.NET Performance Professional ASP.NET Perfor

Introduction

If you want to build ASP.NET applications that run as quickly as possible, that can scale to process a greater number of simultaneous users, but can also appear to the user to be running quickly, then this is the book for you.

In this book, we will look at the many different aspects of improving the performance of ASP.NET applications – designing, coding, testing, and monitoring.

We begin with a discussion of what performance is, and why it's important. Next we look at the important idea of *perceived* performance – after all, no matter how many statistics you have that suggest your application is racing along, if the user feels that your site isn't performing well, then put simply, it isn't. We then move on to look at coding for superior performance, and improving your data performance. The next part of the book deals with testing your application, and producing measurable results about the performance of both the application and the web server, under conditions that simulate the workload you expect from your users in production.

What does this Book Cover?

Chapter 1 starts us off with an overview of *what* performance is, *why* we should care about performance, and how we can ensure that we develop a site that performs as well as required. We also look at the distinction between performance and scalability, at the methods of scaling a site, and at how developments throughout the lifecycle of a project can affect the end result. We also introduce the concept of "performance as a process" – how we need to think about performance throughout the project's lifecycle from the initial requirements to the moment when the site goes live, and beyond.

In Chapter 2 we begin by looking at the ways in which we can make performance savings through ASP.NET page coding. Talking initially about the page itself, the chapter examines the performance savings that can be made by managing state and security, and then goes on to look at the different types of controls and their associated issues. Last of all, it considers the @Page directive properties and their impact on page performance.

Chapter 3 deals with managing user expectations of performance, starting with setting expectations for performance at the design stage, including the usefulness of static as opposed to dynamic content. It then goes on to discuss the importance of designing scalable objects, separating the UI from the business model, and the essentials of UI design. This chapter discusses methods for integrating content with external systems and at the same time managing perceived performance, as they relate to .NET Remoting, Web Services, and integration with COM components. Finally, it tackles the issue of perceived performance during background processing, and suggests ways that this might be managed.

In Chapter 4, we cover guidelines and examples for writing high performance code in the .NET environment. We often measure the performance of code by the amount of time it takes to complete a task for a single user. There are times when you can choose a technique or algorithm to improve both the performance and scalability of an application, but there are also times when these two goals are at odds with each other. In this chapter, we will look at such things as conserving resources, improving performance with caching, the effective use of collections and value types, and using the Trace functionality to gauge the time taken for actions on a page.

In Chapter 5 we look at improving the performance of our data-handling; data access, manipulation and presentation. We'll look at how to improve our data-handling with the .NET Framework, and also how to improve the underlying database. We'll cover such things as the choice between the data reader and the DataSet, data binding optimizations and working with strings and XML. We'll also see how to craft more effective queries, make use of stored procedures and improve the performance of the database itself with such things as careful choice of indexes.

Before we deploy our web application, it needs to be appropriately tested – tested with the workload that we are expecting when it has been fully deployed. In Chapter 6 we look at a free utility from Microsoft called the Web Application Stress Tool. With this tool we can simulate a large number of users hitting our site, and then examine the performance of our application and the performance of our web server, although our focus in the chapter is more on the performance of the web server. We take an in-depth look at the WAS tool, and then move on to some further examples of how we can use the tool to test and improve our applications.

The next chapter sees us take a tour of Microsoft's Application Center Test (also known as ACT) – it's designed to simulate multiple web clients making simultaneous HTTP requests to a web server, allowing you to optimize performance by reproducing the behavior of your application under the expected load of the live data center. In the chapter we look at the differences between ACT and WAS, testing ASP.NET applications and Web Services with ACT, and working with cookies, authentication, and other useful ACT hints.

In the final chapter of the book we turn to monitoring the performance of our web applications. Although we may have tested our application before deployment, there is still a need to continue monitoring the performance of our application and servers when they are in production. In the chapter we look at two ways to keep track of our application's performance – Performance Monitor and Performance Counters. We look at how to accurately monitor and diagnose both ASP.NET applications and the system as a whole – we look at how to use the default ASP.NET performance counters to monitor and improve the performance of our ASP.NET applications, create custom performance counters and how to access and use performance counters directly from our ASP.NET applications.

Who is this Book For?

This book is for ASP.NET developers, with a good working knowledge of ASP.NET and Visual Basic .NET, who need to understand of all aspects of building ASP.NET applications that perform well.

This book is aimed at developers who have learned about .NET, and in particular ASP.NET. It would be advisable to have already read *Professional ASP.NET 1.0 Special Edition* (ISBN 1-86100-703-5) also published by Wrox Press.

> **Since the syntax and code examples in this book are coded in Visual Basic .NET, knowledge of that programming language is assumed.**

What do you Need to Use this Book?

A prerequisite for this book is to have a machine with the .NET Framework installed upon it. This means that you'll need to be running either Windows 2000 Professional (or better), or Windows XP Professional, with IIS installed.

The use of Visual Studio .NET Professional (or higher) is also recommended.

Chapter 7 requires the Application Center Test tool that ships with Visual Studio .NET Enterprise Developer and Visual Studio .NET Enterprise Architect editions, and so you will need to have one of these editions to get full value from the chapter.

Chapter 5, Developing for Data Performance, requires a database server – though it can be on the same physical machine as your .NET Framework installation. The database server we use in the book is Microsoft SQL Server 2000.

The sample files can be downloaded from http://www.wrox.com/.

Conventions

We've used a number of different styles of text and layout in this book to help differentiate between different kinds of information. Here are examples of the styles we used and an explanation of what they mean.

Code has several fonts. If it's a word that we're talking about in the text – for example, when discussing a for (...) loop, it's in this font. If it's a block of code that can be typed as a program and run, then it's also in a gray box:

```
Dim sqlConnection As New SqlConnection()
```

Sometimes we'll see code in a mixture of styles, like this:

```
Private Sub Page_Load(ByVal sender As System.Object, _
        ByVal e As System.EventArgs)
```

```
    If Not IsPostBack Then
      Dim done As Boolean
      done = FillData()
      If done Then
        literal1.Text = "Data loaded successfully"
      End If
    End If

  End Sub
```

In cases like this, the code with a white background is code we are already familiar with; the line highlighted in gray is a new addition to the code since we last looked at it.

Advice, hints, and background information comes in this type of font.

> **Important pieces of information come in boxes like this.**

Bullets appear indented, with each new bullet marked as follows:

- ❑ **Important Words** are in a bold type font.

- ❑ Words that appear on the screen, or in menus like Open or Close, are in a similar font to the one you would see on a Windows desktop.

- ❑ Keys that you press on the keyboard, like *Ctrl* and *Enter*, are in italics.

Customer Support

We always value hearing from our readers, and we want to know what you think about this book: what you liked, what you didn't like, and what you think we can do better next time. You can send us your comments, either by returning the reply card in the back of the book, or by e-mail to feedback@wrox.com. Please be sure to mention the book title in your message.

How to Download the Sample Code for the Book

When you visit the Wrox site, http://www.wrox.com/, simply locate the title through our Search facility or by using one of the title lists. Click on Download in the Code column, or on Download Code on the book's details page.

When you click to download the code for this book, you are presented with a page with three options:

- ❑ If you are already a member of the Wrox Developer Community (if you have already registered on ASPToday, C#Today, or Wroxbase), you can log in with your usual username and password combination to receive your code.

- ❑ If you are not already a member, you are asked if you would like to register for free code downloads. In addition you will also be able to download several free articles from Wrox Press. Registering will allow us to keep you informed about updates and new editions of this book.

❑   The third option is to bypass registration completely and simply download the code.

Registration for code download is not mandatory for this book, but should you wish to register for your code download, your details will not be passed to any third party. For more details, you may wish to view our terms and conditions, which are linked from the download page.

Once you reach the code download section, you will find that the files that are available for download from our site have been archived using WinZip. When you have saved the files to a folder on your hard drive, you will need to extract the files using a de-compression program such as WinZip or PKUnzip. When you extract the files, the code is usually extracted into chapter folders. When you start the extraction process, ensure your software (WinZip, PKUnzip, etc.) is set to use folder names.

Errata

We've made every effort to take sure that there are no errors in the text or in the code. However, no one is perfect and mistakes do occur. If you find an error in one of our books, like a spelling mistake or a faulty piece of code, we would be very grateful for feedback. By sending in errata you may save another reader hours of frustration, and of course, you will be helping us provide even higher quality information. Simply e-mail the information to support@wrox.com; your information will be checked and if correct, posted to the errata page for that title, or used in subsequent editions of the book.

To find errata on the web site, go to http://www.wrox.com/, and simply locate the title through our Advanced Search or title list. Click on the Book Errata link, which is below the cover graphic on the book's detail page.

E-mail Support

If you wish to directly query a problem in the book with an expert who knows the book in detail then e-mail support@wrox.com, with the title of the book and the last four numbers of the ISBN in the subject field of the e-mail. A typical e-mail should include the following things:

❑   The **title of the book, last four digits of the ISBN** (7558), and **page number** of the problem in the Subject field.

❑   Your **name**, **contact information**, and the **problem** in the body of the message.

We won't send you junk mail. We need the details to save your time and ours. When you send an e-mail message, it will go through the following chain of support:

❑   Customer Support – Your message is delivered to our customer support staff, who are the first people to read it. They have files on most frequently asked questions and will answer anything general about the book or the web site immediately.

❑   Editorial – Deeper queries are forwarded to the technical editor responsible for that book. They have experience with the programming language or particular product, and are able to answer detailed technical questions on the subject.

❑   The Authors – Finally, in the unlikely event that the editor cannot answer your problem, they will forward the request to the author. We do try to protect the author from any distractions to their writing; however, we are quite happy to forward specific requests to them. All Wrox authors help with the support on their books. They will e-mail the customer and the editor with their response, and again all readers should benefit.

The Wrox Support process can only offer support to issues that are directly pertinent to the content of our published title. Support for questions that fall outside the scope of normal book support is provided via the community lists of our http://p2p.wrox.com/ forum.

p2p.wrox.com

For author and peer discussion join the P2P mailing lists. Our unique system provides **programmer to programmer™** contact on mailing lists, forums, and newsgroups, all in addition to our one-to-one e-mail support system. If you post a query to P2P, you can be confident that it is being examined by the many Wrox authors and other industry experts who are present on our mailing lists. At p2p.wrox.com you will find a number of different lists that will help you, not only while you read this book, but also as you develop your own applications.

To subscribe to a mailing list just follow these steps:

1. Go to http://p2p.wrox.com/.

2. Choose the appropriate category from the left menu bar.

3. Click on the mailing list you wish to join.

4. Follow the instructions to subscribe and fill in your e-mail address and password.

5. Reply to the confirmation e-mail you receive.

6. Use the subscription manager to join more lists and set your e-mail preferences.

Why this System Offers the Best Support

You can choose to join the mailing lists or you can receive them as a weekly digest. If you don't have the time, or facility, to receive the mailing list, then you can search our online archives. Junk and spam mails are deleted, and your own e-mail address is protected by the unique Lyris system. Queries about joining or leaving lists, and any other general queries about lists, should be sent to listsupport@p2p.wrox.com.

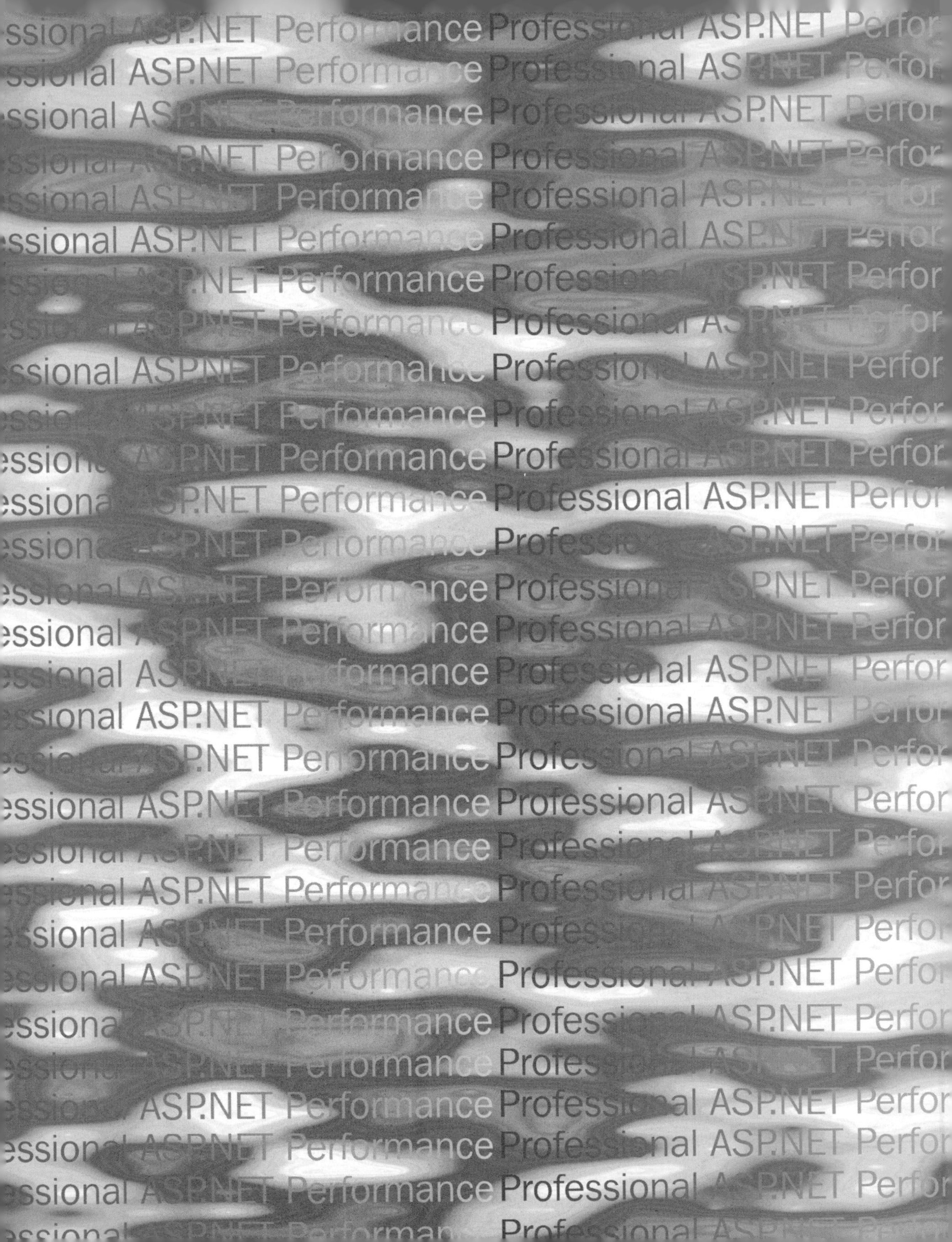
ssional ASP.NET Performance Professional ASP.NET Perfor

What is Performance?

No matter how good your ASP.NET application, or how many cool new features you've added to your web site, it won't impress your users if they have to wait even for a few seconds while it processes their requests. In fact, if they have to wait too long, they'll just give up and go to another site instead. In this book, we'll look at the many different aspects to improving the performance (and, probably more importantly, the *perceived* performance) of ASP.NET – how to ensure that the application runs as quickly as possible, that the application can scale to process a greater number of simultaneous users, and also that the application not only runs quickly, but also *appears* to the user to be running quickly. We'll also look at the different tools and methods for analyzing performance and for testing the scalability of our applications, so that we can identify (and therefore alleviate) the bottlenecks in our system.

In this introductory chapter, we'll take an overview of *what* performance is, *why* we should care about performance, and how we can ensure that we develop a site that performs as well as required. We'll also look at the distinction between performance and scalability (the ability of the site to process multiple requests simultaneously without degrading performance too severely), and at the methods of scaling a site, and how developments throughout the lifecycle of a project can affect the end result. Finally, we'll introduce the concept of "performance as a process" – how we need to think about performance throughout the project's lifecycle from the initial requirements to the moment when the site goes live, and beyond.

Why Does Performance Matter?

Before we go on to look in detail about what we mean by "performance", and introduce briefly some of the ways we can measure it, let's first take a moment to consider *why* performance is so important – probably second only to how a site functions. A poorly performing site is not a usable site, and you'll soon find that potential customers are voting with their feet if your site is too slow.

From the End-User Perspective

Visiting a web site that does not respond as you want it to is frustrating. How many times have you filled in a form and hit a submit button only for the site to sit there, churning away without responding? More than likely on the web, where you are just one click away from somewhere else, you leave. Usability experts (check out Jacob Nielson at www.useit.com) tell us that site response times are one of the most important factors in ensuring site usability. General guidelines are that 10 seconds is the maximum time that people are prepared to wait for a page to download. Any longer than this and people will start to get bored and move on. Obviously, the faster the site, the less people will move on before a page has downloaded. If you're operating an e-commerce site, this has a direct impact on your turnover.

From a user's perspective, no matter what else a web site offers – fantastic design with magnificent visual effects, great products at cut-down prices with next-day delivery, or quality information – if the site performance is not acceptable, all the other hard work will be wasted. However, there's obviously a trade-off here – there's no point spending $1 million ensuring fantastic scalability and performance, if the site only generates an extra $500,000.

The Economic Case

A high-performance web site can also reduce costs and add value. Despite falling hardware costs and improving performance, it always makes sense to ensure that high performance software makes the best, most efficient use of hardware. As well as the initial cost of purchasing hardware, the total ongoing cost of ownership should be considered. This includes the personnel costs of maintaining and monitoring it, hosting costs, licensing costs, connectivity costs, and power consumption costs. Out of these, licensing costs now often overshadow hardware costs.

Let's just do the sums for a moment and see how much poor performance can cost. Consider two web sites, site A and site B. Site A has been designed using best practices throughout. The site is highly optimized, uses caching where appropriate and is highly scalable. The other site has been developed in an ad hoc manner with little or no quality control. One server can handle 1,200 concurrent users on a single server for site A, and scales well. Site B on the other hand, can only handle 300 concurrent users per server, and scales badly.

Assume that the site needs to handle 3,000 concurrent users at peak usage. Assume also that software licensing costs are $5,000 per server, that the servers themselves cost $3,000 and that power, hosting and connectivity costs per unit of rack space are $250 per year.

❑   Site A requires three servers, so the cost for the first year is $24,750.

❑   Site B, because it does not scale as well, requires 15 servers, at a cost for the first year of $123,750. The difference is five-fold, over 500% more expensive for the poorly designed, poorly performing site. This figure doesn't include the costs of installing, configuring or maintaining the additional servers (or of the space required to house them).

With three servers, site A handles the peak usage comfortably. Site B however, is on the limits of its ability to scale, and if usage moved above 3,000 concurrent users, its performance would start to degrade. Adding new servers to a site at this point brings diminishing returns because the database has started to become a bottleneck. With Site A, however, one or more additional servers would be all that's needed to keep handling more traffic. Site B, through its poor performance and inability to scale, has not only been costly, but has also placed a limitation on the ability of the business to expand.

The following figure shows the general pattern – although Site B was cheaper to develop, the costs quickly ramp up, and the poor scalability soon restricts further development. The costs of Site A, in contrast, remain relatively steady, so it quickly provides better value for money:

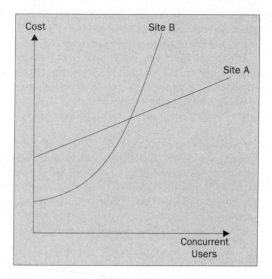

A site that has been carefully developed to make good use of hardware, for which performance metrics and its ability to scale is known, is extremely valuable – and reduces costs.

Ability to Grow

The ability of a site to grow with a business is critical. If a site can't expand to cope with the growing demands of a business, whether it is internal or external, it will limit the business. This shows how critical it is to ensure that scalability and performance concerns are taken seriously.

What Does Performance Mean?

Performance denotes the speed and efficiency with which the system performs its tasks. There are many different ways to look at the performance of a web site. The most important factor in web site performance must be *how it appears to the user*. This is where web performance becomes interesting because performance over the web is subject to many different interpretations. A user on a 500K ADSL broadband connection could view a particular web site as very responsive and high performance, whereas a user on a standard 56K modem connection could view that same web site as nearly unusable – it depends on content type and connectivity.

It's worth taking a little time first to explore exactly what constitutes a high-performance web site. One of the most significant metrics is the number of *pages-per-second* that can be served (sometimes also referred to as "page throughput"). Depending on their characteristics (for example, what resources they need to access), different pages will have different throughputs. The more pages per second that can be served, the more users your site will be able to service simultaneously. The pages-per-second metric is often coupled with two others:

❑   TTFB – time to first byte

❑   TTLB – time to last byte

On its own, the pages per second that a site serves only tell half the story. To be useful, we also need to know how the site is performing when serving up those pages. The smaller the TTFB and TTLB values and the closer together they are, the more responsive a site feels. As the number of users to a site increases, TTFB and TTLB will start to increase (and from a user perspective, the site will feel sluggish). There will come a point where TTFB and TTLB increase to a level that is not acceptable (what is acceptable depends on the nature of the application you're developing and expected response times); at this point, your site has effectively reached maximum capacity. It will continue to serve pages, but from a usability perspective, performance will degrade so much as to render the site unusable.

Usually a site's peak capacity will be reached at a certain CPU usage, so keep an eye on this while you're running tests or monitoring a live site. If the site starts to peak out at 100% CPU capacity, response times will drop, because requests will have to wait for CPU cycles to fulfill them. I've found that a sweet spot for peak capacity is usually 80-90% CPU usage, because if CPU usage is constantly in the 90s, it is likely to hit 100% every now and then. However infrequently it does this, it will cause performance degradation for those periods, and once this starts to happen it can become a vicious circle because users get frustrated and hit Refresh, compounding the problem.

How is Maximum Capacity Measured?

The maximum capacity of the site is the total number of concurrent connections it can cope with while maintaining acceptable response times. The maximum capacity is always a guideline rather than a precise figure because the value will change depending on the nature of the usage (a topic I explore in more detail later in the chapter).

Because HTTP is a stateless mechanism, there isn't a concept of people being "connected" to a web site – all we know is that someone has requested one or more pages. We have no idea if they will request another, or whether they have gone for good. Because of this, sites use methods of approximating concurrent users. For example, the figure in Windows 2000's Performance Monitor for IIS assumes that if a client was active (requested something) on a site within the past 20 minutes, the connection is still considered active; as soon as 20 minutes have passed without activity, that connection is removed from the count. In many ways, this is similar to ASP.NET sessions, but this count is used regardless of whether sessions are enabled on the site.

Different sites have different capacities depending on their nature. A dynamic site will usually have a lower capacity than a static site, and in general the more dynamic a site, the greater the potential for it to be slower. Obviously, there are other factors involved – for example, a static site that serves multimedia content may well be slower than a dynamic site. The key to a high-performance dynamic site is to use the most efficient techniques available to you, as described in this book, to mitigate the extra processing required.

Performance and Scalability

Scaling a web site means adding new servers (horizontal scalability) or upgrading existing hardware (vertical scalability) to increase capacity. A well-written, scalable application will allow the addition of new resources to increase capacity without any changes being required to the application itself, and with little impact on system behavior or performance.

If performance is the speed at which a system (such as a web site) operates, then surely performance and scalability are the same thing, right? Almost.

At any one time a web site will have certain performance characteristics. This depends on the conditions under which the site is operating – and specifically, the number of requests that the site must deal with. Suppose there are 500 concurrent users browsing an e-commerce site. The system will behave in a specific way: requests will take a certain amount of time to be processed and responded to. What if the number of users doubles, or trebles, or increases ten-fold? How does the site perform then?

The importance of scalability depends on the nature of your web application. If you're designing an intranet for a small company with only a dozen employees, scalability is unlikely to figure highly in your mind – performance with a small number of concurrent users is more important than the ability to expand the intranet to process hundreds or thousands of users. However, if you are designing a public web site, then scalability should be very high on your list of priorities. Inability to scale will often equal inability to operate – when a site's traffic increases rapidly, a web site that cannot scale with it will be available to **no-one**, not just the extra traffic! This is worth bearing in mind when developing your application.

Is a High-Performance Web Site Always a Highly Scalable One?

Usually, but not always. The characteristics of a highly scalable site are not always correlated with a high-performance web site. There is nothing to stop a web site that performs well with a certain number of users degrading into a poorly performing one if the site does not scale or cannot be scaled out. Similarly, there is no point in having a site that has been designed to be high-performance and allow scaling if extra servers are not installed to cope with demand.

Generally, if you design for high-performance, and you use efficient means of performing tasks, the system you create should be scalable. There should not be any "trade-off" between scalability and performance – it is unusual to have a situation where writing for performance will seriously impact the scalability of the system.

Scaling a Site

Let's take a scenario: you have a basic web site configuration of a single front-facing web server and a separate database server. You know the performance of your site under different loads and you know the maximum capacity of your site in terms of concurrent users. You are running at 40% average CPU usage at peak capacities at the moment and visitor growth is static. By stress-testing your site (using a tool to simulate many concurrent connections), you know that with double the current peak number of visitors, CPU usage goes above 85%, and performance degrades below acceptable response times.

Your boss comes to give you the good news – your marketing department has struck a deal with a major portal and you can now expect traffic to triple while you have prominent featuring. The current set-up will not handle the extra traffic. It's up to you to make the site scale to the new requirements. Let's examine the options.

Vertical Scalability

Vertical scalability, or scaling up, means replacing, upgrading or adding new hardware to an existing system. There are obvious limits to how far a single machine can be taken by upgrades alone (there are limits to CPUs, memory, subsystems such as disk I/O, and so on), as well as the effect such upgrades have on performance.

Moore's law, which states that hardware (specifically CPU) performance is doubling roughly every eighteen months, is really the backbone of vertical scalability. Relying on Moore's law and vertical scalability is not a good idea – you are limited by advances in technology, there is a limitation to how fast a single piece of hardware can be or how many "upgrades" it can take, and it is costly because you will often end up discarding replaced hardware. Having said that, Microsoft has put a lot of work into ensuring that recent products such as Windows 2000 and the .NET Framework (including ASP.NET) are able to scale up with the addition of more processors. ASP.NET and even classic ASP on Windows 2000 will scale well with the addition of up to eight processors. Previous versions of ASP on Windows NT did not scale well with the addition of new CPUs – usually, the returns on more than two CPUs would be rapidly diminishing because of bottlenecks in the code execution.

Bear in Mind Licensing Costs

Keep in mind licensing costs when considering any sort of scalability. Most Microsoft licensing is currently per CPU rather than per machine, so scaling up (vertical) is rarely much cheaper than scaling out (horizontal). However, there could be savings in incidental costs such as the space to house the machines.

Horizontal Scalability

Horizontal scalability, or scaling out, means adding new servers to an installation and spreading the load amongst them. This is the preferred method of scaling for many reasons: it is possible to scale much further, it gives the system redundancy (web servers can be taken out of the web farm if they develop faults and replaced when fixed), and it can be achieved cheaply. A web farm consisting of a number of standard PC-based servers is a cost-effective option. One of the largest web farms is at Google with over 10,000 PCs in the cluster. This type of scalability simply could not be achieved with a single powerful machine, and it is also hugely redundant. Scaling out is the only way to be able to handle such a huge number of highly intensive requests and guarantee 100% uptime. There is no alternative.

There are many options available for achieving horizontal scalability. Windows 2000 Advanced Server has Network Load Balancing (NLB) built-in, which allows up to 32-nodes in a web farm. In this case, the distribution of traffic between machines is handled by the operating system, which allows the nodes to communicate among each other and spread the load evenly (or to pre-defined levels). It's worth noting that ASP.NET's new session-management capabilities allow session data to be stored in a database, which means that sessions can be used while load-balancing a session across multiple machines. Using sessions on ASP required incoming requests to be directed back to the same server, because the session data was stored in memory. This was not only unreliable (some ISPs use proxy farms with a potentially different IP address for each request), but also reduced redundancy, because if that server was taken out of the cluster, the session data would be lost. Use of the `Session` object was not generally a recommended way to store such data on ASP.

Hardware load balancing is another option, using equipment such as BIG IP or Cisco's Local Router. To ensure that the hardware load-balancer doesn't become a single point of failure, they are usually deployed in pairs to allow a hot-standby to take over automatically in the event of failure of the live machine.

Microsoft's NLB allows programs such as Application Center to be used to manage and maintain the cluster. Application Center also includes other useful functionality for such as performance monitoring and testing, replication across nodes, and the ability to raise notifications in the event of issues with any of the nodes.

Other Advantages of Horizontal Scalability

The addition of multiple web servers has other benefits. It reduces the chances of bottlenecks on the web server itself by poorly written or threaded software. It increases power and capacity linearly, not just in terms of the CPU, but also in disk I/O, memory and network connectivity. Most importantly, it adds redundancy. If one web server falls over, others are available to take over. As well as being vital if a web server fails, this is also useful for routine maintenance such as installing updates (which usually require a reboot).

Code Optimization

An alternative to scaling with hardware is to look for optimizations in the code. There are limitations to this approach, and ideally of course, code should be written properly to begin with. How much can the code be optimized? Will it affect the quality of the code? How long will the optimization take? These are all questions that need to be carefully considered. The cost of code optimization is often neglected – it requires careful analysis to see which areas of the system are suitable for optimization, analysis of how changes will affect overall performance, the re-working itself, and then re-testing and re-deploying. Only rework existing code if there are *major* problems, and you can be sure that the reworks will have a *major* and calculable improvement. Programming time is expensive, and you may not get a return on the investment – investing in hardware generally gives a better and more predictable return.

Whenever analyzing an existing system, look first for major bottlenecks. These could be poorly written components (either in-house or third-party), poor data access, or simply an individual page that has issues. This emphasizes the importance of stress testing on a page-by-page basis: it allows you to pinpoint exactly those areas that are most in need of improvement. Using the page performance calculation allows you to go one step further. This method takes into account page usage (as a percentage of overall site usage), so that a frequently accessed page has a higher cost than a rarely accessed page, assuming that performance is identical. Done properly, this method of analysis is extremely powerful, because it allows potential impact to be accurately modeled. For example, it allows you to ask questions such as, "If I dedicate a programmer to this task and we increase the efficiency of a single page by 30%, what impact does that have on the total site capacity, and therefore how cost effective is it?" The page performance calculation is described in detail in Chapter 6.

Often, to gain major improvements in performance from an existing system that has been poorly designed and implemented, it will be necessary to step back and consider changes at the architecture level. Specifically, look for ways of "doing less work": is caching used in all appropriate areas? Has a caching architecture or framework been defined for the site? How is data access being handled? How many database calls per page are being made? What is the nature of these calls and can they be consolidated?

By considering "performance as a process", the approach I detail later in this chapter, you should avoid having to rework code on systems built with this principle in mind.

Deciding on the Approach to Use

Deciding on which approach to use to scale your site depends very much upon your individual circumstances. If you have inherited an existing site or application, it is always worth spending time analyzing the existing architecture and code to see if there are any areas suitable for major improvement. Undoubtedly, the best approach to scaling is to scale out horizontally. This is the only way that will enable massive scalability.

Databases are hard to scale (although there are many ways we can improve performance, such as the proper use of indexes). They can be clustered for redundancy, but they cannot be load-balanced unless they are read-only (in which case, a better alternative would usually be to hold the data cached on the web servers). When your database becomes a bottleneck and is hindering your ability to scale out by adding new web servers, consider upgrading your database server. Ensure that you test to see exactly what on the server is causing the problem – is it the I/O subsystem, the CPU, a lack of memory, or maybe network connectivity? In many cases, an overloaded database server can be indicative of a poorly designed application with too many database calls or a poorly-designed database – we'll talk more about this in Chapter 5.

How to Measure Scalability

In the real world, a perfectly scaled site is never achievable on a single server. It just can't happen – there are inherent limitations to the number of pages that can be served. The next best thing is a site that scales out linearly with the addition of new servers as the graph below illustrates:

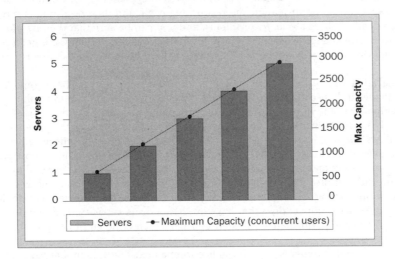

For a site to scale linearly with the addition of new servers, as well as having a connection to the Internet that is suitable for carrying the traffic, it must have no back-end database calls or calls to application servers. As soon as it does, it has the potential for these off-server calls to become a bottleneck, and the linear scaling from the addition of servers will start to degrade. A site serving static HTML pages can be scaled out nearly limitlessly. Because no processing takes place, as long as it is being scaled out correctly (for example, new servers are added before performance degrades), it will also be high-performance. Conversely, consider an ASP.NET application with multiple database calls per page. The more back-end database calls and the more data transferred between database and web server, the less likely the site will be to scale out well. The database will become a bottleneck and adding new web servers will only scale up to a point – after that point has been reached, there will be diminishing returns. The following graph illustrates this:

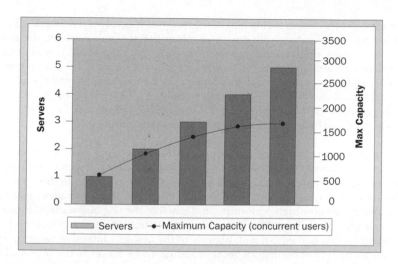

When designing for scalability, it must be kept in mind that the closer to static HTML (and I *don't* mean using static pages; I mean keeping all off-server calls to a minimum), the better the site will scale out. Caching is a fantastic tool to help keep to this doctrine; it also follows the principle of "only process when necessary". If you are performing processing on one page, can the result be used on subsequent requests or on other pages? If it can, that data/output should be cached. Even caching data for small amounts of time can greatly increase site performance and scalability.

It is possible to test specifically for scalability, but for various reasons it is rarely done. Test against one server initially and record the results. Then test against two servers; then against three. You can keep working up if you want, but usually it's possible to get a good feel for scalability just by testing a small web farm. Look at the difference in performance between the individual server and a dual-server configuration. If performance nearly doubles, you have a site that scales nearly perfectly. If performance only goes up marginally, you have a site that scales out poorly and you will gain little by adding additional servers. It is wise to find this out sooner rather than later!

To demonstrate how the ability to scale is affected by the type of processing a page does, try this simple test. Create two simple web pages, one of which displays "Hello World" three times, and one that reads from a database table three times. (Check out Chapter 6 on performance testing with the Web Application Stress tool to find out how to run stress tests against a page.) See how the pages-per-second varies between the two pages. If you have a web farm in operation, see the difference between the two pages when the tests are run on multiple servers. Only by experimenting and continually testing code yourself will you develop a real feel for how to develop scalable, high-performance applications.

Bottlenecks

There will always be bottlenecks in a system. The key to having a high-performance, highly scalable web site is to reduce the bottlenecks. It only takes one small aspect of a system to become a serious bottleneck, and an entire web site can be affected. Let's look at an example to make this clear.

Suppose we have a transactional shopping site that displays a catalog and various means of browsing and searching it. The catalog is cached and the ASP.NET pages created dynamically are also cached. They are high performance, and tests have shown that they scale well when new servers are added. Each server can deliver approximately 100 browsing pages per second.

17

The checkout process however, is highly database-intensive; it involves five pages, all using SSL, and each of these has multiple database calls during processing. Prices and discounts are calculated on each page as new options, such as gift-wrapping and special postage, are added. As part of the calculation process, when discounts are applied, a .NET component queries against a database table of discounts. This is constantly added to as new promotions appear on the site, and currently contains tens of thousands of records, all of which are loaded into memory on the web server. Because of the nature of the checkout pages, these can only be delivered at three pages per second. In addition, because of the number and nature of database calls, these pages do not scale well.

Adding a second server only brings the number of checkout pages per second that can be served to just under four, whereas it almost doubles the number of catalogue pages that can be served. In this case, the *maximum* number of people who can check out from the site is limited to three a second. If any more than this try to purchase, the performance of the checkout pages degrades rapidly, until no one can check out. No matter how high-performing and scalable the rest of the site, this one problem area has limited its overall effectiveness. This is an example of a bottleneck that affects both maximum performance of the site on one server, and, because of the multiple intensive database calls, its ability to scale. This is the worst kind of bottleneck because adding a new server to the front-end has a limited effect on overall site capacity.

If a site is being constantly monitored and tested, problems like this should not suddenly become apparent. Ongoing performance work should allow such issues to be identified, before they become a problem, and dealt with properly.

In this example, there are many ways to look at improving performance – trim the database tables of old promotional data; don't load the entire table into memory when performing the check; only recalculate the total, rather than each individual price, among many others.

Performance in Context

Performance of applications running over the Internet must be considered in context. It is worth taking a little time to look beyond what you control and explore the impact of the Internet itself on performance. If you are hosting an application on an Intranet, you have more control, but some of these issues will still apply.

We'll start at the beginning, typing a URL into our browser. What happens?

1. A DNS lookup is performed to translate the name (for example www.google.com) into an IP address that can be contacted over the network.

2. Once we have the IP address, a TCP/IP connection will be established between the client and the server. Our TCP/IP packet will pass through any number of routers to reach the destination.

3. Once a TCP/IP connection is established, HTTP communication can occur. This starts with our browser sending the HTTP request to the server.

4. The request is handled by the resident web server, in our case IIS. If the page is dynamic, the page is executed (at which point, calls to databases or other components off the web server may occur), and the resultant HTML is served.

5. The server will respond with the requested object (say an HTML file). The client will parse the HTML and request any additional linked items: HTTP has a "keep-alive" property so that the initial connection we established is used for all the remaining images/JavaScript files, or whatever else is contained on the page to be downloaded.

6. The client (your browser) has to render the HTML. With most modern browsers this happens during download.

7. The HTTP and TCP/IP connections are closed.

Delays can occur at any point in this process. A DNS lookup server may be slow to respond; there may be delays on routers between ourselves and the server; the connection to the Internet that our server is on may be overloaded; the connection to the Internet that the client is on may be slow. There is always latency over the network; there are often delays.

Be aware that you will never have total control of your destiny and that if you run any large, public web site, you will get regular queries related to your site's performance. You should be able to determine whether these are within normal limits or whether there is something under your control that you are able to do to resolve them.

There are, however, options available for reducing the risk and impact of areas outside your control.

Consider the Impact on Code Quality – Don't Sacrifice!

When designing for performance, be realistic and do not degrade the overall quality of the code or the construction. It is easy to take short-term views on performance without considering their effect as a whole on future development. I have seen applications developed using ADO where fieldnames have not been used because the developer heard they were "poor-performing". The code instead indexed the recordset fields by column number. Although this "tweak" has a *tiny* (between 2-5%) impact on performance, it had a *big* impact on the readability of the code (and therefore on ongoing maintenance costs). Always take an overview of how any changes you make in the name of performance affect the project as a whole.

Code Is Not the Only Place

There are areas that you can control that are outside of the coding effort, but which still need to be considered. Where your site is hosted and how you deliver rich content are two of these issues. In some circumstances, these will have just as much impact as developing for performance.

Sites which serve a large amount of rich content, such as images or video footage, will require a different approach to the standard dynamic web sites, where the main effort is on improving the speed of dynamic page processing and scalability issues associated with dynamic pages. High-bandwidth sites may also suffer from bandwidth problems on the local web site network, the user's Internet connection, and the traffic on the Internet between the two. In these circumstances, there are potential performance benefits to be gained by using a third party to host the bandwidth-intensive resources. These companies, the most well-known of which is probably Akamai, host your images/footage/HTML at multiple data centers around the world. They have technology that tries to ensure that a data center located closest to the recipient serves them with that content.

As well as reducing load on your own servers, and therefore potentially reducing the number of servers you need to scale out to, this can potentially decrease download times over the Internet, because the data is often hosted with close connections into major ISPs so that bottlenecks on the Internet are side-stepped.

It's Not Always a Technical Matter

Technical issues aren't the only factor affecting performance of a site. Often, human factors play a major role. What size are the pages on your site? Who is responsible for these? In many businesses, there is often negotiation between departments to ensure that pages are kept to reasonable, usable limits. It is always worth stating assumptions of the size of pages when testing during development – assume that they may have a tendency to "bloat", and ensure that everyone is aware of the impact this may have. Even the best-designed web site will appear to crawl along to a modem user if the pages are too large.

Some sites offer different content or look-and-feel depending on the user's bandwidth. Given the difference in speed between modem and broadband, this can have a performance impact: for the modem user, it keeps download and therefore response times low, and for the broadband user it allows a richer experience.

In addition, well-written HTML can make the difference between a page that appears to load slowly and one that appears to load quickly. Internet Explorer waits and renders HTML tables individually, so if a page is formatted using tables, it makes sense not to add everything to one big table, because the page will only be rendered when everything in the table is rendered. This may not increase the overall time for the page to be rendered, but users are more likely to be patient if they can see something happening – the *perceived* performance will be better, even if the actual performance isn't.

Hosting

Obviously, where you host your site can affect performance. When choosing a host, ask questions about connectivity to the Internet. Where in the network is your host located? The best hosts will have multiple dedicated links to different geographic regions. What sort of redundancy does the host offer in terms of Internet connectivity? There is no point in having a high-performance web site if its availability is limited or degraded by connectivity issues.

With regard to bandwidth, ask about how peak-capacity charging works. This allows you to go above your usual bandwidth limit for short periods without paying extra for potentially unused bandwidth.

Most hosts are now trying to offer value-added services as a way of generating extra revenue. Sometimes these take the form of partnerships with third parties; in other cases they are offered directly by the host. These can range from the most basic (being alerted if a web server fails to respond in a timely fashion) to more advanced performance monitoring, and even stress-testing facilities.

Performance Monitoring In Context

As well as monitoring and testing your site locally, it's worth considering getting a third party to test your site from other locations, particularly if you have a global presence. Subscribing to one of these services allows you to monitor how your site responds from locations around the globe, from DNS lookups, through response times, to overall page download times. The breakdown of response time by content is useful because it allows you to see how long your HTML takes to download, compared to other content such as images, JavaScript, and so on, and how these all make up the total download time. Plus, the option of throttle testing to emulate a specific connection (modem, DSL, cable, T1) allows you to see how total download times vary.

These services also allow you to monitor performance by the hour, day, and month – thus you will be able to see if your site is slowing down during peak usage times – and if there is any downtime or are any connectivity issues. In addition, because all these services do is use electronic agents which request web pages like any other visitor, it is possible to use them to monitor competing websites.

Measuring performance in context also means performing usability testing on the computers and connections that average users will use! It is easy to forget.

Application-Specific Issues

Taking performance in context also means focusing on issues specifically related to your application. Consider what "application type" your application falls under, and the sort of questions you need to consider.

High-Bandwidth Content

This type of application is either tailored specifically for broadband users, or with a large amount of high-bandwidth content. Carefully assess the physical site implementation: bandwidth and hosting infrastructure will play a key part. Should a third party be used to host the content? Or should a dedicated local server be used – and dynamic content separated from static content?

Low-Bandwidth But Highly Dynamic

This type of application makes use of lots of dynamic content, often pulled from disparate sources: web services, databases, XML files. Caching will be key to ensuring that performance is kept high. Analyze what data can be cached, and what is user-specific and *must* be generated for each request. Ensure that the architecture specifies how caching is to be used, and that caching is implemented in the most appropriate tier.

Intranet

An intranet application is quite different to a public web site. Often, these will display custom reports and play host to custom applications. Here, scalability is less of a concern than performance.

Highly Transactional

For a highly transactional site, such as online gambling or share dealing, the database will be key. These types of sites require up-to-the-second information, so caching cannot usually be heavily used.

Performance as a Process

Performance is often thought of as just a task for developers to worry about. Often, it's just forgotten about completely. It's not just for developers, and it shouldn't be forgotten about. In this section, I'll look at what it means to consider performance through a project's lifecycle and beyond. From my own experience, I believe this is the best and most reliable way to create high-performance web sites.

Introduction to This "Holistic" Way of Thinking

Throughout this chapter, I have emphasized the importance of thinking of performance as a whole. Good quality, fast code will come from the information contained in this book, but to be of real use it should be applied in a framework where considerations of performance are taken across all disciplines and levels; from the initial requirements of a site or application through to it's deployment and monitoring.

Over the past few years and particularly during the DotCom boom period of 1998-2000, there were some spectacular failings in sites unable to cope with visitor numbers, or with response times that seriously affected the sites' ability to work in a usable manner. In many cases, initial failure required significant re-working of the site, and caused delays ranging from days to months.

In the UK this year, the spectacular failure of the 1901 census site (which allowed access to information on the 32 million people in the UK who completed the census during that year) on its launch in January 2002 means that at the time of writing it is still offline over seven months later. The site was designed to handle 1 million hits daily: in reality, on its first day, it accepted over 30 million hits and the response time was so poor that it was rendered unusable. The initial failure and the subsequent delay in fixing the problem shows that the problems were manifest, from initial requirements and capacity planning through to the side design and architecture. The site was simply not designed to scale beyond initial, wildly conservative estimates. Gathering realistic requirements from the start is key to a well-performing site.

These problems were nearly all due not to a single, isolated problem or to sections of poor coding, but to a failure to work with performance in mind as a whole. In many cases, DotCom companies fruitlessly spent millions of dollars on powerful hardware (often unable to scale horizontally) and on re-working web sites on different platforms (on the misguided basis that a platform is the issue). In all cases, initial failure was costly, and resulted in delays to sites launching, reduced usability (and therefore reduced customer numbers), and bad publicity.

Requirement Gathering

Requirements planning is a crucial area of determining site performance and planning. As we've seen already, get it wrong at this stage, and the project could be doomed without development even having started.

It is important to know the "hidden" requirements for the site or application in terms of capacity. There are many reasons why capacity planning is often not taken seriously: it is not as "sexy" as designing the user interface (although, that too should be undertaken as an engineering task), and it is often forgotten about in the haste to "get busy" and appear productive. It shouldn't be.

Before starting out on architecture work and coding, it is important to know the requirements for the site in terms of response times, expected number of visitors, expected growth rate and any exceptional events likely to cause problems. It may be that these figures are initially hard to come by. If that is the case, there will be a need to work back from business plans and objectives. Look at expected traffic and work out what peaks in capacity are likely to be – using the 80/20 rule that 80% of your traffic will occur only 20% of the time, ensure that you can handle peaks greater than five times average peak capacity. If you are unsure of what traffic your site will be getting, try to work out what would be needed to satisfy predicted revenues if you're operating an e-commerce site: assume pessimistic conversion ratios and work back.

Planning for exceptional events is as important as planning for long-term growth. It is exceptional events (usually planned ones!) that cause the majority of web sites to crumble under traffic. Examples of exceptional events are those that lead to significant numbers of visits to your site, over and above normal peaks during the day. These peaks in traffic are usually between 5-10 times average peak traffic, although the exact nature will depend upon the circumstances. Running a web site that normally peaks during the day at 85% CPU usage is *no use* if you get a peak once or twice a month that increases the visitors five-fold. Examples of peaks include: site launches (related to publicity), television/radio features, high-profile portal features, and special dates (such as high profile betting events, holidays, and celebrations). Close liaison with whoever in the business is responsible for arranging or coordinating these events is vital before the site goes live in order to understand and plan for them at the early stages of architecting and designing the site.

During the requirements gathering and planning stage, good practice is to include time during the early-to-mid stages of development to test that development has proceeded according to architecture and design, and that this can be verified with stress-testing on as many completed parts of the site as possible. Spending a little time being diligent at the early stages, and taking this into account in the project plan can prevent a crisis developing further down the line.

The Software Architecture

Architecture is a sometimes-misunderstood concept, and is often ignored on small projects. Architecture defines the structure of the system, the overall "bird's eye view" of the subsystems that are being used – what they do, how they are used, and how they interact with each other. Getting the right approach for architecture is critical: it should not dive into how the components work, or the details of their implementation, but it should be detailed enough to be applied at a practical level.

When designing an architecture, always keep in mind performance issues and how they can be mitigated. How will data be accessed? What is the caching strategy? It's useful to map out principles for data design and storage at the architecture stage – and to point development in the correct direction. How will components communicate with each other? How does the software architecture map out to the physical implementation? Will there be a physical application layer or will all components be hosted on front-end servers? These are the type of questions you should be considering when architecting the site.

Coding the Site

As long as you have been diligent during the requirements gathering and architecture phases, at this stage you should know exactly what needs to be delivered to ensure that you can meet performance and capacity requirements. It is easy to develop poor code and it is just as easy to develop poorly performing code. A best-practice process is to have performance as a specific review point during peer-review sessions.

What is Peer Review?

If you don't already use peer review as part of a development process, consider it. There are many ways of holding a peer review, but the basis remains the same: programmers review other programmers' code. It can be a group meeting or a one-on-one session. The aim of peer review is to check for anything from coding standards, to good programming practices, to developing for performance. It is also a great forum for sharing best-practice techniques and better ways of tackling problems!

Testing

Stress testing, described in detail in Chapters 6 and 7, is an integral part of "performance as a process". The biggest mistake is to leave stress testing until development has finished, and just before the site goes live, in the assumption that everything will *probably* be fine, and if it isn't it will *probably* be easy enough to tweak a bit and fix. If you know the requirements up-front and have developed your architecture to allow for performance and scalability, you should be in good shape. But don't just assume this.

Keep on Testing

As development progresses, testing of the site both from a functional and a performance perspective should be continuing in parallel and feeding back into the development process.

Pages should be tested as they are finished: do not wait until the complete site is ready to start stress-testing. As much as anything else, lessons learned at this stage can help improve the performance of pages yet to be created.

It is important to test using different visitor profiles, especially a worst-case scenario where the user behavior imposes the greatest possible load on the web site (usually, highly transactional). The behavior that visitors to your site exhibit does not remain static. It changes depending on a multitude of factors, and this in turn has potential for affecting site performance. I personally experienced this while working on an e-commerce site. Following publicity on national TV, site traffic went up by a factor of two or three, but actual purchases increased significantly – upwards of 10 times what would be considered normal for that time of day. The change in visitor profile characteristics meant that the site was under significantly more strain than usual because of a combination of increased requests for pages using SSL and more intense database work.

Test from User-Experience

As well as performing your own tests on the site, it is good practice to ensure that regular testing of the performance of the web site takes place in the context in which it is usually used.

Because performance over the Internet is relative (as we mentioned above in the *Performance In Context* section), it is helpful to get an insight into how your site performs from different locations around the world in real-use scenarios. There are many different ways of doing this, from using online feedback forms to recruiting users to report back.

As IT professionals with (usually!) high-performance PCs and high-bandwidth connections at work, we often forget that the majority of people still connect to the Internet using dial-up. I also wonder how many times company executives have been dazzled by demonstrations that are performed from local servers over a network, and which make high-graphic sites with Flash and other multimedia content seemingly appear instantly. The reality when these sites go live and are viewed by people at home, and when the servers are under real-life load is very different.

Testing in context should also apply to usability tests. There is little point in conducting these on connections that the majority of people don't use. Delays, download times, and general connectivity issues are all part of the real usability of your site. If you expect the majority of your users to be modem users, ensure that the tests are performed over a modem link.

The Database

Earlier on in this chapter, we talked about scalability and how the database is a potential source of bottlenecks and may reduce the ability to scale out horizontally. Because of this, database design is a critical part of the development process.

As part of "performance as a process", databases should be tested during development. It is important to load databases with example data too, to ensure that the effect of growth is known. There are a number of ways to review database performance, from analyzing query execution plans, to stress-testing against the data access layer. Ensure that your developers know about these techniques and make use of them. Take advantage of your DBA, if you have one available, during the database design and implementation phases, especially if it is usually a developer's task. A DBA will usually have more experience of how queries can be optimized. We'll look into these issues in much greater depth in Chapter 5.

Database Server Hardware

Always go for a top-of-the-range server for the database machine. Because a database is difficult to scale out horizontally and is always a potential bottleneck in the system, consider a multi-processor machine and always one with plenty of memory, so that the database software can cache as much as possible.

It's an Ongoing Process

The site you've developed has gone live. The launch went well and the servers coped with everything that was thrown at them. This is the time to relax and forget all about performance... right?

Wrong.

To think of performance as a process, you need to keep thinking of performance once the site is live. As with the requirements and planning stage, the work from now on involves close liaison with the business as well as technical diligence. It is also at this point that any failures will be embarrassingly, and usually spectacularly, revealed!

From a technical perspective, there needs to be ongoing monitoring of the web site and the various metrics it produces. This is covered in detail in Chapter 9. One of the main tasks resulting from the monitoring should be regular analysis to gauge how much spare capacity the servers have. If the servers are coming close to reaching peak capacity when peaks of usage occur, it is time to start planning to add a new server to the web farm. It is always critical to stay one step ahead of current capacity. This also includes ensuring that the associated infrastructure (hosting, power, connectivity) and business matters (licensing, hardware, and hosting costs) are taken care of well in advance.

Also, stay closely involved with the business. Ensure that the technical team is aware of any future developments that will affect traffic to the site. If there is going to be significant marketing activity that will drive site traffic, ensure there is a process in place to be made aware of it – otherwise there is the risk that it will happen when there is routine maintenance and a web farm that is not operating at full capacity.

Also, gather non-technical metrics – if you have a call center or solicit feedback via e-mail or other means, any feedback pertaining to problems on the web site should be logged, and those related to site performance should be logged separately. It is often difficult to solicit information from an irate customer, so ensure that call center staff know exactly what information to ask for and how to solicit it. For example; What ISP is the user using? Where are they clicking through to the site from? What exactly is slow – connecting, downloading, or some other feature?

To show why it's important to ask these questions: at a company I worked at, we suddenly started getting an increase in queries from people complaining about site performance. They told us that ours was the only web site they were having problems with. We were baffled; remote checks of the site and ongoing monitoring of the usual metrics told us that the site should be operating perfectly. Eventually, we narrowed it down to the fact that the majority of complainants were using the same ISP and all were clicking through the same link. When we tracked down the problem, it turned out that an ISP's portal was serving up our site via a proxy that parsed our site and served it up itself. This allowed them to integrate their own shopping basket and affiliate tracking technology. The problem was brought to the portal's attention, and eventually resolved to a standard click-through!

Keep an Eye On Growing Databases

Web sites don't stay still for long. If they are database-driven, they are constantly changing as data is added and updated. This raises potential performance issues.

When you are developing the database for a dynamic website, be aware of the database tables which are likely to grow exponentially, and particularly those that are both being added to and required for read-access. Try to keep web databases "pruned" – not only do bloated tables increase read-access times (make sure you have the optimum indexes!), they also present backup and storage problems. If there is old data that needs to be kept, archive it off to another non-transactional server.

Summary

It's worth summarizing what performance as a process means, and why it's important. Without taking a holistic view of performance, your web site will only be able to perform as well as its weakest link. Ensure that what is required is clear, that development follows the best practice recommendations in this book, and that testing throughout the project lifecycle ensures that what is finally delivered lives up to expectations.

- ❑ **Define** what the performance and scalability requirements are.
- ❑ **Architect** the site with performance in mind.
- ❑ **Implement** according to the best practices contained in this book. Carry on performance testing as new pages/components are finished.
- ❑ **Test** the application and determine its capacity and scalability metrics.
- ❑ **Monitor** on an on-going basis and plan for future capacity.

This chapter gave an overview of performance and scalability concerns and how they fit into the overall context of performance on the Internet. We also explored the concept of taking performance as a process during and after development.

Hopefully, by using the information contained in this chapter throughout this book, you will be able to create applications and sites that perform as expected and scale to your requirements.

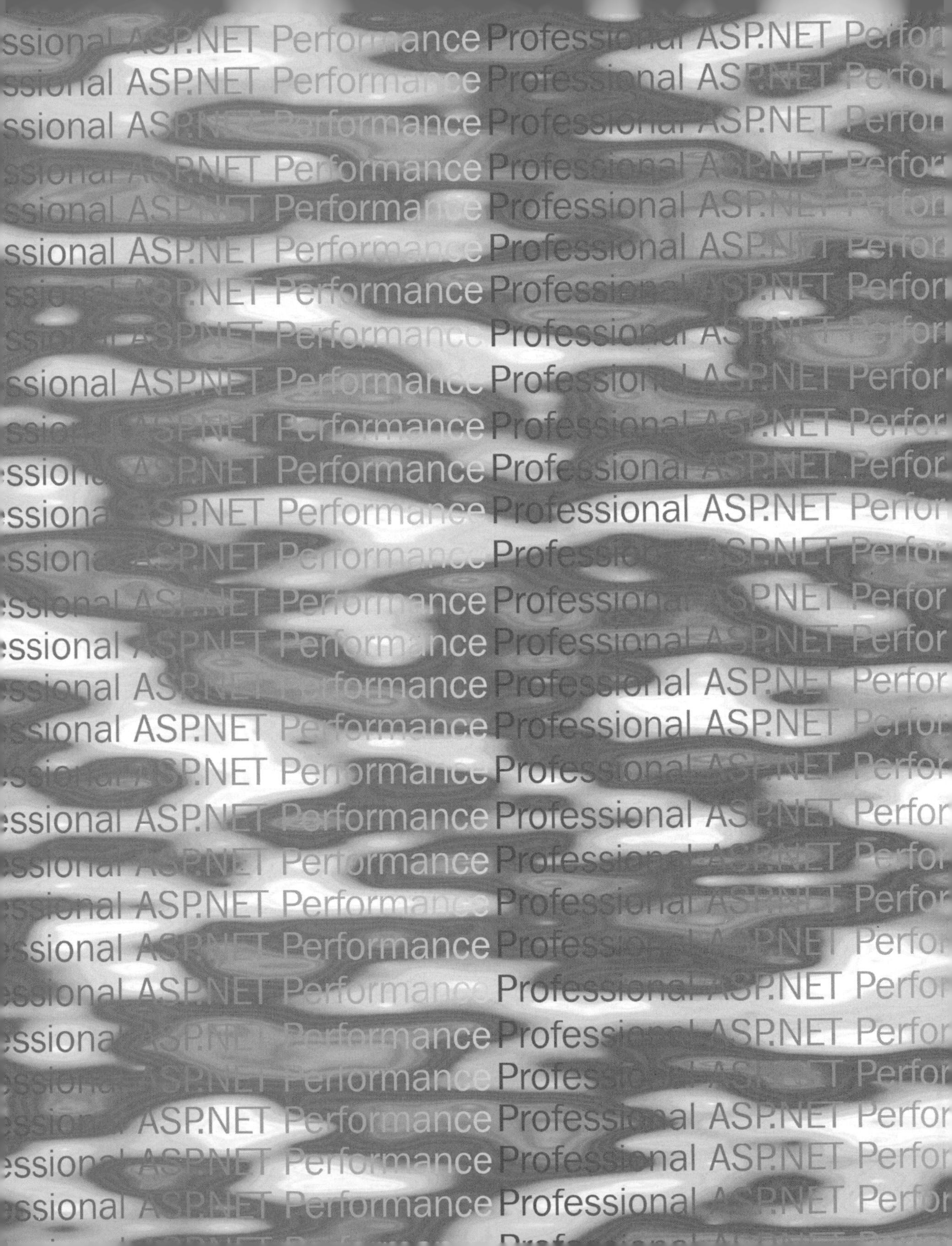
Professional ASP.NET Performance

2

Performance in ASP.NET

As the functionality and complexity of computing platforms increases, so do the different methods for looking at performance. Gone are the days where you could count on the fact that your application ran on a single web and you pretty much controlled the entire request process. In today's line of business Internet applications, it's almost guaranteed that your application is distributed across multiple presentation, object, and database servers. In the past, you only had a couple of things to examine to correct poor performing web applications. You could either find out how to optimize the existing language code, or re-code the slower portions with assembly code that performed faster.

Now, developers have a lot more to worry about. With distributed systems, there are many connection points that can be the culprit in a case of poor performance.

It can be very surprising to listen to many managers when discussing how to improve performance. Since hardware prices for the current technologies are always declining, managers almost always (incorrectly) begin by trying to throw more hardware at the performance problem. While this may end up being the final solution, we must first start by looking at the system itself and any external systems that communicate with it.

Fortunately, ASP.NET provides a plethora of ways to help customize your application for your existing infrastructure, all without incurring the increased expense of throwing additional hardware at the problem.

In this chapter we will cover:

❑ How ASP.NET pages are processed and what techniques you can use to return pages more quickly.

❑ The various Page attributes, such as view state, and how they can best be used to improve performance.

❑   The best use of session, application and cache to achieve maximum performance.

❑   The various properties for ASP.NET Server Controls that will aid performance, and when it's best and best not to use them on your page.

❑   ASP.NET @Page directives and how they impact performance.

.NET Languages

As of this writing, the .NET Framework and the Visual Studio .NET (VS.NET) development platform come with support for the following languages as standard:

❑   Visual Basic .NET

❑   Visual C#

❑   Visual C++ .NET

❑   Visual J#

There are many companies that are providing .NET support for other languages, like COBOL, Fortran and Perl (to name a few), but we'll be concentrating on the languages that come as standard with the .NET Framework and development tools. Since all .NET languages are built on top of the Common Language Run-Time (CLR), they will enjoy the majority of the features that these core languages have to offer.

You're probably asking, "What guarantees that the .NET language I'm using is really as good as another?" The reason is the **Microsoft Common Language Specifications (CLS)**. The CLS is a set of specifications that dictate the minimum set of features that a language must have in order to be a .NET compliant language.

As you probably already know, .NET applications are not native processor applications. When you compile an application in .NET, you are actually compiling the application to an intermediate language called **Microsoft Intermediate Language (MSIL or IL for short)**. Although it does depend on the implementation of the .NET language, generally each compiler will create pretty much the same IL for the compatible statements. Each language can carry forward its own idiosyncrasies, but performance of managed code can generally be considered equal between all of the core .NET languages.

Let's take a peek under the covers of how a compiled .NET application works. After you compile a .NET application you end up with a **Windows PE** (Windows portable executable) file. The structure of the .NET PE file is the same as the Win32 PE file format, with several extensions. When a computer receives a request to run a .NET application, it loads the PE file. The first instruction in the PE file is actually a load statement for the .NET CLR. Once loaded the .NET CLR loads the remainder of the PE file.

ASP.NET applications defined in IIS are run in an **Application Domain**. Application Domains run inside a physical operating system process. While the operating system process provides physical isolation from other processes, Application Domains provide logical isolation from other Application Domains. Application Domains consume far fewer resources and less processing power than ordinary Windows' processes, yielding better performance for an ASP.NET server running multiple applications that are isolated from each other.

To see how well core .NET languages stack up against each other, let's create a test program in two different .NET languages. Our test program will compute the prime numbers all the way up to 20,000. We'll place a start time and end time as part of each program, so that we can record the amount of time that they took to run. Granted, this is a simple test of one facet of a platform, but it is designed to show you that VB.NET and C# are on common performance ground.

First, let's create two different .NET console applications – one in C# and the other in VB.NET. To do this using VS.NET, you will need to create a blank solution and then two separate projects, since VS.NET does not currently allow you to mix the languages of your code-behind files per project (although you can create class files in different languages within a project). The code for the VB.NET and C# versions of our console application will look like the code shown below. Both versions should be compiled for Release mode in order to remove any debugging information that may affect performance (use **Build | Configuration Manager** to change this setting in VS.NET). You can find the code for these examples in the PrimeNumbers folder of the code download for this chapter:

```vb
'****************************************************
' VB.NET Prime Number generator
'****************************************************
Class PrimeNumber
  Private m_Value As Integer
  Public Sub New(ByVal Value As Integer)
    MyBase.new()
    Me.Value = Value
  End Sub

  Public Property Value() As Integer
    Get
      Return m_Value
    End Get
    Set(ByVal Value As Integer)
      m_Value = Value
    End Set
  End Property
End Class
Class PrimeNumberCollection
  Inherits CollectionBase
  Public Sub Add(ByRef objPrimeNumber As PrimeNumber)
    InnerList.Add(objPrimeNumber)
  End Sub
End Class
Module Prime
  Sub main()
    Dim dtStart As DateTime
    Dim i, j As Integer
    Dim boolIsPrime As Boolean = True
    Dim objCurPrime As PrimeNumber
    Dim objPrimeNumbers As New PrimeNumberCollection()

    dtStart = DateTime.Now
    For i = 2 To 20000
      ' Find out if there are any evenly divisible numbers
      For j = i - 1 To 2 Step -1
        ' Check to see if the number is evenly divisible
```

```
        If (i Mod j) = 0 Then
          boolIsPrime = False
          Exit For
        End If
      Next
        If boolIsPrime Then
          objCurPrime = New PrimeNumber(i)
          objPrimeNumbers.Add(objCurPrime)
        End If
          boolIsPrime = True
      Next
      Console.WriteLine("There were: " & _
                        objPrimeNumbers.Count & " primes counted")
    Console.WriteLine("Total Time (sec) = " & _
                      ((DateTime.Now.Ticks - dtStart.Ticks) / 10000000.0))
  End Sub
End Module
```

And here is the C# version of this code:

```csharp
// ****************************************************
// C# Prime Number Generator
// ****************************************************
using System;

namespace PrimeNumbersCS
{
  public class PrimeNumber
  {
    private int m_Value;
    public int Value
    {
      get
      {
        return m_Value;
      }
      set
      {
        m_Value = value;
      }
    }
    public PrimeNumber (int value)
      {
      Value = value;
      }
  }

  public class PrimeNumberCollection:System.Collections.CollectionBase
  {
    public void Add (PrimeNumber objPrime)
    {
    InnerList.Add(objPrime);
    }
```

```
    }
  class Class1
  {
    [STAThread]
    static void Main(string[] args)
    {
      DateTime dtStart;
      int i,j;
      bool boolIsPrime = true;
                  PrimeNumber objPrimeNumber;
      PrimeNumberCollection objPrimeNumbers;

      objPrimeNumbers = new PrimeNumberCollection();
      dtStart = DateTime.Now;
      for (i=2; i<=20000; i++)
      {
        // Find out if there are any evenly divisible numbers
        for (j=i-1; j>=2; j--)
        {
          // Check to see if the number is evenly divisible
          if ((i % j) == 0)
          {
            boolIsPrime = false;
            break;
          }
        }
        if (boolIsPrime)
        {
          objPrimeNumber = new PrimeNumber(i);
          objPrimeNumbers.Add(objPrimeNumber);
        }
        boolIsPrime = true;
      }
      Console.WriteLine
        ("There were: " +
                      objPrimeNumbers.Count + " primes counted");
      Console.WriteLine("Total Time (sec) = " +
        ((DateTime.Now.Ticks - dtStart.Ticks) / 10000000.0));
    }
  }
}
```

Now, let's run each version from the operating system command line a couple of times (in order to get the best performance benchmarks, you should run each application multiple times under the same conditions and record each result). Your results may differ from those that you see in the table below (these test results were run on a 500MHZ Pentium with 256MB of RAM running under the Windows XP Professional operating system), but as you'll notice there is no significant difference in performance times.

Language	Run #1 (sec)	Run #2 (sec)	Run #3 (sec)	Run #4 (sec)	Run #5 (sec)	Avg (sec)	Std. Dev
VB.NET	5.9682	5.9370	5.9213	5.9371	5.9370	5.9401	0.017112
C#	6.0151	5.9526	5.9526	5.9370	5.9526	5.962	0.030454

These test applications assess the time taken by the program's looping capabilities, some of the mathematical operations, and object management (including time spent on garbage collection). While this is by no means a comprehensive collection of the features that are available to you in .NET languages, it does serve its purpose as a quick and dirty comparison for some of the most commonly used building blocks of an application development language. Although out of the scope of this book, you will also find that .NET applications perform just as well as, if not better than, applications built with VB6, VC, and especially ASP.

Please note that these results were not run under the strictest of test lab conditions, but it does demonstrate that .NET languages are basically equal. It also clearly shows that .NET languages are all equal when it comes to performance. To generate a better real-world test case scenario, you should use Application Center Test (ACT), which comes standard with VS.NET Enterprise Edition, or the Windows Application Stress (WAS) tool. We will be discussing application test and stress tools in Chapter 6.

The ASP.NET Page

The ASP.NET page is pre-compiled to IL so that when the browser requests it, the IL is executed by the .NET framework. A deployed ASP.NET application will typically contain only the front-end ASPX files and core object DLLs, along with ASP.NET configuration files. Language code-behind files are not required on the deployed server, since they have already been compiled into a .NET object DLL (which, for local objects, will reside in the \BIN directory for the ASP.NET application).

When an ASP.NET page is requested for the first time (for example after a new version of the ASP.NET page is deployed to the web server), it is just-in-time compiled by the .NET CLR and then run. This is why you will experience a small delay the very first time you execute an ASP.NET page after you compile it. After that, the compiled page is cached and utilized for all subsequent requests.

Pages are similar to Forms in the VB6 development environment. Pages in ASP.NET have their own event model. Understanding the event model is critical to understanding why a page performs as it does. If you're not familiar with the Win32 application event model, not to worry – we'll provide a summary here so that you can come up to speed. It's really not that difficult to understand.

When a page is requested, the following events are fired:

- ❑ Page_Init
- ❑ Page_Load
- ❑ Server Control Event Causing Postback (if necessary)
- ❑ Page_PreRender
- ❑ Page_Unload

There are a few other less common page events that are also part of the page event model. A couple of these are Error and Transaction (Abort and Commit). The Error event is fired whenever a page encounters an unhandled exception (one for which the developer has not provided some "handling" logic"). The Transaction event will be fired, as the page processing sections marked as being transactional are either committed or aborted. The following figure shows the order in which ASP.NET fires these events.

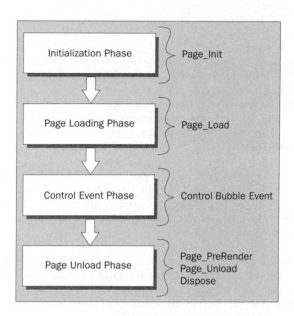

In addition to these events, there are several application-level request events that are fired. These are events like Application_BeginRequest, which is fired at the start of all page requests, and Application_EndRequest, which is fired after all information has been sent to the browser. You can also use the old ASP event names for these events: Application_OnBeginRequest and Application_OnEndRequest. We mention them here so that you don't think that we've left them out of the sequence model. We'll be talking about both Page-level and Application-level events, and their impact on the performance of ASP.NET pages, later in this chapter.

For those who want to be more adventurous and learn everything there is to know about page and control events, and how they're fired, Adam Wayne of divine Managed Services has constructed a web page that lists in exacting detail the event hierarchy of all possible server and control events for a page. The URL for this outstanding resource is: http://www.digitalbanzai.com/aspnet/. You can also research events on your particular page by enabling page tracing (discussed later in this chapter). As you'll see throughout this book, understanding the event hierarchy is critical to understanding how to create a high-performance ASP.NET application.

Since a page can have any number of server controls, you can see that there can be numerous events that fire when a page is requested. We'll talk about the performance impacts of server controls later, but this should give you an idea of how the number of server controls and events that they fire can have a significant impact on your application's performance.

If you are familiar with Visual Basic 6 programming for the Win32 platform, you can see that this event model is pretty similar to the Forms event model you were exposed to. Instead of events on a Form (as in VB6), we're working with events on a web page. For example, VB6 has form events like Form_Initialize and Form_Load/Form_Unload. However, if you're not familiar with this type of event-driven programming, you'll have a significant learning curve over that of working with classic ASP and VBScript/JavaScript.

Page Events

Let's talk more about each event from above in detail so that we can better understand the techniques for ensuring good performance of our pages.

The `Page_Init` event is the first event fired when a page is requested, either the first time or via a page postback. During the `Page_Init` process, all controls are set to their default state, but the view state is not restored at this time. This means that `Page_Init` should not be used to handle the processing of server control values and states.

The `Page_Load` event is the most commonly utilized event in ASP.NET programming. It is invoked after the `Page_Init` event. The main difference between `Page_Load` and `Page_Init` is that the view state for all server controls on the page will be restored by the time the `Page_Load` event is fired. This makes this event the ideal candidate for manipulating controls and preparing the content of the page, before it is rendered to the client.

Server Controls are handled after the page initialization phase. It is important to realize that only one server control can issue a postback, but multiple events can fire once the postback has occurred. For example, if you have a page with an `<asp:button>` server control and the button is clicked, the postback will be issued and the button's event handler will be executed (after the `Page_Init` and `Page_Load`).

It's also possible to nest controls within each other. An example of this would be a data grid that has nested server controls (like a list box or textbox) within the cells of each row. You might want to do this to provide a richer user experience, rather than just displaying plain text in cells within a data grid. The controls being nested are called the child controls, where the top control is called the container control.

The code for our initial Voting Booth page will look like the code shown below. This is the first iteration of our Voting Booth web application, which we'll use throughout this section to demonstrate several key areas that can help improve ASP.NET application performance. You can find this example in the `VotingBooth` folder of the code download.

```
<form id="Form1" method="post" runat="server">
  <STRONG><FONT color="maroon" size="5">
    <DIV ms_positioning="FlowLayout">Vote For Your Favorite M&amp;M Color!</DIV>
    <DIV ms_positioning="FlowLayout"><asp:DataGrid id="DataGrid1"
        AutoGenerateColumns="False"
        runat="server" BorderColor="#DEBA84" BorderStyle="None"
        CellSpacing="2" BorderWidth="1px" BackColor="#DEBA84"
        CellPadding="3">
    <SelectedItemStyle Font-Bold="True" ForeColor="White"
        BackColor="#738A9C"></SelectedItemStyle>
    <ItemStyle ForeColor="#8C4510" BackColor="#FFF7E7"></ItemStyle>
    <HeaderStyle Font-Bold="True" ForeColor="White"
        BackColor="#A55129"></HeaderStyle>
    <FooterStyle ForeColor="#8C4510" BackColor="#F7DFB5"></FooterStyle>
    <Columns>
      <asp:BoundColumn DataField="Key" HeaderText="Name"></asp:BoundColumn>
      <asp:BoundColumn DataField="Value"
          HeaderText="# of Votes"></asp:BoundColumn>
      <asp:ButtonColumn Text="Vote" ButtonType="PushButton"
```

```
        HeaderText="Vote" CommandName="Vote"></asp:ButtonColumn>
      </Columns>
      <PagerStyle HorizontalAlign="Center" ForeColor="#8C4510"
        Mode="NumericPages"></PagerStyle>
    </asp:DataGrid>
    </DIV>
    </FONT></STRONG>
    <asp:Button id="btnReset" runat="server" Text="Reset Votes"></asp:Button>
  </form>
```

In this example, we'll create a sample voting web form in which we'll allow our users to vote for their favorite color of M&M. This will give you an idea of how controls are nested, the events that they end up firing, and an overall baseline of the performance of an ASP.NET page that utilizes nested controls with a data grid. We'll start by creating a web form with a data grid and a dynamic number of rows, depending upon the number of M&M colors specified when the application runs.

In the Page_Load event we either create initial zero values for all vote counts, or we retrieve them from the application cache. If a server control, such as a button in the data grid or the Clear Votes button, caused the postback, then their event handler is invoked and we either increment the vote count or we clear all vote counts.

```
Public Class Vote
    Inherits System.Web.UI.Page
    Protected WithEvents DataGrid1 As System.Web.UI.WebControls.DataGrid
    Public VoteTally As Hashtable
    Protected WithEvents btnReset As System.Web.UI.WebControls.Button
    Public Shared Candidates As String() = _
        {"Red", "Green", "Yellow", "Brown", "Black"}

    Private Sub Page_Load(ByVal sender As System.Object, _
        ByVal e As System.EventArgs) Handles MyBase.Load
      Dim strKey As String
      VoteTally = New Hashtable()
      ' Always retrieve vote counts from cache
      ' There may be multiple concurrent voters
      For Each strKey In Candidates
        ' Check to make sure cache key exists
        If Cache.Get(strKey) Is Nothing Then
          ' If not, initialize vote count
          VoteTally.Add(strKey, 0)
        Else
          VoteTally.Add(strKey, Cache.Get(strKey))
        End If
      Next
    End Sub
End Sub
```

When the page unloads, we cache off these values so that all other browsers of this page will be able to vote as well.

```
    Private Sub Page_UnLoad(ByVal sender As System.Object, _
                    ByVal e As System.EventArgs) _
                    Handles MyBase.Unload
```

```
      ' Save off vote tally for other voting booths
      Dim strKey As String
      For Each strKey In Candidates
        Cache.Insert(strKey, VoteTally(strKey))
      Next
    End Sub
```

When the user votes on a color by pressing the command button on one of the data grid rows, the ItemCommand event of the data grid is fired (after the Page_Load event). This is known as **event bubbling**, where the child control within a container control causes an event for that container control to fire. Remember, the control events fire after the Page_Load fires (because the view state needs to be loaded in order to be able to be manipulated).

```
    Protected Sub DataGrid1_ItemCommand(ByVal sender As System.Object, _
                                 ByVal e As DataGridCommandEventArgs)_
                                 Handles DataGrid1.ItemCommand
      Select Case e.CommandName
        Case "Vote"
          VoteTally(e.Item.Cells(0).Text) += 1
      End Select
    End Sub
    Private Sub Page_PreRender(ByVal sender As Object, _
                         ByVal e As System.EventArgs) _
                         Handles MyBase.PreRender
      ' Bind the data just before we render the HTML
      DataGrid1.DataSource = VoteTally
      DataGrid1.DataBind()
    End Sub
    Private Sub btnReset_Click(ByVal sender As System.Object, _
                         ByVal e As System.EventArgs) _
                         Handles btnReset.Click
      Dim strKey As String
      For Each strKey In Candidates
        VoteTally(strKey) = 0
        Cache.Insert(strKey, 0)
      Next
    End Sub
End Class
```

The application, when run, should look like this.

*When setting up the download code, don't forget to set VotingBooth as a virtual application. You can do this by right-clicking on the **Properties** of the folder containing the application in IIS, and selecting the **Create** button next to the application name.*

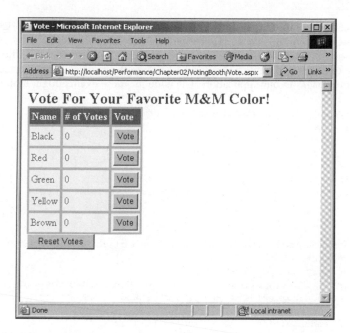

One of the changes that you'll notice related to performance is that we waited to bind our data source to the data grid during the `Page_PreRender` event. We want to eliminate having to bind the data grid twice (once in `Page_Load`, and once in `ItemCommand`), which we would have had to do because we need to cover the case where the user just refreshes the page and the values need to be loaded. By putting the bind in the `Page_PreRender`, we only have to put code to bind the data grid in one place, and it covers all cases. This also eliminates the annoying side-effect of doing multiple data binds during a single postback – a common error in a number of online examples out there today.

We'll be taking a more in-depth look at server controls and how they impact performance later in this chapter, but you can see from this example that the event code within server controls can be a performance bottleneck. The more code you include in an event handler, the longer it will take for that event handler to return, and the longer it will take for the overall page to return. As a general performance rule, you should strive to eliminate any code that does not need to be executed during the page's event processing. A great example of this would be averaging or computing statistics in our application. There is really no need to expend client CPU cycles updating averages or statistics when the user votes. A separate server-side process can easily be written to be notified when a vote occurs, and then perform these computations. Removing the logic to perform these computations will return the page to the user more quickly, without sacrificing a business requirement.

The `Page_PreRender` event is the final event called before the contents of the page are rendered to the requesting client. As we saw from our example above, you would use this event as the last stop to affect any of the server control data (or just render some additional HTML) before it is sent out to the client. ASP.NET actually uses this very same event when you enable tracing. ASP.NET hooks into that event and appends extra page tracing information at the end of your rendered page to show various statistics and states for the execution of your page.

Other examples of when to use this event would be to add a common footer, copyright, or logo to the end of a page. The best way to do this on an application basis would be to use the `Application_BeginRequest` and the `Application_EndRequest` events in the `Global.asax` file. What we're going to do throughout this chapter is hook into these events to give us some primitive timing statistics for all of the pages in our application. The code for these events might look similar to this:

```
Sub Application_BeginRequest(ByVal sender As Object, _
    ByVal e As EventArgs)
  ' Fires at the beginning of each request
  ' Use Application variable since Session
  ' is not available at this time
  If timingstats Then
    Application(Me.Request.UserHostAddress.ToString) = Now()
  End If
End Sub

Sub Application_EndRequest(ByVal sender As Object, ByVal e As EventArgs)
  If timingstats Then
    Dim dtStart As New DateTime()
    dtStart = CType(Application(Me.Request.UserHostAddress.ToString), DateTime)
    Application.Remove(Me.Request.UserHostAddress.ToString)
    Response.Write("<hr>")
    Response.Write("Total Page Processing Time = ")
    Response.Write((DateTime.Now.Ticks - dtStart.Ticks) / 10000000.0)
    Response.Write(" Seconds")
  End if
End Sub
```

If we applied our new `Global.asax` to the `VotingBooth` project above, we'd see a screen that looked similar to the one below. Now, in the real world we'd just use the page tracing feature built-in to ASP.NET, but we'll make our own just to show how to hook into these events and what, if any, consequences come with using these events.

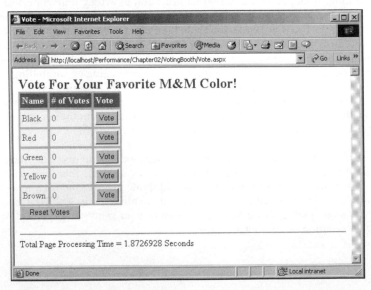

The `Page_Unload` event handles all of the page cleanup and disposal. It is important to note that any server processing that happens here will not impact the rendered page since it has already been sent to the client. The main reason that you would utilize this event is to do cleanup for items manipulated during the page processing process. This would include things like closing open file connections, closing database connections, and explicitly flagging objects as ready for garbage collection by calling their `Dispose` method.

No doubt you've noticed that we've been using the `Handles` keyword when defining our page and control event handlers:

```
Private Sub Page_Load(ByVal sender As System.Object, _
                ByVal e As System.EventArgs) _
                Handles MyBase.Load
```

ASP.NET allows you to chain multiple methods to a single event. For example, you could put the following in a code-behind file:

```
Private Sub Page_Load1(ByVal sender As System.Object, _
                ByVal e As System.EventArgs) Handles MyBase.Load
   ...
End Sub
Private Sub Page_Load2(ByVal sender As System.Object, _
                ByVal e As System.EventArgs) Handles MyBase.Load
   ...
End Sub
```

This will not end up generating an error, as you might think at first. What ASP.NET will do is invoke one method after another. The event list is actually a linked list of callbacks that ASP.NET invokes in a serial fashion. This is where performance comes in. Since the events are executed serially, the more event handlers you daisy chain to a single event, the slower your overall code will be.

It is also possible to dynamically add an event handler. You can do this in VB.NET by using the `AddHandler` method:

```
AddHandler MyControl.event, AddressOf EventHandlerSub
```

Keep in mind that the more event handlers you add, the longer it will take for an event to complete processing and for the page to return to the user. You should only use this dynamic event manipulation to solve a specific business requirement, and not use it just because it looks 'cool'. As with many 'cool' things, they do come at the expense of performance. In the case of event handlers, ASP.NET does not limit the number of event handlers that can be attached to a given event. This means that you could inundate ASP.NET with the servicing of your own event handlers, rather than the timely performance of business logic. Microsoft recommends that to improve performance, you minimize event handler code wherever possible – possibly by standardizing on the inclusion of your event handler code in a single core ASP.NET event, rather than creating your own events and event handlers.

The performance of many business systems are sacrificed by the well-meaning developer who adds that last "cool" UI feature, that works fine in development but it could end up costing an extra 2-3 seconds of page loading time in a production with hundreds of simultaneous users. While the solution is not revolutionary, keeping things simple not only helps maintainability, but also generates better performing code.

ASP.NET Page View State

As you will have seen with active ASP.NET applications, one of the first things that you'll notice is the postback feature mentioned above. This is a real benefit for developers because it eliminates the need for the developer to manually save off information between trips to the server. View state is provided by ASP.NET for all server controls (a server control is designated by the `runat="server"` property). When ASP.NET renders a page as HTML, it creates a hidden form field called _VIEW STATE. This field is an encrypted, tokenized string that contains the name/value pair for every control on the ASP.NET page. The value stored per control is actually the value(s) associated with the control, and any state information for it as well. When the page is sent back to the server (a postback), ASP.NET can easily use these values and reconstruct the page controls, their values and states, all without developer code.

Let's take a look at an example of this using a simple data entry screen for an address book. We'll have name, address, city, state, and zip code fields, followed by an OK and Cancel button. In classic ASP, the creation of this screen is easy enough, but when the OK button is clicked the developer needs to do some background work. This additional code is required in order to restore the data field values since the server does not know anything about the previous page's data.

Let's create this page in ASP.NET. Start off by creating a new ASPX page in VS.NET called `PageViewState.aspx` (we name it `PageViewState` just in case we run into any name resolution problems with the reserved word `VIEWSTATE` in .NET). This page will simply be a single ASP.NET textbox with two buttons that will hide and unhide the textbox to show how the values of the view state field works. You can find this code in the `PageViewStateExample` folder of the code download:

```
<form id="Form1" method="post" runat="server">
  <DIV><br><br><br><br><br></DIV>
  <DIV style="DISPLAY: inline; Z-INDEX: 101; LEFT: 16px;
    WIDTH: 70px; POSITION: absolute;
    TOP: 25px; HEIGHT: 15px" ms_positioning="FlowLayout">Test Field</DIV>
  <asp:TextBox id="txtName" style="Z-INDEX: 106; LEFT: 101px;
    POSITION: absolute; TOP: 23px" runat="server"></asp:TextBox>
  <asp:Button id="btnHide"
    style="Z-INDEX: 111; LEFT: 15px; POSITION: absolute; TOP: 59px"
    runat="server" Width="61px" Text="Hide"></asp:Button>
  <asp:Button id="btnShow"
    style="Z-INDEX: 112; LEFT: 94px; POSITION: absolute; TOP: 59px"
    runat="server" Width="62px" Text="Show"></asp:Button>
</form>
</body>
</HTML>
```

You might have noticed that we're using some extra style properties with our server controls, most notably the `style` property. This allows us to specify exact positions of the controls when they are rendered on the HTML page. While this makes your application look more Windows-like, it does come at a small performance penalty since the size of the rendered HTML increases to support the extra tables, rows, and columns that are created to put the controls in their defined locations. The performance impact is solely dependent upon the number of controls on your page and where they are located.

For the previous example, the additional HTML rendered is negligible, but for a page with 20 controls, all with their own set of position coordinates, the extra HTML can be 5K-20K. While this may seem small, it is the attention to these details that will help you build better performing ASP.NET applications. Many developers will ignore this "low hanging fruit" in favor of looking for the bigger fish. While the bigger fish will certainly help more, these other techniques that we will also be showing are so simple to include, that it would be a shame to not take advantage of them.

The code-behind file is very simple, in that it just hides or shows the text box based on whether the Hide or Show button was clicked.

```
Public Class PageViewState
    Inherits System.Web.UI.Page
    Protected WithEvents btnHide As System.Web.UI.WebControls.Button
    Protected WithEvents btnShow As System.Web.UI.WebControls.Button
    Protected WithEvents txtName As System.Web.UI.WebControls.TextBox

    Private Sub btnHide_Click(ByVal sender As System.Object,
        ByVal e As System.EventArgs) Handles btnHide.Click
      txtName.Visible = False
    End Sub

    Private Sub btnShow_Click(ByVal sender As System.Object,
        ByVal e As System.EventArgs) Handles btnShow.Click
      txtName.Visible = True
    End Sub
End Class
```

Now, it's time to run the ASPX file. To do this you can use the View in Browser command by right-clicking on the ASPX file in the Solution Explorer in VS.NET. After the ASPX page is returned, view the browser source (View | Source in Internet Explorer). It should look something similar to the rendered HTML below:

```
<!DOCTYPE HTML PUBLIC "-//W3C//DTD HTML 4.0 Transitional//EN">
<HTML>
  <HEAD>
    <title>Page ViewState Example</title>
    <meta content="Microsoft Visual Studio.NET 7.0" name="GENERATOR">
    <meta content="Visual Basic 7.0" name="CODE_LANGUAGE">
    <meta content="JavaScript" name="vs_defaultClientScript">
    <meta content=http://schemas.microsoft.com/intellisense/ie5
        name="vs_targetSchema">
  </HEAD>
  <body MS_POSITIONING="GridLayout">
  <form name="Form1" method="post" action="PageViewState.aspx" id="Form1">
  <input type="hidden" name="__VIEWSTATE"
      value="dDwtMTYzMTkzNDY5OTs7Ph1PlyXIDyJpuVrIrElRO03+lDBf" />
  <DIV><br><br><br><br></DIV>
  <DIV style="DISPLAY: inline; Z-INDEX: 101; LEFT: 16px; WIDTH: 70px;
      POSITION: absolute; TOP: 25px; HEIGHT: 15px" ms_positioning="FlowLayout">
      Test Field</DIV>
  <input name="txtName" type="text" id="txtName" style="Z-INDEX: 106;
      LEFT: 101px; POSITION: absolute; TOP: 23px" />
```

```
        <input type="submit" name="btnHide" value="Hide"
            id="btnHide" style="width:61px;Z-INDEX: 111; LEFT: 15px;
            POSITION: absolute; TOP: 59px" />
        <input type="submit" name="btnShow" value="Show" id="btnShow"
            style="width:62px;Z-INDEX: 112; LEFT: 94px;
            POSITION: absolute; TOP: 59px" />
    </form>
    </body>
</HTML>
```

Next, let's click the **Hide** button and see what happens. View the rendered HTML again after clicking the **Hide** button and you should get something similar to the HTML below:

```
<!DOCTYPE HTML PUBLIC "-//W3C//DTD HTML 4.0 Transitional//EN">
<HTML>
  <HEAD>
    <title>Page ViewState Example</title>
      <meta content="Microsoft Visual Studio.NET 7.0" name="GENERATOR">
      <meta content="Visual Basic 7.0" name="CODE_LANGUAGE">
      <meta content="JavaScript" name="vs_defaultClientScript">
      <meta content=http://schemas.microsoft.com/intellisense/ie5
          name="vs_targetSchema">
  </HEAD>
  <body MS_POSITIONING="GridLayout">
    <form name="Form1" method="post" action="PageViewState.aspx" id="Form1">
      <input type="hidden" name="__VIEWSTATE"
          value="dDwtMTYzMTkzNDY5OTt0PDtsPGk8MT47PjtsPHQ8O2w8¬
          aTwxPjs+O2w8dDxwPHA8DxWaXNpYmxlOz47bDxvPGY+O¬
          z4+Oz47Oz47Pj47Pj47PgUS3K7P0/zNI4xkfIAaakuwG1zu" />
      <Div><br><br><br><br><br></DIV>
      <DIV style="DISPLAY: inline; Z-INDEX: 101; LEFT: 16px; WIDTH: 70px;
          POSITION: absolute; TOP: 25px; HEIGHT: 15px"
          ms_positioning="FlowLayout">Test Field</DIV>
      <input type="submit" name="btnHide" value="Hide" id="btnHide"
          style="width:61px;Z-INDEX: 111;
          LEFT: 15px; POSITION: absolute; TOP: 59px" />
      <input type="submit" name="btnShow" value="Show" id="btnShow"
          style="width:62px;Z-INDEX: 112; LEFT: 94px;
          POSITION: absolute; TOP: 59px" />
    </form>
    </body>
  </HTML>
```

Notice the difference? The value of the hidden field _VIEWSTATE is completely different from before. That's because we changed the property of one of the ASP.NET fields. Note, though, that changing values within the fields will not change the view state, since values are not stored there, but they are available to ASP.NET by looking at the fields themselves.

You can also add items to the view state through the use of **state bags**. State bags allow you to define your own key/value pairs and store them in the view state so that the values will be persisted across page postbacks. For example, if you wanted to count the number of times the page has been refreshed, you could do it like this:

```
    Private Sub Page_Load(ByVal sender As System.Object, ByVal e As System.EventArgs)
        Handles MyBase.Load
      Dim i As Integer
      If IsPostBack Then
        ' Get the count of refreshes
        i = CType(ViewState("RefreshCount"), Integer)
        i += 1
        lblCount.Text = "Page has been refreshed " & i.ToString & " times"
        ViewState("RefreshCount") = i
      Else
        ' Make sure to initialize the count
        ViewState("RefreshCount") = 0
      End If
    End Sub
```

This example stores the number of times a refresh (postback) occurred. The developer can enhance the Page_Load event to do things like customization based upon the number of times the user manipulates the page – possibly a poor man's ad rotator.

As we'll find out later in the chapter, you can store any object directly in the view state. However, you should be careful when attempting to store anything but a value type since storing reference types comes with a performance penalty. If you need to store a reference type, make sure that the class implements the ISerializable interface, or manually call a serialize and de-serialize method for your class when storing a reference type. We'll learn more about serialization and de-serialization when we talk about Session, Application, and Cache objects later in this chapter.

View state is a real timesaver for developing web pages. However, as you can see this can come at a performance cost. As you saw from our example above, the slightest change to a property for a server control can drastically change the size of the view state. Add in 10-20 more simple server controls and several advanced server controls on a page, and you can see how the size of the rendered HTML may become a bottleneck for your application, especially for those users with limited bandwidth capabilities.

You might be saying to yourself, "So, what? An extra 100 bytes can't affect performance THAT much." The things you need to consider are that the 100 bytes that you've just seen are for a single person. Now multiply that by 1000 concurrent users, all asking the server to process those extra 100 bytes at the same time. Additionally, add into that the extra bandwidth time on your server and your Internet connection for those extra 100 bytes times those 1000 concurrent connections. Finally, add in the perceived performance differences to the end user. Look at those factors, and you can understand how something that seems so insignificant to start with can end up causing real performance problems in the end. Plus, we haven't even talked about the real performance problems with sending data to wireless devices like cell phones and pagers, through severely bandwidth-restricted Internet gateways.

To help improve performance in your ASP.NET application, it is a good idea to regulate the use of server controls in order to reduce the size of the rendered HTML, thereby reducing the negative impacts discussed above. One good tactic for regulating the use of server controls is by using static HTML controls whenever you don't need to interact with the control during server-side code execution.

A great example is the use of labels on ASP.NET pages. You might have noticed that we chose to use a <DIV> tag to show the label for our textbox in the last example. This was not by accident. Since the label will always remain static in our example, it makes no sense for us to use the <asp:Label> server control to create it. The table below gives you some common HTML mappings for ASP.NET server controls that you can use when you know that the values will be static and you won't be manipulating the objects with server-side code. However, be aware that if you use the runat="server" property in conjunction with a normal HTML control, it will become accessible within server-side code and carries the same performance penalties that the ASP.NET server controls do.

ASP.NET Server Control	HTML Static Control
<asp:label>	<div>
<asp:textbox>	<input>
<asp:datagrid>	<table>
<asp:datalist>	
<asp:datareader>	
<asp:image>	<img>

Another way to reduce (or even eliminate) the size of the view state is by eliminating it for an individual control, or for the entire page. You can eliminate the view state for an individual control by setting the EnableViewState property to False, as shown below:

```
<asp:textbox id="MyTextBox" runat="server" EnableViewState="False">
</asp:textbox>
```

This will eliminate the ASP.NET text box called MyTextBox from saving any information in the view state. However, it does not impact the view state information of any of the other controls on the page, or the page itself.

It's also possible to disable view state for the entire page or the entire web. The reason you would want to disable view state is if it is not necessary to save and restore the values of your page and its controls between postbacks. For example, if you are developing a page that requires "live" results which must hit the database with each visit to the page, you can do without page view state since you will be overwriting the saved values anyway.

You can disable view state for all the controls on an entire ASP.NET page or control by setting the EnableViewState property to False within the @Page directive or @Control directive (for ASP.NET user controls), as shown below.

To disable view state for an entire page (and any inherited controls), you can modify the @Page directive as follows:

```
<%@ Page Language="vb" Codebehind="MyPage.aspx.vb" EnableViewState="False"%>
```

To disable view state for a specific user control, you can modify the @Control directive as follows:

```
<%@ Control Language="vb" EnableViewState="False"%>
```

To disable view state for an entire web, you must edit either the Web.Config (for a single web) or the Machine.Config (the default settings for all webs on that machine):

```xml
<?xml version="1.0" encoding="utf-8"?>
<configuration>
  <system.web>
    <pages enableViewState="false" />
  </system.web>
</configuration>
```

Page Postbacks

Each time a page is refreshed through an action on a server control, like via a button click or data grid sort command, you're issuing a postback to the original ASP.NET page. During a postback, ASP.NET restores the values and states on all the ASP.NET server controls, and then fires the events that caused the postback. As we discussed earlier, the Page_Init and Page_Load events fire first, then the server control events will fire, followed by the cleanup events Page_PreRender and Page_Unload.

One of the most common performance problems that we see from developers new to .NET is the exclusion of checking for a postback during the Page_Load event. Let's take the typical example of a page that will query information from a database to populate an ASP.NET dropdown list box control. Our example will make use of the Authors table in the infamous Pubs database, which gets installed as part of SQL Server. The data for the list box is fairly static in nature, but we want to query it from a code table in our database so that we don't have to recompile every time a new author is eventually added. So, when we develop our first ASP.NET page we crank out code that looks like the code below, which you can find in the PageLoadExample folder of the code download:

```vb
Private Sub Page_Load(ByVal sender As System.Object, _
    ByVal e As System.EventArgs) Handles MyBase.Load
  'Put user code to initialize the page here
  Dim objConnection As SqlConnection
  Dim objCommand As SqlDataAdapter
  Dim strCommand As String
  Dim ds1 As New DataSet()

  ' Connect to SQL Server and query for a list of authors
  objConnection = _
        New SqlConnection("server=(local);uid=sa;pwd=;database=Pubs")
  strCommand = "SELECT au_lname from authors ORDER by au_lname ASC"
  objCommand = New SqlDataAdapter(strCommand, objConnection)
  ' Fill the dataset with the results
  objCommand.Fill(ds1, "authors")
  ' Bind the list box to the results
  lstAuthors.DataSource = ds1.Tables("authors")
  ' Set the field to display in the list box
  lstAuthors.DataTextField = "au_lname"
  lstAuthors.DataBind()

End Sub
```

The problem with this code is that we will end up re-querying the database every time there's a page postback. While this may be the intent, you'll need to think long and hard before doing it this way. How often will the data source be updated? Below is an example of an improved `Page_Load` routine that checks the `IsPostBack` property of the current page to determine whether or not this is the first call to this page. If this is a postback operation, ASP.NET will restore the value and state of the drop-down list box from the page's `_VIEWSTATE` variable (remember that if you've turned off view state for a page, the contents of the list box will not be saved between page postbacks).

Now, let's re-code the above example, but this time let's add the simple check for the `IsPostBack` property. Your code should look like the sample below. Don't get too hung up on the fact that we're using straight SQL embedded in our queries – we'll be focusing on how to improve your database query performance later in Chapter 5.

```
Private Sub Page_Load(ByVal sender As System.Object, _
                        ByVal e As System.EventArgs) Handles MyBase.Load
    'Put user code to initialize the page here
    Dim objConnection As SqlConnection
    Dim objCommand As SqlDataAdapter
    Dim strCommand As String
    Dim ds1 As New DataSet()

    ' Check to see if this is a page postback
    If Not IsPostBack Then
        ' Connect to SQL Server and query for a list of authors
        objConnection = _
                New SqlConnection("server=(local);uid=sa;pwd=;database=Pubs")
        strCommand = "SELECT au_lname from authors ORDER by au_lname ASC"
        objCommand = New SqlDataAdapter(strCommand, objConnection)
        ' Fill the dataset with the results
        objCommand.Fill(ds1, "authors")
        ' Bind the list box to the results
        lstAuthors.DataSource = ds1.Tables("authors")
        ' Set the field to display in the list box
        lstAuthors.DataTextField = "au_lname"
        lstAuthors.DataBind()
    End If
End Sub
```

A major performance gain can be achieved just by checking the `IsPostBack` property of a page and using the cached values in the view state instead of querying them again. We've just eliminated the creation of a SQL Server database connection and a SQL query each time the page is refreshed. Think of the busy SQL Server that's five hops away from the web server. Or maybe the data you're retrieving is coming from a web service, or a COM object. Sure, querying the `Pubs` database repeatedly on a local server seems to run fine when you test it on your local development machine, but you need to remember that enterprise applications rarely query something so simplistic! Queries from these applications tend to be quite complex in nature, so you should only execute them when absolutely necessary.

Page Smart Navigation

A seldom-documented feature of ASP.NET is called **Smart Navigation**. Smart Navigation was introduced to solve the annoying problem of refreshing every control and losing the current control's focus that you get when refreshing a browser page. This feature performs a type of smart refresh that only refreshes the necessary controls when a postback occurs. This setting can be extremely useful for improving perceived performance, since it brings the user right back to where they were before the page refresh was due to complete a postback.

Smart navigation utilizes embedded DHTML and client-side JScript as part of your rendered ASP.NET page to provide these capabilities. As such, smart navigation is only supported on Internet Explorer 5.0 and higher, but other browsers will be unaffected by this property since ASP.NET auto-detects the browser's capabilities and will disregard Smart Navigation for browsers that cannot support it. It is important to note that you might experience browser errors for those browsers (such as Opera or Mosaic) that can disguise themselves as an Internet Explorer browser from the server's perspective. Therefore, you should really only use smart navigation when you can guarantee the end-user community is completely IE 5.0 or higher (this means that smart navigation is not a good technique for Internet applications, no matter how much market share Internet Explorer has at the time).

To enable smart navigation for a page, you enable the `smartNavigation` property of the `@Page` directive like this:

```
<%@Page Language="vb"  AutoEventWireup="true"
       codebehind="WebForm1.aspx.vb" Inherits="WebForm1"
       smartNavigation="true" %>
```

You can also enable smart navigation for an entire web by using the `smartNavigation` property of the `pages` setting in the web site's configuration file (`Web.Config`), or you can specify it as the default for all web sites on a particular machine by setting the same value in the `Machine.Config` settings file.

The code below shows you how you can modify the `Machine.Config` file to enable smart navigation for all of the web pages for ASP.NET application:

```
<configuration>
  <system.web>
    <pages smartNavigation="true" />
  </system.web>
</configuration>
```

To the end user, although they will notice that the page has been refreshed, it will keep focus on the same field and all server control states (like the currently selected list box item) will remain the same. The user will be very appreciative that this information stayed the same, instead of having to re-enter the information – thus, the perception of improved performance will be better than the page that forces the user to keep scrolling back to their original page location after each page postback.

Page Exception Handling

All .NET languages now provide a mechanism for structured exception handling (particularly a boon for VB developers who can now eliminate the GOTO statement forever). This exception handling mechanism allows the developer to "catch" errors that would have otherwise generated a fatal exception and exited the program. Exceptions can also be nested within scope, so as you nest deeper into subroutine and method calls, the exception handling can either be specified at the deepest level, or inherited from the exception handling provided by one of the callers on the stack.

Although exception handling is considered good programming practice, you should always try to catch as many potential "known" exceptions as possible so that the exception handler code is not generally run. There is a significant amount of overhead involved with the CLR generation and catching of exceptions. So, for example, if you are trying to open a connection to the database, you should check return codes from the various methods that you use, in addition to creating a generic exception handler that will take care of the out of the ordinary exceptions.

Let's take a typical example of where you should provide your own error checking, instead of letting ASP.NET generate exceptions for you to handle. In this example, we have a Loan class that exposes a simplistic method for calculating the payment amount of a loan, specifying the number of months to pay off the loan (you'll also notice that our bank is very generous in the fact that we don't charge interest, but that's why we're developers and not financiers!).

```
Public Class Loan
   Private m_LoanAmount As Integer
   Public Property LoanAmount() As Integer
     Get
        Return m_LoanAmount
     End Get
     Set(ByVal Value As Integer)
        m_LoanAmount = Value
     End Set
   End Property

   Public Function MonthlyCost(ByVal iMonths As Integer) As Double
     ' Check to make sure that a valid duration is specified
     If iMonths <= 0 Then
        Return 0.0
     Else
        Return CType((Me.LoanAmount / iMonths), Double)
     End If
   End Function

End Class
```

As you can see, we provide a quick check to make sure that the number of months passed in is not zero (or negative). If we didn't check this and the consumer passed in zero, an exception would have been generated. Now, we could have used the Try...Catch mechanism, but that consumes more resources when an exception is thrown than the simple If check that we've implemented here. The lesson here is that if you can think of a case where your code may generate an error, you should provide some type of check within your code – it ends up saving cycles when exceptions do get thrown.

> **This doesn't mean that you shouldn't use ASP.NET exception handling features. The point is that if you recognize that a situation is likely to occur (such as a null pointer reference, division by zero, etc.) then you should plan for it in your code and not wait for the exception to hit your exception handling code.**

As you can see, understanding page events and page processing is a key concept to understanding how your ASP.NET application performs, and what steps you might need to take in order to make it perform even better. Without a sound grasp of how ASP.NET processes pages and the events that pages can fire, you will probably find yourself on the short end of the stick when it comes to designing high performance ASP.NET applications.

ASP.NET State Management

In the pioneering days of web development, web pages were distinct and separate from each other. They rarely needed to know information about the other's contents (and if they did, they were passed via the query string). As the Internet grew in popularity, so did web pages. Suddenly, it was just not enough to browse to a page and view its contents. Now, it is expected that web sites are designed with a workflow in mind – purposely moving you from one page to the next.

Thus **session state** was born. Session state variables allow a web page to save information linked to the user's specific browser "session". Pages downstream, within the same session, can reference these session variables as they need to. This information is tied to a user's browser session. Once the browser session is closed, the information is deleted. This information is stored on the web server so that it persists across all of the numerous calls that a client's browser makes.

When a postback occurs, ASP.NET can retrieve session information by using the unique cookie ID created by ASP.NET when the user first connected (if the browser supports cookies and the ASP.NET web page is configured to use them), or via an encrypted cookie string that is appended to the URL by ASP.NET (for those browsers that do not support cookies, or when the ASP.NET web page is configured not to use cookies).

Classic ASP had a simplistic session management feature that allowed the programmer to store string values. As you'll see below, ASP.NET enhances this feature by allowing you to store any .NET data type. The persistence value (how long inactive session information is stored) of session data is also configurable through the timeout setting in the Web.Config file.

```
<sessionState
    mode="InProc"
    stateConnectionString="tcpip=127.0.0.1:42424"
        sqlConnectionString="data source=127.0.0.1;user id=sa;password="
        cookieless="false"
        timeout="20"
/>
```

ASP.NET also provides the capability to store session information in a central repository, such as a common file area or SQL Server, without having to provide additional state management code. This provides support for web pages that are stored on multiple web servers (web farms) for load balancing purposes. The concept behind a web farm is that a user will be directed to the server with the lowest utilization at that time. Since you are never guaranteed to be directed to the same server between page hits (unless the web site is configured to do this – a setting called "sticky sessions"), your session information may be lost to you if stored on a single web server.

In this next section, we'll talk about how ASP.NET implements session and application state. Then, we'll delve into some performance topics that will help you get the best performance from your ASP.NET applications when you need to use ASP.NET state management features.

ASP.NET Session State

As in ASP, session state is used to create and manage session information. This information persists as long as the current browser session is valid and has not expired. Session state differs from the State Bag discussed earlier, since it persists across pages and is stored at the server level and not as part of a page's view state.

Previously, in ASP when you wanted to add a new session variable, you added the following script line somewhere in your ASP application. This assumes that the page was called with a `QueryString` parameter called `USERNAME`.

```
<% Session("UserName") = Request.QueryString("USERNAME") %>
```

Then, to use the value, you would get the value of the session variable using a script block like this:

```
<FORM METHOD="POST" ACTION="http://myserver.com/process.asp">
  <INPUT TYPE="TEXT" NAME="txtName" VALUE= <% Session("UserName") %> >
</FORM>
```

If you're familiar with ASP, you'll undoubtedly remember that this is pretty much all you can do with session variables. In ASP, the `Session` object is pretty vanilla. You can set and retrieve session string information, but nothing more.

Now in ASP.NET, `Session` is a true .NET object with methods and properties. You can now store any data type, including user-defined classes and structures in a .NET session state object. However, these new capabilities do come at a performance price, dependent upon how much session information you keep and whether it is value type information (primitive types) or reference type information (user objects).

Let's create a simple example of how session information is stored and used. First, create a new VS.NET project called `SessionExample`, then and add two separate Web Forms pages. The first ASPX page will be called `Entry.aspx` and it will handle collecting the user data. The second ASPX page will be called Results.aspx and will handle the display of results.

The `Entry.aspx` file will contain two text fields that allow you to enter a new session variable and its value, and then store them in session state by clicking an **Add Session Variable** button. There will also be a **View Session Variables** button that will send the user to the `Results.aspx` file.

```
<form id="Form1" method="post" runat="server">
  <asp:TextBox id="txtSessionVariable" style="Z-INDEX: 101; LEFT: 140px;
      POSITION: absolute; TOP: 55px" runat="server"></asp:TextBox>
  <asp:TextBox id="txtSessionValue" style="Z-INDEX: 102; LEFT: 140px;
      POSITION: absolute; TOP: 87px" runat="server" Width="303px"></asp:TextBox>
  <DIV style="DISPLAY: inline; Z-INDEX: 103; LEFT: 18px; WIDTH: 116px;
      POSITION: absolute; TOP: 57px; HEIGHT: 22px"
      ms_positioning="FlowLayout">Session Variable:</DIV>
  <DIV style="DISPLAY: inline; Z-INDEX: 104; LEFT: 18px; WIDTH: 70px;
      POSITION: absolute; TOP: 88px; HEIGHT: 15px"
      ms_positioning="FlowLayout">Value:</DIV>
  <asp:Button id="btnAdd" style="Z-INDEX: 105; LEFT: 19px; POSITION: absolute;
      TOP: 128px" runat="server" Text="Add Session Variable"
      Width="188px"></asp:Button>
  <asp:Button id="btnView" style="Z-INDEX: 106; LEFT: 21px; POSITION:
      absolute; TOP: 167px" runat="server" Width="188px"
      Text="View Session Variables"></asp:Button>
</form>
```

In the code-behind file, we'll write event handlers for the **Add** and **View** buttons. The **Add** button will add or update the session variable's value. The view button will redirect to the `Results` page so that we can see the values of all session variables. A coding performance tip is also here. Notice how we use the `Server.Transfer()` method instead of the `Response.Redirect()` method. `Server.Transfer()` will yield better performance, since it does not require a postback before it executes.

```
    Private Sub btnAdd_Click(ByVal sender As System.Object, ByVal e As
        System.EventArgs) Handles btnAdd.Click
      ' Make sure that the key is not null before adding it
      If txtSessionVariable.Text <> "" Then
        ' Add it to the session object
        Session(txtSessionVariable.Text) = txtSessionValue.Text
      End If
    End Sub

    Private Sub btnView_Click(ByVal sender As System.Object, ByVal e As
        System.EventArgs) Handles btnView.Click
      ' Transfer control to results page.
      ' Server.Transfer is faster than Response.Redirect
      Server.Transfer("results.aspx")
    End Sub
End Class
```

We can see the results of this code below:

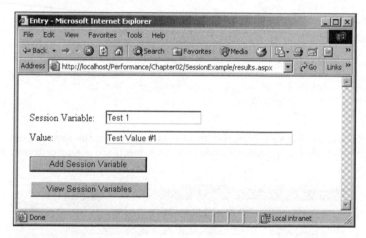

The `Results.aspx` page will go through all of the session state variables and print them out. This will give you a good idea of how to manipulate session information in an ASP.NET application. Your code should look similar to the code below:

```
    <form id="Form1" method="post" runat="server">
      <asp:TextBox id="txtSessionInfo" style="Z-INDEX: 101; LEFT: 17px;
          POSITION: absolute; TOP: 49px" runat="server" TextMode="MultiLine"
          Width="321px" Rows="10"></asp:TextBox>
      <DIV style="DISPLAY: inline; Z-INDEX: 102; LEFT: 16px; WIDTH: 164px;
          POSITION: absolute; TOP: 17px; HEIGHT: 23px"
          ms_positioning="FlowLayout">Session Information</DIV>
      <asp:Button id="btnBack" style="Z-INDEX: 103; LEFT: 20px;
          POSITION: absolute; TOP: 227px" runat="server" Text="Back"></asp:Button>
    </form>
```

The code-behind looks like this:

```
Private Sub Page_Load(ByVal sender As System.Object, ByVal e As
    System.EventArgs) Handles MyBase.Load
  'Put user code to initialize the page here
  Dim sbEntries As New StringBuilder()
  Dim strKey As String

  ' Go through the list of session keys
  For Each strKey In Session.Keys
    ' Append key name and value to stringbuiler
    ' NOTE: Use stringbuilder becuase it is faster
    ' than the normal &/+ appending process
    sbEntries.Append(strKey)
    sbEntries.Append(" = ")
    sbEntries.Append(Session(strKey))
    ' Add CR/LF
    sbEntries.Append(Convert.ToChar(13))
    sbEntries.Append(Convert.ToChar(10))
  Next
  ' Put the results into the text box
  txtSessionInfo.Text = sbEntries.ToString
End Sub

Private Sub btnBack_Click(ByVal sender As System.Object, ByVal e As
    System.EventArgs) Handles btnBack.Click
  ' Clear out session information for next pass
  Session.Clear()
  ' Transfer back to the entry page
  ' Server.Transfer is faster than Response.Redirect
  Server.Transfer("entry.aspx")
End Sub
```

Notice that as you add session variables, the list of values grows on the results page. There is technically no limit to the number of session variables you can store, but there is a price to pay for storing items in session variables.

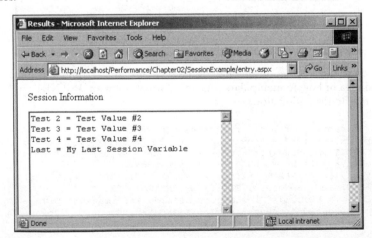

Another performance consideration when you're working with session information (and application/cache information as we'll see in a moment), is that you should not store anything that relies on external connectivity or critical resources. For example, you should not store database connections as part of a session because they are a critical resource. Keeping the database connection open between postbacks will lead to very poor performance. You never know when the next postback will happen, so you'll end up keeping the database connection active for very long periods of time. Other examples of critical resources you should not store in session state are open file handles, file I/O streams, Directory Service connectors (like ADS & LDAP) and WMI (Windows management instrumentation) connections.

ASP.NET Application State

ASP.NET provides another object called `Application` to manage application-level information. Information stored in an `Application` object is static across all connections to the ASP.NET application. The `Application` object information is stored as a hash table of name/value combinations. This is information that you'd rather not hard code, and is not tied to a specific user's session. This might be something like your application's SQL connection string.

There are two ways that you can set application-level information. The first is by using the special section in the `Web.Config` file. In the example below, we've set an application-level variable called `dbConnect` with the value of our SQL Server database connection string. As you can see, you can only initialize the value this way. There's no way for you to manipulate this information during the lifetime of the web application. What is interesting to note, however, is that ASP.NET is alerted whenever `Web.Config` changes, so that you can change values within `Web.Config`, and these new values will be picked up by subsequent browser page requests, all without having to reset IIS.

```
<configuration>
  <appSettings>
    <add key="dbConnection"
         value="server=MyServer;uid=sa;pwd=;database=MyDatabase" />
  </appSettings>
</configuration>
```

In order to retrieve this value you would use the `AppSettings` method of the `ConfigurationSettings` class in your code, similar to the way that we referenced the `Session` object earlier.

```
Dim strConnection As String
strConnection = _
      Ctype(ConfigurationSettings.AppSettings("dbConnection"),string))
```

The other way to set values for application-level information is through the use of the `Application` object in code. The best place to set the values for an application variable is in the `Application_Start` event handler in the `Global.asax` file. This event is fired whenever the application is first started for example, when the first web page request is made since the application was loaded, last reset, or since IIS was last reset. This event will only fire once throughout the life of a web application and will not fire for subsequent web user requests, until the application or IIS is stopped, or until ASP.NET detects a change in the `Web.Config` file. The following code is a sample of how you would set the same variable `DBConnection` using the `Application` object, and then retrieve it later in your code:

```
    Application("dbConnection") = _
        "server=MyServer;uid=sa;pwd=;database=MyDatabase"

    Dim strConnection As String
    strConnection = CType(Application("dbConnection"),string)
```

It is important to note that you must lock and unlock the Application object in order to ensure the integrity of the data since multiple instances of the application can be attempting to update the value at the same time. This is done through the use of the Lock() and Unlock() methods of the Application object.

```
    Public Function Login(ByVal strUserId As String, _
                          ByVal strPassword As String) As Boolean
      ' Increment the number of online users
      Dim intUserCount As Integer

      ' Check to make sure user is valid
      If UserIsValid(strUserId, strPassword) Then
        ' Lock to ensure nobody updates at the same time
        Application.Lock()
        intUserCount = Application("UserCount")
        intUserCount += 1
        '  Update current user count
        Application("UserCount") = intUserCount
        Application.Unlock()
        Return True;
      Else
        Return False;
    End Function
```

However, this also comes as a performance penalty, since any other ASP.NET application instances can be essentially frozen while waiting for an Application object to be unlocked before they can access it. Therefore, it is recommended that if you are going to use the Application object in a read/write fashion, you make sure that there is a minimum amount of code to be executed while a key value is locked. It is not a good idea to spin off threads or run long executing queries inside a lock. If possible, you should try to work with state management in a read-only mode, as described earlier.

In the example above, notice that the check for user validity is carefully done outside the lock so that only the critical logic of retrieving the current user count and incrementing it are locked to ensure the integrity of the user count value. As any VB6 developer who has worked with threads before will tell you, this is a critical component of application performance when sync-locking shared information.

ASP.NET Cache

ASP.NET provides the programmatic capability to cache information on an ASP.NET application-level basis. It is similar to the Application object we looked at earlier, but it provides the capability to dynamically maintain the cache information during the lifetime of the ASP.NET application. Caching data in your application can significantly improve performance, since the data is local to the server and can quickly be retrieved, rather than re-querying the original source of the data. This can save seconds to even minutes (depending on the performance of the process to re-query the data) in your page load time.

A great example of this is the use of caching in a performance monitoring system that provides 30 minute roll-ups of data. Since the data will only be updated every 30 minutes, there's no reason to re-query it every time. Let's assume that the initial performance hit to get the data for a specific customer takes 30 seconds. We can save 30 seconds of page load time immediately by caching off this data for all subsequent requests for this customer over the next 30 minutes. This is a huge performance increase!

The Cache object supports the ability to implement dependency-based expiration, and callback notifications that can allow you to manage the cache as items are manipulated within the cache (by other users of the application, or by ASP.NET itself). With the Cache object, you also have the capability to store anything (value types or reference types), and then update them or remove them at a later time. Cache is a more flexible object than the Application object we looked at earlier. It supports:

❑ Dependency-based expiration and removal – the Cache object provides the ability to tie the automated expiration and removal of a cache value based on a file event, a specific or relative date/time, or another cache key.

❑ Automated Lock management – the Cache object includes internal lock management to provide synchronization for atomic updates (those that can be placed in a single computing operation).

❑ Callback mechanism – the Cache object provides the ability to set a function callback to be invoked when a cache item is removed.

A great example of using the Cache object to solve a business problem would be the storage of a code table value in memory that rarely changes. For example, let's say we have an XML file for an external system that contains our sales regions. We can cache that information in our application, rather than querying it each time:

```
Dim dsRegions As New DataSet()
dsRegions.ReadXml(Server.MapPath("Regions.xml"))
Cache("Regions") = dsRegions
```

You'll notice that we're caching the entire data set in this example. This can be a negative performance factor, as well find out in the next section.

Session, Application, and Cache State Performance

So now that we know the basics of ASP.NET session and application state management, how does that help us with understanding performance? By now, you should be seeing a common theme that adding new server-side resources can and will affect the performance of your application.

An easy way to increase performance for an ASP.NET application is to explicitly turn off session state if it is not used within the application (ASP.NET enables session state by default). To disable session state for a page, you can set the EnableSessionState property as part of the @Page directive.

```
<%@ Page Language="vb" EnableSessionState="False" AutoEventWireup="false"
    Codebehind="Entry.aspx.vb" Inherits="SessionExample.Entry"%>
```

Keep in mind that this property has no impact on the Cache or Application object. This property will apply to the specific web page only (or any user controls that are inherited from it). A page exception will be thrown if you attempt to set or retrieve a session variable with this property set. Microsoft recommends the disabling of session state for any pages or applications that do not access session variables. Depending on the size of the page, this can produce a noticeable increase in the load time of your page, since ASP.NET will not incur the state management overhead required to work with ASP.NET session objects.

If you have an ASP.NET page that requires access to session variables but never manipulates them, the next best setting for EnableSessionState is "ReadOnly". This means that you can access session variables, but not set them. It will not provide as large an increase in performance as completely disabling session state, but it will perform better than enabling complete session state management capabilities. A page exception will be thrown if you attempt to set a session variable with this property set.

```
<%@ Page Language="vb" EnableSessionState="ReadOnly" AutoEventWireup="false"
    Codebehind="Entry.aspx.vb" Inherits="SessionExample.Entry"%>
```

You can also disable session state for an entire web by editing the Web.Config file:

```
<configuration>
  <system.web>
    <sessionState mode="Off" />
  </system.web>
</configuration>
```

> The session state setting in **Web.Config** overrides any **@Page** directive setting, so putting this setting in **Web.Config** guarantees that session state will be disabled for the virtual web covered by this particular **Web.Config** file. This setting can also be applied machine-wide in the **Machine.Config** file.

With ASP.NET, you get the flexibility to control the manner in which session state information is stored. By default, ASP.NET stores session state using a model called In-Proc. This means that the session state is stored in the same process that is used to execute the ASP.NET worker process (aspnet_wp.exe). This is the same model that ASP utilized. This, of course, doesn't work very well when your application is running on a web farm. A web farm is a distributed set of web servers that all have the same copy of the web application, but are front-ended with a load-balancer (either a hardware device or software service) that sends your request to the server with the lowest overall utilization. This is unless a value like "sticky sessions" is enabled which routes all requests from the same browser session to the same server for a specified interval, for example, as required by SSL web sites.

In ASP, developers had to manually code their way around the web farms issue. Many a third party utility was sold capitalizing on this hole in the ASP development platform. To solve this problem, ASP.NET provided two other session state models that give the developer the functionality to persist session state across web farms without any additional coding.

The first mode is called **state server**. This mode stores session state on an external state server process on the local web server, or on a remote server. The state server is really a Windows service called aspnet_state.exe which can be managed using Windows Services on any machine with .NET installed. To change the session state mode to state server, you can edit the Web.Config file for a particular web, or set it as the default for all webs on the machine in the Machine.Config file.

```
<configuration>
  <system.web>
    <sessionState mode="StateServer"
        stateConnectionString="tcpip=127.0.0.1:42424" />
  </system.web>
</configuration>
```

If you want to use a remote machine to be the state server, then you would change the value in your stateConnectionString:

```
stateConnectionString="tcpid=www.mystateserver.com:42424"
```

Notice that the state server uses the port 42424 to communicate. In order for this to work the state server service must be running on the remote machine, and port 42424 must be open between the requesting web server and the state server machine. This port value can be configured on the state server machine by editing a registry key on the remote state server machine:

```
HKEY_LOCAL_MACHINE\System\CurrentControlSet\Services\aspnet_state\Parameters\Port
```

Of course, there are performance penalties when choosing state server over In-Proc as your session state mode. This is because the data being stored and retrieved must cross process or remote to a machine (in the case of using a remote machine). Therefore, ASP.NET must serialize and de-serialize the data and provide cross-process marshaling of the data between the ASP.NET web application and the state server service.

The last session state mode is called SQL Server. This allows the developer to store session state information in a SQL Server database that has been created especially for session state management. The .NET Framework SDK provides you with a script that will create the database and tables that you need for a SQL Server to handle session state information (this file is called InstallSqlState.sql and can be found in the %WINDIR%\Microsoft.Net\Framework\ (version) directory). Once installed, you can choose SQL Server as your session state model by editing the same configuration file as above, but instead choosing the settings shown below:

```
<configuration>
  <system.web>
    <sessionState mode="SQLServer"
        sqlConnectionString="server=mysqlserver;uid=sa;pwd=" />
  </system.web>
</configuration>
```

The SQL Server session state model is the slowest of the three models. However, it is the most robust of the three since it almost guarantees that session state will never get lost – especially if you are clustering the SQL Server with fail-over support, which is being used to store session state.

Both state server and SQL Server models require that session information be serialized and de-serialized. This is because these processes have no direct knowledge of the classes and structures that are being stored. If you attempt to store or retrieve session information without serialization while configured to use either of these models, an exception will be thrown.

Sessions also have a distinct lifetime. This lifetime is configurable in the Web.Config or Machine.config configuration file. Please note that the value specified here is in minutes, which is different than some of the other configuration units in ASP.NET. The default value is 20 minutes, but this default setting is easily configurable:

```
<configuration>
  <system.web>
    <sessionState timeout="5" />
  </system.web>
</configuration>
```

Optimizing session state lifetime for your web application takes some keen usage analysis and guesswork. You'll need to balance the execution time taken for re-creating values that were stored in session state, versus the downstream performance gains from referencing what is essentially a cached value, instead of re-computing it.

We've seen how session state is valuable in storing value types that will persist across page postbacks. What if we were to want to store the value of a user-defined object (reference type) into a session state variable? If we had a class called UserInfo that specified a user's contact information, and we instanced an object called objCurrentUser of type UserInfo, we could just store the entire object into a session state variable like this:

```
Session("CurrentUser") = objCurrentUser
```

What happens when we do this? ASP.NET examines the structure when saving an object in state and stores it using an algorithm that optimizes storage space and makes sure that certain types are on, or within, byte boundaries. When restoring the information, ASP.NET needs to make a copy of the object to examine its structure, and then does the inverse of the same storage process. This is especially a problem when invoking methods outside of the object's scope (for example outside of an Application Domain, or storage of session on a separate State Server process) when the structure of a class is not known.

A better way to do this is to serialize the object and store the serialized data into a state variable like Session, Application, or Cache (serialization is the process of taking a complex data type and storing it into a contiguous storage medium, like a file or memory buffer, in order to persist it so that it can be restored to its original state later). This eliminates the need for ASP.NET state objects to know the specifics about the structure of the object, and encapsulates the serialization/de-serialization code within the class itself.

Binary serialization/de-serialization of the data will provide better performance for your objects because the information has to be marshaled or remoted across process boundaries. If the remote process or machine is required to "know" about the structure of the object, it will spend extra time casting the information, expending processor cycles. By storing the serialized version of the data, the ASP.NET state management subsystem does not need to know anything about the format, other than it's trying to store and retrieve a piece of binary information.

Let's use our voting booth example from earlier to demonstrate this concept. In our original version, we stored the individual vote tallies in cache variables (this same concept would hold true for Application and Session as well). However, what if we updated the application to create a Candidate class that contained the person's name and vote count? The user interface would remain the same, but the updated code-behind file might look something similar to what we have below. We'll create the code without using the serialization method in order to give us a starting reference point. You can find this code in VoteObject.aspx in the VotingBooth folder of the code download for this chapter.

First, we need to create an object that holds the candidate information (for simplicity purposes we're not using properties for Name and Votes, but for a production system we would). Then, we create a collection class that allows us to create a set of candidate objects.

```
Public Class VoteObject
  Inherits System.Web.UI.Page
  Protected WithEvents DataGrid1 As System.Web.UI.WebControls.DataGrid
  Public VoteTally As Hashtable
  Protected WithEvents btnReset As System.Web.UI.WebControls.Button

  Public Class Candidate
    Public Name As String
    Public Votes As Integer
  End Class

  Public Class Candidates
    Inherits CollectionBase
    Public Sub Add(ByVal strName As String)
      Dim objCandidate As New Candidate()
      objCandidate.Name = strName
      InnerList.Add(objCandidate)
    End Sub
    Public Function Item(ByVal strName As String) As Candidate
      Dim objCandidate As New Candidate()
      For Each objCandidate In InnerList
        If objCandidate.Name = strName Then
          Return objCandidate
        End If
      Next
        Return Nothing
      End Function
  End Class
  Public Shared CurrentCandidates As String() = _
    {"Red", "Green", "Yellow", "Brown", "Black"}
  Public objVotes As New Candidates()
```

During the page initialization, we check to see if our cache item exists, if not we reset all values. Otherwise, we load the data from cache. Here is where .NET is taking a performance hit, since it needs to understand the exact structure of the object to restore the data from cache:

```
Private Sub Page_Load(ByVal sender As System.Object, _
    ByVal e As System.EventArgs) Handles MyBase.Load
  Dim strKey As String
  ' Check to make sure cache key exists
  If Cache.Get("Votes") Is Nothing Then
    ' If not, initialize vote count
    For Each strKey In CurrentCandidates
      objVotes.Add(strKey)
    Next
  Else
    objVotes = CType(Cache.Get("Votes"), Candidates)
  End If
End Sub
Protected Sub DataGrid1_ItemCommand(ByVal sender As System.Object, _
    ByVal e As System.Web.UI.WebControls.DataGridCommandEventArgs) _
    Handles DataGrid1.ItemCommand
  Select Case e.CommandName
```

```
      Case "Vote"
         Dim objCandidate As New Candidate()
         objCandidate = objVotes.Item(e.Item.Cells(0).Text)
         objCandidate.Votes += 1
    End Select
End Sub
```

Our pre-render event basically stays the same, except we have to get the information from the collection instead of the hash table, as in the original example. Here we dynamically create a data table to use as the data source. Then, in the page cleanup process, we cache the entire collection. Again, here's where the performance hit takes place, since we're caching a structured object, and not just a serialized stream of information. The ASP.NET state management subsystem must now expend processor cycles getting the structure of the destination object, retrieving the serialized data, de-serializing it to the object, and then repeating the same process to get the object back to the ASP.NET application since they could be out of process. This extra casting and serialization/de-serialization process can be quite a hit, dependent upon the size and structure of your object.

```
    Private Sub Page_PreRender(ByVal sender As Object, _
         ByVal e As System.EventArgs) Handles MyBase.PreRender
      ' Bind the data just before we render the HTML
      Dim dtTable As New DataTable()
      Dim objCandidate As New Candidate()
      Dim drRow As DataRow
      dtTable.Columns.Add("Key")
      dtTable.Columns.Add("Value")
      For Each objCandidate In objVotes
         drRow = dtTable.NewRow
         drRow("Key") = objCandidate.Name
         drRow("Value") = objCandidate.Votes
         dtTable.Rows.Add(drRow)
      Next
         DataGrid1.DataSource = dtTable.DefaultView
         DataGrid1.DataBind()
    End Sub
    Private Sub Page_UnLoad(ByVal sender As System.Object,
         ByVal e As System.EventArgs) Handles MyBase.Unload
      ' Save vote tally for other voting booths
      Cache.Insert("Votes", objVotes)
    End Sub
    Private Sub btnReset_Click(ByVal sender As System.Object, _
         ByVal e As System.EventArgs) Handles btnReset.Click
      Dim objCandidate As New Candidate()
      For Each objCandidate In objVotes
         objCandidate.Votes = 0
      Next
    End Sub
End Class
```

That's the code, and it actually works fine in most cases (we'll talk about two cases where serialization is required in a moment). So, how do I update this example to implement serialization? Actually, it's very easy. We merely need to implement the <Serializable()> attribute for any class that we want to store in a state variable. This way ASP.NET does not need to determine class structures when setting and retrieving state information. Everything is stored as one contiguous stream, and then restored within the class itself, leaving any interpretation out of the equation. Let's make the changes against our existing example and see what it looks like (this is VoteObjectSerialized.aspx in the code download).

```
<Serializable()> _
Public Class Candidate
   Public Name As String
   Public Votes As Integer
End Class
```

Holy hand-cramps, Batman! Look at all that extra code we needed to write just to implement serialization! In all seriousness, though, you will find that a lot of the methods for improving performance are not going to require thousands of lines of new code. Simplicity is the new name of the game with ASP.NET development.

Session state requires you to provide an object that implements serialization when storing session information in session state mode with a mode of State Server or SQL Server. If you attempt to store an object in session state in one of these modes that is not serializable, then you'll get an unhandled exception.

That helps with the session state information, but what about application-level state objects? While serializable classes are not required for Application or Cache, they are still recommended to help improve the performance of your code. It's good practice to just include the attribute for any reference type that you'll be storing in state.

Although there's no way to turn off the Application or Cache objects on a page or web basis (as we saw with Session), we can do (and not do) some things that will help performance. In addition, ASP.NET does not currently support the storage of Application or Cache information other than on the server that is executing the page.

As we saw earlier, the Cache object is the preferred method for setting and updating information that stays the same across all user sessions within the application. The Cache object supports its own internal locking mechanism to ensure the integrity of the data it stores under multi-user conditions, unlike the Application object where you need to manually perform a Lock() and Unlock(). However, this internal locking is only for atomic operations (those that can be placed in a single computing operation). If you need to provide a multi-step update, then you will need to provide your own lock/unlock section. We can do that in VB.NET by using the SyncLock statement (or in C# by using the Lock statement), which guarantees the uninterrupted execution of the code section.

A SyncLock statement allows statements to be synchronized on an expression, which ensures that multiple threads of execution do not execute the same statements at the same time. The expression is evaluated once, upon entry to the block. When entering the SyncLock block, the shared method System.Threading.Monitor.Enter is called on the specified expression, which blocks until the thread of execution has an exclusive lock on the object returned by the expression. The type of the expression in a SyncLock statement must be a reference type.

A simple example of this might be updating a bank account balance after deducting an ATM charge. We would want to make sure that we executed all of the statements as a single transaction, so that no other ATM deduction could run in parallel with ours and allow the customer to withdraw more money than they actually had. The example would look similar to the code below:

```
' The SyncLock variable must be a non-null object accessible
' at the module level
Dim strBalLock As String = "Locked"
```

63

```
Public Function ATMWithdrawl(ByRef objCust As Customer, _
                            ByVal iDollars As Integer) As Boolean
   Dim boolRetVal As Boolean = False
   SyncLock strBalLock
      If (objCustomer.Balance - iDollar) >= 0 Then
         ObjCustomer.Balance -= iDollar
         ObjCustomer.Update()
         BoolRetVal = True
      End If
   End SyncLock
   ATMWithdrawl = boolRetVal
End Sub
```

Granted, the better design would be that the object included the ATMWithdrawl method, but we've purposely coded it this way so that we can show how SyncLock works outside of a class. We're also assuming that we already have a class called Customer, and that it has the methods and properties necessary for getting the customer balance from our repository, then updating to the new balance and finally updating the customer balance in the repository.

An important item to note here is that all other session requests that try to execute this code while a session is in the middle of the SyncLock will be held until the SyncLock is freed. The SyncLock block is implicitly contained by a Try statement whose Finally block calls the shared method System.Monitor.Exit on the expression. This ensures the lock is freed even when an exception is thrown.

You can incur quite a performance penalty if the code section within your SyncLock takes a lot of time to execute. For example, what if we had an object that contained a method called RefreshGrid that re-queried a database and repopulated the data grid. If we applied a SyncLock within the Refresh method, every instance of the ASP.NET web application that called the Refresh method around the same time would be blocked one by one, until a previous instance was completed. The end result would be the serialized processing of all calls to our Refresh method. The time to load for end user pages that used this data grid could easily double or triple over the same page without a SyncLock (depending upon the server load and the number of concurrent requests to a page that utilize the same object and data grid refresh).

Therefore, we recommend that you do not do things like retrieve web service information, execute long running SQL queries, or batch a large section of code together within a SyncLock. If you need to transactionalize large sections of code like this, we recommend using asynchronous calls, which will allow control to be returned to the user more quickly, thereby speeding up the perceived performance of your application. We'll talk more about asynchronous operations in the next chapter when we go into designing a high performance ASP.NET application.

Also mentioned earlier is the Cache object's support of function callback notifications. This callback provides you with the ability to do some cleanup, or other business logic based on the removal of the cache key item. ASP.NET can remove any cache key item at any time based on certain key performance criteria (like system memory usage), so you should be prepared for the fact that a cache item may not be available, instead of waiting for the dreaded unhandled exception error.

Something to keep in mind is that the callback is invoked without regard to the page class that the module lives in. If you include the callback as part of the page class, then the entire page class stays in memory for the lifetime of the cache item, since the callback needs to be accessible from within ASP.NET. In addition, you will not be able to affect existing page controls, even though the callback lives within the page class. That's because the controls have long since been rendered and disposed. This will undoubtedly affect performance, since the amount of memory required for the application to run will increase. Assuming that the object takes up 2K of space, and there are 1,000 users on the system (over the course of the lifetime of the callback), that's an extra 0.2MB of memory that is required just to retain the objects.

Let's take a look at a sample piece of code that demonstrates the callback process. In this code, we'll have an ASP.NET page that allows us to create new cache items and provide a list of the current cache keys and values in memory. You can find this code in the `CacheChange.aspx` file in the `CacheObject` folder of the code download.

```
<asp:DataGrid id="DataGrid1" runat="server" AutoGenerateColumns="False"
              BorderColor="#CC9966" BorderStyle="None" BorderWidth="1px"
              BackColor="White" CellPadding="4">
  <SelectedItemStyle Font-Bold="True" ForeColor="#663399"
                     BackColor="#FFCC66"></SelectedItemStyle>
  <ItemStyle ForeColor="#330099" BackColor="White"></ItemStyle>
  <HeaderStyle Font-Bold="True" ForeColor="#FFFFCC"
               BackColor="#990000"></HeaderStyle>
  <FooterStyle ForeColor="#330099" BackColor="#FFFFCC"></FooterStyle>
  <PagerStyle HorizontalAlign="Center" ForeColor="#330099"
              BackColor="#FFFFCC"></PagerStyle>
  <Columns>
    <asp:BoundColumn ReadOnly="True" DataField="key" HeaderText="Cache Key"
                     runat="server"></asp:BoundColumn>
    <asp:BoundColumn ReadOnly="True" DataField="value" HeaderText="Value"
                     runat="server"></asp:BoundColumn>
    <asp:ButtonColumn ButtonType="PushButton" CommandName="RemoveCache"
                      Text="Remove"></asp:ButtonColumn>
  </Columns>
</asp:DataGrid>
...
<P>Add Key:</P>
<asp:TextBox id="txtCacheKey" runat="server"></asp:TextBox><P>
<asp:TextBox id="txtCacheValue" runat="server"></asp:TextBox><P>
<asp:Button id="btnAdd" runat="server" Text="Add"></asp:Button>
```

The first thing to do is get a list of all of the cache items during the page initialization phase, and as always, we'll bind the data last in the pre-render event:

```
Dim tblCache As New Hashtable()
...
Private Sub Page_Load(ByVal sender As System.Object, _
    ByVal e As System.EventArgs) Handles MyBase.Load
  'Put user code to initialize the page here
  Dim objKey As DictionaryEntry
  For Each objKey In Cache()
    tblCache.Add(objKey.Key, objKey.Value)
  Next
End Sub

Private Sub Page_PreRender(ByVal sender As Object, _
    ByVal e As System.EventArgs) Handles MyBase.PreRender
  DataGrid1.DataSource = tblCache
  DataGrid1.DataBind()
End Sub
```

When the user clicks the Add button, we'll create a new cache item (or update the existing one) and specify a timeout interval of 10 seconds. We'll set the removal callback routine to be the `CacheItemRemovedCallBack` routine in our page class. We'll also supply a Remove button in the data grid that we can use to manually remove the cache key and watch it fire the cache item remove callback.

```
Private Sub btnAdd_Click(ByVal sender As System.Object, _
    ByVal e As System.EventArgs) Handles btnAdd.Click
  ' Create callback pointer
  Dim fnRemoveCallback As New CacheItemRemovedCallback _
      (AddressOf Me.CacheItemRemovedCallBack)
  If txtCacheKey.Text <> "" Then
    ' See if key already present (Add will also update)
    Cache.Add(txtCacheKey.Text, txtCacheValue.Text, Nothing, _
        DateTime.Now.AddSeconds(10), TimeSpan.Zero, _
        CacheItemPriority.Default, fnRemoveCallback)
    If tblCache.Item(txtCacheKey.Text) Is Nothing Then
      tblCache.Add(txtCacheKey.Text, txtCacheValue.Text)
    Else
      tblCache.Item(txtCacheKey.Text) = txtCacheValue.Text
    End If
  End If
End Sub

Private Sub DataGrid1_ItemCommand(ByVal sender As System.Object, _
    ByVal e As System.Web.UI.WebControls.DataGridCommandEventArgs)_
    Handles DataGrid1.ItemCommand
  If e.CommandName = "RemoveCache" Then
    Cache.Remove(e.Item.Cells(0).Text)
    tblCache.Remove(e.Item.Cells(0).Text)
  End If
End Sub
```

Lastly, we supply the callback handler code. Here we'll add an entry to the event log, letting everyone know why the cache item was removed. If its removal reason was `CacheItemRemovedReason.Underused`, it tells us that ASP.NET was running low of system memory and it decided to reclaim an underused cache key ahead of its expiration (which is the reason you can never count that a cache key will be available – you should always check first before referencing its value). This is a good message for any web administrator to receive to alert them of a possible ASP.NET system problem.

```
Public Sub CacheItemRemovedCallBack(ByVal strKey As String, _
    ByVal objValue As Object, ByVal objReason As CacheItemRemovedReason)
  ' Log the reason for removal
  Dim strResult As New StringBuilder()
  Dim eLog As System.Diagnostics.EventLog = New System.Diagnostics.EventLog()
  eLog.Source = "CacheApp"
  strResult.Append("Cache Key Removed. Key=")
  strResult.Append(strKey)
  strResult.Append("; Reason=")
  strResult.Append(objReason.ToString)
  eLog.WriteEntry(strResult.ToString)
  eLog.Close()
End Sub
```

To test this, enable debugging for this page and then compile it and run it in the debugger. Set a breakpoint on the callback routine and then run the ASPX page. Enter a new cache key and value, click Add and then wait. After 10 seconds your debugger will trip with the callback. Now, let's do some investigation in the debugger. Remember that the page has long since been rendered and the memory should have been freed. But, check the debugger when the cache remove callback is invoked. You can access all of the "old" page objects, methods and properties – and they're set to their values at the time of the original cache item add or update! This can only mean that our page class has stayed in memory, or was itself cached and brought back to life when the cache remove callback was invoked.

As you can see, cache expiration callbacks can be quite a resource hog and can lead to extremely poor performance. Imagine setting a cache expiration of three days, and then you get 100,000 page hits in that three day period. If you put the callback within the page class, you'll have 100,000 instances of the page class residing in the ASP.NET process memory space. The controls will have long since been disposed, but the methods and other properties are still in memory. Multiply a few thousand bytes (for even the smallest amount of code and property storage) by 100,000, and you can see that the memory overhead of can be in the megabytes!

In order to compensate for this, we recommend that you move your callback function to its own class module outside of the page class (as a shared method). By doing this, we will eliminate the memory overhead of retaining the entire page class in memory, and since we make the callback a shared method, there will only be one copy of it resident in the memory throughout the lifetime of the application.

In our modified version of the application, UpdatedCacheChange.aspx, we created a small class file to place the callback in, and then explicitly referenced the new class within our page.

To update our example from above, we moved the CacheItemRemovedCallBack routine to its own class file called CacheCallbacks. Since it needs to be called without instantiating the object, we also made it a Public Shared member to cut down on the number of members floating around (remember that the Shared keyword creates a single instance of the method or property to be shared across all copies of the object). You should note that if we were to have made the original callback routine in the Page class a shared member, then we wouldn't have been able to see all of the page properties and members, only those that were shared. However, that still requires more memory than creating your own class file for the callback.

```
Public Class CacheCallbacks
  Public Shared Sub CacheItemRemovedCallBack(ByVal strKey As String, _
      ByVal objValue As Object, ByVal objReason As CacheItemRemovedReason)
    ' Log the reason for removal
    Dim strResult As New StringBuilder()
    Dim eLog As System.Diagnostics.EventLog = New System.Diagnostics.EventLog()
    eLog.Source = "CacheApp"
    strResult.Append("Cache Key Removed. Key=")
    strResult.Append(strKey)
    strResult.Append("; Reason=")
    strResult.Append(objReason.ToString)
    eLog.WriteEntry(strResult.ToString)
    eLog.Close()
  End Sub
End Sub
```

Then, we changed the reference to the callback to point to our new class.

```
Dim fnRemoveCallback As New CacheItemRemovedCallback(AddressOf _
                              CacheCallbacks.CacheItemRemovedCallBack)
```

Here's one last titbit of information about the `Cache` object. ASP.NET uses the same `Cache` object and callbacks to perform page-level caching. It streams the entire result of a page into the `Cache` object and retrieves it later when requested.

As you can see, the `Cache` object is very powerful but must be used with care in order to get the maximum performance from your ASP.NET application.

Application Events

There are a host of default events that can be handled in ASP.NET at the application level. ASP.NET also allows you to generate your own application-level events as well. These events are defined in the `Global.asax` file at the virtual root of the application.

We've already seen how easy it is for you to cache values for use at a later time. And, as we've also discovered, this can come at a performance hit because both the `Application` and `Cache` objects require instantiation and storage/retrieval time. Another way that we can store application-level information is by storing it in the `Global.asax` file, which is in itself a class module.

Let's modify our voting booth example from earlier. What we'll do is move both the `Candidate` and `Candidates` classes to the `Global.asax` file. Then we'll create a public shared instance of the collection that will be accessible throughout the application:

```
Public Class Candidate
  ...
End Class

Public Class Candidates
  ...
End Class
```

Then, we move the initiation code out of the `Page_Load` and into the `Application_Start` event. We no longer need to do any checking for valid values while loading the page, since the value is guaranteed to be available (unlike the cache value).

```
Public Shared objVotes As New Candidates()
Public Shared CurrentCandidates As String() = _
  {"Red", "Green", "Yellow", "Brown", "Black"}
...
Sub Application_Start(ByVal sender As Object, ByVal e As EventArgs)
  ' Fires when the application is started
  Dim strKey As String
  For Each strKey In CurrentCandidates
    objVotes.Add(strKey)
  Next
End Sub
```

Now we can eliminate the retrieval of information from cache, since it will be available to us in our static object. To do this, we named the static variable the same as our old variable (`objVotes`), so it's easy to just substitute `objVotes` for `Global.objVotes` in our code-behind file, `VoteObjectImproved.aspx.vb`:

```
Private Sub btnReset_Click(ByVal sender As System.Object, _
                        ByVal e As System.EventArgs) Handles btnReset.Click
    Dim objCandidate As New Candidate()
    For Each objCandidate In Global.objVotes
        objCandidate.Votes = 0
    Next
End Sub
```

What this code does is create a single instance of these objects for use by all pages within the ASP.NET application. Therefore, they get instantiated once (on `Application_Start`), and then remain in memory until the application terminates. As you should no doubt suspect, retrieving the information from memory will be a lot faster than retrieving it from either the `Application` or `Cache` object.

ASP.NET session and application state can provide you with that extra performance edge for your ASP.NET application by providing a cached medium to store commonly used information that can be retrieved more quickly on subsequent accesses. However, as we've seen, these state management objects are not for use for everything, and they can incur a performance penalty when in use (and an even greater performance penalty if used improperly).

ASP.NET Security

ASP.NET provides a very robust security system that we can easily utilize in order to eliminate the mounds of code we had to write in ASP in order to provide user-level security for our web applications. This means that you need to write less code in order to implement standardized security, and since the functionality is part of the ASP.NET Framework, you are guaranteed to get the highest performing security code for your application.

What does this have to do with performance? Plenty, since you are now freed from the chores of writing your own security check code at the top of each web page. Since the security checking is done by the core ASP.NET subsystem, it is handled much more quickly than any VBScript, `#include`, or COM object ever could in class ASP. The performance of your security code also relies on the speed of your authentication routines. The slower the authentication routine, the slower your overall login process will be. We'll be talking about authentication routines and the various types of authentication repositories that ASP.NET provides native support for in a moment.

To understand how security can help or hinder the performance of your application, let's back up and see how IIS processes requests and passes them along to ASP.NET. When IIS receives a request, it first checks the resource to see how it is secured. It can be secured with anonymous access (which most web sites are), or with the standard local or Active Directory credentials. Next, IIS will check to see if the user has access to the requested resource via the standard access control list (ACL). If any of this fails, IIS will reject the request before it even gets to ASP.NET. During this process, two things happened. The user was **authenticated** (in the case of anonymous access, the authentication came via the standard IUSR_*<machine-name>* account), and then **authorized** (by checking the authentication credentials against the ACL). These two terms are important in understanding the sequence of both the IIS and ASP.NET security process.

If an ASP.NET resource (for example, an ASP.NET page, user control, or web service) is requested and IIS authenticates and authorizes the request, the next step is for ASP.NET to provide its own authentication and authorization. This provides the infrastructure for the developer to provide custom authentication, all without having to develop the security infrastructure from scratch. The following figure illustrates the IIS and ASP.NET security authentication/authorization process.

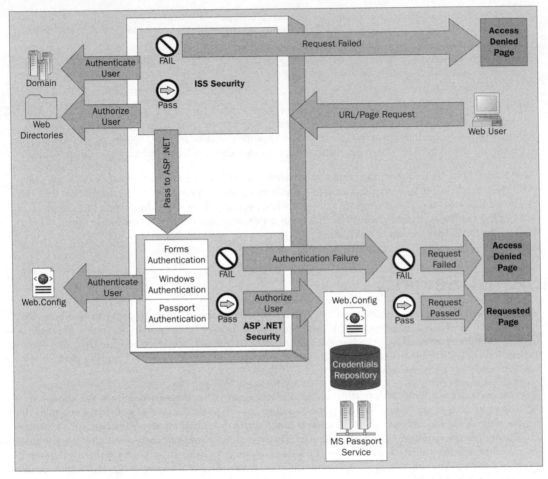

ASP.NET provides three ways for you to authenticate users within your application. These are:

❑   Windows Authentication

❑   Forms Authentication

❑   Passport Authentication

Windows authentication provides integration with traditional Windows accounts (either Active Directory or local accounts). This model works the same way that normal IIS authentication works. In this case, you would disable anonymous access to your web site in order to secure your site against unauthorized users. You would then update the Web.config file to specify Windows authentication and specify that ASP.NET should use the credentials that the user entered when being challenged by IIS as the credentials for this application.

```
<configuration>
<system.web>
   ...
```

```
        <authentication mode="Windows">
          ...
        </authentication>
        <identity impersonate="true">
        </identity>
      </system.web>
    </configuration>
```

From here you can specify groups and access settings by allowing or denying roles, users, or verbs within the <authorization> section of Web.Config. The example below will grant access to the application only to those users in the VIP_Group group of the MyCompany domain. ASP.NET will reject all other credentials and return an unauthorized access page:

```
    <configuration>
    <system.web>
      ...
      <authorization>
        <allow roles="MyCompany\VIP_Group"
        <deny users="*">
      </authorization>
    </system.web>
    </configuration>
```

Windows authentication is the fastest of the authentication models since it relies on what IIS has already queried for. However, it is also the least customizable of the authentication models, since you do not control the login page or credentials source – and, it requires network access to a Windows credential source (Windows local accounts or Active Directory), which means that this model is not very suitable for public web applications where you cannot control the client or network access.

Forms authentication allows the developer to generate their own standard login page and authenticate against entries in the Web.Config file (as in Windows authentication), or from their own authentication source. Forms authentication is the most customizable of the authentication methods, because you are in control of the authentication source and method. Configuring forms authentication is similar to Windows authentication.

```
    <authentication mode="Forms">
      <forms name="MyWebApp" path="/" loginUrl="Login.aspx" timeout=15>
      </forms>
    </authentication>
```

In this example, ASP.NET will call the ASPX page called Login.aspx whenever an unauthenticated request is received. In your login code, you can ask for a user ID and password and perform validation of the credentials.

Once configured, you can specify a list of credentials that can access the web application in Web.Config. This is not very secure, however, since the credentials list is stored in clear text in the XML configuration file. You can encrypt the password values, but this comes at a small performance cost, and the management of the credentials list can become a nightmare.

```
<forms name="MyWebApp" path="/" loginUrl="Login.aspx" timeout=15>
  <credentials>
    <user name="John Doe" password="mypassword" />
    ...
  </credentials>
</forms>
```

A better approach is to create your own authentication method against whatever data source your user IDs and passwords reside. This is usually a call to a stored procedure that takes a user ID and password (either clear-text or encrypted), which returns a valid or invalid response to the authentication request. In your login page, you will call your customized authentication method and manually set the authentication properties for ASP.NET so that it knows that the authentication passed. In the example below, we're checking our authentication routine, and if the credentials pass we're telling ASP.NET to return to the original page that the user requested (that started the authentication process). The last parameter tells ASP.NET whether or not the cookie should be persisted, so that the user can remain authenticated across browser sessions. RedirectFromLoginPage creates this authorization cookie that can either be stored on the client or on the server, based on whether cookie-less mode is enabled for this web application.

```
If (MyAuthentication(strUserid, strPassword) Then
  FormsAuthentication.RedirectFromLoginPage(strUserid, False)
End If
```

Now that we've gotten the basics of forms authentication, we can easily see that performance can be impacted in several areas. The first is the speed of the authentication routine. Unlike Windows authentication, forms authentication requires a separate access to a credentials source (even if it the credentials are stored in Web.Config). You should strive to streamline your authentication routine and eliminate any external items you might be tempted to include (like retrieving personalization items, user pictures, and so on). These can be done at other times and will only slow down the login process. In addition, we've learned that encrypting password data in Web.Config will yield a small performance hit. The larger hit will be taken when you try and convince your web administrator to maintain that file for managing access to the application!

Passport authentication allows you to integrate your application with the Microsoft Passport service. Basically, the way this works is that when an unauthenticated request is detected, ASP.NET sends the login credentials from a Passport login window (which is installed when the Passport service is installed on the web server) to the Passport service.

```
<authentication mode="Passport">
  <passport redirectUrl="<passport_service_url">
</authentication>
```

Passport is the slowest of the authentication methods because is requires a web service-type communication over the Internet in order to validate credentials. Passport does hold some promise because the user needs only remember one set of credentials to log into Passport-protected web sites.

ASP.NET Server Controls

We took a peek at ASP.NET Server Controls a little earlier when talking about the control hierarchy and ASP.NET page events and page view state. Simply speaking, a server control is any control on the page that can be accessed and manipulated by server-side code. Server controls come in the following flavors:

❑ ASP.NET Default Controls

❑ User Controls

❑ Custom Controls

As we saw earlier, the server control event that caused the postback gets fired after the page is initialized. Most controls inherit from a standard base class (like `System.Web.UI.Control`). This makes server controls very easy to implement because they all share the same base properties and events. As you'll see in this section, you can override these properties and events, or create new ones altogether, but this inheritance is really a boon for ASP.NET developers.

You've probably read about .NET garbage collection and how you don't need to worry about disposing your own variables. In a typical page, the developer will create a database connection, query the database for some results, and let the page class go out of scope, which will let the garbage collection know that it can release that unused memory. While there is no way to physically force the garbage collection to run at a specific time (since the garbage collection is non-deterministic), you can tell ASP.NET that you're ready for it to release your resource intensive objects so that it will put them at the top of the priority chain for garbage collection. The standard way of doing this is to ensure the call of the `Dispose` method when you want to release these resources. Calling an object's `Dispose` method will put a higher priority on this object's memory release than other objects (that are just waiting for the standard garbage collection cleanup). This will promote better performance in your application.

Why talk about garbage collection while we're looking at server controls? The reason to bring up garbage collection here is that all server controls implement this `Dispose` event. This event is the final process in a control's life on the page. If you've instantiated objects that have external connections during the page process that consume a lot of resources, it's a good idea to explicitly release them here (like a database connection). Yes, the garbage collection will eventually recover them when the page class goes out of scope, but by explicitly clearing them here, you are guaranteed to release the critical resources ahead of the time that they would have been reclaimed by the garbage collection.

ASP.NET Default Controls

ASP.NET comes with a host of new controls for developers to use to easily create stunning web applications that can now rival their Win32 client counterparts.

The real value behind these controls is that they dynamically render HTML to the browser window, based upon the client browser's capabilities. This eliminates the need for the developer to write specialized code for browsers that may only accept wireless markup language (WML) or may be best suited for an 800x600 display.

All of the information on how to determine a browser's capabilities is registered in the .NET configuration file `Machine.Config`. This configuration file is found in the `%WINDIR%\Microsoft.Net\Framework\(version)\Config` directory (Note: as of this writing v3705 is the current build of the .NET Framework. You will need to substitute *(version)* above for the most up-to-date version of the Framework on your machine).

As we saw earlier, a page's view state captures vital information on the status of the page and the controls that it contains. We learnt that we can improve performance by turning off view state for an entire page. Well, sometimes we can't turn off view state for a page, but ASP.NET gives us the capability of managing view state on a control-by-control basis as well. The same criteria for turning off view state on a page basis (as discussed earlier) should be used for determining whether or not to disable view state on a control basis.

For example, if your control will always reload its data after each postback, there's no reason to save state information for it. For larger controls (like grids and lists), you need to analyze your business requirements and see if they require the saving of state and data between postbacks. If not, your page will receive a performance advantage by eliminating view state for the specific control.

```
<asp:datagrid id="MyDataGrid" EnableViewState="False" runat="server" />
```

The above code will disable view state for the data grid (`MyDataGrid`) being defined. All other controls (including any child controls within the data grid) will not be affected by this property.

As mentioned earlier, ASP.NET provides a large set of built-in controls specifically for use in web applications. These controls can be broken into the following groups:

- ❑ HTML Controls
- ❑ Web Form Controls
- ❑ List Controls
- ❑ Mobile Controls
- ❑ Validation Controls

HTML Controls

HTML controls are merely counterparts of ordinary tags that generate standard HTML in your ASP.NET page. Each of these controls can have the `runat="server"` property, which means that certain properties of the control can be manipulated in server-side code.

However, the benefit of using an HTML server control is a little dubious, since ASP.NET has more fully functional web and list controls that perform the same functionality, and a lot more. A common rule of thumb is that if the information is static in nature and you don't need to interact or reference it from your server side code, then you should use the HTML counterpart for the ASP.NET control. By doing so, you will eliminate the code size, number of event handlers, view state size, and overall page class size – all of which are items that will increase the performance of your ASP.NET web page.

There are very few instances that can be thought of to use HTML server controls instead of using either standard HTML or a web/list control. Any control that will not need to be programmatically controlled during a server-side event should be implemented as standard HTML, since this will yield the highest level of performance due to the elimination of any server-side postback ,and the reduction of data stored in the view state. The only exception to this would be if you needed specific rendering for different clients, in which case you would develop a custom control to create your own rendering. We'll discuss custom controls and their various impacts on performance later in this chapter.

Web Controls

Web Forms controls provide the developer with a standard set of data entry and display controls that are programmatically controlled (and even created) within an ASP.NET page. The following is a sample of web controls available (this list is not intended to be a comprehensive list of all web controls available, since new controls are developed all the time):

- ❑ asp:checkbox
- ❑ asp:hyperlink
- ❑ asp:image
- ❑ asp:label
- ❑ asp:linkbutton
- ❑ asp:panel
- ❑ asp:textbox

The main difference between the web controls and HTML controls is that web controls are all standardized in their interface to the developer, and the web control dynamically renders HTML based on the browser's capabilities. In addition, web controls (along with List controls in the next section) are the most common controls that can be sub-classed or created from scratch to provide the developer with types of controls customized to their needs.

Web controls have events that you can attach event handlers to. Since a control is contained within a page, you can see that the performance of your page is greatly impacted by the number of these controls and what you place in each control's event handler routines.

- ❑ OnInit
- ❑ OnLoad
- ❑ OnDataBinding
- ❑ OnPreRender
- ❑ Disposed
- ❑ OnUnload
- ❑ OnDisposed

Web Forms controls implement a property called AutoPostBack. By setting this value to True within a control's definition, ASP.NET will initiate a postback. By default, this value is set to False since ASP.NET uses event bubbling (which we talked about earlier) to define the events that will cause a postback. However, you may want to issue a postback when the selected item of a list box changes, because you want to repopulate the contents of other fields based on the new selected value.

Below is a typical example of this type of logic. We have a list box for car manufacturers, and then another list box for the models that each manufacturer makes. You can find this code in the `AutoLookup.aspx` file in the `AutoPostback` folder of the code download for this chapter.

```
<form id="Form1" method="post" runat="server">
  <DIV style="DISPLAY: inline; Z-INDEX: 101; LEFT: 14px; WIDTH: 70px;
      POSITION: absolute; TOP: 14px; HEIGHT: 15px"
      ms_positioning="FlowLayout">Manufacturer:</DIV>
  <DIV style="DISPLAY: inline; Z-INDEX: 102; LEFT: 17px; WIDTH: 70px;
      POSITION: absolute; TOP: 48px; HEIGHT: 15px"
      ms_positioning="FlowLayout">Model:</DIV>
  <asp:dropdownlist id="lstMfr" style="Z-INDEX: 103; LEFT: 111px;
      POSITION: absolute; TOP: 14px"
      runat="server" AutoPostBack="True"></asp:dropdownlist>
  <asp:dropdownlist id="lstModel" style="Z-INDEX: 104; LEFT: 112px;
      POSITION: absolute; TOP: 48px" runat="server"></asp:dropdownlist>
  <asp:button id="btnSelect" style="Z-INDEX: 105; LEFT: 17px;
      POSITION: absolute; TOP: 85px" runat="server" Text="Select"></asp:button>
  <asp:label id="lblResults" style="Z-INDEX: 106; LEFT: 19px;
      POSITION: absolute; TOP: 124px" runat="server"></asp:label>
</form>
```

We set the `AutoPostBack` property of the manufacturer list box so we will get an immediate postback, and can populate the models list box based on this new selection. As you can see, this is a perfect example of when to use auto-postback, because the values to be put into the list boxes are local and do not need to be queried from a database source.

```
Imports System.Text
Public Class AutoLookup
  Inherits System.Web.UI.Page
  Protected WithEvents lstMfr As System.Web.UI.WebControls.DropDownList
  Protected WithEvents lstModel As System.Web.UI.WebControls.DropDownList
  Protected WithEvents btnSelect As System.Web.UI.WebControls.Button
  Protected WithEvents lblResults As System.Web.UI.WebControls.Label
  Public strMfr As String() = {"BMW", "Chevrolet", "Ford", "Lexus"}
  Public strBMW As String() = {"540i", "740i1"}
  Public strChevy As String() = {"Caprice", "Suburban"}
  Public strFord As String() = {"4-Runner", "Focus"}
  Public strLexus As String() = {"ES300", "RX300"}

  Private Sub Page_Load(ByVal sender As System.Object, _
      ByVal e As System.EventArgs) Handles MyBase.Load
    'Put user code to initialize the page here
    Dim aryMfr As New ArrayList()
    Dim aryModel As New ArrayList()
    Dim strKey As String
    ' If 1st pass through, then set the listbox defaults
    If Not IsPostBack Then
      For Each strKey In strMfr
        aryMfr.Add(strKey)
      Next
      For Each strKey In strBMW
```

```
            aryModel.Add(strKey)
        Next
            lstMfr.DataSource = aryMfr
            lstModel.DataSource = aryModel
    End If
End Sub
```

During the `Page_Load` event, we get the values for the car manufacturers from our data source and set the secondary list box of models to be the models for the first entry in our manufacturer list box.

```
Private Sub lstMfr_SelectedIndexChanged(ByVal sender As System.Object,_
    ByVal e As System.EventArgs) Handles lstMfr.SelectedIndexChanged
  Dim strKey As String
  Dim aryModel As New ArrayList()
  Dim strSelected As String()
  ' Just set a pointer to the new source
  Select Case lstMfr.SelectedIndex
    Case 0 : strSelected = strBMW
    Case 1 : strSelected = strChevy
    Case 2 : strSelected = strFord
    Case 3 : strSelected = strLexus
  End Select
  ' Populate the model listbox from the new source
  For Each strKey In strSelected
    aryModel.Add(strKey)
  Next
    lstModel.DataSource = aryModel
End Sub

Private Sub Page_PreRender(ByVal sender As Object, _
    ByVal e As System.EventArgs) Handles MyBase.PreRender
  ' Do the bindings last
  lstMfr.DataBind()
  lstModel.DataBind()
End Sub
```

When the selected list box item for our car manufacturer changes, the auto-postback takes over and generates a page postback. After the page initialization process, our list box server control event (`ItemCommand`) gets fired, and we get the value of the selected item and set the values for the car models list box to those for the newly selected manufacturer.

When the user is satisfied with their selection, they press the **Select** button to see their selections.

```
Private Sub btnSelect_Click(ByVal sender As System.Object, _
    ByVal e As System.EventArgs) Handles btnSelect.Click
  ' Display the user selections
  Dim strDisplay As New stringbuilder()
  strDisplay.Append("You Selected: ")
  strDisplay.Append(lstMfr.SelectedItem.Text)
  strDisplay.Append(",")
  strDisplay.Append(lstModel.SelectedItem.Text)
  lblResults.Text = strDisplay.ToString
End Sub

End Class
```

Auto-postback can be a performance bottleneck and can also cause quite a bit of confusion for the user, if implemented for every server control on your page. For example, let's modify the VB.NET code to retrieve these values from an XML database instead of storing them locally. The modified code-behind would look something similar to the code you see here (this code is in the `AutoLookupXml.aspx.vb` file in the code download):

```
Imports System.Text
Public Class AutoLookupXml
    Inherits System.Web.UI.Page
    Protected WithEvents lstMfr As System.Web.UI.WebControls.DropDownList
    Protected WithEvents lstModel As System.Web.UI.WebControls.DropDownList
    Protected WithEvents btnSelect As System.Web.UI.WebControls.Button
    Protected WithEvents lblResults As System.Web.UI.WebControls.Label

    Private Sub Page_Load(ByVal sender As System.Object, _
        ByVal e As System.EventArgs) Handles MyBase.Load
      'Put user code to initialize the page here
      Dim aryMfr As New ArrayList()
      Dim aryModel As New ArrayList()
      Dim strKey As String
      ' If 1st pass through, then set the listbox defaults
      If Not IsPostBack Then
        lstMfr.DataSource = GetCarManufacturers()
        lstMfr.DataTextField = "Mfr_Text"
        lstMfr.DataBind()
      End If
    End Sub

    Private Sub Page_PreRender(ByVal sender As Object, ByVal e As System.EventArgs)
        Handles MyBase.PreRender
      ' Do the bindings last
      lstModel.DataSource = GetCarModels(lstMfr.SelectedItem.Text)
      lstModel.DataTextField = "Name"
      lstModel.DataBind()
    End Sub
```

Notice that we don't actually have any code that handles the list box selected item changed event (which will be invoked after the `Page_Load`, but before the `Page_PreRender`). All we want is to generate a postback, and our code in the `Page_PreRender` handles what the selected values of the list box are.

```
Protected Function GetCarManufacturers() As DataView
    Dim dsReturn As New DataSet()
    dsReturn.ReadXml(Server.MapPath("Manufacturers.xml"))
    Return dsReturn.Tables(0).DefaultView
End Function

Protected Function GetCarModels(ByVal strMfr As String) As DataView
    Dim dsReturn As New DataSet()
    Dim strFilter As New StringBuilder()
    Dim dsTable
    ' Retrieve all models from the DB
    dsReturn.ReadXml(Server.MapPath("Models.xml"))
```

```
        ' Only retrieve models that match the manufacturer
        strFilter.Append("Mfr='")
        strFilter.Append(strMfr)
        strFilter.Append("'")
        dsReturn.Tables(0).DefaultView.RowFilter = strFilter.ToString
        Return dsReturn.Tables(0).DefaultView
    End Function

End Class
```

You'll see that the second example runs slower than the first because we're incurring additional process time to go and get that external data.

Now, think about a more complicated example. What if your query isn't just a simple XML file retrieval, but a complex SQL query, stored procedure, or worse still, a web service? In this case, the user changes the first list box, the postback starts but the screen doesn't start to change because the query is running and no HTML is being rendered because event code is still being run. So now the user might think that they're free to do more edits on the screen, but as they start editing, the screen refreshes with the postback! Not only is the user confused, they are also a little peeved that they just lost the data that they typed, and now you're sure to get a call about how slow they think your application is.

The moral of this story is use auto-postback with caution. Make sure that any event code that needs to be run for an auto-postback is highly streamlined and does not require access to external systems which are sure to introduce performance dips. You should also look to adopting a postback design policy with your development team. By limiting the number of server controls to one or two at a maximum, you can ensure consistency across your entire ASP.NET application, while ensuring good performance of each page (even when being developed by different members of your team).

List Controls

A set of controls that come as standard with the .NET Framework are the list controls. Currently, the server list controls that come with ASP.NET are the DataGrid, DataList, and Repeater controls. These controls allow you to create lists of information that is then rendered to the client based upon the client's browser capabilities.

One of the most commonly called methods for these list controls is the DataBind() method. This binds the data from the DataSource property to the list control. Since binding data does take time (just how much depends upon the size and structure of the data being bound), you should make sure that you don't have to bind if you don't need to. A great example we've already learned is that as long as a list control has view state enabled, there's no reason to re-bind on a postback, unless there's a chance that the data has been updated by another client since the last page load.

Another common performance penalty comes when you bind data too early in the page process. Let's take our voting booth example from earlier. Remember that we explicitly put the bind logic in the Page_PreRender event to make it the last thing to do. This eliminated us from having to put it in twice just to catch all possible page processing paths. Another reason we did this, though, is that there is a performance penalty in binding a list control in Page_Load that is contained within another control, like a panel or an IFRAME. This is especially noticeable if you've developed a multi-frame browser window application through the use of IFRAMEs, all with their individual page and control events. So, if at all possible, try to avoid binding in the Page_Load event, and try the Page_PreRender event to bind the final results of all of your data.

Since the `DataGrid` is the most customizable of these list controls, it also incurs the most performance overhead. So, if you don't need the additional functionality provided by the `DataGrid` control, use the `DataList` or `Repeater` controls.

Mobile Controls

The **Microsoft Mobile Internet Toolkit (MMIT)** was released as an add-on to ASP.NET to provide a set of server controls that are developed specifically for use on mobile devices with smaller screens and bandwidth limitations (cell phones, for example).

Each MMIT control first determines the capabilities of the requesting browser, and then dynamically renders their output (HTML, WML, or whatever format is specified in the control) that best suits the device. Much like device drivers in Windows, this frees up the developer to write business, code instead of writing display code for all possible devices that might access this application.

These controls always optimize their rendered output based on the requesting mobile device, so it's best to use them instead of any other control (server or basic HTML) when developing mobile applications. Since the MMIT controls are also basic server controls, they also carry with them the same properties and potential performance bottlenecks that we've already discussed in the web controls and list controls sections.

Field Validation Controls

Field validation controls provide the ability to tie validation logic to an individual control or page. This means that complex business logic required to validate fields before they are processed can now be stored on the server. What's great about this is that the logic now becomes centralized and compiled on the server, but it is also hidden from the end user. Remember that it's easy for the user to do a View | Source on the browser window to see any client-side JavaScript – so it's a good idea to put that kind of code on the server where its source is not accessible to the user.

Field validation controls should be carefully placed and configured because they can yield a considerable performance hit. This is because field validation generates both client-side and server-side events, and a postback for field validation is required in order for the validation logic to be performed on the server-side. Client-side code can be either JavaScript (the default) or VBScript. Be aware that the generated code (JavaScript and VBScript) is only 100% compatible with Internet Explorer 4.0 and higher. In addition, if you enable client-side validation, you should always back that up with server-side validation, so that clients that cannot handle client-side JavaScript will still have validation rules accessible to them. If the browser cannot handle the client-side script generated, then it will use the server-side event to perform validation.

When both client-side and server-side script settings are enabled, ASP.NET works for you and determines the browser's capabilities. If the browser cannot handle the client-side script generated, then it will use the server-side event to perform validation. You can override these settings in order to customize your application for a target environment, as we'll see in a moment. Care should be taken, however, when using client-side script for validation. You should only use client-side validation script when you can control the browser environment since the client-side code is not 100% compatible with all browsers.

With ASP.NET field validators on the page, it's easy to check the `IsValid` property of the page or the individual validation control before any operations that are sensitive to invalid data are executed.

ASP.NET provides the following control validators:

- ❏ Required Field Validator
- ❏ Comparison Validator
- ❏ Range Validator
- ❏ Expression Validator
- ❏ Custom Validator
- ❏ Summary Validator

Let's look at a simple validation screen that will take a user name, account number, and PIN to demonstrate the various ways to perform field validation. In this first example, it's very easy to associate a validator with the user name text box. However, in this example we have disabled the client scripting feature (EnableClientScript) for field validation. What this means is that this field validator will be run on the server, requiring a page postback. This code is in the Server.aspx file in the Validation folder of the code download.

```
<form id="Form1" method="post" runat="server">
<TABLE id="Table1" style="WIDTH: 512px; HEIGHT: 96px" cellSpacing="1"
    cellPadding="1" width="512" border="0">
  <TR>
    <TD style="WIDTH: 60px">Name</TD>
    <TD style="WIDTH: 265px">
      <asp:TextBox id="txtName" runat="server" Width="251px"></asp:TextBox></TD>
    <TD>
    <asp:RequiredFieldValidator id="RequiredFieldValidator1"
        runat="server" ErrorMessage="Name is a required field"
        Display="Static" ControlToValidate="txtName" EnableClientScript="False">
    </asp:RequiredFieldValidator></TD>
  </TR>
  <TR>
    <TD style="WIDTH: 60px">Account</TD>
    <TD style="WIDTH: 265px">
      <asp:TextBox id="txtAccount" runat="server"></asp:TextBox></TD>
    <TD></TD>
  </TR>
  <TR>
    <TD style="WIDTH: 60px">PIN</TD>
    <TD style="WIDTH: 265px">
    <asp:TextBox id="txtPIN" runat="server"
        TextMode="Password"></asp:TextBox></TD>
    <TD></TD>
  </TR>
</TABLE>
<asp:Button id="btnSubmit" runat="server" Text="Submit"></asp:Button>
</form>
```

Here, we associated the required field validator with a field to validate (txtName). For a test of a required field, we really don't need to do a postback to the server. As we saw with the auto-postback example, the user may become quite irritated with receiving a simple validation message after they hit the Submit button because they expect the system to validate their information before they click the button. Instead, for this type of validation we should let it be handled on the client through the use of automated script generation. By setting the EnableClientScript="True", we can get ASP.NET to generate client-side script to handle the field validation. However, this performance technique should only be implemented if you can guarantee 100% compatibility with your client base (usually in a scenario where you are deploying your application to a corporate Intranet). If not, the potential client-side script errors will do far more damage to your application's reputation than almost any performance improvement.

So, let's move on to server-side validation of controls and pages. For example, let's say we want to check the validity of the account number before allowing the page to be valid. To do this, we'll need to check the account number against our local database to check for validity. In this case, we'll be using a custom validator. We can use the server-side event ServerValidate for this validation control to enter our validation check code. If the field passes your validation check, then the IsValid property for the field validation control should be set to True.

```
<TR>
  <TD style="WIDTH: 60px">Account</TD>
  <TD style="WIDTH: 265px">
    <asp:TextBox id="txtAccount" runat="server"></asp:TextBox></TD>
  <TD>
    <asp:CustomValidator id="AccountValidator" runat="server"
        ControlToValidate="txtAccount" ErrorMessage="Invalid Account"
        EnableClientScript="False">*</asp:CustomValidator>
  </TD>
</TR>
<TR>
  <TD style="WIDTH: 60px">PIN</TD>
  <TD style="WIDTH: 265px">
    <asp:TextBox id="txtPIN" runat="server"
        TextMode="Password"></asp:TextBox></TD>
  <TD>
    <asp:CustomValidator id="PINValidator" runat="server"
        EnableClientScript="False" ErrorMessage="Invalid PIN"
        ControlToValidate="txtPIN">*</asp:CustomValidator></TD>
</TR>
```

We'll also do the same thing for the PIN text box field. In our simple examples, we'll just test for specific values of 1000 and password, but you get the idea that here is where the query to your external source will be performed.

```
Private Sub btnSubmit_Click(ByVal sender As System.Object, _
    ByVal e As System.EventArgs) Handles btnSubmit.Click
  If Page.IsValid Then
    lblResult.Text = "All Validations Passed"
  End If
End Sub
```

```
     Private Sub AccountValidator_ServerValidate(ByVal source As System.Object, _
            ByVal args As System.Web.UI.WebControls.ServerValidateEventArgs) _
            Handles AccountValidator.ServerValidate
       If IsAccountValid(args.Value) Then
         args.IsValid = True
       Else
         args.IsValid = False
       End If
     End Sub

     Private Sub PINValidator_ServerValidate(ByVal source As System.Object, _
           ByVal args As System.Web.UI.WebControls.ServerValidateEventArgs) _
           Handles PINValidator.ServerValidate
       If IsPINValid(args.Value) Then
         args.IsValid = True
       Else
         args.IsValid = False
       End If
     End Sub
```

Note that the server-side validation controls fire before the button click event. This is essential because we need to know the validity of the page (and all controls) before we can proceed with the submit.

Something to keep in mind is that if a field is blank, only the required field validator will fire. So, to make our code more bullet-proof, we'll need to place both a required field validator, and a custom validator against both the account number and PIN fields in order to provide complete validation.

```
     <asp:RequiredFieldValidator id="RequiredFieldValidator2" runat="server"
         ControlToValidate="txtAccount"
         ErrorMessage="Account is a Required Field" EnableClientScript="false">
     </asp:RequiredFieldValidator>
     <asp:CustomValidator id="AccountValidator" runat="server"
         EnableClientScript="False" ControlToValidate="txtAccount"
         ErrorMessage="InvalidAccount">
     </asp:CustomValidator>
     <asp:RequiredFieldValidator id="RequiredFieldValidator3" runat="server"
         EnableClientScript="False" ControlToValidate="txtPIN"
         ErrorMessage="PIN is a Required Field">
     </asp:RequiredFieldValidator>
     <asp:CustomValidator id="PINValidator" runat="server"
         EnableClientScript="False" ControlToValidate="txtPIN"
         ErrorMessage="Invalid PIN">
     </asp:CustomValidator>
```

Now, what if we were to put a Cancel button on this page? By default, pressing Cancel would invoke all of the validation logic. This is a waste of CPU time, since the user doesn't want to validate, they want to exit out of the form. ASP.NET provides a way that you can disable validation when a server control event is fired. This property is called the CausesValidation property.

```
     <asp:Button id="btnCancel" runat="server" Text="Cancel" CausesValidation="False">
```

As you can see, our common theme of streamlining has popped up again. During the postback, we'll need to make sure that our validation code is highly optimized so that it doesn't take away from the performance of the page. We can also improve performance by preventing validation code from running for those control events that should not require the validation of a page or set of controls.

```
Private Sub btnCancel_Click(ByVal sender As System.Object, _
    ByVal e As System.EventArgs) Handles btnCancel.Click
  lblResult.Text = "User Canceled Action"
End Sub
```

The last way to perform validation is by doing a summary validation for the page. The summary validation control provides a way for you to summarize all validation errors for a page. You can either display them in a client-side pop-up window, or as a text-based summary on the rendered page on a postback. This can be especially useful if there are a lot of fields on the page. By providing a summary of any errors, the user will be pleased with the time that they were saved trying to hunt through all of the fields to see what was wrong. Some users might even be oblivious to the control validator message (if you specified one) and continue to press the Submit button, completely unaware that they've entered invalid information.

```
<asp:ValidationSummary id="ValidationSummary1" runat="server"
    EnableClientScript="False"></asp:ValidationSummary>
```

As a default, you don't need any server-side code to make the validation summary work. The result of our sample data entry page with page validation would look something like what you see here:

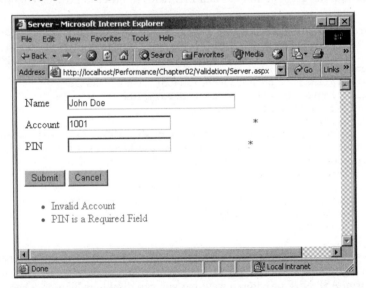

User Controls

User controls provide the capability for the developer to encapsulate a set of functionality that will be used over and over within the project. A typical example of a user control is an error panel that displays information and error messages.

How many times have we seen developers create their own error/information sections on the screen, only to have them be different from the format and placement of what other developers on the team have done? This is where user controls can help. A developer will create a Web Forms page that just contains the visual and code-behind logic necessary to run the control(s) that are going to be shared.

Below is a typical example of an information panel that provides a capabilities form displaying messages to the user. The formatting and placement of the information is obscured from the inheritor so that they can spend development cycles on more important things.

```
<%@ Control Language="vb" AutoEventWireup="false"
    Codebehind="InfoPanel.ascx.vb" Inherits="MyUserControls.InfoPanel"
    TargetSchema="http://schemas.microsoft.com/intellisense/ie5" %>
<asp:Panel id="pnlInfo" runat="server" Width="407px" Height="163px">
  <asp:Label id="lblMsg" runat="server"></asp:Label>
</asp:Panel>
```

This is a very simple ASCX file (InfoPanel.ascx in the MyUserControls folder of the code download) that has a label that we'll use to display messages to the user. The label is within an <asp:Panel> control so that we can group controls (if there were more than one) together.

Next, we develop the "smarts" for the user control. We'll format the message differently for each of the three types of messages that can be used. Notice that we don't use the control's Page_Load event, because we want users to be able to specify messages at any time, and not just during a page load. This is why we expose a Show() and Hide() method for the user control.

```
Public MustInherit Class InfoPanel
   Inherits System.Web.UI.UserControl
   Protected WithEvents pnlInfo As System.Web.UI.WebControls.Panel
   Protected WithEvents lblMsg As System.Web.UI.WebControls.Label
   Public Enum MessageType
      Information
      Warning
      Fatal
   End Enum
   Private m_MsgType As MessageType
   Private m_MsgText As String

   Public Property msgType() As MessageType
      Get
         Return m_MsgType
      End Get
      Set(ByVal Value As MessageType)
        m_MsgType = Value
      End Set
   End Property
   Public Property msgText() As String
      Get
         Return m_MsgText
      End Get
      Set(ByVal Value As String)
        m_MsgText = Value
      End Set
   End Property
```

```
    Private Sub Page_Load(ByVal sender As System.Object, _
        ByVal e As System.EventArgs) Handles MyBase.Load
      'Put user code to initialize the page here

    End Sub

    Public Sub Hide()
      Me.pnlInfo.Visible = False
    End Sub
    Public Sub Show()
      Select Case Me.msgType
        Case MessageType.Fatal
          pnlInfo.BackColor = pnlInfo.BackColor.Red
          pnlInfo.ForeColor = pnlInfo.ForeColor.White
        Case MessageType.Warning
          pnlInfo.BackColor = pnlInfo.BackColor.Yellow
          pnlInfo.ForeColor = pnlInfo.ForeColor.Blue
        Case MessageType.Information
          pnlInfo.BackColor = pnlInfo.BackColor.White
          pnlInfo.ForeColor = pnlInfo.ForeColor.Black
      End Select
        lblMsg.Text = Me.msgText
        Me.pnlInfo.Visible = True
    End Sub
End Class
```

One thing to note is that user controls have an impact on the overall event hierarchy. When a page loads, it then fires the Load event for all subsequent controls. This means that the Page_Load event in a user control should be thought of as a control load event. Another important aspect of user controls is that you should process all of your events in your user control. You should never expect the consumer of the user control to handle your events. This abstracts the inner workings of your control from the consumer, something that all good object oriented developers must do.

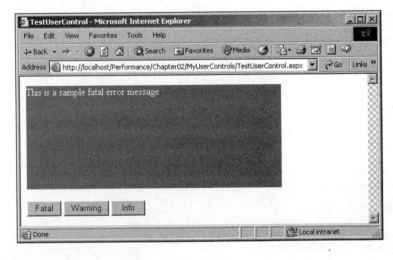

It is important to note that when developing a user control, you should not attempt to create page-level formatting, or inherit from cascading style sheets for the page, since that information should be left for the inheritor of the user control to decide. In addition, you cannot reference user controls outside of your current project. If you want to use a user control from another project, you will need to manually copy it into the project.

Now, for the bad news about user controls. User controls are the slowest performing of all ASP.NET controls for several reasons. First, each user control is kept in a separate ASCX file. This means that if I have three separate user controls on my ASP.NET page, I will have three @Register directives at the top of the page, each yielding a separate HTTP or HTTPS page get. Secondly, the difference between user controls and ASP.NET default controls (and custom controls) is that user controls are not pre-compiled. They are merely a fancy way to standardize a set of ASP.NET code, and then utilize it across a single project. Don't get me wrong though, there are times where user controls make great sense. However, from a performance perspective, user controls are the slowest of all types of controls that can be referenced in an ASP.NET page.

Custom Controls

Custom controls (or sub-classed controls) are another huge feature in .NET. Custom controls provide the developer with the ability to either develop a control from scratch, or subclass from an existing control. This is extremely useful if you want to modify the existing behavior of a server control, or need to develop a control from the ground up.

The effort involved in developing custom controls is greater than utilizing the existing ASP.NET controls, since the developer has to take care of all of the client-side rendering logic, but it can also give your application a performance boost because you can customize for a specific platform or architecture.

When developing a custom control, you would normally inherit from an existing control (like a data grid) and then override to make it work the way that you want it to. This is known as a sub-classed control. It's the easiest custom control to develop, since you get the benefit of all the existing control work, and you get to override only those features that you want to change.

```
Public Class MyDataGrid
  Inherits System.Web.UI.WebControls.DataGrid
  ...
End Class
```

However, you can also build a control from scratch by inheriting from the base object.

```
Public Class MyNewControlType
  Inherits System.Web.UI.Control
  ...
End Class
```

The benefit here is that you get to build the control from a clean slate – you can eliminate any architectural decisions that were imposed on an existing web control (or maybe there just isn't a control quite like yours).

When you develop a web control from scratch, you are responsible for all of the device-specific rendering, properties and events for your control. There can be a lot of code to write, but once written the benefits are endless since the control is now ready for use within all of your development projects (or better yet, for sale for a tidy profit!).

One of the items that you can configure is the number of event handlers that your control supports. You can programmatically define events and handlers for your control by using delegates in your control's class. While this book is not about how to write custom controls, it is important to understand that the event architecture for these custom controls is up to you. One sure way to improve performance is to supply only those event handlers that are absolutely necessary. The best rule is to think about the target functionality that you're trying to provide. If you don't see the need for an event, there's no reason to create a stub for it. Creating just the event signature takes up memory, and will impact performance time since ASP.NET frequently spins through the event handler lists to determine which events to raise.

ASP.NET @Page Directive Properties

We've already mentioned several @Page directive properties that can help the performance of your ASP.NET application. Let's take a look at the @Page directive in a little more detail and see what other goodies have been bestowed upon us by ASP.NET, and how we can use them to power up our applications.

The @Page directive lives at the top of every ASP.NET page and tells ASP.NET what properties are in place for this specific page, and any user controls that the page inherits (for user controls this is the @Control directive, and most of the properties are available for this directive as well). The following is the set of @Page directive properties that affect the performance of an ASP.NET page:

- ❏   AspCompat
- ❏   CompilerOptions
- ❏   Debug
- ❏   EnableSessionState
- ❏   EnableViewState
- ❏   EnableViewStateMac
- ❏   SmartNavigation
- ❏   Trace
- ❏   Transaction

AspCompat is used to allow your ASP.NET page to access classic COM components by setting the page to run in a single thread apartment. By default, ASP.NET pages are run in multi-threaded apartments (MTA). When you enable the AspCompat mode, you're telling ASP.NET to run the page in a single-thread apartment (STA) so that it can safely interact with the COM object.

```
<%@ Page Language="vb" aspCompat="false" Codebehind="MyPage.vb"
    Inherits="MyProj.MyPage"%>
```

This option is sure to hamper performance since you are now basically running the page serially. The best way around this is to create a .NET **runtime callable wrapper (RCW)** for the COM component. This will make .NET feel like the COM object is actually a .NET assembly by providing the assembly that's expected for .NET components. VS.NET automatically creates this wrapper for you when you add a COM object reference to a VS.NET project. You can also do this manually by using the .NET SDK tool called TblImp.exe.

```
C:\> TblImp.exe /out:NewAssembly.dll OldComObject.dll
```

Once the RCW is created, .NET handles all of the interoperability issues, and you won't have to run your page in `AspCompat` mode.

Compiler options allow you to specify the exact compiler options when the ASP.NET page is first compiled using just-in-time compilation. These are normally language compiler command-line switches to inform the compiler how you want this page compiled. For the most part, these settings are handled by VS.NET, but you can tweak the compiler settings to tailor the resulting application to your specific environment. For example, in VB.NET you can use the `/optimize-` parameter to turn off VB.NET compilation optimizations. Normally, you should use the defaults for the language compiler to get the best performance results.

```
<%@ Page Language="vb" CompilerOptions="/optimize-"
    Codebehind="MyPage.vb" Inherits="MyProj.MyPage"%>
```

Debug is a pretty obvious property that enables debug mode for the specific page. This flag is used when compiling the page (using the .NET SDK or VS.NET). As many a developer can attest, you can dramatically improve the performance of any system by compiling it for "production" mode, and eliminating all of the debug information from the final product.

```
<%@ Page Language="vb" debug="False" Codebehind="MyPage.vb"
    Inherits="MyProj.MyPage"%>
```

As we've already discussed, `EnableViewState` and `EnableSessionState` are used to eliminate either view state or session information from a particular page.

```
<%@ Page Language="vb" EnableViewState="false" EnableSessionState="false"
    Codebehind="MyPage.vb" Inherits="MyProj.MyPage"%>
```

`EnableViewStateMAC` tells ASP.NET whether the view state should be checked via a hashing algorithm called **message authentication code**, which generates a checksum for the data in the view state. Upon a postback, ASP.NET will check the checksum against the data to make sure that the view state is not corrupted. This will come at a slight performance hit, since ASP.NET will have to generate the checksum and compare it on the postback.

```
<%@ Page Language="vb" EnableViewStateMac="false"
    Codebehind="MyPage.vb" Inherits="MyProj.MyPage"%>
```

`SmartNavigation` is the property that we discussed earlier that captures more detail on the field of focus and scroll position, so that when the page refreshes, the user is brought back to their original position. This impacts perceived performance the most and does not really have any noticeable server or client-side processing performance impact.

```
<%@ Page Language="vb" SmartNavigation="True"
    Codebehind="MyPage.vb" Inherits="MyProj.MyPage"%>
```

The `Trace` property is a great property to look at the physical execution of your page. When enabled, ASP.NET appends a set of page information pertaining to the execution of that particular instance of the page, and appends this information to the end of your rendered HTML. As we mentioned earlier, ASP.NET hooks into the `Application_EndRequest` event and appends application-level tracing information to the end of the HTML stream.

```
<%@ Page Language="vb" trace="True" Codebehind="MyPage.vb"
    Inherits="MyProj.MyPage"%>
```

Here's a sample page with tracing turned on so that you can see the wealth of valuable debug information that it provides. However, as with any debug code you should remove page tracing since not only does it put debug information at the end of your page, it increases your page's overall response time.

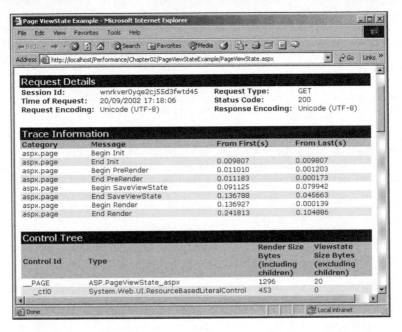

You can also programmatically supply trace information that will appear within the trace section shown above. We will discuss ASP.NET tracing in detail in Chapter 4.

The Transaction property is set to tell ASP.NET that this page is part of a COM+ transaction. The Transaction property can have the following values:

- ❑   Disabled
- ❑   Required
- ❑   NotSupported
- ❑   RequiresNew
- ❑   Supported

An example use for the Transaction property is when your page is doing multiple updates that need to be treated as a single atomic transaction.

```
<%@ Page Language="vb" Transaction="Required" Codebehind="MyPage.vb"
    Inherits="MyProj.MyPage"%>
```

Summary

In this chapter, we've covered the basics of ASP.NET pages and controls, their event hierarchy, how ASP.NET security works, and how all of this impacts your ASP.NET application.

We showed you the overall Page class, including events and what ASP.NET generates for you on the back-end. We learned that everything on an ASP.NET page is an object, and based on the runat attribute, can either be accessible (or not) from server-side code.

We also delved into the various types of controls that we can either utilize or create. We saw that they too have event hierarchies, and how these fit in with the ASP.NET page model.

Lastly, we examined how ASP.NET integrates with IIS to perform security using both authentication and authorization. We covered the three techniques for securing your ASP.NET applications, and how each impacts performance.

From this chapter you should have gleaned the following major performance concepts:

❑ Do not use server controls when you don't need to programmatically interact with the control during server-side events.

❑ Turn off session state for any objects or the entire page, if not needed.

❑ Turn off view state for any objects or the entire page, if not needed.

❑ Use the right page settings tailored to your application's needs.

❑ Don't forget to turn off debugging.

❑ Explicitly call the Dispose method to tell ASP.NET to collect free memory sooner, which helps the garbage collection process through the use of an explicit request for memory deallocation.

In the next chapter, we'll take a look at how to start the design of your ASP.NET application, and select those techniques that will really make them fly.

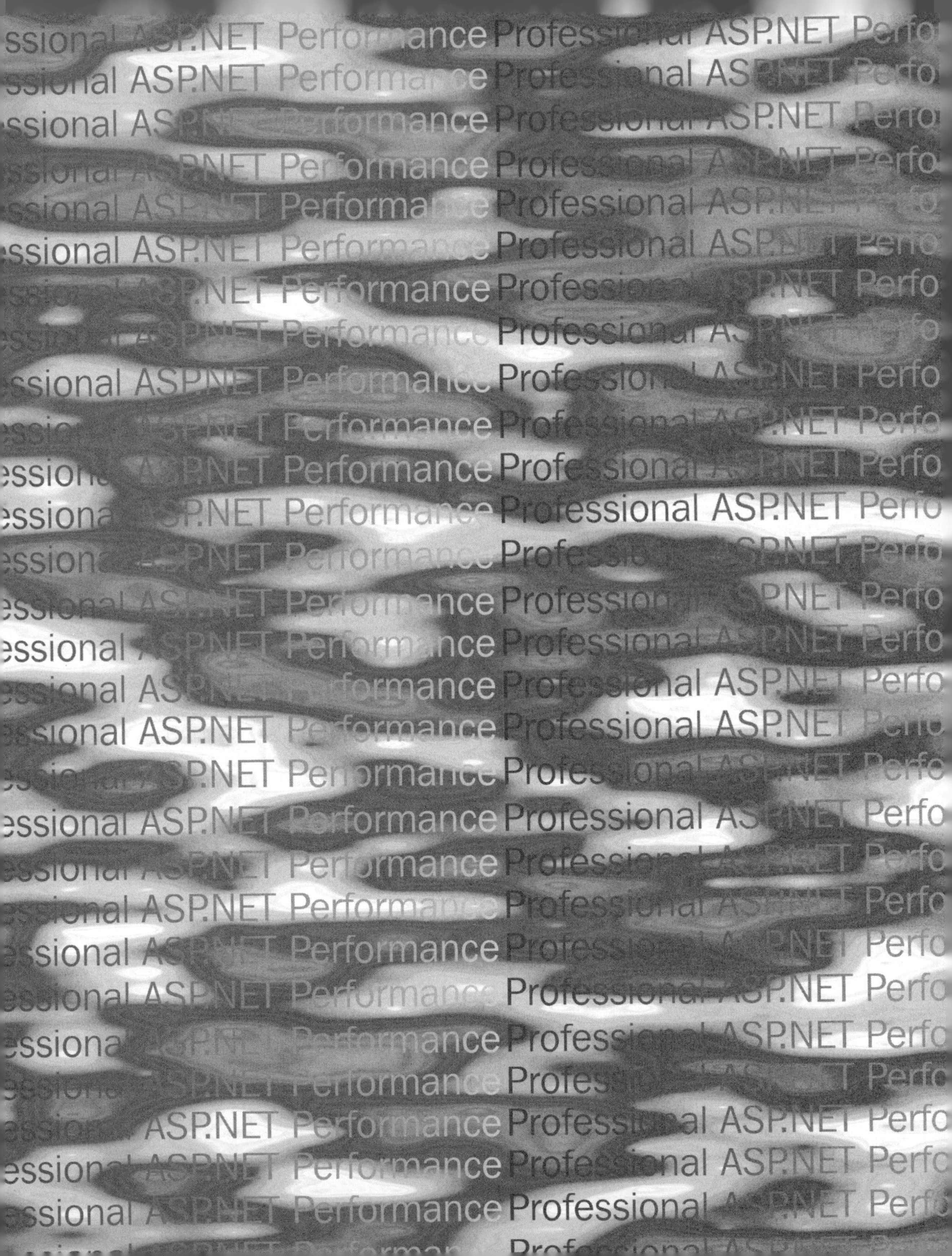
Professional ASP.NET Performance

3

Designing For Performance

As any successful software development team will tell you, the success of any software project starts with a good design. Without good design, the software team will end up spending an inordinate amount of time patching problems that were not thought out ahead of time. Sometimes, large parts of the system will even need to be re-written because they were not designed properly and cannot handle some aspect of performance or functionality.

A perfect example of this is a system that performs database updates. As silly as it may seem, some developers don't create a standard database layer for manipulating their data. This is a critical mistake, since it exposes a huge hole in the design when multiple users attempt to update the same data at the same time. Once this hole is discovered, the development team must scramble to "patch" this hole since it leads to data corruption. Then, they'll probably end up spending a lot of time rewriting pieces of the system to handle multi-user updates. In the end, the time involved in fixing this problem is much longer than if the development team took the time to design the system properly in the first place (sometimes by factors of 5 times or more!).

The same can be said of performance. If the development team does not think about the potential impact their design decisions will have on performance, they'll end up spending most of their post-release time patching up these performance holes, and re-writing sections of the system to improve performance. In addition, the application will never run cleanly, and it will eventually be destined for the application "junk-heap" (something that, unfortunately, happens to too many enteprise applications).

The pressure is on the developers to ensure that this does not happen to the project, otherwise they will probably end up overhauling the system soon after its release (if management allows them to do this at all).

In this chapter, you will be taken through the various design decisions made by the typical software development team. We'll look at how ASP.NET programs can be structured, configured and designed, in order to gain the maximum level of performance without the aid of additional hardware. This chapter is about making the right architectural choices for ASP.NET applications, and not about ASP.NET coding alone. As in any enterprise application, design considerations must come first. You've probably already seen first-hand that a poor design cannot be made up for by excellent code, no matter how much of a superstar development team you have.

Determining the User Expectations

One of the first things to do is to determine what the user's expectations are. As we discussed earlier, the user primarily determines the overall performance of an application or web site.

> **If the user perceives that performance is poor, the performance is poor – no matter how many statistics we can show them about transactions per second, CPU utilization, or user load.**

Thus, in order to understand what performance is for our web site or application, we need to talk to a representative base of the user community who will actually be using it (in the case of commercial software, this will be a team of individuals responsible for providing the feature set). This user committee is usually selected at the project kickoff meeting by a group of executives who sponsor the project. It should be the development team's responsibility to guide the selection so that only meaningful contributors participate on the team (of course, sometimes company politics play a role in this selection, eliminating a "perfect world" scenario).

This representative base should be able to speak for the needs of the entire user community and be able to make decisions on their behalf. It is unrealistic that you will be able to meet with each and every user of your system in a lot of cases, so these user community representatives will be critical to the success of your system in the user's eyes.

Another important thing to consider is that unless it's important to the integrity of the architecture system, if the user community doesn't feel it's important, we shouldn't spend a lot of time on it. Always look for the path of least resistance (or in our case, development time) to solve a problem. A good example occurred to this web development team I worked with just after the public release of ASP.NET. There was a particular administration page that was taking 5-8 seconds to load, and the users remarked that it might be confusing to wait that long without some type of sign that the page was still processing. The lead developer suggested placing a "Working ..." graphic on the screen while the page was processing, which all the users agreed would solve the problem. However, a senior staff member was convinced that 5-8 seconds was just too slow, and ordered the development team to tear apart the infrastructure to further improve performance. In the end, the development team spent over 100 hours of re-architecture time on an area of the system that was infrequently used, where the simple solution of a "Working ..." image would have sufficed. What is the moral of the story? Never over-complicate design issues when the user community agrees that the more simplistic solution will satisfy their needs.

Perceived Performance

So, how do you eliminate perceived performance problems? Well, there are a few tricks and they all happen during the design phase. Waiting until the application is released and in the user's hands is too late to affect anything of substance with regard to perceived performance. Here are some of the techniques that you can use during the design phase in order to help get that Holy Grail of user acceptance on performance:

- ❏ Set expectations up front
- ❏ Keep users informed

Set Expectations Up Front

This may sound simple, but the fact of the matter is that most users don't know what to expect from an application until they actually use it in user acceptance testing or production for the first time. This is one of the most common problems with the coordination of any development project with the user community.

Let's look at a common example of this problem. You are in charge of development for an enterprise system that is replacing an existing legacy system that the users are currently working with. Although the current application is a Windows-based application, you are developing a replacement system that is a web application, so that it can be run across a multiple client base, without having to manually distribute and install application updates to all of the users.

Sounds ideal, doesn't it? In a perfect world, yes, but this type of transition can set you up for failure. In this case, the user community is used to an application that stays up on their desktop all of the time and gives almost immediate access. The end system that is provided to them is a web application, which means that page requests can take seconds, if for no other reason than HTTP response times are inconsistent, at best. Even if the entire work process (for example entering an order into the system) takes less overall time within the web application, the user will perceive a poor response time because they are used to having screens transition more quickly.

So, how do we set the user expectations before they actually see the product? One of the first ways is to generate early throw-away prototypes that will represent the screen flow, once it is mapped out. The important point to make here is that the prototype must reflect the performance goal that your team sets, so you'll probably need to enter some delay code in your prototype to simulate the expected performance of any back-end business logic. Then, take the user through the business use of the new system, and compare it to the old one (if necessary). Any questions will be brought up in this forum, well ahead of the software release, so it's very easy to determine whether the user community is bought-in to the new product.

The key here would be to involve the user in the exercise of designing the system to the extent that they know the pitfalls of the new technologies being worked with (the negative aspects of networked applications, network speed and latency, and so on).

Keep Users Informed

How many times have you clicked on a web page, just to watch that Internet Explorer globe spin for what seems like an eternity? Did your Internet connection go down? Was there any error connecting to a back-end system? Or is the system just that slow? These are the questions that your user community asks as well.

The easiest way to help get the users back on your side is by providing them with messages along the way to let them know that the system is working on their request. These messages reassure the user that the system is working and helps them to be a little more patient. Let's take a look at a couple of methods that we can utilize in ASP.NET to keep users informed of application status.

One of the easiest ways to do this is by controlling the browser's status bar. You can easily add information to the Internet Explorer status bar by including a simple piece of JavaScript for every page you plan to issue a call from.

```
<SCRIPT LANGUAGE="JavaScript">
  var msg = 'Processing Page Request'
  function ScrollMarquee()
    {
      window.setTimeout('ScrollMarquee()', 250);
      defaultStatus = msg
      msg += '.'
    }
</SCRIPT>
<body Onbeforeunload="javascript:ScrollMarquee()">
  <FORM id="Form1" method="post" runat="server">
    <P>
    <asp:Button id="btnGo" runat="server" Text="Go"></asp:Button></P>
  </FORM>
</body>
```

Notice that we're using the JavaScript's OnBeforeUnLoad event, so that we get the message as soon as the request to Unload the page has happened, but before the Unload has actually occurred. If we were to use the UnLoad event, then the message would only appear (very briefly) after the destination page finished processing and was just about to load. This is the same reason we don't put JavaScript in the Load event of the destination page, because that code will not fire until ASP.NET has rendered the page and sent it to the user – making any status display useless when waiting for a page to process.

The problem with this approach is that is requires each and every browser to implement the status message bar the exact same way. Some versions of Netscape, and other older browsers, do not provide this support.

Another way to give a user status messages, and to do it independently of a browser, is to create a standard page processor. It is the job of the page processor to put up an informational message, while in the background it will be processing the page results. Once the results are available, the informational message is replaced by the desired page. Here's one way we can accomplish this.

We create a page loader called PageLoad.aspx. In it we enter the following client-side JavaScript and HTML code:

```
<script language="javascript">
  var iLoopCounter = 1;
  var iMaxLoop = 6;
  var iIntervalId;

  function BeginPageLoad()
  {
```

```
      /* Redirect the browser to another page while keeping focus */
      location.href = "<%=strPageToLoad %>";
      /* Update progress meter every 1/2 second */
      iIntervalId = window.setInterval
          ("iLoopCounter=UpdateProgressMeter(iLoopCounter,iMaxLoop)", 500);
    }
    function EndPageLoad()
    {
      window.clearInterval(iIntervalId);
      ProgressMeter.innerText = "Page Loaded - Now Transfering";
    }
    function UpdateProgressMeter(iCurrentLoopCounter, iMaximumLoops)
    {
      iCurrentLoopCounter += 1;
      if(iCurrentLoopCounter <= iMaximumLoops)
      {
        ProgressMeter.innerText += ".";
        return iCurrentLoopCounter
      }
      else
      {
        ProgressMeter.innerText = "";
        return 1;
      }
    }
  }
</script>
<body onLoad="javascript:BeginPageLoad();"
    onUnload="javascript:EndPageLoad();">
<form id="frmPageLoader" method="post" runat="server">
  <table border="0" cellpadding="0" cellspacing="0"
      width="99%" height="99%" align="center" vAlign="middle">
    <tr>
      <td align="center" vAlign="center">
        <font color=Navy size=5>
        <span id="MessageText">Loading Page - Please Wait</span>
        <span id="ProgressMeter"
            style="width:25px;text-align:left;"></span>
        </font>
      </td>
    </tr>
  </table>
</form>
</body>
```

What this page does is take a parameter as part of the querystring called Page, and redirect the browser to that page. However, what's different about this page is that it sets location.href in JavaScript, to set the URL for the current window to be the web page value (Page) passed in and read during the Page_Load event:

```
    Public strPageToLoad As String
    Private Sub Page_Load(ByVal sender As System.Object, _
        ByVal e As System.EventArgs) Handles MyBase.Load
      'Put user code to initialize the page here
      strPageToLoad = (Request.QueryString("Page"))
    End Sub
```

The BeginPageLoad JavaScript function keeps the current window open and retrieves the results. No postbacks are made, so the end result is the display of a progress message until the resultant page is fully processed and loaded. We also included some JavaScript to make the message appear more dynamic by adding dots to make the message look more like an animated progress meter.

The end result is a very useful "In Progress" meter page that informs the user that something is happening in the background. Better still, you only need to create this page once and then use it anywhere in your project just by entering the following code when you want to move to a page that might take some time to load.

```
Server.Transfer("LoadPage.aspx?Page=Results.aspx")
```

This call would yield the progress meter page shown below:

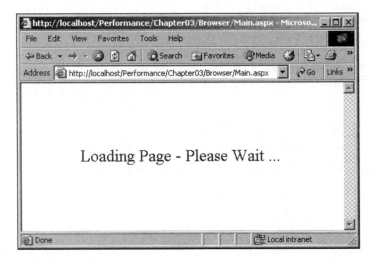

And then it would display the desired end page:

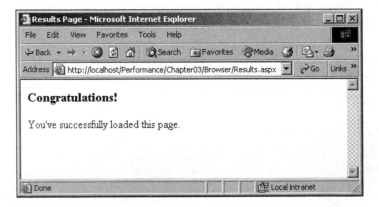

As you can see, with just a small amount of client-side code, you can keep the user informed as to the progress of your application and what it is doing. By keeping the user informed, their level of perceived performance increases and your ASP.NET application will gain a better reputation.

A big key in determining whether or not to use client-side coding techniques is to understand the best technological fit for the requirement. You should utilize client-side scripting when you're working with navigational requirements or formatting code that you don't mind the user being able to capture. The one caveat to this is if you cannot guarantee your browser base, then you should provide server-side code to backup your client-side code, just in case the browser does not support it. Business rules should be implemented using server-side code and rarely, if ever, be implemented using client-side code.

Dynamic versus Static Content

It's no secret that static content is faster to serve than dynamic content. We saw this earlier when we learned to use HTML controls instead of ASP.NET Server controls when creating static labels (or other static information) on an ASPX page. The same logic applies at the page level as well. A static page that does not need to be processed and is just "served" to the requestor, is going to be many times faster than any compiled page, no matter how fast the operating system or how tightly compiled the code is.

Reports are a great example of functionality that can benefit from the creation of static content. Most web reports are not expected to be real-time, so it's easy to build static pages that represent the most common reports. We'll be covering ASP.NET content caching in a later chaper, but let's go over a sample of how we can include caching as part of our design in order to improve performance.

Let's say that we need a report, which will show us a list of job openings for a company. This type of report is probably a great candidate for caching, but you should always check with your user community to ensure that their expectations are set correctly. This will eliminate communication problems down the road where the user might expect a real-time view of the data, and the design implements a cached view. These kind of requirements need to be fleshed out during the design phase, so that the right technology can be implemented to solve the business requirement.

Since we probably don't expect the customer report to change over the period of an hour, we'll create a web page to generate the report and then cache the entire page for an hour. All subsequent requests for this report will be served from the static content and will be instantly available – plus no additional load on the web server will be created by re-querying the database for these results.

Let's take a look at how we can accomplish this. We'll create an ASPX report page that can be called from within any existing page in our application. We'll be using the Jobs table in the Pubs database as the source of our data.

The page is very easy to create. It should look something similar to the one shown below:

```
<%@ Page Language="vb" AutoEventWireup="false" Codebehind="Openings.aspx.vb"
    Inherits="Jobs.Openings"%>
<%@ OutputCache Duration="3600" VaryByParam="none" %>
...

<form id="Form1" method="post" runat="server">
  <DIV ms_positioning="FlowLayout">
    <FONT size="5"><STRONG>Company XYZ Job Listings</STRONG></FONT>
```

```
    </DIV>
<asp:DataGrid id="DataGrid1" runat="server" AutoGenerateColumns="false"
    BorderColor="#DEBA84" BorderStyle="None" CellSpacing="2" BorderWidth="1px"
    BackColor="#DEBA84" CellPadding="3">
    <SelectedItemStyle Font-Bold="True" ForeColor="White"
        BackColor="#738A9C"></SelectedItemStyle>
    <ItemStyle ForeColor="#8C4510" BackColor="#FFF7E7"></ItemStyle>
    <HeaderStyle Font-Bold="True" ForeColor="White"
        BackColor="#A55129"></HeaderStyle>
    <FooterStyle ForeColor="#8C4510" BackColor="#F7DFB5"></FooterStyle>
    <PagerStyle HorizontalAlign="Center" ForeColor="#8C4510"
        Mode="NumericPages"></PagerStyle>
    <Columns>
      <asp:BoundColumn HeaderText="Job ID" DataField="job_id"></asp:BoundColumn>
      <asp:BoundColumn HeaderText="Title" DataField="job_desc">
      </asp:BoundColumn>
      <asp:BoundColumn HeaderText="Min Salary" DataField="min_lvl">
      </asp:BoundColumn>
      <asp:BoundColumn HeaderText="Max Salary" DataField="max_lvl">
      </asp:BoundColumn>
    </Columns>
</asp:DataGrid>
</form>
```

Our code-behind is the straightforward fetch of data from the SQL Server Pubs database.

```
If Not IsPostBack Then
    Connect to SQL Server and query for a list of jobs
    objConnection = New SqlConnection("server=;uid=;pwd=;database=Pubs")
    strCommand = "SELECT job_id, job_desc, min_lvl, max_lvl FROM Jobs"
    objCommand = New SqlDataAdapter(strCommand, objConnection)
    ' Fill the dataset with the results
    objCommand.Fill(ds1, "jobs")
    dgJobs.DataSource = ds1
    dgJobs.DataBind()
End If
```

The one difference is the addition of the @OutputCache page-level directive that we reviewed in Chapter 2.

```
<%@ OutputCache Duration="3600" VaryByParam="none" %>
```

What this line does is tell ASP.NET to cache off the results for this page the first time it is requested, making it basically a static page for a duration of 3600 seconds (1 hour). Each cached page in memory is stamped with the time of its creation, as well as the expiry interval. When the page is requested next, ASP.NET first looks in the cache and if the cache has expired, it executes the page again, otherwise it just pumps the cached page to the output stream. The static page is served for any future requests within one hour. After one hour, the static page is discarded and a fresh page is cached on the next page request.

As you can imagine, this type of caching will serve as a great performance benefit, since serving up a static page costs almost no server resources at all. Compare the first hit to this page and a successive hit (from another browser session) and you'll immediately notice how much faster other browsers receive the page. When implementing a design for pages that have long lists or reports, look to page caching to help improve performance.

If caching does not fit the user's requirements (for example, if the user requires real-time access to the data), then you're better off creating a reporting data warehouse that receives periodic (scheduled or real-time) updates from the application's database. This reporting system can then be used to provide real-time access for reporting against any piece of data in the system, all without affecting the performance of your ASP.NET system.

We've just scratched the surface of caching in ASP.NET, and what it can do for the performance of your system.

We'll take a detailed look at caching and ASP.NET application development in the next chapter.

Making the Move to OO

In ASP.NET, the page and controls are all objects, which inherit from a common base class. By developing these base classes, we eliminate the need to reinvent the wheel and develop similar code across all of our similar objects. Writing this kind of reusable code is a big key to eliminating code bloat, a predominant problem in today's enterprise applications.

Designing Scalable Objects That Perform

While we are looking toward object orientation as a way to achieve better performance, let's examine how we can build scalable objects that have the highest level of performance. Many times a developer thinks they have to choose between a system that is scalable and one that performs well. To achieve performance, a lot of developers feel that they need to cut all the corners that they can find in order to tune the system for the specific architecture, and by doing so, lose all potential scalability. It basically comes down to doing what makes the best sense for a high-performance system that solves the business requirements.

The fact is that most performance gains are achieved during the design phase. A poor design (be it architecture or user interface) is harder to compensate for than a code performance faux pax.

The first rule of developing a high-performance object is that the object should be designed to fill a single requirement. A class should encapsulate one, and only one, role (an entity). Too often, an object is initially created to serve a single function, but the base class is then altered to handle multiple duties. Take the following book object, for example:

```
Public Class Book

    Private m_ID As Integer
    Private m_Title As String
    Private m_ISBN As String
    Private m_Publisher As String
    Private m_Cost As Double
    Private m_Owner As String
    Private m_AtWork As Boolean
    Private m_Notes As String
    Private m_PurchaseDate As DateTime
    Private m_CheckOutStatus As Boolean
    Private m_CheckOutDate As DateTime
```

```
Public Property ID() As Integer
End Property
Public Property Title() As String
End Property
Public Property ISBN() As String
End Property
Public Property Publisher() As String
End Property
Public Property Cost() As Double
End Property
Public Property Owner() As String
Public Property AtWork() As Boolean
End Property
Public Property Notes() As String
End Property
Public Property PurchaseDate() As DateTime
End Property
Public Property CheckOutStatus() As Boolean
End Property
Public Property CheckOutDate() As DateTime

   ...

End Property
Public Function Save() As Boolean
   Dim strSQL As String
   Dim objConnection As New SqlConnection(SQLDB.strConnection)
   Dim objCommand As New SqlCommand()
   Dim objSQLDataReader As SqlDataReader

   ' Make a call to the DB and update this specific record
   ...
End Function
Public Function Insert() As Book
   Dim strSQL As String
   Dim objConnection As New SqlConnection(SQLDB.strConnection)
   Dim objCommand As New SqlCommand()
   Dim objSQLDataReader As SqlDataReader

   ' Make a call to the DB and update this specific record
   ' and return the fully populated object with new record id
   ...
End Function


End Class
```

While this is an extreme example, you should strive to eliminate properties and methods from your class that do not directly deal with the class. You shouldn't be concerned that we're not showing the implementation for our properties and methods, since we're talking about the design of the objects right now.

A typical extension of this example is the addition properties and methods to that class to support a collection (say Books). This object should be treated as a separate class, which could live in the same namespace but its logic is separated. The Books class would utilize the Book class, but its operations do not revolve around manipulating a book object (at the database level, for example), but how to manipulate a list of books.

When we design a class, we also need to look at how people will consume it. Take the previous Books class. Let's assume that instantiating this class will go and retrieve a list of all contacts in the database. The end result is a collection of contacts, each of type Book.

```
Public Class Books
  Inherits CollectionBase
  Public Enum ItemRetrievalType
    DB
    Collection
  End Enum
  Public ReadOnly Property Item(ByVal iColIndex As Integer, _
                Optional ByVal iType As ItemRetrievalType _
                  = ItemRetrievalType.DB) As Book

      ...

  End Property
  Public Function Add() As Integer
      ' Now Insert the Book into the collection
      ' Make sure to call the Book Insert method

  End Function

  Public Function Delete(ByVal iRecIndex As Integer) As Boolean
  ...
  End Function

  Public Function LoadDataSet() As DataSet
  ...
  End Function

  Public Function RefreshList(Optional ByVal strFilter As String = "") _
        As Boolean
  ...
  End Function

End Class
```

Since our class inherits from the Collection class, we get the Count property for free. This property lets the consumers know how many contact objects are in the collection. This count comes at a price, though. In order to get at the count, we'll need to instantiate the entire collection and create a new contact object for each item in the collection. This is a lot of overhead if we just wanted to know the number of contacts that fit a certain criteria (say for a status or reporting page).

```
Dim objBooks as new Books()
Response.Write("There are " & objBooks.Count & _
            " in the database")
```

If you will have consumers that want to know the number of items in a collection without actually using the items in the collection, then there's a better way to implement this count. We can create our own ReadOnly Shared CurrentCount property. This means that there will only be one value of this count property for all of the instances of the Contacts collection. Within the CurrentCount property we can specify a call to a stored procedure that merely does a SELECT COUNT(*) on the Books database table (called usp_GetBookCount).

To do this, we would implement this new shared property to our Books class like this:

```
Public Shared ReadOnly Property CurrentCount() As Integer
  Get
    Dim objConnection As New SqlConnection(SQLDB.strConnection)
    Dim objCommand As New SqlCommand()
    Dim objSQLDataReader As SqlDataReader
    Dim iCount As Integer
    objCommand.CommandText = "exec usp_GetBookCount"
    objSQLDataReader = objCommand.ExecuteReader
    iCount = objSQLDataReader("Count")
    objConnection.Close()
    Return iCount
  End Get
End Property
```

We can avoid the overhead of instantiating the collection by using our new CurrentCount property. The code would look like what you see below:

```
Dim objBooks as Books()
Response.Write("There are " & objBooks.CurrentCount() & _
             " in the database")
```

Notice that we couldn't specify the New keyword when declaring objContacts, since we didn't want to instantiate the collection. We only wanted to create a reference to the class so that we could use its shared property CurrentCount. Since this a shared member, we don't need a same type class reference – it's an unnecessary performance hit; we merely need a variable that matches the return type of the shared member. Since CurrentCount returns an integer type, we can specify any variables that are set to this property as Integer to get this performance gain.

In summary, to get the best performance out of your objects, they need to have a good object-oriented design.

A good resource for more information about object-oriented design in the .NET world is "Professional Design Patterns in VB.NET - Building Adaptable Applications" (ISBN 1861006985, from Wrox Press or "VB.NET Class Design Handbook" (ISBN 1861007086), also from Wrox Press.

Separating the UI from the Code

Another large leap forward for ASP.NET over previous application platforms is its use of code-behind files to separate presentation logic from business logic through the actual UI page (called an ASPX file or ASCX file if you are developing a user control) and the code-behind file (called an ASPX.vb, ASPX.cs, or other extension based on what language you've defined for your project). While the ASPX/ASCX file contains the graphic layout of the page, the code-behind file contains the server-side activities that are performed as events for each of the controls (including the page) are fired.

Separation of code from user interface is the easiest way to provide structured team development, and a manageable product to maintain.

Imagine an enterprise development project where you have a team of developers assigned to the user interface, and another team of developers assigned to the architecture, database, and business logic. It also impedes progress when you have a group of design artists who perform the UI design, and know nothing about application development. Without code separation, you will ultimately end up with the development teams stepping on each other. The result can range from a longer development cycle to bug-ridden code. Change management in this type of environment is also difficult, at best, because each team needs access to the same files at the same time to do their job.

From a performance perspective, what code-behind provides is the ability to generate code more quickly and with more quality. This is because we're focusing on end-user presentation in the ASPX file, and on business logic in the code-behind file.

Another reason to utilize the code-behind metaphor is to increase the serving of ASP.NET pages during the page compilation process. When you request an ASPX page in ASP.NET, the first thing the ASP.NET worker process does is look to the compiled cache for that page . Compiled pages can be found in the following directory:

```
%WINDIR%\Microsoft.NET\Framework\v1.0.3705\
    Temporary ASP.NET Files\<application name>.
```

ASP.NET will either serve the pre-compiled page from this private directory, or compiles it again if it has changed. This compiled page is different from the compiled assembly that you create when you compile the project, and the .NET Framework compiler places the DLL in the bin folder (this file is actually inherited from the compiled ASPX page). The version in the bin folder is actually the latest compiled version, while the version cached in ASP.NET's private assembly directory is the cached version (providing ASP.NET with a performance gain by executing against cached copies of the .NET executable).

So, let's assume that you've got some server-side script inside an ASPX page (remember this code from Chapter 2?):

```vb
<SCRIPT language="VB" runat="server">
        Dim i As Integer
        Dim objSessionCollection As HttpSessionState
        Dim strSessionVarName As String
        Dim strSessionVarValue As String
        Dim sbEntries As New StringBuilder()

        ' Get the current session object
        objSessionCollection = Session.Contents
        ' Go through the list of contents
        For i = 0 To objSessionCollection.Count - 1
            ' Append key name and value to stringbuiler
            ' NOTE: Use stringbuilder becuase it is faster
            ' than the normal &/+ appending process
            sbEntries.Append(objSessionCollection.Keys(i).ToString())
            sbEntries.Append(" = ")
            sbEntries.Append(objSessionCollection.Item(i))
            ' Add CR/LF
            sbEntries.Append(Convert.ToChar(13))
            sbEntries.Append(Convert.ToChar(10))
        Next
        ' Put the results into the text box
        txtSessionInfo.Text = sbEntries.ToString
    </SCRIPT>
```

These variables are now created as public at the page-level. But what's worse, is that if you change anything in the ASPX page (even outside the <SCRIPT> tag), you'll end up forcing ASP.NET to parse through the entire page. If we were to move the VB code to the code-behind file, where it belongs, then we'll alleviate the extra processing time it takes to parse through all of that extra code. By putting the code in the code-behind, it will be pre-compiled with the project and only the UI code will need to be generated off of what server controls are placed in the ASPX file.

There is a smaller issue not quite related to performance, but which does relate to fault tolerance. Let's assume that you create the following variable in <SCRIPT> tags in the ASPX page:

```
<SCRIPT language="VB" runat="server">
  dim iNumber as Integer = 5
</SCRIPT>
```

iNumber is now declared as a variable with a page-level scope. If you create the same variable name in the code-behind file for this page, you won't get a VB.NET compiler error, but you will get a run-time compiler error when ASP.NET attempts to compile the page for the first time. This is because you now have two variables with the same name in the same namespace (the page). The compiler did not know about the other variable, but when ASP.NET first attempts to compile the ASPX page, it will find the naming conflict.

Microsoft now recognizes the code-behind as the new standard for ASP.NET development. You should strive to utilize code-behind for all server-side code in all of your ASP.NET pages, in order to provide maintainability and consistency within your application.

The Essentials of a Good User Interface

A good user interface is also a necessity in a high-performance web application. You might be asking yourself, "What does the organization of graphics and cool colors have to do with performance"? The answer to that question lies in good versus bad web user interface design. You see, web application user interface design is very different from its fat-client counterpart. You can get away with a lot of truly bad UI design on a desktop application, which will absolutely kill the performance of a web application, simply because the desktop application is always connected. Remove that connectivity and make the transitions between screens stateless, and you have the potential for a real mess.

The very first thing you must do as a team is create an application screen flow tree or hierarchy. What you need to define is all of the work screens that your application will have, and how they are navigated to. It is not important that the screens are completed, we only need to know of their intended existence in order to start organizing them.

Once the screens are all sketched, you should organize them into functional areas and show possible flows. The goal here is to keep the flows simple and distinct. It will be hard to debug a flow design where Page A may call Page B one time, but Page B calls Page A another time (this could also lead to other bugs because the developer may not have tested for that type of cross-linking).

The first thing to consider in screen flow is how many mouse clicks it will take for the user to get to their intended destination. If possible, your design team should set a policy that limits the number of clicks for a user to get from point A to point B. For example, having a nested set of popup windows that force a user to click on a bank account to pop a window, then a balance to pop another window of check numbers, and then finally a check to pop up a set of check details would be a bad UI design. This forces the user to pop up 3 to 4 (depending on what consistutes the main window) just to get information on a check. The better approach would be to provide a search mechanism that allows the user to enter criteria, and then they can click on the desired check would pop up a single window.

The next thing to consider when implementing your page flow, is to properly specify your page URLs. As we've already learned in Chapter 2, we should use the `Server.Transfer()` method to move to another internal page. You should also implement the following standards when specifying the move from one page to another:

- ❑ Implement relative URL addressing
- ❑ Add the ending slash ("/") to any web site or directory

A relative URL is one where we pass only the necessary parts of the URL to get to the destination page, based on where the current page is on the same server or server farm. For example, if you are currently in `http://localhost/app1/MyDir` and your page is `Page1.aspx`, you should set your URL to `../GuestDir/Page2.aspx` to reference a page in the `GuestDir` directory at the same level as the `MyDir` directory. Using `http://localhost/app1/GuestDir/Page2.aspx` is not only a little slower, but it is not very scalable since this won't deploy to another hosting server, nor will it work if the name of the application changes from `App1` to something else.

Adding the ending slash to a URL is the appropriate way to specify loading the default page in a web directory. For example, the following is the RFC 1808 standard for loading the home page on the Wrox site:

```
http://www.wrox.com/
```

Now, we all know that we can drop the ending slash and still get the page. However, what you might not know is that this causes an extra round trip from the browser to the server. When the browser contacts a server without the ending flash (and there's no specific filename at the end), the server responds back to the browser that it requested a directory and not a file. The browser then adds the ending slash to the URL and retries the http `GET` operation. Again, this doesn't apply when specifying files as part of the URL (such as `http://www.wrox.com/default.htm`).

We also need to look at individual pages themselves to see how much information they contain. A common pitfall is to create a large dumping ground for any information related to the screen at hand. Clutter on the screen not only leads to user confusion, but also extra time to load all of that extra information.

Let's take a look at an example to demonstrate this point. This web page was designed to show a customer and their interactions with our company. We want to be able to see the customer information, a contact list for the company, their order history, and a list of currently open support incidents. The first iteration of this page's design might look similar to the one below shown in the VS.NET IDE. Notice that we can't even fit all of the information on one screen without having to scroll. The problem with scrolling is that it has a negative impact on perceived performance. Therefore, you should attempt to design your UI screens to work with the various screen sizes of your customer base. This information will most likely be determined during the customer interview sessions, unless you are building commercial software, in which case you'll need to support the most populate screen sizes and resolutions.

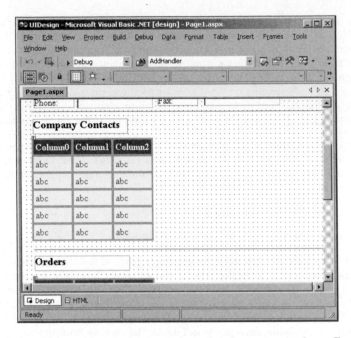

The problem with this design is that it presents too much information up-front. Even shifting the data grids so that they're side-by-side still make this screen unwieldy. A user generally comes to a page to see and do a single operation. Putting this much information all at once can be confusing. In addition, from the performance angle we can take quite a hit if the information comes from multiple sources. We'll need to do at least four separate queries just to get the screen back to the user, and these queries will probably be against different data tables (and they may even be against external systems if our system doesn't host this information). What if the user just wanted to find their phone number?

The better way to do this is to provide a main customer contact screen with separate action tabs for viewing purchasing information. We will allow the user to bring up a modal window with this information in it. The modal dialog box will allow the user to slice and dice the data locally, so they don't have to go back to the customer contact page and enter different criteria. Once they've got what they're looking for, they close the modal window and are returned to the customer contact screen, where they can now move off to perform some other action. The revised screen and modal window are shown as so:

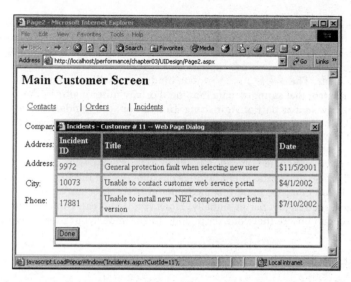

Here's the code that accomplishes this technique. The first thing we'll do is to add a navigational tab structure to the top of the page using the ASP.NET hyperlink server control. We'll use these hyperlinks to allow the user to select the details that they want, which will bring up a modal browser window with the detail information.

```
<TABLE id="Table1" style="Z-INDEX: 118; LEFT: 17px; POSITION: absolute;
    TOP: 58px" cellSpacing="1" cellPadding="1" width="300" border="0">
  <TR>
    <TD><asp:hyperlink id="HyperLink1" runat="server">
        Contacts</asp:hyperlink>
    </TD>
    <TD>|</TD>
    <TD><asp:hyperlink id="HyperLink2" runat="server">
        Orders</asp:hyperlink></TD>
    <TD>|</TD>
    <TD><asp:HyperLink id="HyperLink3" runat="server">
        Incidents</asp:HyperLink></TD>
  </TR>
</TABLE>
```

Next, we'll add code to the Page_Load event to set the NavigateUrl property for each ASP.NET hyperlink server control to the desired destination page. This property will actually be a JavaScript command (instead of a physical URL), which will instruct JavaScript to open up a new browser window with no frame, help, toolbar, or resize capabilities. We'll also add the customer ID, which is retrieved from the txtID variable, as part of the URL query string to the new page, so that it can query the detailed information for that customer ID.

```
' Set the URL for the navigation tabs to be JavaScript popups
HyperLink1.NavigateUrl =_
    "javascript:LoadPopupWindow('Contacts.aspx?CustId=" & txtID & "');"
HyperLink2.NavigateUrl = _
    "javascript:LoadPopupWindow('Orders.aspx?CustId=" & txtID & "');"
HyperLink3.NavigateUrl = _
    "javascript:LoadPopupWindow('Incidents.aspx?CustId=" & txtID & "');"
```

You might be asking why we needed to put this information in the code-behind, and not directly in the ASPX file, using the "<%# ... %>" data binding evaluator tags. This is a common misconception amongst ASP.NET developers. The reason we can't use the data binding evaluator is because the ASP.NET HyperLink control does not support data binding. In many of today's ASP.NET books, this topic is not made clear. The "<%# ... %>" data binding tag will only be evaluated within an ASP.NET server control that supports data binding. For any other controls, the tag is ignored and you end up getting the raw text as part of your string. In addition, the standard script section tags "<% ... %>" will not work since the section is embedded inside of a server control, and the information is pre-rendered by ASP.NET.

Another user interface technique you can implement to improve performance is to offload as much of the user interface processing to the client layer as possible. As we discussed in Chapter 2, when talking about server validation controls, there is some trade-off here, since not all browsers implement client scripting languages, such as JavaScript, equally. However, if you can control your client's browser capabilities, or you can ensure that your script code works under your user's environments, then this technique is for you.

Some of the most common user interface operations that we can offload from the server to the client layer are:

❑   Input validation

❑   Advanced UI effects

❑   Page navigation functions

Beware that implementing code at the client layer will give your client complete visibility to your code and how it works. Some of the items that we should not implement at the client level are:

❑   Core business logic

❑   Interaction with other business systems

The key to this is to balance any client-side coding with the requirements. A lot of systems provide flashy interfaces that implement drag and drop for web applications, or some other Windows-type UI features. The fact is that the majority of your users care about functionality and performance in comparison with feel. So, before you start adding client-side code to perform some advanced UI effects, make sure that it fulfills a business need, and is not implemented just because it's cool. As a prominent commercial goes, "Cool is what costs me money" – and so it is with enterprise application development.

A common performance problem you'll see a lot in web applications is the retrieval of all information up-front during the Page_Load process. There may be times when the user absolutely does not want to have window pop-ups (as in our earlier example), and wants to have access to the information from one screen.

As we saw in Chapter 2, we can use the IsPostBack property for the page to make sure that we don't re-query information when it's stored in the viewstate for us. However, this still doesn't solve the problem of performance the very first time that page is brought up. The main problem with this page is that it requires us to provide many different queries to different data sources to populate all of the data up-front. We'll assume that we can't use the filter criteria for a data set and do a single query, since the information for each queue might be in a different repository. The reason that we have to re-query isn't important, only that it has to be done. The problem is that this page will load slowly because we have to do all queries up-front. Caching or performing a background query will not work since this is the information that the user wants to see in an up-to-the-minute fashion.

Let's take a look at our example from earlier. Remember that we designed a customer main screen that had the customer information, and then modal dialogs for each of the specific areas of information (contacts, orders, and support tickets). We can modify this example to have the best of both worlds by putting placeholders on the screen and fetching data only when the placeholder is clicked. Let's take a look at this example in action.

On the initial screen, the user would receive the customer details, followed by three tabs which are all collapsed. The screen loads very quickly because we haven't loaded any information other than the customer details.

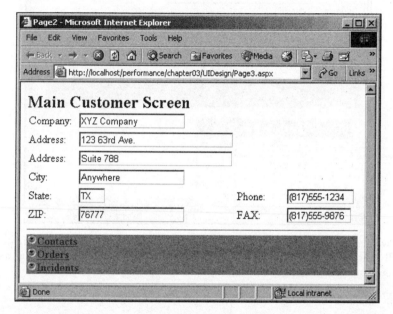

Now, when the user clicks on one of the tabs, it "expands" to show them the details underneath. What's cool about this is that the data is not brought until the user clicks on the tab. This means that if the user only cared about orders, we wouldn't waste any CPU cycles on fetching support ticket or contact information.

So, how did we accomplish this? Actually it's quite easy. The first thing we did is create some JavaScript code that will generically expand and contract a DIV tag, whose name is passed in as a variable. The JavaScript function called ExpandSection is found below:

```
function ExpandSection(DivTag, FrameTag, FrameSource)
{
  DivSel = eval("document.all." + DivTag);
  FrameSel = eval("document.all." + FrameTag);
  if (DivSel.style.display == "none")
  {
    DivSel.style.display = "block";
    FrameSel.src = FrameSource;
  }
  else
  {
    DivSel.style.display = "none";

  }
}
```

This function takes the DIV tag's name and set's the style to "none", to give the impression of collapsing the section. Within the DIV tag, there's a borderless IFRAME, whose source is the same ASPX pages for Contacts, Orders, and Incidents (with the exception of the **Done** button). Only when the DIV tag is expanded, will the frame selection source be enabled, firing off the IFRAME to go get the data from the remote page (which is also passed in as a parameter).

```
<table width="100%" border="0" cellpadding="0" cellspacing="0">
  <tr>
    <td width="250" nowrap bgcolor="#999999">
    <a href="javascript:"onclick="ExpandSection('DivSection1','FrameSection1',
        'Contacts_Expando.aspx'); return false;">
      <img src="images/Collapse.gif" border="0">
      <span><b>Contacts</b></span>
    </a>
    </td>
  </tr>
</table>
<div id="DivSection1" style="DISPLAY:none">
  <iframe id="FrameSection1" scrolling="no" height="auto" width="auto"
      style="WIDTH: 499px; HEIGHT: 197px" frameBorder="no">
  </iframe>
</div>
<table width="100%" border="0" cellpadding="0" cellspacing="0">
  <tr>
    <td width="250" nowrap bgcolor="#999999">
    <a href="javascript:"onclick="ExpandSection('DivSection2','FrameSection2',
        'Orders_Expando.aspx');return false;">
      <img src="images/Collapse.gif" border="0">
      <span><b>Orders</b></span>
    </a>
    </td>
  </tr>
</table>
<div id="DivSection2" style="DISPLAY:none">
  <iframe id="FrameSection2" scrolling="no" height="auto" width="auto"
      style="WIDTH: 499px; HEIGHT: 197px" frameBorder="no">
  </iframe>
</div>
<table width="100%" border="0" cellpadding="0" cellspacing="0">
  <tr>
    <td width="250" nowrap bgcolor="#999999">
    <a href="javascript:"onclick="ExpandSection('DivSection3','FrameSection3',
        'Incidents_Expando.aspx');return false;">
      <img src="images/Collapse.gif" border="0">
      <span><b>Incidents</b></span>
    </a>
    </td>
  </tr>
</table>
<div id="DivSection3" style="DISPLAY:none">
  <iframe id="FrameSection3" scrolling="no" height="auto" width="auto"
      style="WIDTH: 499px; HEIGHT: 197px" frameBorder="no">
  </iframe>
</div>
```

By passing in the IFRAME's source as a parameter when expanding the DIV tag, we ensure that we're not spending any time retrieving the data for that section, until the user clicks on the DIV tag to expand. The end result is a page that loads more quickly, and then responds with individualized data queries as the user selects their area of interest.

What we've shown you in this section is that there's natural balance in any ASP.NET user interface, between client-side code and server-side code. As we've outlined earlier, you should utilize client-side code for those operations like formatting and navigation that do not require back-end information. You should strive not to implement core business logic on the client-side, and keep all of that logic compiled and running on the server side.

Integrating External Systems

A typical enterprise system requires information from other external systems. For example, an HR/Payroll system might need access to the Accounting system for account codes and cost center numbers, so that it doesn't have to duplicate this information. But, what if this information isn't on the same server? What if it's across the country? What is it's not even on the same operating platform as your application?

Integrating (or calling) these external systems, be they local or across the world, is almost a necessity in today's enterprise systems. Since almost all enterprise systems require this integration, it is also imperative that we look at the performance of both the external system itself, and any interface that we develop which communicates with it. While performance tuning of external systems themselves is out of the scope of this book, we will discuss performance improvement techniques for integration with them.

Before .NET, the only way to do this was through DCOM (distributed COM) or RPC (remote procedure) calls (just before .NET was released, a SOAP toolkit for VB6 was also released to provide support for remote communication via SOAP). Both COM/DCOM and RPC are slow and require direct network access to the machine, since they required the archaic NetBIOS protocol, which does not work over the open Internet and over most WAN/VPN connections (for security reasons).

In .NET development, we now have the following options when attempting to integrate with our external systems:

- ❑   .NET Remoting
- ❑   Web Services
- ❑   COM Interop

.NET Remoting

.NET Remoting is the process of remotely invoking .NET objects/methods across Application Domains. The integration occurs between processes via an object that has a shared assembly. The shared assembly actually exists on the local and remote machine, and at runtime .NET determines whether to create a local or remote instantiation of the object. This is so that the metadata for the remote assembly is available to the calling machine. The actual objects, methods and properties are never actually locally accessed.

Communication between the objects happens over channels, which can be either HTTP or TCP. You should use a TCP channel when communicating between servers within the same network. Use HTTP over an open network (like the Internet) since HTTP is the most non-blocked protocol available to us.

Creating a .NET Remoting object is just like creating a regular .NET object, with a few minor exceptions. The first difference is that any class you want to expose to remoting must inherit from the `MarshalByRefObject`. This tells .NET that this class should always stay in its Application Domain, and will never move.

```
Public Class ServerTime
    Inherits MarshalByRefObject
    Public Sub New()

    End Sub
    Public Function GetTime() As DateTime
        Return Now()
    End Function
End Class
```

Next, you must create a server service that sets up listening on a particular HTTP or TCP channel and registers the objects as a WellKnownServiceType, which allows consumers to pass information back and forth being marshaled by reference. The code below shows how we can register a service that will listen on a particular TCP channel in order to process server time requests:

```
dim objChannel as iChannel = new TCPChannel(9000)
ChannelServices.RegisterChannel(objChannel)
RemotingConfiguration.RegisterWellKnownServiceType (GetType(ServerTime), _
    "ServerTime.rem", WellKnownObjectMode.Singleton)
```

Utilizing a .NET object for remoting is very simple. First, the object must be available on the calling machine so that a reference can be made. This is usually done by registering the assembly with the GAC (global assembly cache). It's best to put these assemblies in the GAC, since they should be shareable amongst projects (eliminating duplicate code scattered throughout the client machine), and because .NET will search the GAC first (just after searching the bin folder) for any unresolved objects. This will speed up execution time, since the search is higher in the chain.

Now that we've discussed the basics of .NET Remoting, let's talk about a few rules of performance for using it in your ASP.NET applications.

First, you should use TCP channels to communicate serialized, binary information using .NET Remoting when both the server and the client are within your own private network. TCP channels are a more lightweight protocol, utilize fewer resources, and communicate more quickly than their HTTP channel siblings.

You can also perform asynchronous .NET Remoting for long-running operations. This helps speed up perceived performance, since control of the application is returned more quickly to the user, and the long-running operation is processed in the background. The results can then be retrieved during the next page load, or by placing some JavaScript on the client side to communicate with an IFRAME or other hidden HTML object (as we showed earlier in this chapter).

```
Delegate Function GetUSCurrencyConversionDelegate _
    (ByVal strCurrency As String, ByVal dblValue As Double) As Double
Dim USCurrencyConvertDel As GetUSCurrencyConversionDelegate = _
    AddressOf objMyRemote.ConvertToDollars
Dim iasr As iAsyncResult
Dim dblDollars As Double
iasr = USCurrencyConvertDel.BeginInvoke("YEN", 1000000.00, Nothing, Nothing)
' Do your parallel processing here
dblDollars = USCurrencyConverDel.EndInvoke(iasr)
```

In this example, we've created a delegate to the .NET remoting object objMyRemote, which contains the method ConvertToDollars. The signatures for the delegate and the remote object method must match. We call the BeginInvoke method for the delegate (a method automatically created when declaring a delegate) to start the call to the remote object. We get back an iAsyncResult object so that we can keep tabs on the status of the remote call. We use the EndInvoke function to retrieve our results back. Between the BeginInvoke and EndInvoke, we can do as much or as little parallel processing as we want.

If we call EndInvoke before the remote object is finished, .NET will block our thread until the remote object completes. We can eliminate this wait time by checking the value of IsCompleted on the iAsyncResult object.

```
While iasr.IsCompleted = False
   ' Do some processing
End While
```

We can also provide a callback mechanism so that we will get notified when a remote method call returns, instead of trying to poll the iAsyncResult object.

```
Public Sub RemoteObjComplete (byval iasr as iAsyncResult)
   Dim Dim dblDollars As Double
   dblDollars = USCurrencyConverDel.EndInvoke(iasr)
End Sub
Delegate Function GetUSCurrencyConversionDelegate _
     (ByVal strCurrency As String, ByVal dblValue As Double) As Double
Dim USCurrencyConvertDel As GetUSCurrencyConversionDelegate = _
     AddressOf objMyRemote.ConvertToDollars
iasr = USCurrencyConvertDel.BeginInvoke("YEN", 1000000.00, _
     AddressOf RemoteObjComplete, Nothing)
```

We pass a function pointer to the BeginInvoke method, letting it know that it should call our RemoteObjComplete method when the remote object returns. Then, in our callback routine, we can retrieve the value of the currency conversion using the EndInvoke method.

The subject of .NET Remoting is very complex and a complete description of all the capabilities is beyond the scope of this book. The basics that you should know about .NET Remoting for the design phase is that it is the fastest of all the external system integration options. So, if at all possible, you should look to .NET Remoting as your primary inter-process communication option (even over Web Services) whenever possible.

For more information on .NET Remoting, there's a great section on the topic in "Professional VB.NET 2nd Edition" (Wrox Press, ISBN 1-86100716-7) and a deeper look in the "VB.NET Remoting Handbook", (Wrox Press, ISBN 1-86100-704-X).

Web Services

You can't read any developer magazine these days without seeing some type of article on Web Services. You can't have a discussion about how to communicate with an external system, without someone talking about how "cool" web services are. Before we get into Web Services and performance, let's talk a little bit about how Web Services can be used in today's distributed applications.

Web Services make it very easy to communicate with external systems by providing "wrappers" around them, which can then pass back native XML to the ASP.NET application for processing. A typical example of this is the integration of an ASP.NET application with the company Help Desk ticketing system (which may be a third party vendor solution). We might want to allow our web application to add, update and delete support ticket information.

We can easily wrap any existing integration points that the Help Desk ticketing system has (like native API calls, or even direct database access) with a Web Service. All we need is a .NET server on the wire that can directly communicate with the third party system's integration point. Then, we wrap Web Services around these integration points to provide the objects and methods that best suit our ASP.NET application.

```
<WebMethod()> Public Function FindTicket(ByVal TID As Integer) As Ticket

    ... Help Desk API wrapper

End Function
```

Some manufacturers are also including their own Web Services as part of their product, so we can end up consuming their Web Service regardless of what platform it is build on. What's great about Web Services is that they are fast becoming a standard. Yes, there are variations here and there, but for the most part you can integrate a .NET Web Service with a web service written in Java and running on a UNIX platform.

Web Services are the slowest of the three external system integration mechanisms that we're discussing in this chapter. This is because of the overhead involved in making HTTP/SOAP requests from the client to the server and back to the client again. However, Web Services are the only real standardized solution to integrate disparate solutions over the open Internet, since they utilize the standard HTTP protocol. As you no doubt already know, the HTTP protocol is the really only "clear" communication channel available over the Internet, since it is generally not blocked by firewalls.

The decision on whether to use Web Services or .NET components to integrate disparate systems is an easy one. If you are integrating with a system that is within your own company's back-end environment, and the client requires no interaction with this integration (which it shouldn't), then you should be using .NET Remoting. As we learned earlier, .NET Remoting is the easiest to develop and work with, since it is just another .NET object that you work with. Since .NET Remoting runs all under managed code, it doesn't incur the overhead of the stateless Internet or unmanaged code calls in COM (we'll discuss COM integration with .NET in just a moment). In addition, there is extra overhead for processing of the SOAP headers and messages sent via plain or encrypted text over standard HTTP.

If you've decided that Web Services are they best design for integrating with another system, then there are some key points to making sure that your:

❑   Web Service runs as fast as possible

❑   ASP.NET application is not impacted by Web Service performance spikes

When we talk about performance and Web Services, we will be finding out ways to make them fulfill these design needs.

One of the lowest common denominators in communicating with an external system is a method known as screen scraping. This technology was in vogue ten years ago when PC developers were trying to integrate their applications with mainframe applications. Third-party tool developers carved out a niche by providing various HLLAPI (High Level Language Application Programming Interface) tools that would help make a mainframe connection, simulate the pressing of keys, and return screen information to the calling application. The PC application would actually be simulating the typing of information over a mainframe communication channel in order to provide integration.

The same technique is possible over the Web. Although, it should be reserved as a last resort because of its performance restrictions, you can simulate screen scraping as a method for retrieving data from an external system that doesn't provide any integration points, other than the web pages that it serves. Let's look at an example of this technique and how we can improve its performance as we add the integration to our ASP.NET application.

You've probably already ordered books from Amazon.com or at least browsed their web site (http://www.amazon.com/). You might be surprised to learn that there is no way to directly integrate with their system to retrieve book information. So, we ended up reverting to old-fashioned screen scraping in order to get at the information we desired. The goal of the Web Service was to provide a book's title, cost, publisher, and a link to the cover image when the caller provided an ISBN. This made it easy for us to perform data entry when entering books. All we had to do is enter the book's ISBN, and then the rest of the information would be auto-updated via the results from the Web Service. Let's take a look at our first stab at this Web Service:

```
<WebMethod()> _
Public Function FindBook(ByVal strISBN As String) As BookItem
  Dim objBook As New BookItem()
  Dim strURL As String = "http://www.isbn.nu/" & strISBN
  Dim strResponse As String
  Dim strBookName As String
  Dim strBookPrice As String
  Dim strBookPublisher As String
  Dim strBookCover As String
  Dim index As Integer
  Dim index2 As Integer
  Dim strTitleHeader As String = "<title>"
  Dim strTitleHeaderEnd As String = "</title>"
  Dim strCoverSearch As String = _
    "<img src=" & Chr(34) & "http://images.amazon.com/images/P/" & _
    strISBN.Replace("-", "")

  Try
    ' Get the response string for this ISBN search from isbn.nu
    strResponse = ReturnHTTPResponseString(strURL.Replace("-", ""))

    ' See if anything was found. Search for 2 key strings that
    ' indicate that the book wasn't found
    If (strResponse.IndexOf("No title or book details") <> -1) Then
      objBook.Title = "Book Not Found: " & strURL
      Return objBook
    End If
    If (strResponse.IndexOf("Invalid ISBN or UPC") <> -1) Then
      objBook.Title = "Invalid ISBN: " & strURL
```

```
    Return objBook
End If


' Search for title. It's right after the Title tag
index = strResponse.IndexOf(strTitleHeader)
index2 = strResponse.IndexOf(strTitleHeaderEnd)
If index = -1 Or index2 = -1 Then
  objBook.Title = "Couldn't find Title Tag: " & strTitleHeader
  Return objBook
End If
Dim i As Integer
index += strTitleHeader.Length
For i = index To (index2 - 1)
  strBookName = strBookName & strResponse.Chars(i).ToString
Next
objBook.Title = strBookName

' Set ISBN to be the ISBN value passed in, but stripped of dashes
objBook.ISBN = strISBN.Replace("-", "")


' Now get pricing information.
' It's right after the string "Full Retail Price:"
index = strResponse.IndexOf("Full retail price:")
If index <> -1 Then
  While strResponse.Chars(index) <> "$"
    index += 1
  End While
  index += 1
  While (Char.IsDigit(strResponse.Chars(index)) Or _
      (strResponse.Chars(index) = "."))
    strBookPrice = strBookPrice & _
            strResponse.Chars(index).ToString
    index += 1
  End While
  objBook.Cost = strBookPrice
End If


' Now find the book publisher.
' It's the string right before the ISBN listing
index = strResponse.IndexOf("Published by")
If index <> -1 Then
  While strResponse.Chars(index) <> "y"
    index += 1
  End While
  index += 2
  While strResponse.Chars(index) <> "(" And _
      strResponse.Chars(index) <> Chr(10)
    strBookPublisher = strBookPublisher & _
              strResponse.Chars(index).ToString
    index += 1
  End While
  objBook.Publisher = strBookPublisher
End If
```

```
    ' Now find the pointer to the book cover image. Amazon.com has
    ' the most cover images, so go there to look for it.
    strURL = "http://www.amazon.com/exec/obidos/ASIN/" & strISBN
    strResponse = ReturnHTTPResponseString(strURL.Replace("-", ""))

    index = strResponse.IndexOf(strCoverSearch)
    ' Get to the opening double-quote
    While strResponse.Chars(index) <> Chr(34)
      index += 1
    End While
    ' Now pass it to get to the start of the pointer link
    index += 1
    While strResponse.Chars(index) <> Chr(34)
      strBookCover &= strResponse.Chars(index)
      index += 1
    End While
    objBook.CoverPointer = strBookCover

    Return objBook

  Catch
    objBook.Title = "Error Finding Book :" & Err.Number.ToString & _
          " , Text='" & Err.Description & "'"
  End Try
End Function
```

This is a pretty simple Web Service, with the exception of all the text manipulation code. We basically call the ISBN.NU web site to get information on the book, and then we call Amazon.com to get the image of the book cover. We've created a common function called `ReturnHTTPResponseString`, which will open an HTTP session to the desired URL and return a string of text that represents the response to the HTTP GET. Once we get the response from the web site, we manually parse through the string to find the information that we need.

Once parsed, we return the information back to the user in XML. We actually create a `BookItem` structure so that the caller can use the same structure instead of needing to understand the internals. The format is automatically determined by the fact that we declared the return value as type `Book`. Behind the scenes, VS.NET has already written all the code necessary for the web proxy, the UDDI (Universal Description Discovery and Integration), Disco (Web Services Discovery) and XML serialization to and from the Web Service. With all of that built for us, all we have to do is add a web reference in our calling ASP.NET application and then provide a call to the Web Service.

To consume this Web Service, a consumer needs only to create a Web Reference within a project in VS.NET. This is done by right-mouse clicking on the project in the Solution Explorer and selecting **Add Web Reference**. VS.NET displays an **Add Web Reference** wizard, as follows, where you will enter the address to the Web Service file (in our case it will be http://localhost/Performance/Chapter03/BookService/FindBook.asmx).

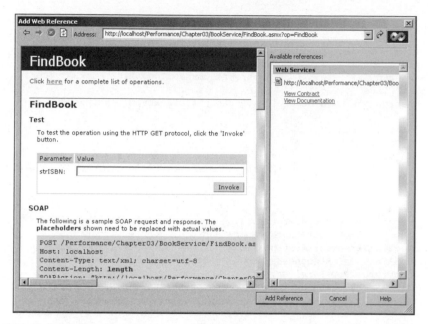

Once the Web Service has been created, it's extremely easy to reference it and invoke it from within your ASP.NET application. Let's take a look at the snippet of code we can use to invoke our Web Service:

```
Dim objService As New localhost.FindBook()
Dim objBook As localhost.BookItem
objBook = objService.FindBook("000000000000")
```

As you can see, screen scraping is not a very fault tolerant solution. Should either ISBN.NU or Amazon.com decide to revamp the format of their web pages, or move book covers to another page, we'll need to update our Web Service. This is an emergency just waiting to happen, and we should avoid this type of design, unless no other solution is possible.

One of the biggest problems that we found was the time it took for the Web Service to return this information. Even more performance problems awaited us should we allow the Web Service to search for multiple books. The way to improve performance in this scenario is to enable the Web Service to complete asynchronously. We'll be talking about asynchronous page processing for controls that use this same Web Service later in the chapter, but what we're talking about here is the ability to make a call to a Web Service, move on to the next task in the code, and have the Web Service notify us via a callback once it is completed.

Creating an asynchronous Web Service is really not that different from creating a synchronous Web Service, with the exception that we'll be dealing with a callback routine to return the results. As a matter of fact, it's downright easy to do. Since we created the Web Service using VS.NET and the <WebMethod> tag, the asynchronous methods have already been created for us.

VS.NET creates a Begin and End asynchronous Web Service method for every web method defined. It also creates all of the SOAP wrapper code that the consumer needs to invoke the Web Service synchronously or asynchronously. Let's take a look at the code that was generated for us when we created our FindBook Web Service. You'll find this wrapper code in the Reference.vb file located under the Web References/<server> folder of your project.

```
Namespace localhost
  <System.Diagnostics.DebuggerStepThroughAttribute(),  _
   System.ComponentModel.DesignerCategoryAttribute("code"),  _
   System.Web.Services.WebServiceBindingAttribute(Name:="FindBookSoap", _
   [Namespace]:="http://localhost/Performance/Chapter03/BookService")> _
  Public Class FindBook
    Inherits System.Web.Services.Protocols.SoapHttpClientProtocol

    Public Sub New()
      MyBase.New
      Me.Url =
          "http://localhost/Performance/Chapter03/BookService/FindBook.asmx"
    End Sub

    '<remarks/>
    <System.Web.Services.Protocols.SoapDocumentMethodAttribute _
     ("http://localhost/Performance/Chapter03/BookService/FindBook", _
     RequestNamespace:="http://localhost/Performance/Chapter03/_
     BookService",ResponseNamespace:="http://localhost/Performance/_
     Chapter03/BookService",_
     Use:=System.Web.Services.Description.SoapBindingUse.Literal, _
     ParameterStyle:= _
            System.Web.Services.Protocols.SoapParameterStyle.Wrapped)> _
    Public Function FindBook(ByVal strISBN As String) As BookItem
      Dim results() As Object = Me.Invoke("FindBook", _
                                          New Object() {strISBN})
      Return CType(results(0),BookItem)
    End Function
    Public Function BeginFindBook(ByVal strISBN As String, _
                  ByVal callback As System.AsyncCallback, _
                  ByVal asyncState As Object) As System.IAsyncResult
      Return Me.BeginInvoke("FindBook", New Object() {strISBN}, callback, _
                      asyncState)
    End Function
    Public Function EndFindBook(ByVal asyncResult As System.IAsyncResult) _
          As BookItem
      Dim results() As Object = Me.EndInvoke(asyncResult)
      Return CType(results(0),BookItem)
    End Function
  End Class
  <System.Xml.Serialization.XmlTypeAttribute( _
  [Namespace]:="http://localhost/Performance/Chapter03/BookService")> _
  Public Class BookItem

    '<remarks/>
    Public Cost As String

    '<remarks/>
    Public CoverPointer As String

    '<remarks/>
    Public ISBN As String
```

```
'<remarks/>
Public Publisher As String

Public Title As String
End Class
```

If you're generating a web reference to a server named APOLLO, the Web Service would have the namespace of APOLLO and you would reference items in the Web Service through an explicit declaration like APOLLO.BeginFindBook().

> A little known fact about web references is that you can combine all of the web references into a single **Reference.vb** file under a single namespace by copying and pasting all of the VS.NET generated code from all the different files into a single one. This way, you don't need to have multiple web reference names in your application. This also eliminates the need to rename the web reference and re-compile when moving Web Services and their accompanying code from your development machine to production.

Invoking an asynchronous Web Service is just about as easy as invoking a synchronous Web Service. The only difference is that you need to specify a delegate that the web method can contact when the Web Service is finished, and then you can perform your logic and invoke the End method. Let's take a look at invoking the same FindBook Web Service from above, but using the asynchronous method:

```
Dim objService As New localhost.FindBook()
    objService.BeginFindBook("1861007035", _
                        AddressOf Callbacks.WebServiceCallBack, Nothing)
```

Then, as before, we'll create a separate class file to contain our callback functions so that we're leaving as small of a footprint as possible in memory.

```
Public Shared Sub WebServiceCallBack(ByVal iasResult As IAsyncResult)
    Dim objBook As localhost.BookItem
    Dim objService As New localhost.FindBook()
    objBook = objService.EndFindBook(iasResult)
End Sub
```

This mechanism let's us return control to the caller as soon as possible, so that other processing can be done while waiting for the Web Service to return.

We can also cache results from a Web Service very easily by including a single attribute as part of the WebMethod tag on any function exposed as part of the Web Service. Let's do this for our FindBook web method from above. We'll set the cache duration to be 120 seconds.

```
<WebMethod(CacheDuration:=120)> _
Public Function FindBook(ByVal strISBN As String) As BookItem
```

This will cache the web results indexed by the value of strISBN. Each new strISBN value will generate a new cache value. When the cache expires for a specific value, the next call will execute the entire Web Service. We can also manage our own caching by using the Cache object we learned about earlier (instead of having the Web Service manage it), and use the CacheItemRemoved event handler notify us when the Web Service data has expired.

One last thing we can do to help performance is to set a timeout value for the completion of Web Services. This is most beneficial for synchronous Web Services, which might hang if connectivity or the external system is unavailable. Instead of waiting for the default HTTP timeout (which is `Timeout.Infinite` seconds by default), we can customize this value by setting the `Timeout` property of the Web Service that we're creating a reference to. Note that even when the timeout value is set to infinite, the server running the Web Service can still force a timeout on the Web Service based on its web server settings (the default setting for IIS is 90 seconds). What about the browser timeout value? For performance reasons, you should never force a Web Service to run indefinitely.

Let's go back to our original `FindBook` example Web Service. If we wanted to force a timeout after 10 seconds with no response, then we'd update the Web Service code to update the `Timeout` property as you see below:

```
Dim objService As New localhost.FindBook()
Dim objBook As localhost.BookItem
objService.Timeout = 10000
objBook = objService.FindBook("1861007035")
```

If the Web Service times out, the return value will be `Nothing` since there was no XML data received from the Web Service. This property is only applicable for synchronous web methods. If you want to utilize a timeout property for asynchronous web methods, then you'll need to add your own code to the `Reference.vb` Web Services wrapper to expose some type of `Cancel` method and timer callback as a kind of a roll-your-own Web Services timeout value.

Although we've covered the key performance characteristics of .NET Web Services, we cannot cover all aspects of them in this book. For a good reference on ASP.NET Web Services, please see "Professional ASP.NET Web Services with VB.NET", published by Wrox Press (ISBN – 1-86100-775-2).

Integrating With COM Components

During any enterprise software development project, you will undoubtedly encounter the need to call existing COM code previously written. The truth is that it's not necessary to port all of your code at once to .NET in order to provide a clean enterprise solution.

A good example is a legacy Win32 Help Desk system written for use by internal employees to manage support tickets for the company. Let's assume that this system was written internally a few years back, and provided several COM objects to expose system functionality. Now let's fast forward to today, where the CIO has mandated that your group create an Internet customer portal that provides them one-stop access to all of your company's interactions with them – one of these being Help Desk support. Now, you could re-write the Help Desk system on .NET, but why would you do that if the system works just fine? The better solution is to utilize the existing COM technology that's part of the system into the new customer portal that you've just been given two weeks to develop.

Calling COM components from .NET does incur a significant amount of overhead. This is because the .NET CLR has to marshal information from managed .NET code to unmanaged code – the existing legacy code. This marshalling is done via a .NET runtime-callable wrapper (RCW) that .NET puts around the COM object. The RCW is responsible for creating and disposing of the instanced COM object, and marshalling information back and forth between it. The marshaling of data is time consuming, since the data needs to be serialized, sent, and then de-serialized, between each inter-process communication.

VS.NET makes it relatively easy to integrate with your existing COM components by generating the RCW when you create a reference to the COM object in your project. All you need to do is to add a reference to the COM object using the `Add Reference` command. After that, VS.NET will add all of the wrapper code necessary to marshal information back and forth between managed and unmanaged code. This wrapper code is compiled and put into the `bin` folder. There will be an `Interop.<COM DLL>.dll` file for each COM object referenced.

Let's do a simple example here. If we wanted to incorporate some MS Excel manipulation as part of our ASP.NET application, all we need to do is to import a reference to the Excel COM object. Once imported, we can reference all of the objects exposed by the COM object just as if they were part of a .NET object. For example, we could create a new instance of an Excel Application using the following code:

```
Dim objExcel As New Excel.Application()
```

As you can see, it's now very simple to integrate with COM objects. No more creation of COM wrapper code, because VS.NET takes care of all the details for you. However, that doesn't mean that you should just run out and invoke all the COM objects you want. There is still a significant amount of overhead involved in processing the VS.NET created code that marshals information back and for between managed and unmanaged code. In addition, calls to the COM component still run under the COM platform and run under the same apartment thread initialized by COM.

We can also create what is called a primary interop assembly, which allows us to use the same wrapper from many different .NET applications. Primary interop assemblies have strong names, are usually created by the original COM object developer, since they require a publisher key and are more tightly integrated with the underlying COM object.

Once we've made a reference to the COM component in our project, we're ready to start consuming it. One of the first performance improvements we can make is to make sure that we use early binding when referencing any attribute, property or method of the COM object. In VB6, we could declare things as objects, and then type cast them as they were used. By using early binding, we're eliminating all the processing that takes place in late binding of objects from a generic type to the more specific type.

Since the COM object has the .NET RCW wrapped around it, the entire object itself is exposed to the .NET garbage collection mechanism. Although the COM object itself still uses the traditional reference counter to manage memory, the entire object wrapper will not be garbage collected until the `Dispose` method is called. However, if our COM object holds expensive resources (such as an open file handle), we can manually release the COM object by using the `ReleaseCOMObject` method of the `Marshal` class:

```
Marshal.ReleaseCOMObject(objExcel)
```

This line would force a release of the Excel COM object that we created up above (as long as there was only a single reference to that object).

Another common technique to speed up interoperability with COM is to prepare "chunky" versus "chatty" calls to COM services. Let's say you're working with a remote object with multiple `Get()` and `Set()` properties you wish to use.

```
MyRemoteObject.FirstValue = 1
MyRemoteObject.SecondValue = 2
Dim iValue = MyRemoteObject.ThirdValue
```

It would be a better idea to encapsulate these properties with one remote method that allows us to set or retrieve their values all at the same time.

```
MyRemoteObject.Initialize(1,2,3)
MyRemoteObject.Retrieve(iValue1, iValue2, iValue3)
```

Most likely, you will put this code in your .NET wrapper, since most third party COM components cannot be edited.

Another performance improvement is the use of binary compatible data types (also referred to as blittable) between COM and .NET. If you use a blittable data type, there's no need for a conversion layer when passing result sets back and forth from managed to unmanaged code. Therefore, you should strive to use the following blittable data types when working with COM objects:

System Data Type
Byte
SByte
Int16
UInt16
Int32
UInt32
Int64
IntPtr
UIntPtr

One-dimensional arrays of blittable data types above are also considered blittable data types themselves. We'll see more about blittable data types in Chapter 8.

One last technique for improving performance in communication with COM objects doesn't really deal specifically with .NET, but is nonetheless important. If you manage your COM components under COM+ services, you will automatically receive service benefits such as object pooling and transactions. Object pooling is a specific feature that will help the performance of your COM component, since COM+ will hold open a set number of object connections for use so that when called, the object does not have to be instantiated from scratch. This can be quite useful if the instantiation of the object takes awhile. This topic is almost identical to the database connection pooling feature in ADO.NET.

> *Providing Interop capabilities with COM is an extremely deep and complex topic. For more information on how COM Interop with .NET works, you can read "Professional Visual Basic Interoperability", published by Wrox Press (ISBN – 1861005652).*

Background Processing in ASP.NET Pages

Now that we've discussed the various ways that you can communicate with external systems, it's time to talk about how we can improve their performance when integrating them with our ASP.NET web pages. We've already talked about how to improve the performance of the "wrappers" themselves, but that's just the start. Since we're dealing with external systems, the performance of requests to and from the external systems cannot be guaranteed. Think of the example of a Web Service that queries information out of the HR/Payroll system in the corporate office all the way across the country.

Fortunately, there are several techniques that can be implemented in order to give the user the best "perceived" performance. This involves background processing of information from external systems. What we can do is organize our pages so that external information is grouped together in a section, and we provide an initial page load with either blank or default data. Then, in the background, we go and get the data and load it into the page as it becomes available. The benefit here is that the user gains control of the page almost immediately, and then receives "additional" information as it is retrieved.

This technique is not useful for pages that contain only external system information, since the user will still be staring at page with blank fields. However, it's a great technique when you're displaying external system data in conjunction with information from your system all on the same screen. This way the screen is returned to the user more quickly, and the external system information is loaded automatically afterwards.

Let's take a look at one way we can do this using a couple of real-world examples.

Our first example will be a page that provides a user's bank account information and balance information. We can group critical information that our system holds to be displayed in the foreground, and then retrieve the remaining external system information in the background. This will improve our perceived performance since the page will load that much more quickly.

What we'll do is first construct the results page and include text boxes for entering the user name, address, phone, and account information. Then, we'll create an IFRAME inside the main page to include the detail account information. This IFRAME will point to a separate page that retrieves the detail information. The code for your main page should look like the one below:

```
<body>
<form id="Form1" method="post" runat="server">
  <TABLE id="Table1" cellSpacing="1" cellPadding="1" width="300" border="0">
    <TR>
      <TD>
      <DIV style="DISPLAY: inline; WIDTH: 70px; HEIGHT: 15px"
              ms_positioning="FlowLayout">Name:</DIV>
    </TD>
    <TD>
        <asp:textbox id="txtName" runat="server" Width="235px"
                  ReadOnly="True"></asp:textbox>
      </TD>
    <TD></TD>
    </TR>
    <TR>
      <TD>
      <DIV style="DISPLAY: inline; WIDTH: 70px; HEIGHT: 15px"
              ms_positioning="FlowLayout">ID:</DIV>
```

```
      </TD>
      <TD>
         <asp:textbox id="txtID" runat="server" Width="235px"
                     ReadOnly="True"></asp:textbox>
      </TD>
    <TD></TD>
     </TR>
     <TR>
       <TD>
        <DIV style="DISPLAY: inline; WIDTH: 149px; HEIGHT: 22px"
             ms_positioning="FlowLayout">Check Account #:</DIV>
    </TD>
    <TD>
         <asp:textbox id="txtChecking" runat="server" Width="235px"
                     ReadOnly="True"></asp:textbox>
      </TD>
    <TD></TD>
     </TR>
     <TR>
       <TD>
        <DIV style="DISPLAY: inline; WIDTH: 149px; HEIGHT: 22px"
             ms_positioning="FlowLayout">Savings Account #:</DIV>
    </TD>
    <TD>
         <asp:textbox id="txtSavings" runat="server" Width="235px"
                     ReadOnly="True"></asp:textbox>
      </TD>
    <TD></TD>
     </TR>
   </TABLE>
 </form>
 <DIV style="DISPLAY: inline; WIDTH: 208px; HEIGHT: 27px"
      ms_positioning="FlowLayout"><FONT size="5"><STRONG>
      Latest Transactions</STRONG></FONT></DIV>
 <P>
 <iframe id="frmDetails" style="WIDTH: 455px; HEIGHT: 228px"
         src="AccountDetails.aspx?AccountID=<%# txtID.text%>">
 </iframe>
 </P>
 </body>
```

What this page will do is load, and the target of the IFRAME will be set to an account details page that gathers details for accounts held by the currently assigned account ID (held by the text box txtID). Both the main page and IFRAME will load in parallel, giving us the illusion of background processing. The main page text boxes on the main page will become immediately viewable to the user.

Now, on to our details page. For example purposes, we'll just show the last bank transaction for each, and we'll manually introduce some fake delays in this page to simulate how an actual external system may perform (we'll do this by stopping the thread in the middle of the Page_Load event for 10 seconds – simulating the processing of large amounts of information). The page itself is pretty simple, containing just a DataGrid that returns some rows associated with the account number passed in. The account number is passed in as a variable in part of the querystring. We won't bother to show the actual code here, since we've done this kind of data binding many times before. The main point here is that we've got a page that might take awhile to load, and we'll be loading it as a target within the IFRAME.

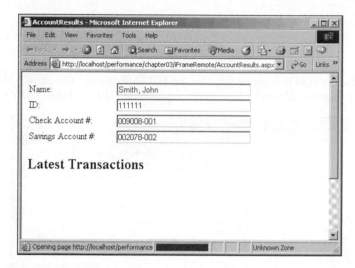

And here is the screen, fully loaded:

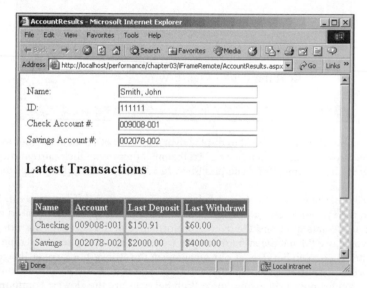

The result of this design is that the user is returned a page almost immediately with information on it for them to review. Then, as the external system responds, more information is presented to the user. This gives the user the feeling that they are actually connected "live" to the system, instead of connected via a web browser. Their perception of performance increases, and so does their satisfaction with the ASP.NET application.

We could even be a little fancier and combine this with our "Page Processing" JavaScript example from earlier in this chapter. By changing the `src` attribute of the `IFRAME` to the page loader that we developed earlier, the `IFRAME` would actually display an in progress meter, giving the user even more information on the status of their request.

```
<iframe id="frmDetails" style="WIDTH: 455px; HEIGHT: 228px"
   src="LoadPage.aspx?Page=AccountDetails.aspx?AccountID=<%# txtID.text%>">
</iframe>
```

This would yield an interim processing page for the IFRAME like the one shown below. This processing tag would then be dynamically replaced with the page results, just as in the earlier example.

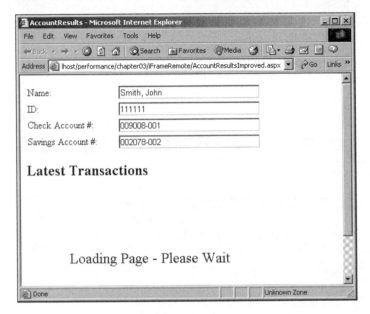

What if you had more than that one field to display dynamically? Let's look at another example. In this example, we'll be displaying books in a `DataGrid` that might represent their current shopping cart. In each row we'll display the book name, ISBN and publisher. In addition, we'll display the picture of the book cover.

However, let's say that our business stores book cover pictures in a different system. We could make multiple calls to the system to get each image, but that could take a long time based on the number of rows displayed in the data grid, and the overall performance of the access to the external system. To make matters worse, we'll have the scenario where we need to actually screen-scrape the image from the Amazon.com site (via a Web Service) as our mechanism to retrieve book cover images (while this mechanism is probably not how a company would get an image, it serves a useful purpose in demonstrating asynchronous processing, since Web Services are the slowest communication mechanism, this means that we'll really be enjoying the benefits of asynchronous processing).

So, let's start by creating a results page (we'll assume that the data from this page is the result of the customer selecting items to put in their cart). For the purposes of this example, we'll just put some book data into a `DataSet` and bind it to the `DataGrid`. We'll add one final column for the image and set its default image to a valid local GIF file, so that results are retrieved immediately. Don't worry about the rest of the properties within the image tag, we'll talk about them in a moment. After the data grid, we'll include some fictional name and address details to show how the user can manipulate fields on the page, even though we're getting data in the background.

```
<body>
<form id="Form1" method="post" runat="server">
  <asp:DataGrid id="DataGrid1" runat="server" AutoGenerateColumns=false
                BorderColor="#DEBA84" BorderStyle="None" CellSpacing="2"
                BorderWidth="1px" BackColor="#DEBA84" CellPadding="3">
    <SelectedItemStyle Font-Bold="True" ForeColor="White"
                       BackColor="#738A9C"></SelectedItemStyle>
    <ItemStyle ForeColor="#8C4510" BackColor="#FFF7E7"></ItemStyle>
    <HeaderStyle Font-Bold="True" ForeColor="White"
                 BackColor="#A55129"></HeaderStyle>
    <FooterStyle ForeColor="#8C4510" BackColor="#F7DFB5"></FooterStyle>
    <PagerStyle HorizontalAlign="Center" ForeColor="#8C4510"
                Mode="NumericPages"></PagerStyle>
  <Columns>
    <asp:BoundColumn HeaderText="Title" DataField="Title">
    </asp:BoundColumn>
    <asp:BoundColumn HeaderText="ISBN" DataField="isbn">
    </asp:BoundColumn>
    <asp:BoundColumn HeaderText="Publisher" DataField="Publisher">
    </asp:BoundColumn>
    <asp:TemplateColumn>
      <ItemTemplate>
        <img src="UnknownBook.gif"
        onerror="javascript:this.src='Unknownbook.gif'"
        onload="javascript:this.src=
                'GetBookImage.aspx?isbn=<%#Container.DataItem("isbn")%>';">
      </ItemTemplate>
      <HeaderTemplate>Book Cover</HeaderTemplate>
    </asp:TemplateColumn>
    </Columns>
  </asp:DataGrid><br>
  <table border=0>
    <tr>
      <td>Name:</td>
    <td><asp:TextBox ID="txtName" Runat="server"></asp:TextBox></td>
    </tr>
    <tr>
      <td>Address:</td>
    <td><asp:TextBox ID="txtAddress" Runat="server"></asp:TextBox></td>
    </tr>
    <tr>
      <td>City,State / ZIP:</td>
    <td><asp:TextBox ID="txtCSZ" Runat="server"></asp:TextBox></td>
    </tr>
  </table>
  <br>
  <asp:Button id="btnBuy" Text="Buy" runat="server"></asp:Button>
</form>
</body>
```

The code-behind for this page is relatively simple in that it just reads the book entries from an XML file in our web directory.

```
Dim dtTable As New DataTable()
Dim dsDataSet As New DataSet()
Dim drRow As DataRow
If Not IsPostBack Then
    ' Add initial data into the database
    dsDataSet.ReadXml(Server.MapPath("Books.xml"))
    DataGrid1.DataSource = dsDataSet.Tables("Book")
    DataGrid1.DataBind()
End If
```

So, what we've done is load some data in the DataGrid, and then create a template column that will hold the book cover GIF that we'll retrieve from a call to another page. This is done via the JavaScript's page OnLoad method, which is the first thing to happen after all information from the ASP.NET page is rendered on the server and sent to the client.

This other page (GetBookImage.aspx) is actually a call to a Web Service that will contact Amazon.com and get the image associated with the ISBN for the book. You can see that if we would have included this in the base page that we'd be waiting for a long time until the user could interact with the page, because the page would not be completely loaded and rendered for the user until all Web Service calls were complete. The number of Web Service calls would be equal to the number of rows in the data grid – not a very appealing solution for the user. They would probably click refresh over and over, or even worse – maybe they'd just leave the site assuming that it was down.

Now that we've seen the page and how we want it to work, let's go back to the original image tag that we put in the results page:

```
<img src="UnknownBook.gif"
 onerror="javascript:this.src='Unknownbook.gif'"
 onload="javascript:this.src=
          'GetBookImage.aspx?isbn=<%#Container.DataItem("isbn")%>';">
```

What this does is immediately load a local default image for every row. This returns a page immediately for the user, since there's virtually no lag time in retrieving a small local image. Notice that we're specifying JavaScript code for the OnLoad and OnError events. The OnError event just says that we want to reset the src attribute of the image tag (Javascript:this.src) to the locally available default image. The OnLoad event is really what makes this all work. When the page is rendered and sent from ASP.NET, the JavaScript OnLoad event is fired. What we're doing here is setting the src attribute to be the results of our GetBookCover.aspx page (which is the call to the slow Web Service).

The end result is a page that initially loads with default images, as follows:

Once loaded, the images will load in the background, but the user can begin to manipulate the screen by typing in the text boxes, or even pressing the Buy button. The user has been given control of the screen earlier, and their perspective on performance has been affected because of it. The actual time it took to load all of the information (including all book covers) is probably the same, but because the user can get control of the screen more quickly, they feel that the application performs better.

One last way we can improve performance with external systems is by running background (batch) processes to do bulk business logic, and then cache off those results in a database table local to our system. An example of a perfect requirement for this technique is the updating of currency conversion data for purchasing and order management systems.

In such an example, we need to provide the latest currency conversion in order to get an accurate price/cost. However, you should never develop a .NET Remoting component or Web Service to dynamically query for the values as the screen is brought up, even if it is in the background. The better design for this type of requirement is to develop a Windows Service application in VS.NET that is responsible for retrieving the information and placing it into a local database area in your system. Then, you can develop a system-wide Currency object that will expose the properties and methods you need for currency management.

The great thing about this solution is that the service can be run at whatever time interval the business requires, and it has no impact on the ASP.NET application, unless the Windows Service is so processor intensive that it takes too much processor utilization. If this is the case, then performance for the Window Service needs to be examined because there is only one copy of it running, so its impact on CPU utilization should be minimal.

Summary

In this chapter, we've talked about the design considerations for your ASP.NET applications. It is imperative that you prepare a good design, since a bad design will always yield a poor result, no matter how well-written the code is.

We discussed the importance of a good user interface and how user perceived performance is just as important as the raw performance of the code within the application itself. We provided an overview of ADO.NET and how the data providers and connections are best suited for each type of back-end database. We also looked at how stored procedures, indexes, and triggers can all be used to design the best performing back-end database to make your ASP.NET applications fly.

We examined the various types of integration points for external systems. We looked at the performance differences between COM, Web Services, and .NET Remoting. We reviewed when to use (and more importantly, not use) each type of integration point.

We also discussed how to offload the long-running processes asynchronously so that the user can re-gain control of the application more quickly, thereby increasing the level of perceived performance. Implementing asynchronous processing for long-running processes is a key concept in designing high performance applications. Just like multi-threading of traditional Windows applications, asynchronous processing can help stabilize the perceived performance of your application against the "unknowns" of the open Internet.

If you take away just one thing from this chapter, you should understand that the best performing applications are ones that address the following areas during the design phase:

- ❏ Work on perceived performance as much as raw performance
- ❏ Replace your T-SQL with compiled stored procedures
- ❏ Make the move to object orientation
- ❏ Perform long-running operations in the background

In the next chapter we'll look at specific coding guidelines for the development of your ASP.NET applications.

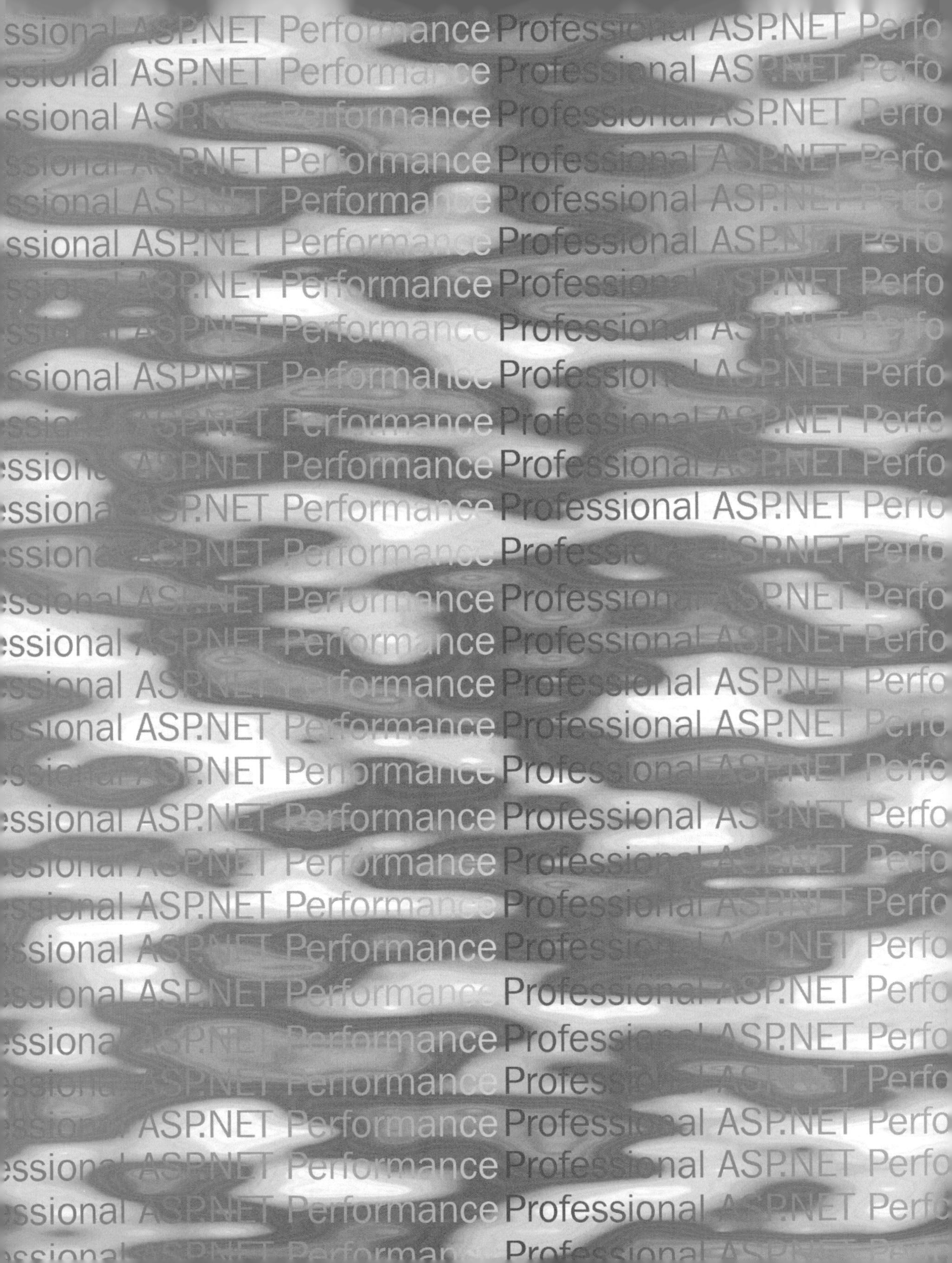
Professional ASP.NET Performance

4

Developing for Performance

In this chapter, we will cover guidelines and examples for writing high-performance code in the .NET environment. We often measure the performance of code by the amount of time it takes to complete a task for a single user. However, as we discussed in Chapter 1, we must also keep scalability in mind for web applications. There are times when you can choose a technique or algorithm to improve both the performance and scalability of an application, but there are also times when these two goals are at odds with each other.

For example, imagine you have a large amount of text to sort. You could allocate a large buffer to sort all of the text in memory and have the fastest performance possible for a single user. But if the allocated memory consumed 80% of the local machine's RAM, chances are that you are hurting the performance of any other concurrent users who could use memory for their requests and limiting your scalability.

Evaluating gains in performance versus scalability is not the only tradeoff to examine when optimizing your application. For example, you might find yourself writing extra code to achieve better performance, and trading off some of the simplicity in your existing algorithm. You will also need to make time during your development process to examine code for performance optimizations. Taking the time to review code will certainly take away time from implementing features. Although we would all like to have the time to review and perfect every feature in an application, we never have this luxury. Fortunately, the .NET Framework and ASP.NET architecture provide a fast and scalable foundation to build upon. Use the design topics covered in the last chapter to make sure you are implementing a fast and scalable solution when you begin writing code. A good design goes a long way in creating a high-performance application.

When you are finished with the implementation, there is an old rule of thumb to apply: 20% of an application's code is executed 80% of the time. Using the monitoring and testing techniques covered in the later chapters of the book you can find the 20% of your application where optimizations will have the most impact. We call these areas the **hotspots** of an application, and these are the areas you will want to optimize with every method available.

You can apply the techniques presented in this chapter to your application hotspots and also use them as general guidelines for coding throughout your application. Specifically, we will cover the following topics throughout this chapter:

❑ Writing 'lazy' code by avoiding unneeded work

❑ Conserving resources – for example, using less memory

❑ Improving performance with caching

❑ Effective use of collections and value types

❑ Performance implications of COM Interop

Before we launch into these topics, let's take a look at the .NET tools and runtime, and how these tools give us a high-performance foundation to build on.

.NET Framework Performance

Two of the key pieces in the .NET Framework are the just-in-time (JIT) compiler, and the garbage collector (GC). By taking a look at these components in a bit more depth, we can gain a better understanding of how and when to look for performance improvements.

JIT Compiler

When you compile any .NET application, the compiler transforms your source code into Microsoft intermediate language (MSIL). MSIL does not execute on any specific processor; in fact, MSIL is designed to be processor-independent. To execute the application in a specific environment, a JIT compiler takes the MSIL output and transforms the instructions into native instructions for the host processor. The JIT compiler compiles the code just in time for the application to start execution.

A JIT compiler does not have as much time to make optimizations as, say, a C++ compiler. Unlike a traditional compiler running on machines during development, an end-user is waiting on the JIT compiler to finish for the program to run. Still, the JIT compiler finds the time to perform a number of optimizations by only compiling small pieces of the program at a time. Whenever execution reaches a method in your assembly that has not been JIT compiled, the JIT compiler will compile only the method currently waiting to execute, then save the result for future calls to the same method until the application terminates. This technique means the application never wastes compilation time on unused methods.

JIT Optimizations

The JIT compiler performs a number of optimizations when generating native instructions, including sub-expression elimination, loop unrolling, and method inlining. These optimizations are outside of our control, and also outside the scope of the book, but let's look briefly at one of them:

Inlining is an optimization where the compiler replaces a call to a method with the instructions for the method itself. The compiler will inline a method when it sees the opportunity for a significant saving. Small methods are the best candidates for inlining because the overhead of a stack frame setup, a branch, and a return, are often greater in cost and size than the amount of code in the method itself.

Also, there are a number of advantages in compiling just before execution. The compiler will know the exact characteristics of the runtime environment and can target the host CPU with specific instructions, say, for an Intel Pentium 4 or an AMD Athlon chip. The compiler can make aggressive memory optimizations on platforms where RAM is limited (such as a handheld computer), while using the processing power of a faster machine to look for optimizations in speed.

There are many opportunities for optimization as your program moves from source code to MSIL and then to native code for the host CPU. The point of this discussion is to encourage you to let the compilers work on these small optimizations and keep your code simple and maintainable. For instance, don't try to inline methods yourself, as this might only add to the amount of code in your program and make the source harder to read. Let the runtime do the work until you have identified a trouble area in a hotspot.

The Garbage Collector

The .NET runtime provides memory management services – a feature Visual Basic developers have been accustomed to for some time, although the service is new and improved in .NET. When you create an object, the runtime allocates memory from an area known as the **managed heap**. Periodically, the garbage collector (GC) will decide it is time to run and clean up the managed heap. The GC releases memory reserved by objects no longer in use by the application. To know which objects are still in use, the GC works closely with the JIT compiler and the common language runtime (CLR).

GC Optimizations

The garbage collector is a highly tuned engine, so highly tuned there are two versions of the GC. The workstation version works best with client applications, such as a Windows form application. This version strives to keep applications as responsive as possible by working in the background to try to avoid creating a noticeable pause. The server version, in contrast, works best in multi-processor environments. This version favors throughput over responsiveness and might introduce some latency to a program. The ASP.NET runtime will select the appropriate version for the host platform.

The GC allows the runtime to allocate and release memory in a fast and efficient manner. Once again, the best advice is to not over-engineer a solution or try to out-think the runtime. Although the GC class allows you to force the start of a garbage collection, it is best to let the engine itself determine the best time to run. Later in the chapter we will look at a few techniques that help to conserve memory by working with the garbage collector. For now, we are ready to start taking a look at a few of the recommended practices for writing faster code.

Do The Same Work With Less Code

It may sound obvious, but high-performance code will do as little work as possible. Take the earlier discussion on the JIT compiler, for example. Instead of transforming *all* of the MSIL in an assembly to native code before starting execution, the compiler only works one method at a time – jumping into action when execution reaches an uncompiled method.

There are two performance advantages to the JIT compiler approach. First, this technique spreads the cost of compilation over a longer period of time. Since execution will appear to begin more quickly than if the JIT compiler took the time to compile all the MSIL, the *perceived performance* of the application is increased. Often, perceived performance is just as important as actual performance. If you can hide long pauses or wait times from your user by breaking them into smaller chunks and spreading them out, the user remains happier with the performance of your application.

The second advantage to this approach is that the compiler doesn't perform any unnecessary work by compiling methods not used during execution. Any time that you can eliminate unneeded processing, you have found a true performance gain. Let us take a look at reducing the amount of work needed to produce the following ASP.NET Web Form (`WebForm1.aspx` in the download):

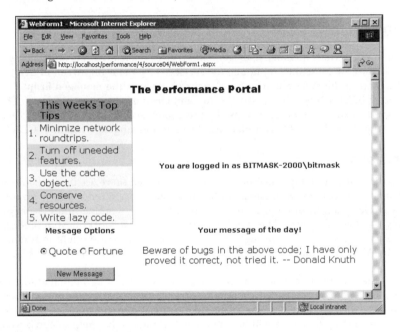

Using IsPostBack

In the top left of the Web Form shown above, we have a `DataGrid` control. During the `Page_Load` event of the Web Form, we populate the grid with the contents of an XML file containing our performance tips. Although we load these strings from an XML file in this example, the data could just as easily come from a database query or web service call.

Once we have populated the grid control with data, the grid control will automatically save its state into the view state. View state, remember, is a hidden form variable used by Web Forms to save and restore the state of controls between page requests. When a form posts back to the server, the runtime recreates the state of the controls from the information in the view state. This means that we do not have to reload our grid control from the XML file during a postback operation.

As shown in the code excerpt from `WebForm1.aspx.vb` shown below, the `Page.IsPostBack` property will allow you to determine if the current request is the result of a post back operation or not. On the initial page request (or if the user refreshes the page), the `IsPostBack` property is `False`. If the user clicks the **New Message** button in the lower left of the form, the form will post back to the server and raise an event for the server-side button control. At this time, the `IsPostBack` property is `True` and we let the runtime restore the data in the grid from the view state. We will cover the `DisplayLoginName` call in a later section.

```
Private Sub Page_Load(ByVal sender As System.Object, _
                      ByVal e As System.EventArgs) _
                      Handles MyBase.Load

   If Not (IsPostBack) Then

      Dim dataSet As New DataSet()
      dataSet.ReadXml(MapPath("tips.xml"))
      TipGrid.DataSource = dataSet
      TipGrid.DataBind()

      DisplayLoginName()

   End If

   Dim funText As New FunText()
   If FunnyRadioButton.Checked Then
     MessageLabel.Text = funText.Quote
   Else
     MessageLabel.Text = funText.Fortune
   End If

End Sub
```

The `IsPostBack` property is a good idea. It allows us to be "lazy", and avoid rebinding the data grid when we don't have to. We will return to this specific example later in the chapter to look at an additional optimization. For now, we will move on to look at additional areas of this same Web Form. Our next example is also inside `IsPostBack`: the method to display the current login name.

Lazy Evaluations

You might come across the term **lazy evaluation** with a number of different definitions. For our purposes, lazy evaluation means that an expression is evaluated only if the program *requires* a result to continue execution. We can implement this technique ourselves, as well as use some lazy features built into the language.

AndAlso / OrElse

Visual Basic .NET offers two logical operators with the ability to conditionally evaluate. These operators, `AndAlso` and `OrElse`, when given two Boolean expressions, will perform the least amount of work necessary to determine the result.

As an example, consider the implementation of `DisplayLoginName` below. In this code we want to set the text of a label to the name of the logged-in user, but only if the system authenticated the user *and* we have a non-null username.

```
Private Sub DisplayLoginName()

  With Page.User.Identity
    If (.IsAuthenticated AndAlso Not .Name = Nothing) Then
      GreetingLabel.Text = String.Format( "You are logged in as {0}", .Name)
    Else
      GreetingLabel.Text = "You have an unknown identity"
    End If
  End With

End Sub
```

If the `IsAuthenticated` property in the above code is `False`, the `AndAlso` operator 'short-circuits' and does not bother evaluating the `Name` property to see if the string is equal to `Nothing`. After all, if you `And` a `False` with either a `True` or a `False`, the result is still `False` – there is no need to evaluate the second half of the expression. Similarly, with an `OrElse`, if the first expression evaluates to `True`, the operator does not evaluate the second expression, it knows the result of the operation will be `True` in either case.

The VB.NET operators `And` and `Or` do not short-circuit; they will always evaluate both expressions. C++ uses only one set of operators for the computation (`&&` and `||`), and always short-circuits when possible. These may seem like small optimizations, and in this example they are. However, if you can use short-circuit operators inside of tight loops, or where the second expression is costly to calculate, you can see a performance increase with the smallest of changes in your code.

Lazy Properties

Exposing an object's data fields as properties instead of allowing direct access is not only a solid programming technique, it also allows us to delay the computation of a field until we are sure a program really needs the information. For example, the Web Form we have been working with displays a random message to the user – either a funny quote or a fortune depending on the user's preference in the radio buttons on the left of the form. We instantiate the following class to retrieve the text for this message (`FunText.vb`).

```
Public Class FunText

  Protected FortuneField As String
  Protected QuoteField As String

  Public ReadOnly Property Fortune() As String
    Get
      If FortuneField Is Nothing Then
        FortuneField = GetNewFortune()
      End If
      Return FortuneField
    End Get
  End Property
```

```
      Public ReadOnly Property Quote() As String
        Get
          If QuoteField Is Nothing Then
            QuoteField = GetNewQuote()
          End If
          Return QuoteField
        End Get
      End Property

      Protected Function GetNewFortune() As String

        'implementation not shown

      End Function

      Protected Function GetNewQuote() As String

        'implementation not shown

      End Function

    End Class
```

Notice we do not show the implementations for GetNewQuote and GetNewFortune, as the implementations are really not important to us. Imagine these methods make a web service call, a database query, or some other relatively expensive operation to return a string to the caller.

What is important to note is that we could have initialized both of our data fields (QuoteField and FortuneField) during construction of the FunText class. But this is a waste of processing time and memory unless the application is going to use both of the fields – the Web Form in this example only uses one of the two properties each time the class is instantiated. In this class, the calculation only occurs if the program requests the value, and once the class makes the calculation we save the value in a member variable for future calls to return the same value.

As a class designer, it is sometimes difficult to predict just how consumers of your class will put your code to work. Any expensive computation you can delay, and thereby sometimes avoid, will result in a performance win. In the next section, we will discuss another improvement we can make in building the message of the day label.

Making Less Work for the Runtime

Underneath the covers, the .NET and ASP.NET infrastructures are doing a fair amount of plumbing work to make our jobs easier. Although it is nice to use the architecture as a black box, it is also sometimes useful to know some of the implementation details that make everything work so seamlessly. With this extra information, we can often use the runtime more efficiently and gain an advantage in speed.

View State Optimizations

Another optimization we can take advantage of is with the label control containing the message of the day. If you refer back to the Page_Load method we listed earlier for this Web Form, you'll notice we reset the MessageLabel control on each page request, even during a postback request.

Remember from our view state discussion earlier in this chapter that the view state for a control is only useful if we want the state of a control restored for reading during a postback operation. Saving and retrieving information from the view state adds some extra processing time, and adds additional bytes on the network payload sent to the client. Since we never read the state of the `MessageLabel`, we will turn off view state processing for the label with the `EnableViewState` property (in `WebForm1.aspx`).

```
<asp:label id="MessageLabel"
           runat="server"
           EnableViewState="False">
</asp:label>
```

Anytime you don't need to read the state of a control, consider disabling the control's view state to save processing and bandwidth. If you happen to build a Web Form that does not need to perform any postback operations, you should consider disabling view state for the entire page in the @ Page directive of your ASPX file. An example is shown below.

```
<%@ Page Language="VB" EnableViewState="false" %>
```

View state generally only uses a small number of bytes, depending on the amount of data in the control. If you are placing a large amount of data, HTML, or script into a control, the savings can be more substantial. The best way to see how much view state each control produces is to enable tracing in your page by adding `Trace="True"` in the @ Page directive. As shown in the trace below, the trace reports view state size for each control on the page (as the column header on the far right mentions, the total view state size here does not include the view state size of the child controls), allowing you to pinpoint which controls generate large amounts of data.

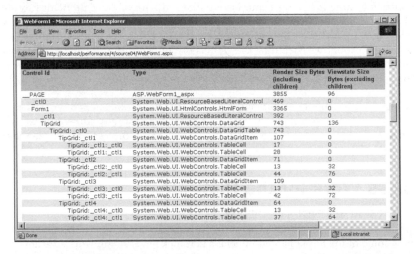

Minimize Server Controls

In the same vein, you should also strive to keep the number of server-side controls on a page to a minimum. Not only do server-side controls generate view state, they will also need additional run-time processing to bind to member variables, render, and then unload.

In our first Web Form, for example, text labels such as the Your Message Of The Day heading are all simple HTML elements we placed in the form. Even the table on our web form is a normal HTML <TABLE> tag, and does not have the runat="server" attribute for server-side controls. Notice how, even though the table itself is not a server control, we can still place server controls inside the table where they will render correctly and we can still reach them programmatically.

Session State Considerations

Obviously a major challenge in building a web application is maintaining state across page requests, for instance, knowing what items a customer has placed in their shopping cart. There is a wide variety of mechanisms to mix and match in order to achieve state persistence: cookies, view state, query string parameters, and of course, the built-in ASP.NET session infrastructure.

The ASP.NET session features are simple to use and familiar to previous ASP technology. ASP.NET vastly improves session features by offering three different session state providers. The in-process session state provider is by far the fastest of the three. You can also choose to store session state in memory on a central server, and while this technique is not as fast, you will be able to share session state in a web farm among multiple servers. Finally, you can have ASP.NET keep session state in a SQL Server database, which is the most robust solution, but also the slowest. We talked about these considerations in more detail in Chapter 2.

Whichever session state provider you decide to use, try not to abuse the session features by storing large amounts of data or objects. The definition of large will depend on the number of users you need to support and the type of hardware running your application, so you will need to do some testing. Just be aware that without using the session in moderation you run the risk of limiting your scalability.

If you are using ASP.NET session state in your application, but not on a specific page, you can disable session state for the page in the @ Page directive. This can slightly reduce the overhead in processing for the page. The following directive is from our first example Web Form.

```
<%@ Page Language="vb" AutoEventWireup="false" Codebehind="WebForm1.aspx.vb"
        Inherits="source04.WebForm1" EnableSessionState="False"
        Trace="true" %>
```

If you do not use ASP.NET session state anywhere in your application, be sure to change the sessionState mode attribute in web.config.

```
<configuration>
  <system.web>
    <sessionState mode="off"/>
  </system.web>
</configuration>
```

Minimize Exceptions

Exceptions are an extremely useful device for communicating errors during the execution of a program. Unlike return codes, a program cannot ignore exceptions – they *will* alter the flow of execution. Programmers have often shunned exceptions in performance- and memory-critical applications to avoid additional overhead. In the managed environment of the .NET runtime, however, there is only a negligible performance cost in setting up exception handling blocks with Try and Catch. Exceptions are an integral part of the .NET Framework design, so make sure you add robust error handling to your application. Throw exceptions when the situation is exceptional, for instance, if you cannot complete a request due to insufficient security permissions or a missing file.

145

What you don't want to do is to use exceptions unnecessarily. While there is nearly no cost to adding a
`Try...Catch` block to handle exceptions, there is a performance penalty to pay when a program
throws an exception. The runtime needs to walk the stack and gather information about the exception,
in addition to whatever logging or other additional processing your application adds to processing an
exception. Consider the code snippet below:

```
Dim myStringLen As Integer
Try
   myStringLen = CStr(Session.Item("MyString")).Length
Catch exception As Exception
   ' initialize Session.Item("MyString")
End Try
```

If the `Session` object does not contain the key `MyString`, the runtime throws an exception when we
use the `Length` property on a null object reference. Session variables in ASP.NET always have the
possibility of being empty – this is not an exceptional circumstance. Instead of trying to control the
logical flow of the method with a possible exception, the same code becomes easier to read, will throw
fewer exceptions, and runs faster with an `If` statement.

```
Dim myStringLen As Integer
Dim myString As String

myString = CStr(Session.Item("MyString"))
If Not myString Is Nothing Then
   myStringLen = CStr(Session.Item("MyString")).Length
Else
   ' initialize Session.Item("MyString")
End If
```

Use Early Binding

VB.NET projects in Visual Studio .NET support both early and late binding by default. With late
binding, you are using variables of type `Object` to access object references whose types are not known
until run time. In the following example, we have declared a variable without a type and the runtime
will complete all of the processing using late binding.

```
Module Module1

  Sub Main()

    Dim s
    s = "This is a string"

    Console.WriteLine(s.Length)

  End Sub

End Module
```

Late binding offers a great deal of convenience for developers. Many popular languages, including VBScript and Visual Basic, owe some part of their successes to the conveniences of late binding. These conveniences come with a price of course, not the least of which is a performance hit. To perform late binding, the runtime needs to use reflection and query objects about their type and their methods, and also perform conversions between objects of different types.

With VB.NET, there is a statement to ensure your code does not use late binding: `Option Strict`. With this directive all undeclared variables, variables declared without an `As` clause, or late binding expressions will result in a compiler error. The compiler will generate the following errors for the lines highlighted above when compiling the above program with `Option Strict` on.

```
Module1.vb(5): Option Strict On requires all variable declarations to have an 'As'
clause.
Module1.vb(8): Option Strict On disallows late binding.
```

To enable `Option Strict` for a specific page or user control, use an attribute of `Strict="true"` in the @ `Page` or @ `Control` directives. We can add this attribute to our first example Web Form as shown here:

```
<%@ Page Language="vb"
        AutoEventWireup="false"
        Codebehind="WebForm1.aspx.vb"
        Inherits="source04.WebForm1"
        EnableSessionState="False"
        Trace="true"

        Strict="true"

%>
```

In Visual Studio .NET you can also set the default compiler options for a project to include `Option Strict`. Right-click the project in Solution Explorer and select **Properties** from the context menu. Navigate to the **Build** node under **Common Properties**, as shown below, and set the **Option Strict** drop-down option to **On**. This will set the default for a project, meaning you can still change the behaviour of an individual file with the `Option Strict` statement.

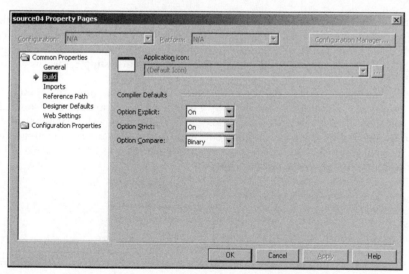

With early binding, the compiler knows what type of object reference we are using. Although some behavior is still not resolved until run time (virtual method calls, for example), the compilers are still in a much better position to make optimizations. In addition, the runtime does not need to use reflection during execution, which leads to a substantial performance enhancement.

This section has outlined a number of techniques to perform the same amount of work using less processing. In the section, we will touch on a related subject, namely, how to perform the same amount of work using fewer resources.

Using Memory Efficiently

Earlier in the chapter, we highlighted some of the features of the .NET garbage collector and gave you a rule of thumb: let the runtime do the work for you. Trying to outsmart the runtime may only create more work for both of you. In this section, we will give you some tips on how to use memory, one of the most precious resources, in an efficient manner using features of the .NET platform.

Jagged Arrays

There are three types of arrays you can use in .NET: single-dimensional arrays, multidimensional arrays, and jagged arrays. **Jagged arrays**, also known as arrays of arrays, offer not only space savings in certain conditions, but also a performance enhancement, as we will demonstrate.

In WebForm2.aspx, we are going to use a multidimensional array and a jagged array to hold random numbers for each day of the year. Two dimensions will allow us to reach any day of the year by providing the index of the month, and the index of the day. We declare the arrays using the syntax shown below.

```
Private multi(12, 31) As Integer
Private jagged(12)() As Integer
```

Notice that for the multidimensional array we need to declare the second dimension of the array with the maximum number of days possible in a month (31). With two dimensions, you can think of a multidimensional array as a square, since each row has the same number of columns. This leads to wasted space, as not all of the array entries correspond to a valid day; for example, there is no 31st day in April.

Jagged arrays, on the other hand, allow you to allocate a different number of columns for each row. In the CreateArrays subroutine shown below, we populate both arrays inside of loops. Notice the jagged array initialization includes the extra step to allocate an array of days for each month. Using the exact amount of storage required for a month saves a small amount of memory in comparison to the multidimensional array. The savings to represent a calendar year as an array are small, but other applications might find more significant savings.

```
Private Sub CreateArrays()
    Dim i As Integer
    Dim j As Integer
    Dim random As New Random()

    ' initialize multi dimension array with random data for each day
```

```
    For i = 0 To 11
      For j = 0 To DateTime.DaysInMonth(DateTime.Now.Year, i + 1) - 1
        multi(i, j) = random.Next(100)
      Next
    Next

    ' allocate and initialize jagged array with random data
    For i = 0 To 11
      jagged(i) = New Integer(DateTime.DaysInMonth(DateTime.Now.Year, i + 1)) {}
      For j = 0 To DateTime.DaysInMonth(DateTime.Now.Year, i + 1) - 1
        jagged(i)(j) = random.Next(100)
      Next

    Next
  End Sub
```

Obviously, a jagged array, when compared to a multidimensional array, might require slightly more time to create with the extra allocation steps inside the loop. However, you might be surprised to know a jagged array will generally outperform a multidimensional array when it comes time to access it and iterate the arrays. In version 1.0 of the .NET Framework, better optimizations exist in the JIT compiler for jagged arrays. To demonstrate, let's look at the two test subroutines we run each time the Web Form executes.

```
Private Sub TestSquareArray()
  Trace.Write("Beginning TestSquareArray")

  Dim i As Integer
  Dim j As Integer
  Dim k As Integer
  Dim sum As Int64

  sum = 0
  For i = 0 To 65525
    For j = 0 To 11
      For k = 0 To DateTime.DaysInMonth(DateTime.Now.Year, j + 1) - 1
        sum = sum + multi(j, k)
      Next
    Next
  Next

  Trace.Write("Ending TestSquareArray")
End Sub

Private Sub TestJaggedArray()
  Trace.Write("Beginning TestJaggedArray")

  Dim i As Integer
  Dim j As Integer
  Dim k As Integer
  Dim sum As Int64

  sum = 0
  For i = 0 To 65525
    For j = 0 To 11
```

```
      For k = 0 To DateTime.DaysInMonth(DateTime.Now.Year, j + 1) - 1
        sum = sum + jagged(j)(k)
      Next
    Next
  Next

  Trace.Write("Ending TestJaggedArray")
End Sub
```

Each subroutine sums up the values inside of each array. We do this repeatedly inside of another large loop to lengthen the computation time and extract more meaningful timing information. After we enable tracing we can look at the timing information for the page, shown below. The numbers in the far right column display the amount of time, in seconds, elapsed since the last trace entry. The routine accessing the jagged array is consistently around 20% faster than the multidimensional version.

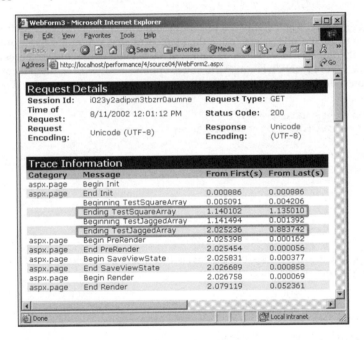

Weak References

When you assign an object reference to a variable, the variable holds a **strong reference** to an object. The garbage collector will not reclaim an object with a strong reference outstanding. Only when the variable goes out of scope, or you explicitly assign Nothing to the variable, is the strong reference removed.

Weak references give you a way to keep a reference to an object while still allowing the garbage collector to free the object and reclaim memory when it decides the time is right for garbage collection. Let's imagine you have an object that is relatively inexpensive to create but consumes a large quantity of memory. You'd like to keep the object around to use whenever needed by your application, but you also would like to be able to tell the garbage collector to reclaim the memory for use by other areas of functionality if required.

Weak references are available using the WeakReference class. In the sample code below, we create a 32-kilobyte string when the ASP.NET application starts. We assign the string to a WeakReference instance, and place the weak reference in the Application object to retrieve later. After the bigString variable in Application_Start goes out of scope, no strong references to the string instance will exist.

```
Sub Application_Start(ByVal sender As Object, ByVal e As EventArgs)
    ' Fires when the application is started

    ' create a 32KB string
    Dim bigString As New String("A"c, 32768)

    ' create a weak reference to the string
    Dim weakReference As New WeakReference(bigString)
    Application.Add("BigString", weakReference)

End Sub
```

Next, we will look at the code for WebForm3.aspx (found in WebForm3.aspx.vb). If we can reach this Web Form before garbage collection occurs, the form should tell us it can successfully retrieve the string from the Application object via the WeakReference. The Target property of the WeakReference object will hold an object reference to the string. If this property is empty, the weak referenced object has been garbage collected, and we would need to rebuild the string in order to use it. Otherwise, we can extract the Target property and create a strong reference with the bigString variable, then use the string object we created in the beginning of the application.

```
Private Sub Page_Load(ByVal sender As System.Object, _
                      ByVal e As System.EventArgs) _
                      Handles MyBase.Load
    'Put user code to initialize the page here

    If Not IsPostBack Then
        GetBigString()
    End If

End Sub

Private Sub GetBigString()

    Dim weakReference As WeakReference

    If Not (Application.Item("BigString") Is Nothing) Then
        weakReference = CType(Application.Item("BigString"), WeakReference)

        Dim bigString As String
        bigString = CType(weakReference.Target, String)

        If Not (bigString Is Nothing) Then
            MessageLabel.Text = "BigString retrieved from WeakReference"
        Else
            MessageLabel.Text = "BigString was garbage collected"
        End If
```

```
    Else
      MessageLabel.Text = "Unable to retrieve BigString From Application"
    End If

  End Sub

  Private Sub CollectButton_Click(ByVal sender As System.Object, _
                                  ByVal e As System.EventArgs) _
                                  Handles CollectButton.Click
    GC.Collect()
    GetBigString()

  End Sub
```

A button on the form will allow us to force garbage collection using the static `Collect` method of the `GC` class. We still recommend you let the garbage collector determine the best time to run, and include this call only for demonstration purposes. After garbage collection, the `WeakReference Target` will be empty.

Although memory becomes more plentiful in every new machine, we still need to make the best use of this resource. In the next section we will again weigh the tradeoffs of memory usage versus performance when we discuss caching in ASP.NET.

Caching

Caching in ASP.NET has the ability to provide the biggest wins in performance and scalability. With an effective cache in place, you can avoid network round trips to the database, bypass expensive calculations, and generally save server resources while improving response time and latency. Design and iterative testing are the best methods for finding the most effective caching strategy for your application. In this section, we will discuss two caching strategies in ASP.NET: caching application data, and caching pages.

Caching Application Data

In each ASP.NET application there is an instance of the `Cache` class. Similar to the `Application` object, the `Cache` object begins existence when the application starts, and all contents are lost when the application halts or restarts. Also like the `Application` object, the `Cache` is a dictionary style object, giving you the ability to store a value paired with a key, which you use to later retrieve the value.

Unlike the `Application` object, however, the `Cache` object offers a number of intelligent features designed for highly scalable web applications. For instance, you can prioritize items you insert into the cache. Later, if the system is under heavy load and memory is becoming scarce, the cache will begin to unload values with a low priority or infrequent accesses.

You will need to test your application under realistic load to obtain the proper balance. If you do not cache enough, your application will not realize its full performance potential. If you cache too aggressively, you can hurt the scalability of your application by using too many resources on caching instead of processing requests.

The following code excerpt is the `Page_Load` method for `WebForm4.aspx` (found, as expected, in `WebForm4.aspx.vb`) a revised version of the first example Web Form in the chapter. Remember, there is a grid control we populate with the contents of an XML file. Since the XML file contents rarely change, there is no reason to constantly open the file and read it from the disk into a `DataSet`. Instead, we will use the `Cache` object.

```
Private Sub Page_Load(ByVal sender As System.Object, _
                      ByVal e As System.EventArgs) _
                      Handles MyBase.Load

    If Not (IsPostBack) Then

        Dim dataSet As DataSet
        dataSet = CType(Cache("Tips"), DataSet)

        If (dataSet Is Nothing) Then

            dataSet = New DataSet()
            dataSet.ReadXml(MapPath("tips.xml"))

            Cache.Insert("Tips", dataSet, _
                New Caching.CacheDependency(MapPath("tips.xml")))

        End If

        TipGrid.DataSource = dataSet
        TipGrid.DataBind()

        DisplayLoginName()

    End If

End Sub
```

The first step is to try to retrieve the `DataSet` from the cache by asking for the value with a key of `Tips`. If the cache returns an object reference, we can cast the object reference to a `DataSet` and continue with our data binding. Otherwise, we will create a new `DataSet`, ask the `DataSet` to read the XML file, and then insert a reference to the `DataSet` in the cache. Notice we only attempt these steps if the request is not a postback operation. From our discussion earlier in the chapter, you should remember how the view state will populate the `DataGrid` during a postback operation automatically.

The `Insert` method of the `Cache` class will replace a cache entry, if the key already exists. Another method, the `Add` method, will not overwrite an existing value if the key exists in the cache, and instead will return an object reference to the existing value.

Notice how we can pass an instance of a `CacheDependency` class to the method. A `CacheDependency` will track files, directories, or keys to other cache objects and determine when to invalidate a cache entry. In this example, if the XML file changes, the cache will remove the existing `DataSet` from the cache, which will force us to reload the XML during `Page_Load`.

Overloaded versions of these `Insert` and `Add` methods allow you to add a value to the cache with a specific priority, with an absolute expiration time, and with a sliding expiration time. You can use the last parameter to have an item removed from the cache if the application has not accessed the value for a specified amount of time. You can even pass in a delegate for the runtime to notify you when it removes an item from the cache.

The Cache object is a great deal more powerful than the Application object for storing application data, particularly when the data has a limited lifetime due to external dependencies, or the data requires a large amount of memory needing prioritization.

Page Caching

Page caching can realize an even greater performance gain by caching the entire response for a Web Form request. Once a page with caching has executed for the first time, the runtime stores the result in the cache. The runtime can then fulfill subsequent requests by pulling the cached version of the page, and thereby avoid execution of the page's code, including all the database queries, file I/O, and other processing in the page. Skipping all of this processing can dramatically increase the number of requests your application serves per second.

@OutputCache Directive

The easiest way to control caching for a page is with the @ OutputCache directive in your ASPX file. There are two required parameters. The first, Duration, specifies the amount of time in seconds to hold the page results in cache. This is an absolute expiration time. Finding the optimum duration for the different pages in your application will require stress testing and performance monitoring as described over the final few chapters of this book. Performance counters monitoring cache hits and cache turnover are invaluable in tuning the duration parameter.

The second required parameter is VaryByParam. Dynamically generated pages are not going to look the same for every request because there is generally a query string or form parameter input by the user to modify the look of the page. For instance, you might have a page with a DataGrid displaying employees by city. One of the form parameters posted to the page (with the name of city) eventually ends up in the WHERE clause of a SQL query, and thereby changes the contents of the page. To cache different versions of the page, based on the city parameter, use the following cache directive:

```
<%@ OutputCache Duration="120" VaryByParam="city" %>
```

We will now have as many versions of the page in cache as we have unique city parameters. When you need to track more than one parameter, separate the parameters with a semicolon. For example, to vary by city and country, use the following:

```
<%@ OutputCache Duration="120" VaryByParam="city;country" %>
```

If you need to vary the cache on all parameter values, specify the VaryByParam attribute as an asterisk (*). This option can result in the runtime attempting to cache a large number of page versions, so take extreme care by watching the number of parameters you have and the number of different values they might carry. You can also use VaryByParam="None" and the runtime will only cache request results with no query string or form parameters.

An optional attribute, VaryByHeader, allows you to cache different versions of the page depending on one of the client's HTTP headers. For example, every web browser should send a User-Agent header in the HTTP request indicating the name and version of the browser. If you wanted to cache versions of the page depending on the User-Agent, use the following directive:

```
<%@ OutputCache Duration="120" VaryByParam="none" VaryByHeader="User-Agent" %>
```

Using VaryByCustom

The final optional attribute is `VaryByCustom`. This attribute allows you to vary cache versions of a page based on a custom string you define. Let's examine a screenshot of `WebForm5.aspx`:

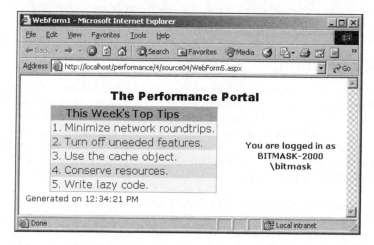

If we decided to cache this Web Form we would need to vary the cache based on the user's identity, since the form displays a login name (our forms are under a virtual directory requiring Windows Integrated authentication). Since identity is not a parameter or an HTTP header, we will need `VaryByCustom` to achieve this trick. The cache directive for our page is shown next:

```
<%@ OutputCache Duration="120" VaryByParam="none" VaryByCustom="identity" %>
```

When a page uses `VaryByCustom`, the runtime will call the `GetVaryByCustomString` function of the `HttpApplication` to retrieve a custom string. This string symbolizes the version of the page. Imagine the runtime using the string you return from `GetVaryByCustomString` as the key to a value in the cache table, just as we used `Tips` in the last sample to find our `DataSet`. If the runtime does not find an entry with the custom string, it can add a new version of the page to the cache using the custom string as the key. In order to implement our own custom strings, we only need to override `GetVaryByCustomString` in our `global.asax` file. The incoming `arg` parameter will tell us the `VaryByCustom` string we need to compute and return.

```
Public Overrides Function GetVaryByCustomString(ByVal context As HttpContext, _
                                    ByVal arg As String) As String
  If (arg = "identity") Then
    Return context.User.Identity.Name
  End If
End Function
```

Notice that all we need to do to cache a different version of the page for each user login is simply return the login name itself. The runtime passes the string from the `VaryByCustom` attribute (`"identity"`) as the second parameter. This allows us to identify which custom string we need to compute when multiple pages are using different `VaryByCustom` strings. If multiple pages needed to cache pages by the user's identity, all of them could use a `VaryByCustom` string of `"identity"`.

Caching pages on a per-user basis might not be the best caching strategy, but this example illustrates a simple case of caching using a custom string.

Page caching is a great feature in .NET, but can sometimes become difficult to implement. When a single ASPX page uses many parameters across different areas of the screen, the number of versions to cache becomes too great. Fortunately, .NET provides infrastructure to cache smaller pieces of a page.

Partial Page Caching

The performance tips grid in the upper left of our form is a perfect candidate for partial page caching, also called **fragment caching**. Here is a piece of our Web Form that is not dependent on any parameters or the name of the logged-in user. We might use this grid on quite a few pages, yet the pages themselves might not be favorable for page caching due to a large number of parameters. Although we already have the DataSet to construct the grid cached, it would be nice to cache the output of the grid itself and avoid the creation of a DataGrid, the databinding, the HTML generation, and other behind the scenes work required to display the grid.

The first step in taking advantage of fragment caching is moving the sections of your page to cache into user controls. In our example project, we have added a new web user control (TipControl.ascx). The ASP.NET tags and markup from the ASPX file have moved into the ASCX file, while the code to load XML into the DataSet and bind with the DataGrid has moved into the code-behind file for the user control (TipControl.ascx.vb), the code is shown below.

```vb
Private Sub Page_Load(ByVal sender As System.Object, _
                    ByVal e As System.EventArgs) _
                    Handles MyBase.Load

    If Not (IsPostBack) Then

        Dim dataSet As DataSet
        dataSet = CType(Cache("Tips"), DataSet)

        If (dataSet Is Nothing) Then

            dataSet = New DataSet()
            dataSet.ReadXml(MapPath("tips.xml"))

            Cache.Insert("Tips", dataSet, _
                New Caching.CacheDependency(MapPath("tips.xml")))

        End If

        TipGrid.DataSource = dataSet
        TipGrid.DataBind()

    End If

    TimeLabel.Text = "Grid generated on " + DateTime.Now.ToLongTimeString()

End Sub
```

WebForm6.aspx, shown below, looks similar to our previous forms, but underneath it is using the new user control in the upper left hand side. Notice we also have placed labels in both the user control and the Web Form and generated time stamps to place when the code executes. Both the form and the control are using the cache. The duration for the form cache is set to 10 seconds with the following directive in WebForm6.aspx.

```
<%@ OutputCache Duration="10" VaryByParam="none" VaryByCustom="identity"%>
```

The duration for the control cache is set to 20 seconds with the following directive in TipControl.aspx.

```
<%@ OutputCache Duration="20" VaryByParam="none"%>
```

By loading the form, waiting more than 10 seconds, and then pressing the refresh button in the browser, we should see the page regenerated by executing the form while the runtime fetches the user control from the cache. Notice the time stamps in the screen shot below verify the correct behavior:

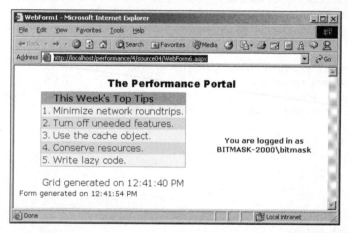

The @OutputCache directive for the tip user control is shown next. Caching with user controls has a few twists compared to page caching. For starters, you cannot use VaryByHeaders with fragment caching, but you can still use VaryByCustom with the same behavior we described earlier. VaryByParam will still work to vary the cache on GET and POST parameters, while a new attribute for fragment caching, VaryByControl, will also vary the cache based on the value of the web server controls contained within the user control.

```
<%@ OutputCache Duration="20" VaryByParam="none"%>
```

> One caveat when caching user controls: never try to programmatically access a user control with a cache directive. The first time the user control executes, the programmatic access will work because the runtime creates the control to execute. However, if the runtime can pull the page fragment from the cache it will not instantiate the user control, and attempting to access the control from code will result in an exception. The only safe place to reference the user control and its contents is from within the user control code.

Partial page caching is an excellent way to speed up the menus, navigation bars, and those other common elements in your application. Isolate these areas into user controls and apply a cache directive to increase the throughput of your application.

Using Collections

When choosing how to hold and process a collection of items in .NET, there are a number of tradeoffs to evaluate. Let's discuss the tradeoffs between an `ArrayList` from the `System.Collections` namespace versus using an array variable. The biggest tradeoff is how the capacity of an `ArrayList` can grow as you add new items, while the capacity of an array is fixed.

While a simple array does not have all the features of an `ArrayList` class, it does have better performance. The performance delta can be considerable, depending on the types you are using in the containers. Let's imagine we need to store a collection of integers. Integers are a value type in .NET. The compiler places value types such as `Integer` and `Double` on the stack, and access to a value type is direct. A reference type derives from the `Object` class, and the runtime will create storage for a reference type on the heap. You always access the storage via a reference, and the garbage collector tracks the storage for later collection.

While you can declare an array to hold value types or reference types, an `ArrayList` will only hold reference types. So how are value types placed into an `ArrayList`? To find out, let's look at the next listing, an excerpt from `WebForm7.aspx`. Notice we are able to call the `Add` method of an `ArrayList` object, which accepts an `Object` as a parameter, but we pass an `Integer`.

```
Private Sub Test_ArrayList_Int()
   Trace.Write("Begin Test_ArrayList_Int")

   Dim i As Integer
   Dim arrayList As New ArrayList()

   For i = 0 To NUMITEMS
     arrayList.Add(i)
   Next

   For i = 0 To NUMITEMS
     arrayList(i) = CInt(arrayList(i)) + 1
   Next

   Trace.Write("End Test_ArrayList_Int")
End Sub
```

Boxing

In order to treat the `Integer` as a reference type, the compiler will **box** the `Integer`. Boxing creates a new object and copies a value type's bits into the managed heap, then returns a reference to the new storage location. This is an implicit operation, and also relatively expensive. There is also an unboxing operation which turns a reference type back into a value type. Think about what happens when the following line of code from the above subroutine is executed:

```
arrayList(i) = CInt(arrayList(i)) + 1
```

First, we unbox the `ArrayList` element with a `CInt` cast. Remember, the `ArrayList` will give us back a reference to an `Object`, so we need `CInt` to coerce the type to an integer. We then add one and assign the integer back into the same `ArrayList` element. To do this, however, requires another implicit boxing, since the integer is again copied into an object reference on the manage heap. All of this boxing and unboxing takes a toll on performance, as we will soon demonstrate. It is important to be on the lookout for implicit boxing when you are using value types. In tight loops such as this example, the performance hit is noticeable, as we will demonstrate shortly.

Another subroutine in the `WebForm7.aspx` code-behind uses an array of integers to perform the same calculations. This subroutine is shown below. With our trace statements in place and tracing enabled, we will be able to compare the time required to execute both methods.

```
Private Sub Test_Array_Int()
  Trace.Write("Begin Test_Array_Int")

  Dim i As Integer
  Dim array(NUMITEMS) As Integer

  For i = 0 To NUMITEMS
    array(i) = i
  Next

  For i = 0 To NUMITEMS
    array(i) = i + 1
  Next

  Trace.Write("End Test_Array_Int")
End Sub
```

What you will see when executing the form is the `ArrayList` version of the subroutine is consistently around 20 times slower than the subroutine using an array. Some of this overhead is attributable to boxing, and some of this overhead is attributable to the `ArrayList` growing dynamically. Let's do some additional timing tests to see how other techniques compare.

Avoiding Boxing

The choice between `ArrayList` and `Array` isn't made just looking at performance numbers, as we pointed out earlier. If you do not know how many items you may need to store, the `ArrayList` or other dynamically sized collection class is still going to be a top choice. Let's say we have decided on an `ArrayList` but want to avoid the boxing. All we need is a reference type we can use the same way as we use the `Integer` types above. For this example, we will use the following class. The class wraps an integer member variable inside a property (`Value`) that we can use to get and set the value.

```
Public Class IntWrapper
  Dim valueField As Integer

  Public Sub New(ByVal value As Integer)
    valueField = value
  End Sub

  Property Value() As Integer
    Get
```

```
      Value = valueField
    End Get
    Set(ByVal Value As Integer)
      valueField = Value
    End Set
  End Property
End Class
```

Next, we will build the same logic we used earlier, only this time using our reference type:

```
Private Sub Test_ArrayList_Object()
  Trace.Write("Begin Test_ArrayList_Object")

  Dim i As Integer
  Dim arrayList As New ArrayList()

  For i = 0 To NUMITEMS
    arrayList.Add(New IntWrapper(i))
  Next

  Dim intWrapper As IntWrapper
  For i = 0 To NUMITEMS
    intWrapper = CType(arrayList(i), IntWrapper)
    intWrapper.Value = intWrapper.Value + 1
  Next

  Trace.Write("End Test_ArrayList_Object")
End Sub
```

Executing this subroutine and examining the trace results shows this method is about 14 times slower than using an array of `Integer`. While still slower than an array, it is an improvement over the version using boxing, which was 20 times slower because of the boxing and unboxing taking place.

The tradeoff for the performance and flexibility is more complex and less readable code. You'll need to evaluate this tradeoff based on how badly you need to avoid the performance hit of boxing.

Next, let's try to make more of an apples to apples comparison by using an array with the integer wrapper class we wrote. This method is shown next:

```
Private Sub Test_Array_Object()
  Trace.Write("Begin Test_Array_Object")

  Dim i As Integer
  Dim array(NUMITEMS) As IntWrapper

  For i = 0 To NUMITEMS
    array(i) = New IntWrapper(i)
  Next

  Dim x As IntWrapper
  For i = 0 To NUMITEMS
    x = array(i)
```

```
    x.Value = x.Value + 1
  Next

  Trace.Write("End Test_Array_Object")
End Sub
```

This method is around 11 times slower than using an array of `Integer`. Obviously, value types offer much higher performance than reference types in this situation. You can create your own value types by defining a `Structure` instead of a `Class`. This is a useful and performance enhancing technique to use when you have a type in your program which acts like a primitive type such as `Integer` or `Double`. A good example would be a complex number, or a structure holding x, y, and z coordinates. Just remember value types are *copied* by value into method calls, so a large structure might result in more of a performance hit than a reference type (which only copies a reference) when used in a large number of method calls.

Finally, let's try one more trick to increase the speed of our `ArrayList` algorithm. Typically, you do not know how many elements you will place in an `ArrayList`; this is one of the overriding problems to solve when using an `ArrayList`. But since we do know how many items we will use in this example, let's pre-allocate the `ArrayList` to hold all of our items using the constructor syntax shown in the following code excerpt, and then measure the results to see the overhead of expanding an `ArrayList`. Even when you construct an `ArrayList` with an initial capacity as seen here, you can always add more items than initially requested.

```
Dim arrayList As New ArrayList(NUMITEMS)
```

The subroutine with the above code runs 13 times slower than our base case (the array of `Integers`). This is, however, pretty close to the speed of the algorithm using an array of objects. Obviously there is still a small overhead in using an `ArrayList` instead of an array. To see one reason for the overhead, we will take a closer look at the two methods in the next section.

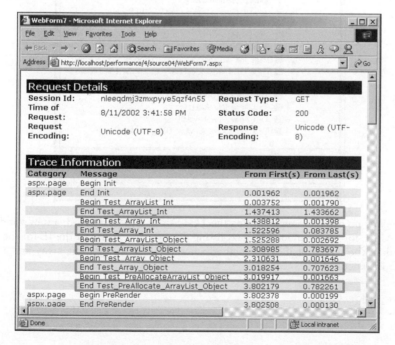

Using ILDASM

The Intermediate Language Disassembler (ILDASM) allows you to look inside an assembly and see the MSIL code the compiler generates. This is a good tool to use if you really need to look under the covers and examine what is happening in minute detail. ILDASM will also show you the assembly manifest, and the types and interfaces contained in an assembly.

You can find ILDASM in the Bin directory of your .NET Framework installation. Run the program and select Open from the File menu, then navigate to the Bin directory for the chapter's example web application. Open the source04.dll, expand the source04 node, and finally expand the WebForm7 node. You should have a display similar to the following screenshot:

If we double-click on the node representing the Test_Array_Obect method, a new window will open showing the MSIL for the method. The next listing displays an excerpt of the IL for the method. This section of code is the second half of the method where we loop through the array and add one to each IntWrapper instance.

```
IL_0036:  ldc.i4.0
IL_0037:  stloc.1
IL_0038:  ldloc.0
```

```
IL_0039:   ldloc.1
IL_003a:   ldelem.ref
IL_003b:   stloc.2
IL_003c:   ldloc.2
IL_003d:   ldloc.2
IL_003e:   callvirt      instance int32 source04.IntWrapper::get_Value()
IL_0043:   ldc.i4.1
IL_0044:   add.ovf
IL_0045:   callvirt      instance void source04.IntWrapper::set_Value(int32)
IL_004a:   nop
IL_004b:   nop
IL_004c:   ldloc.1
IL_004d:   ldc.i4.1
IL_004e:   add.ovf
IL_004f:   stloc.1
IL_0050:   ldloc.1
IL_0051:   ldc.i4        0xf4240
IL_0056:   ble.s         IL_0038
```

Without going into detail on every instruction, let's examine a few critical pieces. We start with the instruction at offset 36. This instruction is an LDC (load numeric constant) instruction where the i4 stands for the type (32-bit integer), and the 0 is the value to push on the stack. The CLR is a stack-based machine, so if we want to load a value into a variable, we push the value on the stack first. If we want to call a method to add integers, we push the two integers on the stack before calling the method. Remember also the JIT compiler will transform these instructions into machine instructions for the target CPU, so the instructions we are reading here are not instructions executed on the CPU.

The instruction at offset 37 is a STLOC, which pops the top value off the stack into a local variable – in this case local variable 1. There are three local variables in this method; you can see them in the full disassembly listing at the top of the method. Local variable 0 is array, local variable 1 is i, and local variable 2 is x. This instruction pops the zero off the stack and into i – our loop counter is initialized and we are ready to begin.

The next three instructions will fetch an element from the array. Offset 38 uses LDLOC (load local variable) to place local variable 0 (Array) on the stack. Offset 39 uses LDLOC to place local variable 1 (i) on the stack. The next instruction (LDELEM – or load array element) uses the two parameters pushed on the stack to pull a reference type out of the array (the .ref part of the instruction) and onto the stack. We can imagine the LDELEM instruction is rather efficient – needing only some simple arithmetic given the address of the array and the index into the array.

The next instruction (stloc.2) pops the reference off the stack and into the second local variable (x). We can see the calls to get and set the value in our IntWrapper class at offset 3e and 45, with the 1 added in between. Instructions from 4c to 4f add 1 to i, while instructions between 50 and 56 compare the value of i to one million, which is the value of NUMITEMS, and branch back to offset 36 if the value is less than or equal. Next, let's take a look at the Test_ArrayList_Object method with ILDASM. You'll notice the excerpt of the loop shown below is nearly identical, except for two lines.

```
IL_0034:   ldc.i4.0
IL_0035:   stloc.1
IL_0036:   ldloc.0
IL_0037:   ldloc.1
```

```
IL_0038:  callvirt    instance object
                       [mscorlib]System.Collections.ArrayList::get_Item(int32)
IL_003d:  castclass   source04.IntWrapper
IL_0042:  stloc.2
IL_0043:  ldloc.2
IL_0044:  ldloc.2
IL_0045:  callvirt    instance int32 source04.IntWrapper::get_Value()
IL_004a:  ldc.i4.1
IL_004b:  add.ovf
IL_004c:  callvirt    instance void source04.IntWrapper::set_Value(int32)
IL_0051:  nop
IL_0052:  nop
IL_0053:  ldloc.1
IL_0054:  ldc.i4.1
IL_0055:  add.ovf
IL_0056:  stloc.1
IL_0057:  ldloc.1
IL_0058:  ldc.i4      0xf4240
IL_005d:  ble.s       IL_0036
```

Instead of LDELEM, we need a virtual function call to retrieve an element from the ArrayList. This instruction appears at offset 38. The callvirt instruction invokes virtual methods and instance methods on a class, in this case invoking get_Item on the ArrayList object to retrieve our value. Following this call is a castclass operation at offset 3d, which will cast the reference on the stack from type Object to type IntWrapper, We can be pretty sure these two calls are more expensive than a LDELEM instruction, thus explaining some of the additional time spent inside the ArrayList methods.

Using ILDASM, you can find implicit boxes made by the compiler, the effects of using a With expression (hint: it helps performance), and other secrets hidden in the intermediate language by the compiler. We're not going to go into all of these now, but it's useful to know we can pick up on them if we need to.

Interop

There is still a tremendous amount of software we can use packaged as COM components . The .NET Framework allows us to use this software through an interoperability (called **interop** for short in .NET) layer. Of course the key word here is 'layer', which is key to understanding that interop does not come for free: you will pay a price in performance. In this section, we will offer some details on how interop works and some techniques for achieving faster interop.

The Runtime Callable Wrapper

If you have previously used COM interop you'll know the first step is to create an interop assembly with the IDE's Project Reference menu or the command line Type Library Importer (TLBIMP). The metadata contained in this assembly allows you to create the COM component and invoke methods as if the COM object was a native .NET object. This behavior is made possible by the runtime callable wrapper (RCW) generated by the .NET runtime.

The RCW is responsible for creating COM components and managing their lifetimes through the reference counting function `AddRef` and `Release`. The RCW also marshals parameters between managed code and COM, allowing you, for instance, to pass a .NET `System.String` where the COM component expects a `BSTR`. The RCW also map COM `HRESULTS` into .NET exceptions and retrieve additional error information when an error occurs. The runtime creates exactly one RCW to manage each instantiated COM object.

The choice of porting COM components into managed code is a tough decision. On the one hand, it is hard to change existing code you have tested and verified. On the other hand, if you are using COM interop in a performance-critical situation, porting the COM code into managed code will certainly provide a performance boost. You might choose to find a middle ground by porting the most frequently used components to managed code. You should try to use COM components which do not require multiple accesses to achieve an operation. For example, a method you call once and pass five parameters will perform faster than a component requiring you to set five properties and then call a method. Try to minimize the number of transitions into unmanaged code.

COM Apartments

Being aware of COM apartment types in .NET programming is important to achieving optimum interop performance. Many existing COM components (including components built using Visual Basic 6) run in a single threaded apartment (STA). An STA requires that all access to a component happens from the same thread. The STA protects instance data from multithreaded access by serializing calls on this single thread. This is in contrast to a COM component supporting the multithreaded apartment model (MTA), which has no such restrictions and forces the developer to write additional code to protect instance data from multithreaded access. COM components can support both and be created in either apartment type.

The components you need to be extremely careful with are the components that only support the single threaded apartment model. You can use these components in .NET but the performance hit is severe. ASP.NET pages run in an MTA by default. Imagine going to a grocery store for the first time and using register number three when you check out to leave. In an STA world, the analogy is that every time you go back to this grocery store, you need to use register number three – even if register three is full with other customers while register four sits idle. STA components require access from the same thread every time, so if the required thread is currently executing another request, the runtime has no choice but to block and wait for the thread to become free.

If you have no choice but to execute STA components in your ASP.NET page, there is some help. In the @ Page directive of your ASPX files using STA components, set `aspcompat="true"`. The `aspcompat` attribute forces the page to execute on an STA thread. Another tip when using `aspcompat` is to never construct a COM component until after the constructor of your page has finished. The runtime does not place the request into STA mode until after the constructor has completed, and creating an STA COM component before this time will lead to additional marshalling overhead between apartments. Creating the component in the `Page_Load` method or other event handler will avoid this problem.

Summary

Over the course of this chapter we have discussed many coding techniques and concepts that will help you increase the performance of your ASP.NET code. We'll summarize them here:

❏ The JIT compiler and garbage collector perform a number of optimizations, which means that you don't have to. Trying to out-think the framework will rarely result in any performance gain.

❏ High-performance code will do the minimum amount of work necessary. Save time and increase perceived performance by breaking long wait times into smaller chunks. And leave unnecessary work until it's actually called for, rather than initializing everything all at once.

❏ Use `IsPostBack` to see whether certain processing needs to be done on a page, or whether you'll just let the view state take care of it.

❏ Lazy evaluation operators like `OrElse` and `AndAlso` save time by not evaluating the second clause if the first clause makes the result obvious.

❏ Exposing an object's data fields as properties lets us delay computation until the information is really needed.

❏ Turn off view state for controls that you don't need persisted during a postback. Turn off view state for entire pages if they will never be used to post back.

❏ Minimize the number of server-side controls. Server controls use not only view state, but also have their own associated processing costs.

❏ Don't store more session state information than you need; excessive use of state storage can impact scalability.

❏ Use exceptions wisely. Exception *handling* is cheap, but actual exceptions come at a cost. Only throw exceptions if the situation is actually exceptional. In other situations, consider alternative methods of handling the situation.

❏ Use early binding to avoid unnecessarily stressing the runtime. Late bound objects need to be queried about their type and their methods, whereas with an early bound object these things are already apparent. Turn on `Option Strict` to keep yourself in check.

❏ Jagged arrays provide savings in memory and performance over multidimensional arrays.

❏ Use weak references whenever you have an object that you'd like to keep around as long as you can, but that you don't mind if the garbage collector decides it needs the memory for something else. This way you don't have to keep it open at the expense of other functionality, nor do you have to explicitly throw it away and create a new one every so often.

❏ Cache where possible anything that won't change too often, and which otherwise you would have to keep reading from disk.

❏ You can also cache the response for a Web Form request. Be careful when using the `VaryByParam` attribute if there are a lot of parameters with a lot of options, as you could end up caching far too much. You can also use `VaryByCustom` when you want to vary the cache based on something that isn't a parameter.

❏ Use fragment caching to speed up the common elements in your application, such as menus and navigation bars, by creating user controls and caching those. `VaryByControl` will vary the cache based on the value of the web server controls in the user control.

❏ Do not access user controls programmatically with a cache directive. If the control is found in the cache, the runtime will not instantiate the user control, so you won't be able to access it and an exception will be generated.

❏ Use ILDASM to look into the IL code when you want to know where the compiler is implicitly boxing, as well as other secrets.

❑ When using interop, try to minimize the number of transitions into unmanaged code. Port the most suitable COM components into managed code first, namely those that require the least number of accesses to operate.

❑ Be especially careful with COM components that use the single threaded apartment model. If you have to use them, AspCompat="true" in the @Page directive will force the page to execute on an STA thread.

Try to think of performance implications during implementation. As we learned in the last chapter, a good design is essential for good performance. The idea that we want you to take from this chapter is how it is easier to avoid performance problems when you first write code than it is to test a system and track down bottlenecks.

As a developer, you certainly have deadlines to meet. Make sure you get the biggest return for your investment when optimizing code. Caching is the best way to improve the performance of an ASP.NET application, while you apply the other techniques in this chapter to the heavily used areas of your site. With .NET, don't feel you need to rely on tricky code and magic – keep good principles in mind and use the features of the framework.

5

Developing for Data Performance

Dynamic web applications use a variety of data sources, like relational databases, XML data sources, or simply text input from a user. Retrieving, processing, and presenting this data efficiently is absolutely essential to good performance and scalability. As we said in the last chapter – work with the framework to achieve what you need instead of trying to reinvent the wheel. Starting an application from a good design and using the techniques favored by the .NET Framework will let you satisfy the scalability requirements of your application in less time and with less work. Knowing what the framework has to offer is a considerable part of the battle.

In this chapter we will examine what the .NET Framework has to offer in terms of data access, manipulation, and presentation. Over the course of the chapter we will cover the following topics:

- ❑ Choosing between a data reader and a `DataSet`.
- ❑ Working with `DataSet` schemas and a typed `DataSet`.
- ❑ Effective database queries
- ❑ Database tuning for performance
- ❑ Data binding optimizations
- ❑ Working with strings
- ❑ Working with XML

Throughout the chapter we will also present some timing information for different data access techniques. Be aware that the numbers given during testing in this chapter are not the same kinds of numbers you might see during a heavy load of concurrent users. Although the numbers here are a good rule of thumb, you need to use the testing techniques covered in later chapters to truly uncover the best approach for your application. Our first section will delve into the two workhorses of ADO.NET: the DataSet and data readers.

The Data Reader and the DataSet

In ADO.NET, when you query a database for records, you'll be retrieving the records into either a data reader or a DataSet. Both of these classes work with the .NET managed data providers to expose data to your application, and of course vary widely in the features they offer.

Data Readers

The data reader classes in .NET offer the fastest way to retrieve records with the least amount of overhead. When possible, always use a data reader for the best performance and scalability. As shown in the table below, the specific reader you will use depends on the provider you choose:

.NET Data Provider	Description	Namespace	DataReader class
SQL Server .Net Data Provider	For Microsoft SQL Server 7.0 and higher	System.Data.SqlClient	SqlDataReader
OLE DB .Net Data Provider	For any data source exposed through OLE DB	System.Data.OleDb	OleDbDataReader
ODBC .Net Data Provider (*)	For any data source exposed through ODBC	Microsoft.Data.Odbc	OdbcDataReader
Oracle .NET Data Provider (*)	For Oracle 8i (8.1.7) or later	System.Data.OracleClient	OracleDataReader

* – Both the ODBC .NET and Oracle .NET data providers are available as a download from http://msdn.microsoft.com/vstudio/downloads/vsnetupdates.asp.

The data reader classes give you read-only data with forward-only navigation. We sometimes call these the "fire hose" classes because they move a stream of data quickly and in only one direction. The data is non-buffered, meaning that even if a query returns a huge number of records there is still only one record in the memory of the data reader at a time. When working with large amount of data, the data reader remains highly scalable.

There is one caveat with the data reader classes: you must use the Close method on data reader objects as soon as you are finished with them. The high-performance mode of the data reader requires a dedicated connection to the server – you cannot use the connection to execute additional commands or for any other purpose while the data reader is open. Calling Close will free the connection for other work. If you do not call Close and depend on the garbage collector to clean up for you, the connection remains busy for much longer than is needed – limiting scalability.

One technique to ensure you always clean up properly is to use a Try...Catch block with a Finally clause. As shown below from the source of WebForm1.aspx.vb, this syntax ensures you call Close even when an exception occurs.

```
Private Sub Page_Load(ByVal sender As System.Object, _
        ByVal e As System.EventArgs) _
        Handles MyBase.Load

   If Not IsPostBack Then

      ' open a connection to local sql server's northwind database
      Dim sqlConnection As New SqlConnection()
      sqlConnection.ConnectionString = _
        "User ID=sa;Initial Catalog=Northwind;"
      sqlConnection.Open()

      Dim sqlCommand As New SqlCommand()
      sqlCommand.CommandText = "SELECT ProductName FROM Products"
      sqlCommand.Connection = sqlConnection

      Dim sqlReader As SqlDataReader
      Dim stringBuilder As New StringBuilder()

      Try
         sqlReader = sqlCommand.ExecuteReader()

         While (sqlReader.Read())
           stringBuilder.Append(CStr(sqlReader("PRoductName")))
           stringBuilder.Append("<br>")
         End While

      Catch exception As Exception
         stringBuilder.Append(exception.Message)
         stringBuilder.Append(exception.StackTrace)
      Finally
         If Not sqlReader Is Nothing Then
           sqlReader.Close()
         End If
         sqlConnection.Close()
      End Try

      literal.Text = stringBuilder.ToString()

   End If

End Sub
```

Referencing Columns

You can retrieve a column's value from the data reader by one of the following ways: specifying the column by name, specifying the column by ordinal number, or by using one of the typed methods with an ordinal number for the column. Using some test code, we are going to exaggerate the impact of these various methods. The first method shown below is `TimeReaderString`. This method retrieves column values by passing the column name as a string.

```
Private Sub TimeReaderString()
  Trace.Write("Begin TimeReaderString")

  Dim sqlDataReader As SqlDataReader

  Try
    sqlDataReader = sqlCommand.ExecuteReader()
    While (sqlDataReader.Read())
      Dim i As Integer
      For i = 0 To ITERATIONS
        productName = CStr(sqlDataReader("ProductName"))
        productId = CInt(sqlDataReader("ProductID"))
        discontinued = CBool(sqlDataReader("Discontinued"))
      Next
    End While
  Finally
    If Not sqlDataReader Is Nothing Then
      sqlDataReader.Close()
    End If
  End Try

  Trace.Write("End TimeReaderString")
End Sub
```

Passing the column name as a string forces the data reader to search among the columns of the current row to find the column with the specified name. The search is case-sensitive, but if the search fails a case-insensitive search for the column begins.

Instead of creating overhead by searching with each column access, the second method (`TestReaderOrdinal`) specifies the value to retrieve using the column ordinal. The three lines inside of the `For` loop become the following:

```
productName = CStr(sqlDataReader(0))
productId = CInt(sqlDataReader(1))
discontinued = CBool(sqlDataReader(2))
```

There is still one more piece of overhead we can remove from each statement. The data reader returns the column value as an object reference – even if the native storage format for the column is an integer and we assign the return value to an integer (as is the case with the product ID). You can eliminate these extra type conversions using the typed accessor methods of the data readers. Our last method (`TimeReaderOrdinalTyped`) replaces the three lines shown above with the following:

```
productName = sqlDataReader.GetString(0)
productId = sqlDataReader.GetInt32(1)
discontinued = sqlDataReader.GetBoolean(2)
```

Each improvement we have made couples the code more tightly with the database schema and SQL commands, meaning there is a better chance of breaking the application when the schema or SQL changes. Building a good code-generating tool can help offset this tradeoff by using schema information from the database to create classes for you automatically.

With the number of iterations for the loop set to 100, we obtain the following trace results. Notice how referencing columns by name instead of ordinal is relatively expensive, but this also depends on the number of columns in the reader and how often you are accessing them.

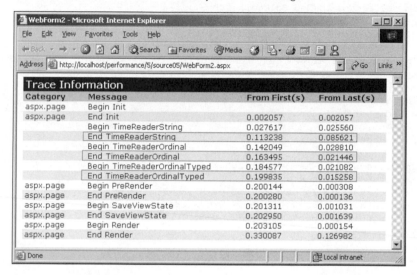

When To Choose A Data Reader

As long as you are not performing an extended amount of processing on the resultset, the data reader is the best choice for performance. Keeping a connection tied up while you perform heavy processing on the data reader is not the best use of resources. Also, because of the dedicated connection, do not try to cache a data reader, or return a data reader as the result of a Web Service call. There are no updates possible with a data reader, nor can you know how many records are available in the object until you've looped through the entire set. To perform any of these tasks you'll need to use the most flexible ADO.NET data container: the DataSet.

The DataSet

The DataSet appears as an in-memory copy of a relational database. This DataSet may contain tables, and the tables may maintain relationships between themselves to expose a hierarchical object model of tables, rows, and columns. In addition, the DataSet may even contain constraints. The real flexibility in a DataSet comes from the ability to read and write XML, and the ability to keep a relational data view in synch with a hierarchical XML view of the same DataSet. If we were to rewrite our first example Web Form with a DataSet, the results might be similar to the following listing from WebForm3.aspx.

```
Private Sub Page_Load(ByVal sender As System.Object, _
        ByVal e As System.EventArgs) _
        Handles MyBase.Load
```

```
If Not IsPostBack Then

    ' open a connection to local sql server's northwind database
    Dim sqlConnection As New SqlConnection()
    sqlConnection.ConnectionString = _
    "User ID=sa;Initial Catalog=Northwind;"
    sqlConnection.Open()

    Dim sqlCommand As New SqlCommand()
    sqlCommand.CommandText = "SELECT ProductName FROM Products"
    sqlCommand.Connection = sqlConnection

    Dim dataAdaptor As New SqlDataAdapter()
    dataAdaptor.SelectCommand = sqlCommand

    Dim dataSet As New DataSet()
    dataAdaptor.Fill(dataSet)

    sqlConnection.Close()

    Dim stringbuilder As New StringBuilder()
    Dim dataRow As DataRow
    For Each dataRow In dataSet.Tables(0).Rows
      stringbuilder.Append(dataRow("ProductName"))
      stringbuilder.Append("<br>")
    Next

    literal1.Text = stringbuilder.ToString()

End If

End Sub
```

Notice how once we have filled the DataSet, there is no longer a need for a database connection. You can work with a set of tables and rows while disconnected from the data source. We can move randomly through the rows to print results, or modify, delete, and insert rows. You can load data from heterogeneous sources into the same DataSet, and then persist the entire object into an XML file for e-mail. All of these features make the DataSet an incredibly flexible alternative to the data reader classes. Just remember the DataSet will require more overhead than the reader classes, and all the rows you retrieve are kept in memory, so be extremely careful with the size of your result sets.

In the example above we are retrieving data values for each column by specifying column names. As we discussed earlier, we can improve performance using ordinals and type-safe methods to retrieve values. With a DataSet, strong typing takes an entirely new turn – the typed DataSet.

The Typed DataSet

Typed DataSet classes derive from the DataSet class to provide strongly typed properties, events, and methods for the underlying data, thereby allowing you to access columns, not by passing the column name by string, but by invoking a property with the name of the column. Not only is strong typing better for performance, you also have increased readability, less risk of type mismatch errors during runtime, and help from the IDE's IntelliSense features. If you do not have schema information available for your data source, however, there is no alternative but to use an un-typed DataSet.

Creating a Typed DataSet

Since there are a number of ways to create a typed DataSet, we will quickly walk through how to create one for our next experiment. The first step is to right-click on the project in the Solution Explorer, select Add Item from the context menu, then select DataSet from the list of templates. Give the item a name of ProductDataSet.xsd and click Open. This sequence of commands should bring us to the XML schema designer.

A typed DataSet is built from an XML schema. If you already have an XML schema file you can generate a typed DataSet using the XML Schema Definition Tool (XSD.EXE) from the command line. In the schema designer you can drag and drop XML schema components from the Toolbox, as well as database elements from the Server Explorer window.

For this example, we will open a connection to the SQL Server Northwind database in the Server Explorer, and drag the Products table onto the schema designer window. Since we do not need all the columns for our query we will delete all but the ProductId, ProductName, and Discontinued columns by highlighting the element in the schema designer and pressing the *Delete* key. The schema designer should look like the following screenshot:

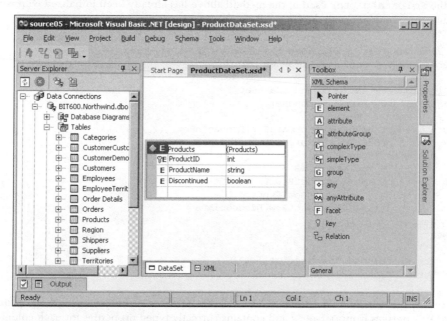

With the schema complete we need only close the designer, and the IDE will generate a new DataSet-derived class and place the source in ProductDataSet.vb. To see the generated code, click the Show All files toolbar button in the Solution Explorer pane and expand the ProductDataSet.xsd node. Underneath this node, you should find the ProductDataSet.vb file. The name of the DataSet derived class should match the name of the schema file, namely ProductDataSet.

Putting The Typed DataSet To Work

In WebForm4.aspx, we will perform an experiment similar to our last experiment with data readers. Firstly, let's use an un-typed DataSet to retrieve product information.

```
Private Sub TestDataSet()
  Trace.Write("Begin TestDataSet")

  Dim dataSet As New DataSet()
  sqlDataAdapter.Fill(dataSet)

  Dim dataRow As DataRow
  For Each dataRow In dataSet.Tables(0).Rows
    Dim i As Integer
    For i = 0 To ITERATIONS
      productName = CStr(dataRow("ProductName"))
      productId = CInt(dataRow("ProductId"))
      discontinued = CBool(dataRow("Discontinued"))
    Next
  Next
  Trace.Write("End TestDataSet")
End Sub
```

Notice the `SqlDataAdapter` used in the method above has already been initialized with a command and connection. In the next method we will use the typed `DataSet` we created.

```
Private Sub TestTypedDataSet()
  Trace.Write("Begin TestTYpedDataSet")

  Dim products As New ProductDataSet()
  sqlDataAdapter.Fill(products)

  Dim productRow As ProductDataSet.ProductsRow
  For Each productRow In products.Products
    Dim i As Integer
    For i = 0 To ITERATIONS
      productName = productRow.ProductName
      productId = productRow.ProductID
      discontinued = productRow.Discontinued
    Next
  Next

  Trace.Write("End TestTypedDataSet")
End Sub
```

Notice that in this version of the function we can use a `ProductRow` object instead of a plain `DataRow`. `ProductRow` derives from `DataRow` and contains correctly typed properties for each column of the row. The code becomes much easier to read and write, and by enabling tracing mode in our ASPX page directive we can also see the typed `DataSet` has better performance for our test.

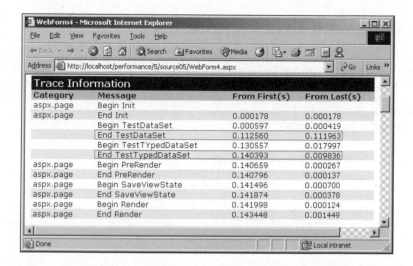

Choosing Between DataSets and Data Readers

Choosing between these data access classes is basically a choice between features. Even though the data reader classes have the absolute best performance and scalability characteristics, there are some tasks you cannot complete with a forward-only, read-only data source. Also remember that the readers require a dedicated connection. If you are going to perform extensive calculations or blocking operations with an open data reader, you may well be limiting your throughput.

When used in the right situation, a DataSet can also help ASP.NET performance by avoiding return trips to the database. Once you have filled the DataSet with the results of an expensive query, you can store the results in the Cache or Session objects, for instance. Consider loading your static lookup tables in a DataSet and storing a reference into the Application object. You'll never have to requery the database to look up simple values. One caveat with a DataSet, as mentioned earlier, is the memory required for queries with a large number of records. Memory is an important resource to keep available in server applications.

Effective Queries

Let's back up one step to the point where you are actually writing your queries. First of all, you might be wondering about the best way to handle small queries, such as queries returning one value (like a sum of all sales), or queries performing data modifications and returning no results. We will give an example of each of these queries in the next section. We will also show how to group together statements and avoid network trips to the database server, as well as some of the classes to avoid in high-performance database applications. We hinted at the need to use effective queries back in Chapter 2 – now we're going to actually see how we do this.

ExecuteScalar and ExecuteNonQuery

The ADO.NET command classes, such as `SqlCommand` for the SQL Server managed provider, offer two methods to execute queries without result sets. `ExecuteScalar` is the method to use when you are looking for a single return value from your query. For example, in `Webform5.aspx` below we have a button to click and retrieve the number of records in the `Shippers` table of the `Northwind` database. We retrieve this single result by performing a query with the `ExecuteScalar` method, as shown below, in the event handler for the button.

```
Private Sub CountButton_Click(ByVal sender As System.Object, _
            ByVal e As System.EventArgs) _
            Handles CountButton.Click

    Dim sqlConnection As New SqlConnection()
    sqlConnection.ConnectionString = "User ID=sa;Initial Catalog=Northwind;"
    sqlConnection.Open()

    Dim sqlCommand As New SqlCommand()
    sqlCommand.Connection = sqlConnection

    sqlCommand.CommandText = "SELECT COUNT(*) FROM Shippers"

    Dim count As Integer
    count = CInt(sqlCommand.ExecuteScalar())

    CountLabel.Text = String.Format("There are {0} shipper records", count)

End Sub
```

The behavior of `ExecuteScalar` is such that even if the query returns multiple rows or multiple columns, the method only gives you the value from the first column of the first row. This method is lightweight and requires less code when you simply need a single value.

Likewise, use `ExecuteNonQuery` when you do not need any results, although the method will return the number of rows affected for `INSERT`, `DELETE`, and `UPDATE` statements. In another excerpt from `WebForm5.aspx` we have two `TextBox` controls and a `Button` for adding a new shipper to the database. Shown below is the event handler for the click event. We use the `ExecuteNonQuery` method to send the `INSERT` statement to the database:

```
Private Sub InsertButton_Click(ByVal sender As System.Object, _
            ByVal e As System.EventArgs) _
            Handles InsertButton.Click

    Dim sqlConnection As New SqlConnection()
    sqlConnection.ConnectionString = "User ID=sa;Initial Catalog=Northwind;"
    sqlConnection.Open()

    Dim sqlCommand As New SqlCommand()
    sqlCommand.Connection = sqlConnection

    sqlCommand.CommandText = "INSERT INTO Shippers(CompanyName, Phone)" _
            + "VALUES(@CompanyName, @Phone)"
```

```
sqlCommand.Parameters.Add("@CompanyName", CompanyName.Text)
sqlCommand.Parameters.Add("@Phone", Phone.Text)

sqlCommand.ExecuteNonQuery()

CompanyName.Text = String.Empty
Phone.Text = String.Empty

End Sub
```

Parameterized Queries

The code sample above uses a parameterized query with Microsoft SQL Server. The exact syntax needed will vary from database to database (specify parameters with a question mark when using the OLE DB provider). Consider an alternative way to build this INSERT statement:

```
Dim sql As String
sql = "INSERT INTO Shippers(CompanyName, Phone) " _
    + "VALUES ('" + CompanyName.Text + "', '" + Phone.Text + "') "
```

In this version, the SQL statement is harder to read and maintain. It also poses a security risk, as concatenating user input with your SQL command runs the risk of a SQL injection attack. Finally, this version will cause most database engines to work a little harder. The database engine needs to compile and optimize an execution plan for each query you send. Compilation and optimization are sometimes expensive for a database to perform, so once the database generates an execution plan, it often will attempt to cache the plan and avoid recompiling when you issue the same query. In many database engines, however, the queries have to match exactly. The first two ad hoc queries below could not share the same execution plan and would require separate compilations, whereas the third query, when satisfied with a parameter in the command object, could compile once and be reused regardless of the ShipperID value.

```
SELECT CompanyName FROM Shippers WHERE ShipperID=1
SELECT CompanyName FROM Shippers WHERE ShipperID=2

SELECT CompanyName FROM Shippers WHERE ShipperID=@ShipperID
```

By using parameter markers instead of actual data values you allow the database to compile and cache your queries effectively. SQL Server 2000 has the ability to auto-parameterize simple queries, but does so very conservatively. Stored procedures offer many of these same benefits, and we will cover them in more detail later in the chapter.

Avoiding Round Trips

Making a trip across the network often requires more time than the time required to execute and process a simple query.

Whenever you can, try to save a trip over the wire by caching data locally or using different logic in your application code, for example to make one trip instead of two.

179

In ADO.NET, it is easy to group together statements into the same command and retrieve multiple results from a single trip to the database.

In `WebForm6.aspx`, we have a form to display both product names and shipper names. Firstly, we will create a command object and assign a command with two queries:

```
sqlCommand.CommandText = "SELECT ProductName FROM Products;" _
              + "SELECT CompanyName FROM Shippers"
```

If we are using a `SqlDataReader`, we can loop through the product names until the `Read` method of the `SqlDataReader` returns `False`; this is the same logic we used earlier in the chapter. Once the product name loop is finished, we can jump to the company names with the `NextResult` method. `NextResult` will return `False` if no more result sets exist, otherwise, we can now loop through the shippers until `Read` again returns `False`.

With a `DataSet` class, the data adapter places each result set into a new `DataTable` in the `Tables` collection. The first result set will be in `Tables(0)`, the second result set in `Tables(1)`, and so on. You can also use the `TableMapping` property of the `SqlDataAdapter` to give specific names to each table.

In the code from `WebForm6.aspx.vb` shown below, we use the same query shown above to fill a `DataSet`, then bind each result set to a Web Form's `DataGrid` control.

```
Private Sub ShowByDataSet()
   Dim sqlConnection As New SqlConnection()
   sqlConnection.ConnectionString = "User ID=sa;Initial Catalog=Northwind;"
   sqlConnection.Open()

   Dim sqlCommand As New SqlCommand()
   sqlCommand.Connection = sqlConnection

   sqlCommand.CommandText = "SELECT TOP 3 ProductName FROM Products;" _
                + "SELECT CompanyName FROM Shippers"

   Dim dataAdapter As New SqlDataAdapter(sqlCommand)
   Dim dataSet As New DataSet()

   dataAdapter.Fill(dataSet)

   ProductsGrid.DataSource = dataSet.Tables(0)
   ProductsGrid.DataBind()
   ShippersGrid.DataSource = dataSet.Tables(1)
   ShippersGrid.DataBind()

   sqlConnection.Close()
End Sub
```

Auto-Generated Commands

The .NET managed providers offer command builder classes (`SqlCommandBuilder`, `OleDbCommandBuilder`) to automatically generate SQL statements at run time. Given a SELECT query, the command builders can generate corresponding INSERT, UPDATE, and DELETE queries for single-table queries. The builders work closely with the data adapter classes and the `DataSet` to provide an easy way to reconcile changes made to the `DataSet` with the database.

In `WebForm7.aspx` below, we demonstrate these capabilities by letting the user enter a query, and then generate `INSERT`, `UPDATE`, and `DELETE` commands using a command builder. After the user enters a query and clicks a button, the following code is executed:

```
Private Sub BuildButton_Click(ByVal sender As System.Object, _
              ByVal e As System.EventArgs) _
              Handles BuildButton.Click
   Dim sqlConnection As New SqlConnection()
   sqlConnection.ConnectionString = "User ID=sa;Initial Catalog=Northwind;"
   sqlConnection.Open()

   Dim sqlCommand As New SqlCommand()
   sqlCommand.Connection = sqlConnection
   sqlCommand.CommandText = QueryTextBox.Text

   Dim sqlAdapter As New SqlDataAdapter(sqlCommand)

   Dim commandBuilder As New SqlCommandBuilder(sqlAdapter)

   Dim stringBuilder As New StringBuilder()

   stringBuilder.Append(String.Format("<b>INSERT COMMAND=</b>{0}<br><br>", _
         commandBuilder.GetInsertCommand.CommandText))
   stringBuilder.Append(String.Format("<b>DELETE COMMAND=</b>{0}<br><br>", _
         commandBuilder.GetDeleteCommand.CommandText))
   stringBuilder.Append(String.Format("<b>UPDATE COMMAND=</b>{0}<br><br>", _
         commandBuilder.GetUpdateCommand.CommandText))

   CommandText.Text = stringBuilder.ToString()

End Sub
```

If we select all columns from the `Shippers` table, we should see the following queries generated:

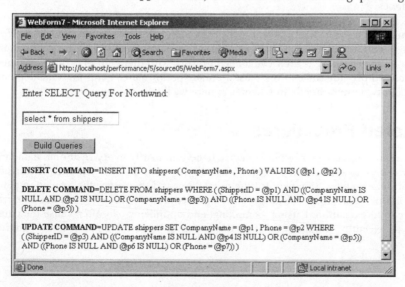

`SqlCommandBuilder` is an extremely useful class to have when you are prototyping or working with a dynamic application where the queries are not known until run time. In these situations the class will save you from writing code. Unfortunately, less work for you is more work for the runtime. In order to build these statements, the command builder requires a trip to the database to retrieve meta-information about the columns, types, and keys in a database table. In SQL Server, the command builder uses `SET FMTONLY ON` and executes the `SELECT` statement to retrieve schema information only and no result set. This information must be retrieved and processed before the command is built.

By examining the generated queries, you can see the command builders favor optimistic concurrency, which is the best choice for a web application, but perhaps not what you intended. With optimistic concurrency there are no locks held on a row when it is read, instead, when updating or deleting the row the query tries to ensure another user has not made changes to the row since the last read. Optimistic concurrency requires the runtime to pass additional parameters containing the original values of the record, and adds additional complexity to the `WHERE` clauses.

If you build your SQL statements at design time, optimistic concurrency checks are an option you can forego. Certainly, there are situations where you won't need the overhead.

> **In general, any time you can create less work for the runtime and the database, your performance will increase, so avoid the command builder classes for production applications.**

Database Performance

In this section we will examine two effective database mechanisms for enhancing database performance:

❑   Stored procedures

❑   Indexes

Although there are a wide variety of techniques and strategies to improve database performance, we highlight these two for special reasons. Stored procedures, when used, will form the interface to the database for your code, and as such you'll need to work with them closely. We cover indexes in detail, since indexes can provide some of the most dramatic performance gains for a database query. We discussed these two topics briefly in Chapter 2; here we'll take a deeper look at them.

Using Stored Procedures

Stored procedures will give you a performance benefit in nearly every relational database system. Typically, when your application executes a stored procedure for the first time, the database will parse, compile, optimize an execution plan for the procedure, and then store the execution plan in a cache before execution. Subsequent calls to the stored procedure will pull an execution plan from the cache and go directly to execution. Parsing, compiling, and optimizing can often cause the database just as much work as executing the query itself, so the savings in processing time can be significant.

Although you can achieve the same caching effect with parameterized queries, stored procedures offer other performance benefits as well. You can often save on the number of round trips and network traffic to the database. For example, you might need to run a simple query to retrieve a result and perform a second query based on the value of the first result. Sending both of these queries from your application will result in two round trips, while encapsulating the same logic in a stored procedure requires only a single trip. Let's take a look at another example using XML and SQL Server 2000.

Batch Inserts With OpenXML

Consider a situation where you need to insert multiple records into a table. This generally involves sending multiple INSERT statements to the database, or making multiple calls to a stored procedure. These round trips can often be as expensive as the record insertion. When your underlying database has strong XML support, consider sending an XML document to the database to insert the records with just one network trip.

In WebForm8.aspx we build an XML document for the Northwind Shippers table using a DataSet. Our first step is to build a DataTable with a schema matching the Shippers table. In production code, we would want to avoid a trip to the database, but for this example we use the FillSchema method of the SqlDataAdapter to build a DataTable matching the Shippers schema. As shown in the code excerpt below, we add new rows to the table and use a DataSet to generate the resulting XML for us. We then store the XML in a Web Form's Literal control to display to the user.

```
Private Sub Page_Load(ByVal sender As System.Object, _
            ByVal e As System.EventArgs) _
            Handles MyBase.Load

  If Not IsPostBack Then

    Dim sqlConnection As New SqlConnection()
    sqlConnection.ConnectionString = _
        "User ID=sa;Initial Catalog=Northwind;"
    sqlConnection.Open()

    Dim sqlCommand As New SqlCommand()
    sqlCommand.Connection = sqlConnection
    sqlCommand.CommandText = "SELECT * FROM Shippers"

    Dim sqlDataAdapter As New SqlDataAdapter()
    sqlDataAdapter.SelectCommand = sqlCommand

    Dim dataTable As New DataTable("Shippers")
    sqlDataAdapter.FillSchema(dataTable, SchemaType.Mapped)

    Dim dataRow As DataRow
    dataRow = dataTable.NewRow()
    dataRow("CompanyName") = "Fly By Night"
    dataRow("Phone") = "3015551212"
    dataTable.Rows.Add(dataRow)

    dataRow = dataTable.NewRow()
    dataRow("CompanyName") = "ByTor Shipping"
    dataRow("Phone") = "7175551212"
    dataTable.Rows.Add(dataRow)
```

```
      Dim dataSet As New DataSet()
      dataSet.Tables.Add(dataTable)
      ShippersXml.Text = Server.HtmlEncode(dataSet.GetXml())

   End If
End Sub
```

The interesting action happens when a user clicks on the insert button on the form. In the event handler below, we retrieve the XML from the `Literal` control and pass the text to a SQL Server stored procedure as a parameter.

```
Private Sub InsertButton_Click(ByVal sender As System.Object, _
               ByVal e As System.EventArgs) _
               Handles InsertButton.Click

   Dim sqlConnection As New SqlConnection()
   sqlConnection.ConnectionString = "User ID=sa;Initial Catalog=Northwind;"
   sqlConnection.Open()

   Dim sqlCommand As New SqlCommand()
   sqlCommand.Connection = sqlConnection
   sqlCommand.CommandType = CommandType.StoredProcedure
   sqlCommand.CommandText = "InsertShippersByXml"
   sqlCommand.Parameters.Add("@ShipperXml", _
                        Server.HtmlDecode(ShippersXml.Text))

   sqlCommand.ExecuteNonQuery()

End Sub
```

The code for `InsertShippersByXml` is shown next. The `sp_xml_preparedocument` stored procedure will parse the text and return a handle (`@hDocument`) to a parsed XML document. With this handle we can use `OPENXML` to return a row set view of information from the XML. The second parameter to `OPENXML` is an `XPATH` pattern to extract the information as rows, in this case the nodes inside of the Shippers elements. The `WITH` clause tells `OPENXML` to use the `Shippers` table as the schema for column mapping. The results of `OPENXML` are given to an `INSERT` statement, and on success we will have two rows inserted with one stored procedure call. At the end of this method, we free up the memory used to store the document with `sp_xml_removedocument`.

```
CREATE PROCEDURE dbo.InsertShippersByXml
   (@ShipperXml ntext)
AS
  DECLARE @hDocument int

  EXEC sp_xml_preparedocument @hDocument OUTPUT, @ShipperXml

  INSERT INTO Shippers
  SELECT *
  FROM OPENXML(@hDocument, '//Shippers',2)
  WITH Shippers

  EXEC sp_xml_removedocument @hDocument

RETURN
```

Many of today's databases are providing more and more XML support. You'll need to evaluate how well your specific database supports XML, both in terms of features and performance. Processing large amounts of XML requires processing power and healthy amounts of memory, and may not be a suitable task to perform on your database server. Bulk loading of data is one area to consider using XML features of your database.

Indexes

Effective indexes are one of the best ways to improve performance in a database application. Without an index, a database engine is like a reader trying to find the word *performance* in this book by examining each page. By using the index in the back of the book, a reader can complete the task in a much shorter time. In database terms, a **table scan** happens when there is no index available to help a query. In a table scan the database examines every row in the table to satisfy the query results. Table scans are sometimes unavoidable, but on extremely large tables they will have an obvious toll on performance.

One of the most important jobs for the database is finding the best index to use when generating an execution plan. Most major databases ship with tools to show you execution plans for a query and help in optimizing and tuning indexes. This section will give you several good rules of thumb to apply when creating and modifying indexes for your database. First, let's cover the scenarios where indexes help performance, and when indexes can hurt performance.

Useful Index Queries

Just like the reader searching for a word in a book, an index helps when you are looking for a specific record or set of records with a WHERE clause. This includes queries looking for a range of values, queries designed to match a specific value, and queries performing a join on two tables. For example, both of the queries against the Northwind database below will benefit from an index on the UnitPrice column:

```
DELETE FROM Products WHERE UnitPrice = 1

SELECT * FROM PRODUCTS
WHERE UnitPrice BETWEEN 14 AND 16
```

Since index entries are stored in sorted order, indexes also help when processing ORDER BY clauses. Without an index the database has to load the records and sort them during execution. An index on UnitPrice will allow the database to process the following query by simply scanning the index and fetching rows as they are referenced. To order the records in descending order, the database can simply scan the index in reverse.

```
SELECT * FROM Products ORDER BY UnitPrice ASC
```

Grouping records with a GROUP BY clause will often require sorting, so a UnitPrice index will also help the following query to count the number of products at each price:

```
SELECT Count(*), UnitPrice FROM Products
GROUP BY UnitPrice
```

By retrieving the records in sorted order through the UnitPrice index, the database sees matching prices appear in consecutive index entries, and can easily keep a count of products at each price. Indexes are also useful for maintaining unique values in a column, since the database can easily search the index to see if an incoming value already exists. Primary keys are always indexed for this reason.

Index Drawbacks

Indexes are a performance drag when the time comes to modify records, and are a particular drag for INSERT statements. Any time a query modifies the data in a table, the indexes on the data must change also. Achieving the right number of indexes will require testing and monitoring of your database to see where the best balance lies. Static systems, where databases are used heavily for reporting, can afford more indexes to support the read-only queries. A database with a heavy number of transactions to modify data will need fewer indexes to allow for higher throughput.

Indexes also use disk space. The exact size will depend on the number of records in the table as well as the number and size of the columns in the index. Generally, this is not a major concern as disk space is inexpensive and is easy to trade for better performance.

Building The Best Index

There are a number of guidelines to building the most effective indexes for your application. From the columns you select to the data values inside them, consider the following points when selecting the indexes for your tables.

Short Keys

Keeping index keys short is beneficial for two reasons. First, database work is inherently disk-intensive. Larger index keys will cause the database to perform more disk reads, which limits throughput. Secondly, since index entries are often involved in comparisons, smaller entries are easier to compare. A single integer column makes the absolute best index key because an integer is small and easy for the database to compare. Character strings, on the other hand, require a character-by-character comparison.

Distinct Keys

The most effective indexes are the indexes with a small percentage of duplicated values. As an analogy, think of a phone book for a town where almost everyone has the last name of Smith. A phone book in this town is not very useful if sorted in order of last name, because you can only discount a small number of records when you are looking for a Smith.

An index with a high percentage of unique values is a **selective** index. Obviously, a unique index is highly selective since there are no duplicate entries. Many databases will track statistics about each index so they know how selective each index is. The database uses these statistics when generating an execution plan for a query.

Covering Queries

Indexes generally contain only the data values for the columns they index and a pointer back to the row with the rest of the data. This is similar to the index in a book: the index contains only the keyword and then a page reference you can turn to for the rest of the information. Generally, the database will have to follow pointers from an index back to a row to gather all the information required for a query. However, if the index contains all of the columns needed for a query, the database can save a disk read by not returning to the table for more information.

Take the index on UnitPrice we discussed earlier. The database could use just the index entries to satisfy the following query:

```
SELECT Count(*), UnitPrice FROM Products
GROUP BY UnitPrice
```

We call these types of queries **covered queries**, because all of the columns requested in the output are covered by a single index. For your most crucial queries, you might consider creating a covering index to give the query the best performance possible. Such an index would probably be a composite index (using more than one column), which appears to go against our first guideline of keeping index entries as short as possible. Obviously, this is another tradeoff you can only evaluate with performance testing and monitoring.

Clustered Indexes

Many databases have one special index per table where *all* of the data from a row exists in the index. SQL Server calls this index a **clustered index**. Instead of an index at the back of a book, a clustered index is closer in similarity to a phone book because each index entry contains all the information you need, there are no references to follow to pick up additional data values.

As a general rule of thumb, every non-trivial table should have a clustered index. If you only create one index for a table, make the index a clustered index. In SQL Server, creating a primary key will automatically create a clustered index (if none exists) using the primary key column as the index key. Clustered indexes are the most effective indexes (when used, they always cover a query), and in many databases systems will help the database efficiently manage the space required to store the table.

When choosing the column or columns for a clustered index, be careful to choose a column with static data. If you modify a record and change the value of a column in a clustered index, the database might need to move the index entry (to keep the entries in sorted order). Remember, index entries for a clustered index contain all of the column values, so moving an entry is comparable to executing a DELETE statement followed by an INSERT, which can obviously cause performance problems if done often. For this reason, clustered indexes are often found on primary or foreign key columns. Key values will rarely, if ever, change.

> *For more information on this and other SQL Server 2000 issues, refer to Professional SQL Server 2000 Programming, ISBN 1-861004-48-6, from Wrox Press.*

Database Providers And Connections

Before you begin writing your .NET application, or porting an application to .NET, you'll need to decide on how you will access your data sources. Choosing your data access provider and API will have an impact on the performance and scalability of your application.

Database Access Providers

If you are writing a new .NET application, there is no doubt you will want to use one of the .NET managed data providers. The OLE DB .NET data provider will allow you to access an amazing number of data sources, including Microsoft Jet databases, DB2, Oracle, SQL Server, Sybase, and any other data source with an OLE DB or ODBC interface.

You will always achieve better performance in .NET by using a provider specific to the data source you are using. These providers are generally more lightweight, use fewer software layers, and are better optimized for a specific database. For instance, you could use the OLE DB .NET data provider to access SQL Server. This provider will use OLE DB interfaces through COM interop for data access. On the other hand, the SQL Server .NET data provider communicates directly with SQL Server using SQL Server's tabular data stream (TDS) format. This efficient packet format will avoid OLE DB and ODBC layers by communicating with SQL Server's native API, and give a substantial performance improvement.

System.Data Interfaces

Fortunately, all of the managed providers for .NET have a core set of classes in common: `Command`, `Connection`, `DataAdapter`, and `DataReader`. If there is a possibility of changing your database vendor, you have a straightforward port to move from one provider to the next.

If you need to program generically while maintaining the performance benefits of a native provider, use the interfaces from the `System.Data` namespace. Instead of using a `SqlConnection` object directly, use a layer of software to create a `SqlConnection` and return an `IDbConnection` to work with. Likewise, `IDbCommand`, `IDbDataAdapter`, and `IDataReader` will provide interfaces for `Command`, `DataAdapter`, and `DataReader` classes respectively. This approach programs to an interface instead of an implementation, meaning we are loosely coupled to our actual data provider.

Porting ADO Code

If you already have a large data-driven application using ADO code, there are several tradeoffs to evaluate before migrating to ASP.NET. The good news is you can still use classic ADO connections and recordsets in .NET. In fact, there is an overloaded version of the `Fill` method on the `SqlDataAdapter` to populate a recordset. It is always a difficult decision to retire well-tested and working code, so this interoperability is a welcome option. The bad news is using ADO from .NET will keep many software layers between yourself and the data source, including the overhead of COM Interop we discussed in the last chapter.

If performance is a high priority for your application port, you'll want to immediately run some tests using ADO and .NET in combination. If you achieve the performance and scalability you require using this combination, the pressure to migrate immediately will not be as great. However, moving to a .NET managed provider, particularly a native provider such as the SQL Server .NET provider, will give you noticeable performance improvements.

Connection Pooling

Database connections are expensive to create and destroy – there are generally several round trips involved in connecting, authenticating, and validating an incoming connection request. Likewise, there are a number of data structures for the runtime to tear down and clean up when an application closes a connection. Constantly opening and closing connections to a database will severely limit scalability.

ADO.NET has a built-in solution to the problem: **connection pooling**. When an application requests a database connection, the runtime creates a connection pool. Requests for a connection will grab an open connection from the pool. When you invoke the `Close` method on a connection object, the runtime does not actually close the connection, but simply returns the connection to the pool where it will be available for future requests. After a period of inactivity, the runtime will close the connection.

Each provider will have a maximum and minimum pool size. If the pool size has reached the maximum size and no connections are free, the request for a connection will queue. You can control some of the pooling features with connection string parameters specific to the provider you are using. For example, with the SQL Server provider, you can control the minimum and maximum pool size by using the `Max Pool Size` and `Min Pool Size` parameters in your connection string.

Pooling Algorithms

In order to use connection pools effectively, you need to understand how connection pools revolve around three parameters: application domains, connection strings, and identities.

A connection pool serves a single application domain. There can be multiple application domains in a single process. For instance, the ASP.NET runtime executes in the ASP.NET worker process (`aspnet_wp.exe`). The runtime loads each ASP.NET application into the worker processes in a separate application domain. Application domains isolate applications and protect them from tampering with each other inadvertently. Connection pools are destroyed when the application domain unloads from memory.

Each ASP.NET application will use a connection pool dedicated to it's own application domain. There may actually be more than one connection pool for each application domain, because connection strings also affect how the runtime uses the pool. If the connection string for an open request does not match the connection string for an existing pool **exactly** (including case), the runtime creates a new pool for the connection. The following code would create two connection pools because of the difference in the initial catalog parameter:

```
Dim sqlConnection1 As New SqlConnection()
sqlConnection1.ConnectionString = "User ID=sa;Initial Catalog=Northwind;"
sqlConnection1.Open()

Dim sqlConnection2 As New SqlConnection()
sqlConnection2.ConnectionString = "User ID=sa;Initial Catalog=pubs;"
sqlConnection2.Open()
```

Furthermore, connection pooling also requires matching identities. If you change the `User ID` parameter between connections, the runtime will create a new pool because the connection string is different. Identity comes more into play when using trusted connections with the following connection string:

```
Dim sqlConnection1 As New SqlConnection()
sqlConnection1.ConnectionString = _
            "Integrated Security=SSPI;Initial Catalog=Northwind;"
sqlConnection1.Open()
```

This connection string, specific to SQL Server, instructs the client-side database software to establish a trusted connection using Microsoft's Security Support Provider Interface (SSPI). A trusted connection does not specify a user ID and password, but instead carries the current execution identity to the database for authentication. In the default ASP.NET setting, this is the identity of the ASP.NET worker process (`ASPNET` is the default account name). You can change this setting in the `<processModel>` section of `web.config`, and presumably you'll configure SQL Server to give the ASP.NET account connect privileges and authorization to the required databases.

This connection string can cause a problem if you configure an ASP.NET application to use impersonation. With impersonation, ASP.NET executes requests with the identity of the client. If your web site is configured using NTLM authentication, and 200 unique users log into the web site using their Windows account username and passwords, none of them will share connections from the same connection pool: the identities now all appear different. This behavior is primarily for security reasons. You would not want a regular user to grab a connection from a pool opened by an Administrator, as the regular user would then have privileges beyond what is expected.

Coding For Connection Pooling

Connection pooling is an extremely effective technique for performance and scalability, but you'll need to follow a few rules to gain the most advantage:

❑ Request a connection as late as possible – don't just open a connection on every page "in case you might need it later on". Connections are valuable resources, so you only want to take one if you are sure you will need it, and take it as close to when you actually need it as possible. Conversely, release the connection as soon as possible by calling Close. The runtime will not close the connection configured for pooling, only hold on to use it for another request. The best rule of thumb is to hold a connection for as short a time as possible.

❑ Make sure you leave all connections in a tidy state – make absolutely sure you have closed any transactions on the connection by committing or aborting work. You do not want to risk leaving any rows locked while a connection sits idly in a pool. Also, drop any temporary objects, such as temporary tables you may have created. Connection pooling is a feature of the client-side software – the database server knows nothing about a pool. The database will not be able to clean up when you are finished with a connection.

Data Binding Optimizations

Data binding is an important feature of .NET, and there are numerous options and features to take advantage of. You can bind any property of a control, such as Text, Color, and Width, to almost any type of data source, for instance relational data, XML data, or an ArrayList object.

One of the keys to performance in data binding is to simply limit the amount of data you retrieve and display. By displaying fewer records, you will cause less work for the database server, less work for the web server, and generate less network traffic. Large result sets are not just a drag on server and network resources, they can also overwhelm a user. Paging results into moderate sized groups of records will work to solve many of these problems.

DataGrid Binding

Let's look at an example of data binding a DataGrid using three different techniques to see the performance differences. In WebForm9.aspx, we have three grids on the form, and our Page_Load method looks like the following:

```
Private Sub Page_Load(ByVal sender As System.Object, _
            ByVal e As System.EventArgs) _
            Handles MyBase.Load
```

```
Dim sqlConnection As New SqlConnection()
sqlConnection.ConnectionString = _
    "User ID=sa;Initial Catalog=Northwind;"
sqlConnection.Open()

Dim sqlCommand As New SqlCommand()
sqlCommand.Connection = sqlConnection
sqlCommand.CommandText = "SELECT ProductName, QuantityPerUnit, " _
                + "UnitPrice, UnitsInStock " _
            + "FROM Products"

Dim sqlDataAdapter As New SqlDataAdapter()
sqlDataAdapter.SelectCommand = sqlCommand

Dim dataSet As New DataSet()
sqlDataAdapter.Fill(dataSet)

BindDataGrid1(dataSet)
BindDataGrid2(dataSet)
BindDataGrid3(dataSet)
sqlConnection.Close()
End Sub
```

In this code, we are going to place the results of a simple query into a `DataSet`, and bind the `DataSet` object to three different grids. The `BindDataGridX` methods to do this look like the following, each one is exactly the same except for binding to a grid and writing different messages to `Trace`.

```
Private Sub BindDataGrid1(ByVal dataSet As DataSet)
  Trace.Write("Begin BindDataGrid1")

  Dim i As Integer
  For i = 0 To ITERATIONS
    DataGrid1.DataSource = dataSet
    DataGrid1.DataBind()
  Next

  Trace.Write("End BindDataGrid1")
End Sub
```

We will place a call to `DataBind` inside a loop with a large number of iterations to examine different binding strategies, including auto-generated columns, template columns, and optimized data evaluation statements. The first grid (`DataGrid1`) is the simplest baseline case. This grid will auto-generate the columns during run time. The ASPX source code for this grid is shown below:

```
<asp:datagrid id="DataGrid1" runat="server"></asp:datagrid>
```

Unfortunately, not many applications can get away with auto-generated columns. We usually need to add specific headers or format the data to a specific format before display. With a `DataGrid`, the most flexible way to present information is through the use of template columns. A template column will give you the ultimate control in how your grid cells look, and how they format data through data binding expressions.

Data Binding Expressions

Our second `DataGrid` uses the following ASPX source full of template columns and data binding expressions to give the same results as our first grid.

```
<asp:datagrid id="DataGrid2" runat="server" AutoGenerateColumns="False">
  <Columns>
  <asp:TemplateColumn HeaderText="Product Name">
    <ItemTemplate>
  <%# DataBinder.Eval(Container.DataItem, "ProductName") %>
    </ItemTemplate>
  </asp:TemplateColumn>
  <asp:TemplateColumn HeaderText="Quantity / Unit">
    <ItemTemplate>
    <%# DataBinder.Eval(Container.DataItem, "QuantityPerUnit") %>
    </ItemTemplate>
  </asp:TemplateColumn>
  <asp:TemplateColumn HeaderText="Price / Unit">
    <ItemTemplate>
  <%# DataBinder.Eval(Container.DataItem, "UnitPrice") %>
    </ItemTemplate>
  </asp:TemplateColumn>
  <asp:TemplateColumn HeaderText="Stocked Units">
    <ItemTemplate>
    <%# DataBinder.Eval(Container.DataItem, "UnitsInStock") %>
    </ItemTemplate>
  </asp:TemplateColumn>
  </Columns>
</asp:datagrid>
```

In our template columns we are using a special expression format: the data binding expression. Inside of the `<%#` and `%>` delimiters we use the `DataBinder` class, which has a shared method named `Eval`. This method will examine the data item we are binding against (`Container.DataItem`) to find a value for `ProductName`. The runtime will invoke these data binding expressions in each column for every row in the data source.

Using `DataBinder.Eval` saves time when writing code because we do not need to worry about the source of our data – the source could be a `DataSet` or could be a data reader. Also, we do not need to worry about the type of object we extract – `Eval` will always convert the object to a string. Thus, `DataBinder.Eval` looks the same extracting `ProductName` (a string) as it does `UnitPrice` (a float).

`DataBinder.Eval` does a fair amount of work underneath the covers with late binding. As we learned in the last chapter, forcing the runtime to use reflection for late binding during execution is a drag on performance. Our template column version of the `DataGrid` is about twice as slow in binding as the first grid. Since we know all of the types involved, we can write a more efficient version of the grid, although there are other trade offs to consider that we will soon see.

The code for our third grid is shown as follows. This version gains back most, but not all, of the original grid's performance by removing some of the burden from the runtime.

```
<asp:datagrid id="Datagrid3" runat="server" AutoGenerateColumns="False">
  <Columns>
    <asp:TemplateColumn HeaderText="Product Name">
      <ItemTemplate>
        <%# CType(Container.DataItem, DataRowView)(0) %>
      </ItemTemplate>
    </asp:TemplateColumn>
    <asp:TemplateColumn HeaderText="Quantity / Unit">
      <ItemTemplate>
        <%# CType(Container.DataItem, DataRowView)(1) %>
      </ItemTemplate>
    </asp:TemplateColumn>
    <asp:TemplateColumn HeaderText="Price / Unit">
      <ItemTemplate>
        <%# CType(Container.DataItem, DataRowView)(2).ToString() %>
      </ItemTemplate>
    </asp:TemplateColumn>
    <asp:TemplateColumn HeaderText="Stocked Units">
      <ItemTemplate>
        <%# CType(Container.DataItem, DataRowView)(3).ToString() %>
      </ItemTemplate>
    </asp:TemplateColumn>
  </Columns>
</asp:datagrid>
```

Our first gain comes from removing Eval and converting the DataItem to a specific derived type. When we are binding with a DataSet, the DataItem is actually a DataRowView. If, instead, we were binding with a data reader, we would convert to an IDataRecord reference. We also reference columns by ordinal instead of column name – this is a performance tip we demonstrated earlier in the chapter. We could have used the following, more readable expression:

```
<%# CType(Container.DataItem, DataRowView)("ProductName") %>
```

Note, if the expression does not return a string, we need to manually convert the object to a string, as is the case with our numerical columns. If we were using a data reader instead of a DataSet, we could achieve the fastest binding to the ProductName column using the typed accessor for a string, as shown next:

```
<%# CType(Container.DataItem, IDataRecord).GetString(0) %>
```

The drawbacks to this approach need serious consideration. Firstly, by not using DataBinder.Eval we have made the application prone to breakage. If we switch to using a DataReader instead of a DataSet as the data source, and do not change our data binding expressions for DataGrid3, our application will fail during run time. Likewise, we could change the column order in our queries, or change the data types in our schema, and the application will throw a run-time error. You might only need to make these tradeoffs in the most critical pages of your application. The following trace results will give you a general idea of the relative costs.

Text Manipulation

Text manipulation always plays a major role in data-driven applications. Text is how you receive user input, and how you display information. The key to effective text manipulation is to remember that string objects are immutable. Any operation you perform to modify a string object will result in a new string object being created. Thus performance can become abysmal if you are using heavy amounts of concatenation to build a large string.

The solution for the problem is to forego the String class and use the StringBuilder class from the System.Text namespace. The StringBuilder object minimizes new memory allocations while automatically expanding to hold additional characters as you add them. If you have a general idea of how large a buffer you need, you can help StringBuilder performance by setting the capacity of the internal buffer through the constructor or the Capacity property.

In WebForm10.aspx we will test the performance of string concatenation using the String class versus the StringBuilder. In the page load method we will build a DataSet of product names from the SQL Server Northwind database and pass the DataSet to the following two methods:

```
Private Sub TestStringConcat(ByVal dataSet As DataSet)
  Trace.Write("Begin TestStringConcat")

  With Literal1
    Dim i As Integer
    For i = 0 To ITERATIONS
      Dim dataRow As DataRow
      For Each dataRow In dataSet.Tables(0).Rows
        .Text = String.Concat(.Text, dataRow(0).ToString())
      Next
    Next
  End With
```

```
    Trace.Write("End TestStringConcat")
  End Sub

  Private Sub TestStringBuilder(ByVal dataSet As DataSet)
    Trace.Write("Begin TestStringBuilder")

    Dim stringBuilder As New StringBuilder()

    Dim i As Integer
    For i = 0 To ITERATIONS
      Dim dataRow As DataRow
      For Each dataRow In dataSet.Tables(0).Rows
        stringBuilder.Append(dataRow(0))
      Next
    Next

    Literal2.Text = stringBuilder.ToString()

    Trace.Write("End TestStringBuilder")
  End Sub
```

As shown in the results below, the `StringBuilder` class has a huge performance advantage in this scenario. Every time we `Concat` a string in the first method, the method creates a new string object and copies all of the characters into the string. By reducing the number of string allocations and string copies, the `StringBuilder` version runs an incredible amount faster, about 500 times as fast in fact.

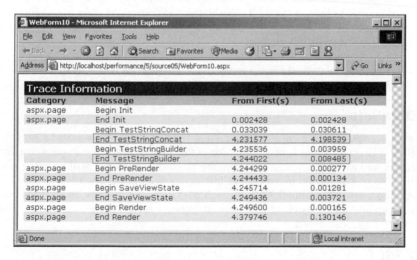

XML is also text-based and continues to be found in more and more applications. In the final section of this chapter we will examine performance tips for XML processing.

Performance and XML

If your application relies heavily on XML, there is good news – so does the .NET Framework; you can see XML just about everywhere. Configuration files are in XML format, a DataSet doubles as an XML document, and entire namespaces are devoted to XML classes and tools. Most of the work in achieving good performance with XML is in selecting the proper classes and methods to use in the appropriate circumstances.

Pull Model and the DOM

Similar to the choice between a data reader and a DataSet, the XmlTextReader and XmlDocument classes offer tradeoffs between performance and features. The XmlTextReader is a lightweight, read-only, and forward-only cursor (a fire hose cursor) for pulling information from an XML document. Particularly when you work with large XML documents, the stream model offered by an XmlTextReader will save considerable resources by moving through the document as you request to read each piece of content – this is known as the **pull model**, because you 'pull in' data when you need it.

Part of the performance gain with an XmlTextReader also happens because no schema or DTD validation occurs. If you want to stick with the lower memory overhead of a reader while performing validation, step up to the XmlValidatingReader class.

The XmlDocument is an in-memory tree representation of an XML document, allowing you to modify, add, and remove nodes. You have random access to information in the XmlDocument instance and can perform XPath queries to extract data. Obviously, the XmlDocument class has a larger memory footprint than the XmlTextReader when loading large documents. When possible, stick with the XmlTextReader for the best performance.

There are also a number of special classes in the .NET Framework to use in specific cases. These classes are outlined below:

XML and DataSets

If you are working with a single set of information as relational data (as in a DataSet) and hierarchically (as in an XmlDocument), then turn to the XmlDataDocument class. Instead of having both a DataSet and an XmlDocument around, the XmlDataDocument will keep the relational and hierarchical views of a DataSet in synch. For instance, you can add new rows to a DataTable inside the DataSet and view the modified XML through an XPath query of the XmlDataDocument. Likewise, you can add elements via the XmlDataDocument methods and see changes reflected in tables of the associated DataSet object.

XPath and XSLT

The .NET designers provided the XPathDocument class specifically for the best performance of XPath queries and XSLT processing. Use this class in combination with the XslTransform class to achieve the fastest XSLT transformations.

The XmlDocument, XPathDocument, and XmlDataDocument classes all implement the IXPathNavigable interface, and provide a CreateNavigator method to return an instance of the XPathNavigator class. One of the advantages to using XPathNavigator on a document is the ability to pass an XPath expression to the Compile method. If you are going to use an XPath expression repeatedly, use Compile with the expression and cache the resulting XPathExpression instance to pass into the Select, Evaluate, and Matches methods.

Schema Caching

Schema files are generally loaded from a file or URL. If you are using the same schema file to validate multiple XML documents, turn to the XmlSchemaCollection class to keep the schemas cached in memory: instead of reloading on every validation. Add the XmlSchemaCollection instance to the Schemas property of the XmlValidatingReader and improve performance.

Summary

During the course of this chapter we have covered a number of techniques to improve the performance and scalability of a data-driven application. Let's recap on them here:

❑ Data readers have less performance overhead, so choose them where your situation allows.

❑ Data readers are still scalable when working with large groups of data.

❑ Remember to explicitly close a Data reader, because waiting for the garbage collector to close it for you will limit scalability. Use a Try...Catch...Finally block, for example.

❑ We can remove overhead when referencing a column by using column ordinals and typed accessor methods, instead of searching on a string for the column title.

❑ The DataSet is more flexible and can read and write XML, and can work in a disconnected state. The overhead is partly dependent on the size of your result set, as it is stored in memory.

❑ The typed DataSet is better for performance, readability, and solid code, so if you have schema information for the data source, use typed DataSets. They can be auto-generated from the XML schema.

❑ Use ExecuteNonQuery and ExecuteScalar for quick queries – ExecuteScalar when you want to return a single value and ExecuteNonQuery when you don't need any results.

❑ Parameterized queries allow efficient compilation and caching of similar queries, and thus reduce database load.

❑ Also, reduce database load by reducing round trips. Group statements into one command and retrieve more than one set of results from one database trip where possible.

❑ Avoid using SqlCommandBuilder in a production environment. It's very useful when prototyping, but comes with unnecessary overheads.

❑ Stored procedures will improve database performance because even parsing, compiling, and optimizing the stored procedure on first execution only takes about as much processing as processing a query. After that, you're just executing the procedure directly, which is a lot faster.

❑ Processing large amounts of XML takes a fair amount of resources, so consider carefully when you should use it. Bulk loading of data is one time to consider using XML.

❑ Indexes can help with finding a specific record, ordering records, and grouping records. However, indexes can slow down modifying records, so consider what kind of database you have: a more static system would benefit from more indexing, whereas one that's modified frequently would benefit more from having just a few well chosen indexes.

❑ Use short, distinct index keys to reduce load on the database. However, covered queries can provide benefits for your most crucial queries. Clustered indexes also reduce lookup time by having the data immediately available instead of as a reference.

❑ Always use the correct data provider for your data source for the best performance, as they use fewer software layers and are optimized for their particular source. If you need loose coupling to your source, use the interfaces from the `System.Data` namespace.

❑ Test existing ADO code in your .NET context to see if performance is up to scratch. Moving to a .NET managed provider can provide performance benefits if you need them because it doesn't use so many software layers, including COM Interop.

❑ Connection pooling requires that the connection string be identical. Differing user IDs or catalog parameters will result in new pools being created. This is especially important when using impersonation, as each unique user will create a different connection pool.

❑ Improve resource utilization by acquiring database connections as late as possible and closing them as early as possible. Make sure you clean up any transactions on the connection and drop temporary objects as soon as you can.

❑ Limit the amount of data you retrieve for data binding operations. Optimize data binding expressions by using specific derived data types, as well as referencing columns by ordinal. However, this makes the application less robust if you change the data source type or column order.

❑ Create and modify large strings with the `StringBuilder` class instead of using concatenation. This reduces the number of string allocations and copies, as well as not having to keep creating new string objects every time you add characters.

❑ The `XmlTextReader` is a fire hose cursor for working with XML. No schema or DTD validation occurs, so you save on memory overhead. If you want validation, use the `XmlValidatingReader`.

❑ Use the `XmlDocument` if you want to add, remove, or modify nodes. It comes with a bigger memory footprint with large documents, though. Use the readers when possible.

❑ The `XmlDataDocument` gives you the benefits of both a `DataSet` and `XmlDocument`. It keeps the relational and hierarchical vies of a `DataSet` in synch. The `XPathDocument` is useful for XSLT transformations. And the `XmlSchemaCollection` class lets you keep a group of schemas cached in memory instead of reloading every time.

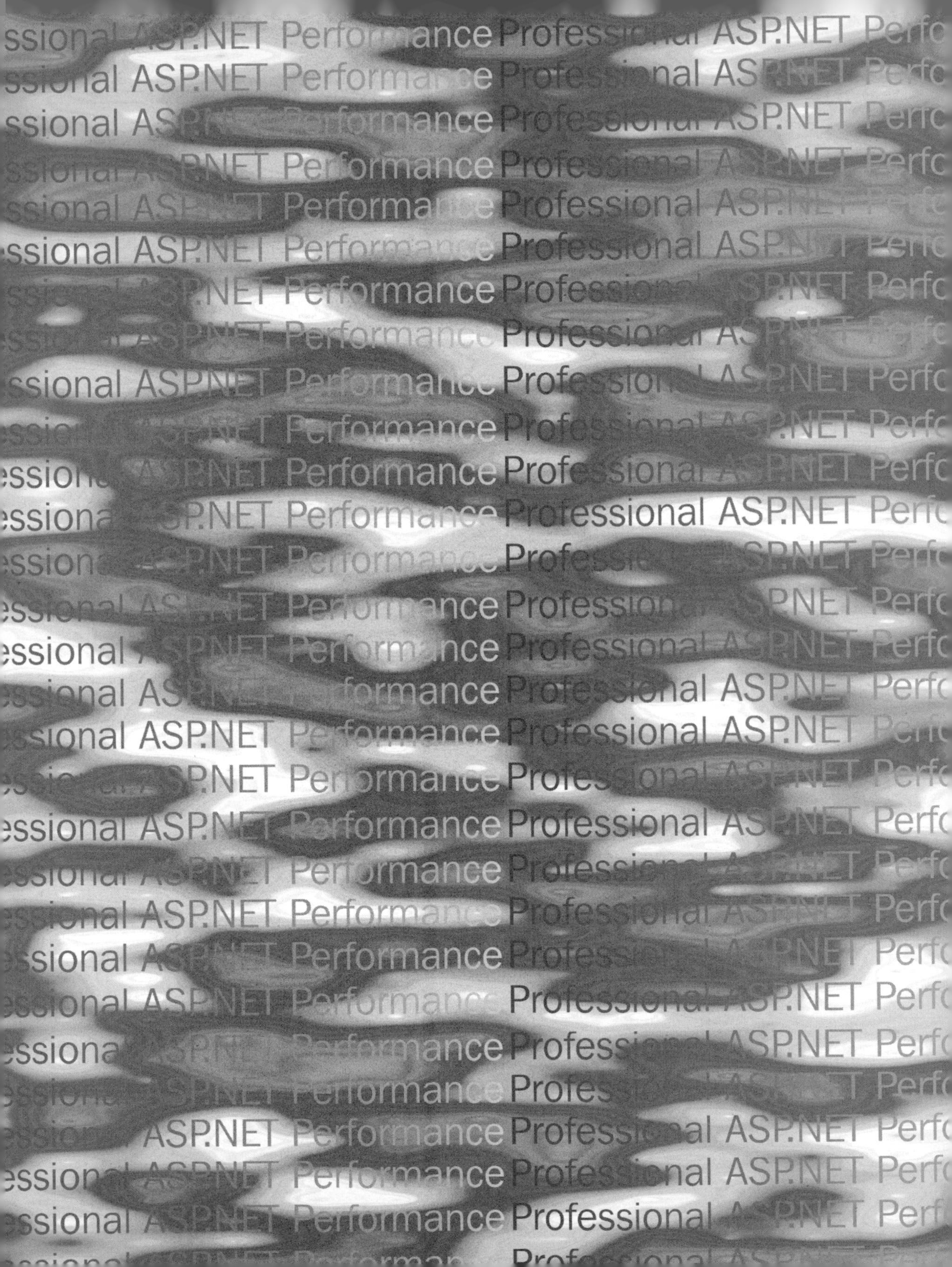
Professional ASP.NET Performance

6

Using the Web Application Stress Tool

One of the most important steps in the successful deployment of our web applications is testing our applications before deployment. All of our hard work in developing our applications can come tumbling down if our deployment is marred by bad performance. Simply testing the application by ourselves is not enough; we need to test the application with the workload that we are expecting. And while we could round up all our friends and tell them what site to hit, it's a lot easier to use a free utility from Microsoft called the Web Application Stress Tool. Using this tool, we can simulate a large number of users hitting our site, and then examine the performance of our applications and the performance of our web server. In this chapter, we will focus more on the performance of our web server as we will be covering more application-based performance in Chapter 10. First we are going to take an in-depth look at the WAS tool, and then we will move on to some practical examples of how we can use the tool to test and improve our applications.

In this chapter we are going to cover the following topics:

- ❑ What is the WAS tool?

- ❑ Creating a script to test the performance of our application.

- ❑ Changing the settings of the WAS tool.

- ❑ Testing the performance of our application with our script. Improving and measuring the performance improvement of our application.

- ❑ Other settings that we can use in our tests.

What is the WAS Tool?

The Web Application Stress tool is a free utility available from Microsoft that can simulate a large number of users and requests for our web application. To use the tool we simply need to specify the pages that we want requested, the amount of mock users to hit our site with, and various other settings. The WAS tool also has a host of other settings and features that we can utilize, including options to specify the querystring values and post data, as well as reporting functionality.

One of the features that the WAS tool provides, that can't be found in the new ACT (we'll look at this in the next chapter), is the ability to coordinate multiple systems to test a single site. Using the WAS tool we can string together multiple client computers to generate very large amounts of traffic toward our site. You can setup up a test on the master client and it will tell the client systems what to do, and what settings to use. This gives us the ability to enterprise level web farms as we can generate the traffic of thousands of users.

The WAS tool is available from Microsoft at http://webtool.rte.microsoft.com. The tool will only run on Windows NT, 2000, or XP. It is about a 10 MB download, but very quick and easy install. You will also find some support features on this site, and I encourage you to take a look around while you are there. It's also a good idea to download the tool and follow along with the chapter, but there will be a good number of screenshots, so it's not essential.

You will also find at that site the knowledge base for the WAS tool. This includes tons of great information, including general information and error- or issue-specific information. If you have any problems or questions with the tool, you should definitely check there first.

An important consideration when installing the WAS tool is that you should not install on the server you are testing – this puts extra stress, irrelevant to the actual testing, on that server, and as such can interfere with your results.

Test Application

A small test application has been included in the code download so that you can follow along with all the examples and tests in this chapter. The application consists of the following files:

❑   `Default.aspx` – Index page, includes links to the other pages.

❑   `Page1.aspx` – Includes a textbox and a button, when text is entered and the button is pressed the length of the text in the textbox is returned. We will use this page to demonstrate using post information.

❑   `Page2.aspx` – This page issues a cookie to the user and records the current data and time in the cookie. When the user returns, it displays the last time the user was at the site.

❑   `Page3.aspx` – We are only going to use this page as a demonstration of a processor intensive page, it simply uses a loop and a literal control to count from one to a thousand.

❑   `Logo.jpg` – This is our logo graphic that we will use to demonstrate dealing with graphics.

To set up this application on your system you simply need to copy all the files to a web directory; no other settings are needed.

WAS Tool Intro

We will start creating scripts shortly, but let's first take a quick look at the main screen of WAS to familiarize ourselves with how it works. To get to this screen, simply start up the WAS tool and select the manual option. We won't be creating a script but simply taking a look around.

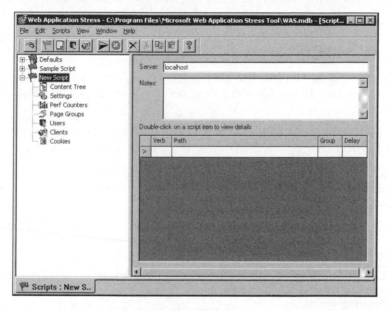

This screen is where we will control all our scripts. It has a layout that you should be familiar with; among other things, the Microsoft Management Console (MMC) uses this configuration. On the left side, each script appears as a node under which a number of subgroups appear. The right side of the screen changes depending on what's selected in the left panel.

Let's take a look at the options we have when entering our pages. The first entry on the page is for our server, which in our case is localhost. This simply means that the tool will look for our pages on the localhost server. We also have a Notes field available for comments about the script.

The next section is where we will be spending most of our time. The first column is for the Verb, or request type. This contains a drop-down which has the values:

❑ GET – A get request simply requests the resource from the server without anything additional. This is the most common type of request.

❑ HEAD – This request only asks for the response headers and not the entire resource. This can be useful if you are just looking for the characteristics or existence of a resource, and not the actual contents of the page.

❑ POST – A familiar request method to most ASP or ASP.NET programmers, the post methods sends information from the client to the server along with the request. Most commonly this is used to send form information to the server from the user.

The second field is **Path**, which is the virtual path of the file page that we wish to test. The third field is called **Group** and specifies what group of files this page is in (we will talk about page groups a little bit later). The last field is **Delay**, which is the amount of time in milliseconds that the tool will wait before processing this request. It simulates the fact that users will hit pages within our site in a random fashion, rather than all at exactly the same time as each other. We can also double-click on the left side of the entry and access even more properties for that entry, which we'll see a bit more later on.

Creating a Script

Let's get started creating our script. Scripts are basically directions for the tool, telling it what pages to hit, where, and how often. The tool provides a number of different ways to create scripts, and we will be covering them all here shortly.

First, we are going to create a script to test our sample application. There are four different methods that the WAS tool has to create scripts, let's take a quick look at the different methods:

❑   Manual – This method requires us to manually add each page that we want to test to the tool. It is very useful when dealing with very small apps, but there is usually an easier and better method available.

❑   Record – This method is one of the most useful when working with ASP.NET. Using this method, we can open our web browser and record the actions including the pages we navigate to, the post data, and more.

❑   Log File – Using this method we can create a script from the IIS log files of our web server. This method is very useful when we want to recreate the level of traffic that we are currently experiencing on our site.

❑   Content Tree – This method is similar to the Manual method because we have to specify the files that we want to test; the only difference is that we can choose the files from a list.

When you start up the WAS tool, you will be presented with the following set of options:

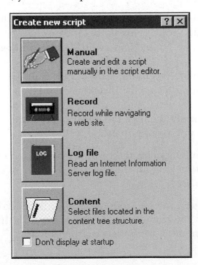

Let's choose **Record**, as this is the script creation method that you will probably use the most. This process is quite similar to recording macros in Microsoft Word, in that we will perform some action, or string of actions, and the system will record what we did in order to recreate it later. WAS lets us go about our business navigating our site, all the while recording which pages we hit and how we hit them. It will then use our navigation as a template for the test, replicating our actions many times. This lets us build up a test that is based more on 'real' user navigation than on just our own choice of what pages we think we'd like to include. It is one of the easier methods and it works great with ASP.NET as it records post information. After choosing **Record**, we will see the following dialog box with some options for us to choose:

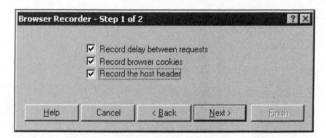

The first option is whether or not we want to record the delays between requests. This depends on what the final goal of our script is. If we want to accurately record how a user moves around the site, then we'd want to check this box and record the delays.

The second option is whether or not we should record browser cookies. This again depends on the goals of our test. If we use cookies and want to include them in our testing then we should include it, but if we do not use cookies and do not think it will impact the performance of our site then we can leave it off.

Our last option is recording the host header of the pages. For this test, let's go ahead and check all of the options, so we can see how each of them affects the test results. The next window gives a **Finish** button which we press and will be presented with our browser. We can now use our browser to navigate to different pages or sites on our local system and record the movements in the tool. For this test, let's browse through our sample application, making sure that we hit each page, and also using the small tool on page1.aspx by entering a string in the textbox and pressing the **Count** button. This will create a postback and we can see how the tool records this information. After navigating through all of the different pages in our application here is what we see:

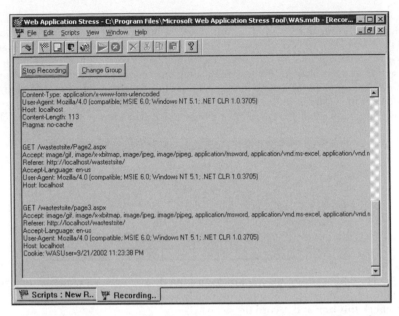

If you take a close look at the above screenshot, you will see that it is recording what page we hit along with the additional request header information such as referrer and cookie. Notice that the cookie information is the cookie that we assign to the user on Page2.aspx.

We now have two options, one to stop recording and the other to change group. The Change Group button allows you to record more hits in a separate page group, which we will be going over later in the chapter. For now, let's Stop Recording and see what type of script has been generated for us:

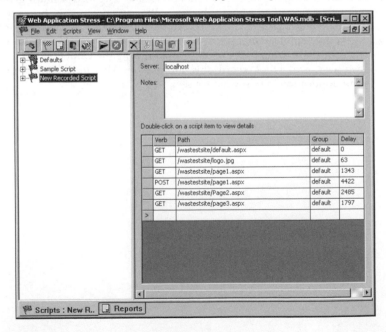

As you can see in the image above, all the pages we've hit (as well as the images) have been added to the script along with their appropriate verbs. The tool has also recorded a delay for each page because we checked that option when setting up the script.

As we mentioned earlier, a benefit of using the recording feature is that it will include settings that you might not otherwise think to change. For an example of this, let's take a closer look at the properties of the one page using the POST method, by double-clicking to the left of that item:

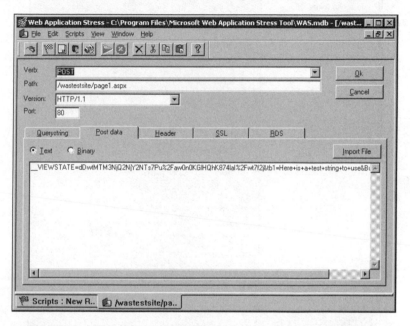

The values of the post have been stored in the properties of the entry (at the top of the large text area), so that during the stress test we will be able to see the effects of the post data on our performance. Let's take a close look at the actual post data in this example:

__VIEWSTATE=dDwtMTM3NjQ2NjY2NTs7Pu%2Faw0n0KGlHQhK874lal%2Fwt7f2j&tb1=Here+is+a +test+string+to+use&Button1=Count

The first part of this data is the view state of this page. Every ASP.NET page contains some view state, even if `EnableViewState` is set to `false`. View state is used to preserve the state of the various web controls on a page when the page posts back to the server. The second part of the above post data is the text that we entered in the textbox on `Page1.aspx`. This data is being sent to the server to be processed by our event handler. This is another added value of using the recording feature. As you can see, using the record feature is a lot easier than manually entering the page information.

Script Settings

Before we run our script, there are a number of settings that we can set to change how our test will be performed. These settings are set for each individual script. We can access the setting of each script in the Settings category beneath the script.

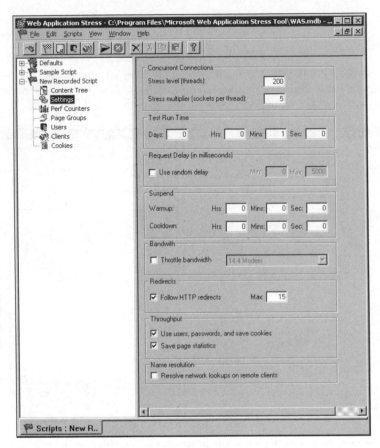

Let's take a look at some of the settings that we will be using:

Concurrent Connections

WAS is designed to stress test our applications and servers, and as such needs to be able to simulate a number of concurrent users. It does this by creating a number of threads, each of which can also have a number of socket connections. Each of these figures can be altered to provide the simulated load you want.

Stress Level (threads) is the total number of Windows threads that the tool will create across all of the client systems. Each thread can create multiple socket connections, and each socket connection represents a concurrent request.

Stress multiplier (sockets per thread) is the number of sockets per thread that will be opened. We will not normally need to use this setting unless we need to hit our site with an extremely large number of requests, since Windows does not like having more than 100 threads. It will work with more threads than that, but tends to slow down. The socket multiplier is included so that we can run 90 threads with 5 sockets per thread for a total of 450 concurrent requests, instead of causing problems by trying to open 450 threads. The problem lies with overloading our client systems, the systems that will be hitting our web server. The web server itself will only see incoming requests and does not care about the number of threads created on the clients.

Test Run Time

This setting is the amount of time in Days, Hours, Minutes, and Seconds that we want the script to run on our server. We will be using short tests of three to four minutes here, but if we wanted to test for small memory leaks or server stability then we would use longer tests, somewhere in the twenty-four hour range.

Request Delay

We saw earlier that we can hard set a delay value in our scripts, where the tool will wait between one request and the next. This setting adds a random delay value between our minimum and maximum settings. This can be very useful when you want to simulate the unpredictability of users.

Suspend

We can set a warm-up and cool-down period here for the test. These are periods of time, either at the beginning of the test or at the end when the test is running, but the report is not collecting data. The warm-up period can be very useful as it allows us to get past the initial processor hit of objects being loaded and caches being filled. This is particularly useful when dealing with ASP.NET, since sometimes our pages may not yet be compiled, and we do not want that resource usage to be recorded in our reports.

Bandwidth

Using this setting we can 'throttle', or limit, the simulated bandwidth available to our incoming requests. Since in the real world a lot of users are still using modems we may want to specifically simulate modem users using our application. When we enable bandwidth we will be able to use more concurrent connections as modem users will not tax our server as much as broadband users will.

Redirects

Using this setting, we can limit the number of HTTP redirects (`Response.Redirect("location")`) that our tool should follow. If you do not allow the tool to follow such redirects, then you would not have a good representation of what your traffic does, since subsequent pages would not be tested.

We want to keep this box checked because it creates the best simulation of real users, as they will also be following these redirects. One issue with HTTP redirects is that the data of the page being redirected to will not be recorded in the report, so we will need to use performance counters to track the impact of those pages.

Running Scripts

You will have noticed that there are some more settings pages under the Script nodes in the left-hand pane of the WAS tool. We will take a look at these later on, after we've run a couple of scripts to get a feel for how it works and what kind of results we will see. The first thing we are going to do is set up the tool to hit a local application. As we are currently using the same system to host the files and run the test, it will be pulling double duty and will affect performance.

> If possible, you should always use a different system to run the test othert than the one
> that is hosting pages – after all, we're not only testing the server, we're testing the
> entire process, so if we put a strain on the server before we start then our test results
> are compromised from the outset.

In this test run, we are going to try and generate the largest number of requests that our server can
handle. This will give us the maximum number of requests that our server can handle per second, and
we can then perform a couple of calculations and get a value that we can compare to future tests. We
can then try and make performance improvements to the site and measure the amount of performance
improvement.

Let's look at the script we set up earlier:

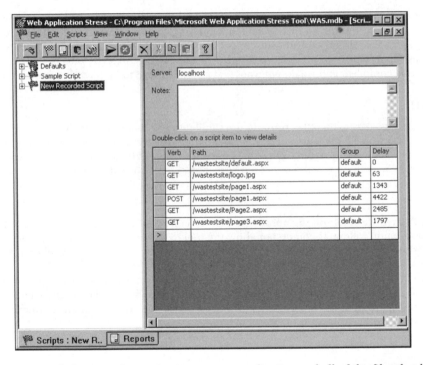

Here we have recorded a script by navigating our test application and all of the files that have been
added to our script. For this example, let's delete the Delay values, because we are going to try and test
the limit of our site rather than trying to simulate actual user interaction. The delay will also cause our
tool to hit a certain page all at the same time, which is not realistic.

We are also going to tweak our script settings to try to get the most effective test that we can, so let's
open up the Settings section of our script:

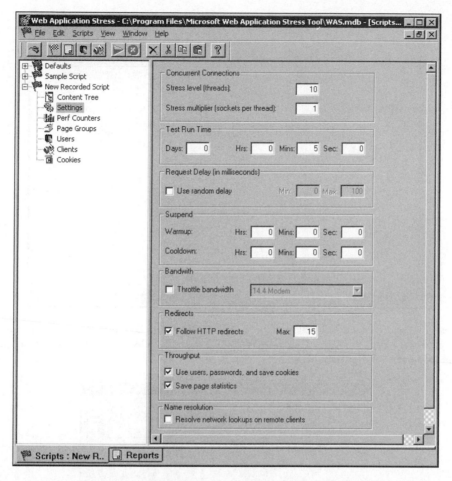

First, we set our stress level, or number of threads, to 10. At this point, this number is really just guesswork, and we will have to run our test and view the results to see if this actually stresses our application. We also set the test run time to five minutes. This should give us plenty of time to get some good performance readings.

Our next step is running the script and observing the performance monitor at the same time. We are going to use the logging feature of the Performance Monitor (we'll go into more detail about the Performance Monitor in Chapter 9) so that we can see the results of the entire test, instead of just the data that can fit on the screen at any one time during the test. The Performance Monitor can be accessed from either the **Administrative Tools** section of the **Start** menu, or by simply typing **perfmon** in the **Start** | **Run...** field. The first thing we need to do in the Performance Monitor is click on the **Performance Logs and Alerts** option on the left, then select the **Counter Logs** option. We will then see a screen like this:

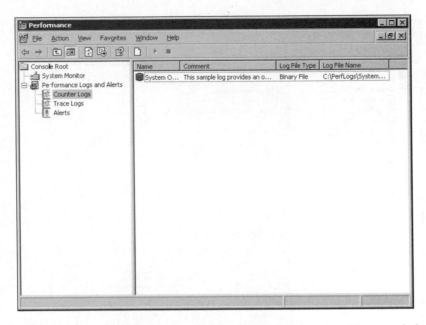

Our next step is to click on the Action menu and select New Log Settings. The next dialog box will ask for a name for the log. We will call this log WAStestlog and hit OK, at which point we are presented with the following settings screen:

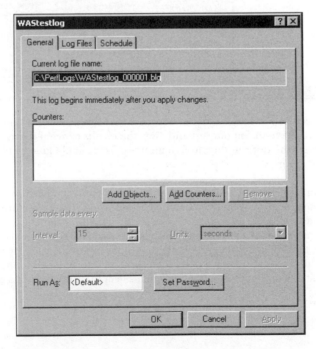

Next, we will click the **Add Counters** button and add the following counters:

- ❑ **Memory | Pages/Sec** – The number of Memory Pages accessed per second.

- ❑ **Physical Disk | Avg. Disk Queue Length** – The average length of the hard drive queue.

- ❑ **Processor | % Processor Time** – The amount of the processor being used.

- ❑ **ASP.NET Applications | Requests/Sec** – The number of ASP.NET requests handled by our application.

We are also going to set the interval time to 1 second. Since this is such a small test length, we want as many readings as possible. Our next step will be to set when we want the log to begin, by changing the **Start Log** setting on the **Schedule** tab to **Manually** and the **Stop Log** setting to 5 minutes:

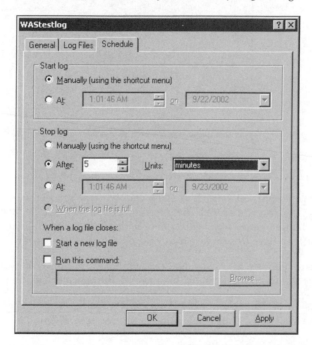

Next, we will start our WAS test and immediately start our log by right-clicking on our log and clicking **Start**.

Now that the test has completed and our log has automatically stopped recording, let's take a look at the results. To do so, we need to pull up the main Performance Monitor screen and right-click on the area where the counter data is viewed. We will be presented with the properties of the monitor. Select the **Source** tab and then change the option to **Log Files**. Add the log file we just completed recording:

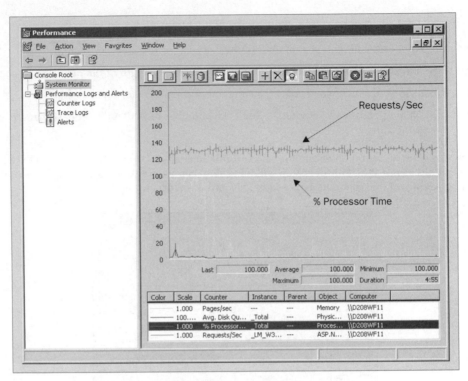

Here we can see our processor was pegged at 100% and we were handling around 130 requests a second – you may be asking is this a good score? The interpretation of this value depends on your server and the application, and the number of users you would be expecting – it is difficult to say if a particular value is a good value; you have to compare it to your other values you record.

We will use this data to generate a single value; the number of (millions) of cycles per request. To get this value, we will use the following formula, the page performance calculation:

$$\frac{\text{(Speed of Processor(s) in MHz)} * \text{(Number of Processors)} * \text{average of \% Processor Time}}{\text{Average of ASP.NET Applications Requests per Second counter}}$$

For our above example it would look like this:

(1800 * 1 * 1.0) / 130

This will give us a value of 13.8 (million) cycles per request. We can also use this value to compare any optimizations we perform on our pages, say using caching or any of the other methods described in this book. We will try optimizing our sample application in a moment, but first let's take a look at the report that was generated by the WAS tool:

Reports

A very informative report is generated after each test is run through the WAS tool. We can access the reports by clicking on the Report button ![icon] in the toolbar. We will then see a list of all the tests that have run for each script, and can select the report for the test we ran in the last section.

Here we have selected the general overview of the report which shows us the number of connections as well as the total bytes sent and received. It also gives us other information such as requests per second and the number of hits, as well as any socket errors we may have received. Our report shows that we hit the application a total of 47,034 times.

Let's also look at the Page Summary section of the report:

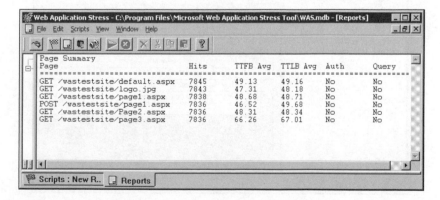

Here we can see the number of hits per page, along with the TTFB and TTLB averages. The TTFB is the time that it takes from when the tool first requests the page to when it receives the first byte of the page. And TTLB is the time is takes from the request to when the last byte of the request is received. This information is very useful to us because we can use it to find out which pages might be taking too long to process, or are too large. Since we want to try and optimize our test application, we can look at this list and find the pages that are taking the longest to load and be processed. It is obvious that page3.aspx, our more processor-intensive page, is taking the longest to be processed and is also one of the larger files. Thus our first step in optimizing the application should be focused on this page. You can find the improved files under the improved directory in the code download.

The first thing we are going to do on the page is disable view state – we've discussed overuse of the view state in an earlier chapter. We are going to simply change the page declaration like so:

```
<%@ Page Language="VB" EnableViewState="false" %>
```

This will cause very little view state to be generated by the page (a small amount is required for the page to still function but it should not affect our performance). We are also going to be adding some page-level caching to this page, which should help cut down on the processor time required to display this page. To do so, we will add the following line right under our page declaration:

```
<%@ OutputCache Duration="100" VaryByParam="none" %>
```

We could also go on to add caching and disabling view state to the other pages in our application, but let's go ahead and run our test again to see what kind of improvement we have.

We will set up our test exactly the same as before, except we will change our /wastestsite/page3.aspx listing to wastestsite/improved/page3.aspx so we will be using the file that we have made improvements on:

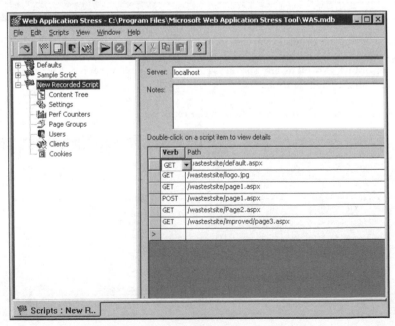

All of our test settings will stay the same. We will also set up the performance monitor log to again monitor our performance. We do not need to make any changes to the log, so let's run the test and take a look at the results:

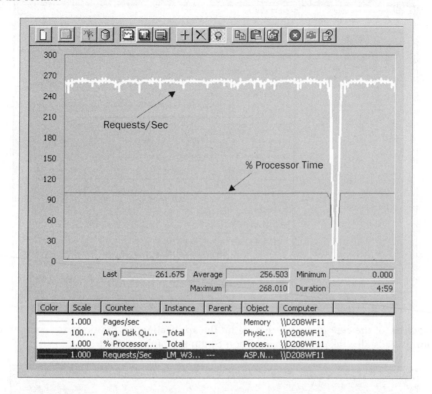

Wow! Look at the difference in how many requests we are handling per second. Our processor is still maxed out at 100%, but we are handling twice the number of requests. Let's perform our page performance calculation again and see what kind of improvement we have:

(1800 * 1 * 1.0) / 256 Gives us a 7 (million) cycles per request. A vast improvement over our first calculation, and all we did was disable view state and enable caching. Imagine what our results could be if we did this on all of our pages!

Let's also take a look at the report generated from this new test:

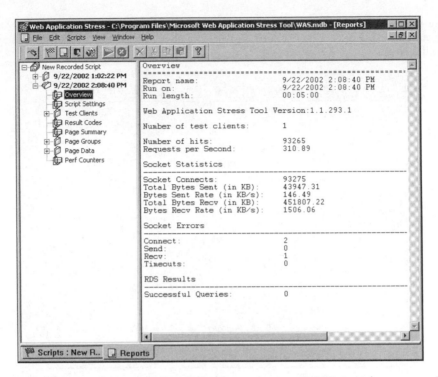

In the Overview of the report, we see that we hit the application 93,265 times (as compared with 47,034 times before)! Let's also take a look at the Page Summary of this report:

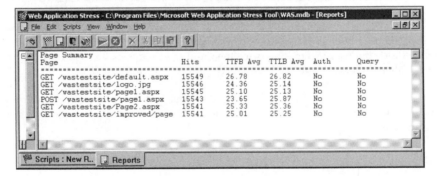

Here we can see that the page3.aspx page is being processed and loading in 50% of the previous time. This also freed up more processor time and improved the loading speed of the other pages as well. As you can see, the Web Application Stress tool is an invaluable resource to measure the improvements in performance that can be achieved by implementing some of the ideas presented in this book. Now that we have seen the WAS tool in action, let's take a look at some of the other features and methods that we did not use in our examples.

Script Creation Methods

We covered the script recording method in our example, but there are three other ways that we can also create scripts. Let's look at these briefly, as they each have their own benefits:

Create Scripts from a Content Tree

From the main menu, which is accessed by clicking the 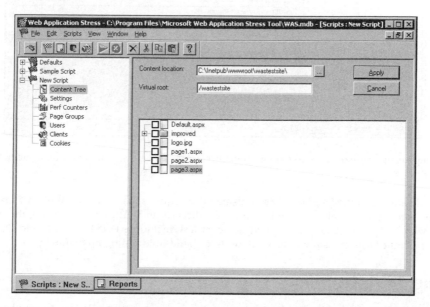 button, select the **Content** option. This will take us to the main screen, shown below:

Content Tree is one of these subgroups, and it is selected by default since we chose the **Content** option.

Firstly, we select the directory containing the files we want to include in our test, and then the virtual directory that is used to access these files. We will then get a list of all the files in that directory (as well as any subdirectories), as you can see above. We can now select the files that we wish to include in our script and click **Apply**. Our script will then be generated using the files that we selected. Let's take a look at our results:

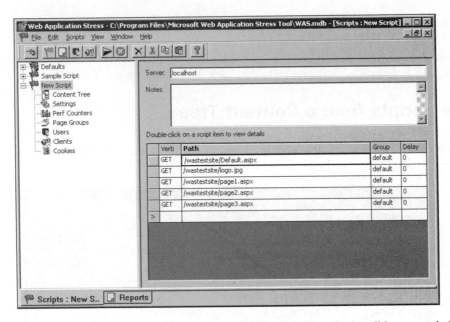

We can repeat the process if we like with other directories and files, which will be appended to the end of our script.

Using this method, all the files are accessed using GET requests. You can edit these manually in the same way as manually creating a script, which we'll discuss later. Alternatively, using the recording method, which we used earlier, will provide a richer test, including POST requests and POST data, cookies, and other aspects that you may not wish to spend time setting up manually.

Creating Scripts from a Log File

It is also possible to use log files to create scripts – this is the most accurate way to simulate real traffic on our applications, because it is created from actual usage data. But since it relies on our application already being deployed, it's not so useful when testing our application in development.

The WAS tool supports Microsoft IIS Log File Format, NCSA Common Log File Format, and W3C Extended Log File Format, and we're going to work with an IIS log. Let's return to our main menu and select the Log File button. A dialog box will pop up asking us for the location of the log we would like to use; you should find your logs in the winnt/system32/logfiles directory. For this example, let's use the log file WAStestlog included in the code download for this chapter. After we have selected our log file, we are presented with these options:

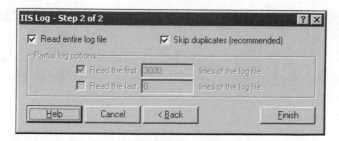

Here, we can choose whether we want to read the entire log file or just part of it. In our case, we will choose the entire log. We will also choose to skip duplicates – since the tool will be hitting each page many times anyway, there is no reason to have multiple entries for each page. Let's take a look at the script generated from our log file when we click on Finish:

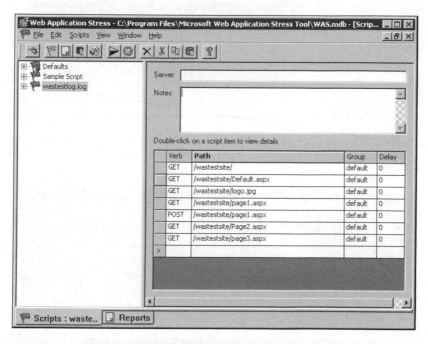

Given a log file, this is a very efficient and accurate method of script creation. The drawbacks to this method are that you do require this log file information of course, and also the POST information posted to the site is not included, which means we would manually need to add that information.

Creating and Editing Scripts Manually

Of course, if you're just trying to create a quick script and you already know which pages you want to include, you can do it manually. Start up a new script in the usual way, this time selecting Manual. We will be dropped to a blank canvas, where we can enter the pages that we want to test. Just type in the details. In the same way, you can edit a script recorded or generated in one of the ways we've already seen.

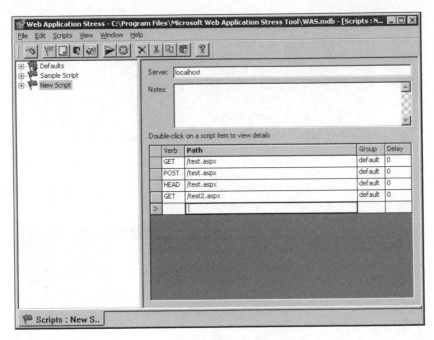

If you double-click on a script item, the following properties screen will appear, where more detailed properties of the item can be altered. We saw this screen earlier when we recorded a script that included a POST request.

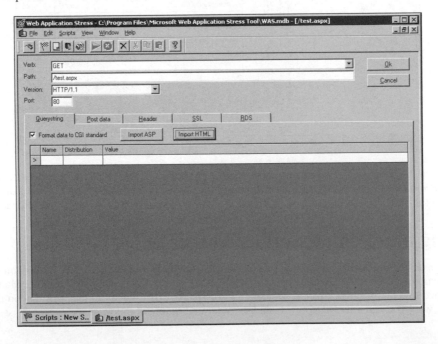

This method of script creation is best for when you are testing a small number of files and you know exactly what files you want to test. This method is not good for large scripts, as it involves a lot of manual labor. This method is also not very precise at representing actual user interaction, since it is mostly guesswork at what pages will be hit by a typical user.

Further Options

Now let's turn our attention to the other pages found under the script node. Here, we will be able to create page groups, user groups, and more.

Page Groups

Page Groups allow us to create groups of files or paths and specify how often each group should be requested. A good example of this is if we have three different main pages in our application, and each of the pages is accessed a different amount of times, then we can add all the elements of each page to a page group. By doing this, we can specify the amount of times that each page should be accessed by using a percentage value. In this way, we can get the most accurate idea of the performance of our application.

Let's take a look at the Page Group page for our WAS.mdb script, accessible by clicking on File | Open. The file, in our case, is in the C:\Program Files\Microsoft Web Application Stress Tool folder:

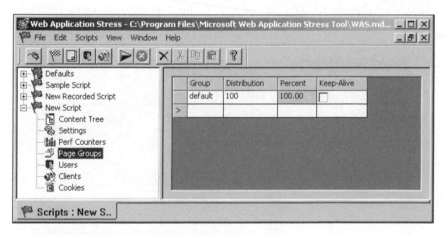

We have a couple of properties that we can set here:

❑ **Group** – the name of the page group that we will use to assign our requests to.

❑ **Distribution** – this changes the percentage value of the total requests that will be used to test this page group.

❑ **Keep-Alive** – this prevents the tool from closing all the sockets between page groups.

Users

We can also specify which users the tool should use when testing. It is very easy to create new users and assign them to our scripts. Firstly, let's look at the Users section under the script node:

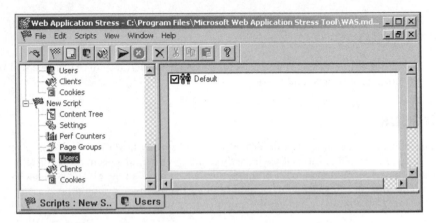

Here, we can set the populations that we want our script to pull its users from - a population is a group of users. Unless you are trying to run tests with a very large number of users, you will not need to create any more as 200 users are installed by default. If we do need more users, then it is easy to create them in the user section. We can access this section by clicking the user icon on the toolbar:

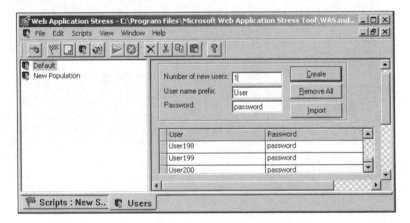

It is easy to add new users to a population. Simply select the population you want to add to in the User tab, and then enter the number of users you wish to create. You can also specify the user name prefix and the password. Then click Create and the tool will create that number of users for you with the user prefix and password specified.

You can also create a new population by right-clicking on the Default population in the User tab, and selecting Add. Each of the users that we create and use in our scripts will be assigned a cookie and other user-specific information. Since this is a rather resource-intensive operation, we want to make sure that we only use the number of the users that we are expecting on our site.

You can also import users from a comma-separated text file. The format of the file should look something like this:

```
Username, password
James, myPassword
Tammy, herPassword
```

Then click the Import button on the user page and browse to the text file. This can be useful if you need to specify certain users, and do not want to do the mouse work of adding each individually. It can also be very useful if you are setting up separate machines with the same configuration, and need to use specific users.

Clients

Client systems are the systems that will be used to perform the testing. When we are dealing with relatively low numbers of requests and stress then we can perform all of our tests using one system. However, if we wanted to test a site using very large numbers of requests, then we would need to use multiple systems to generate these requests. That is where the client options come into play.

This screenshot below shows the clients that might be used for an individual script:

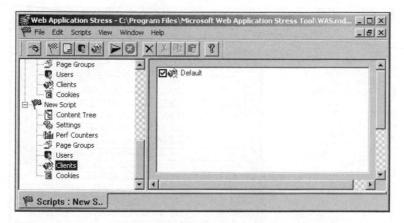

Here, you can select which clients should be used when executing this script. In our screenshot here, we only have Default checked since we will not be using any other systems.

The next screenshot shows the client page that is accessed by clicking the Client button on the toolbar. This page allows us to add new client systems to the tool, which can then be selected in the script as demonstrated in the following screenshot. You simply need to enter the name of the machine that will be used, along with the current one and click Add. You will also be able to see the status of the connection to the system, although it is not necessary to wait until it shows "Connected" to start the test.

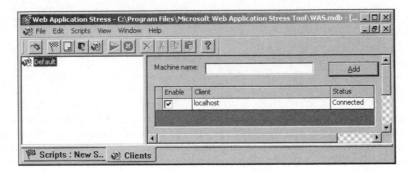

We will not be using more than one client in our tests here, but you will definitely need to incorporate multiple clients if you want to test a site that will be receiving extremely large amounts of traffic. It is also a good idea to use systems of relatively the same speed and performance, as the tool does not seem to test this and expects the other system to perform the same as the master system.

Cookies

Another setting available to us is setting the cookies of the users we will be using:

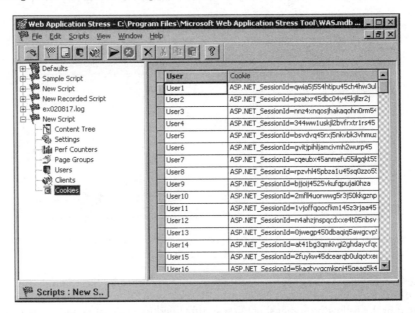

The best way to populate the cookies of your users is to run a test script and point it to the page that assigns the cookie in your application. You could also specify custom post or query string data if it was required. It is essential to incorporate cookies in your tests if you use them in your application, as they add additional performance needs to the application.

Page Properties

The Page Properties options are not found under a separate page under the script node. Instead, they're accessed on the script page itself by double-clicking to the left of the individual page listing that you want to examine. The first tab contains the query string information.

Query string

Let's imagine we have a page that takes the ID of an order in a query string, for example: order.aspx?ID=4, would pull up the order information for job number 4. If we accessed this page without the query string information included in the test then the page would not react the same way as it would when real users access it, or an error might even be generated. When using the query string fields, we can include the query string and not only avoid any possible errors, but also observe the effect that differently queried pages have on our performance. Ideally, we would be able to submit a range of valid values that WAS can use to test our pages. Well, that's exactly what we can do.

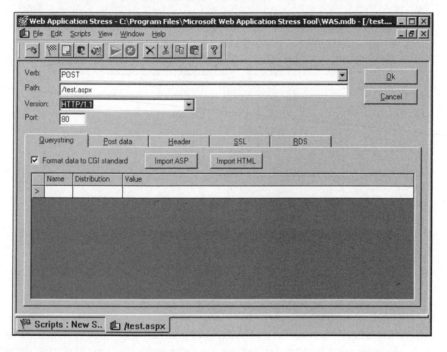

For this example, we could add a query string name and range of values to this properties page and they would be used when requesting the page, giving us a better idea of how this page will act when it is in production, rather than just returning the same page. If the returned page happened to be above or below average in size and complexity, we would be skewing our results. This way, we will be able to monitor performance over a broader range of activity.

The way to do this is simple. There are three fields to consider: Name, Distribution, and Value. In the example we have been using, we would enter ID in the Name column, and Value would contain a list of our valid order numbers. Since our users will be accessing more than one job we can click on the "..." button in the Value field and specify multiple values to be used with the querystring, as shown below. We can then set Distribution to either Don't Use, which will deactivate the entry; Sequential, which will use our values sequentially; or Random, which will use our values in a random order. If you have a page on your site that is accessed using a certain order then you would want to use Sequential, as you could replicate that situation exactly. For example, you might have a page that is first accessed with mypage.aspx?step=1, then when the page is being viewed the second time it is accessed with mypage.aspx?step=2, and so on. You would want such pages tested in the order that they will be viewed by your users. On the other hand, you may also have pages that take an ID or job number, and these pages should be accessed in a random fashion, using the Random setting, as this is essentially how we would model the behavior of users accessing the pages.

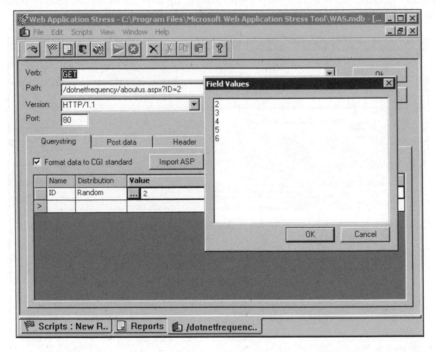

Here we can see the different values that we have specified for this specific field. When we run the test the tool will access the page using the specified querystring name and a random value from the list above.

We can also add multiple querystring names to our page, for instance, order.aspx?ID=4&print=yes, where we might specify a printable view of the page. When we add our first name value, another row will appear where we can enter additional names and values to be used for multiple querystring values.

Post Data

Just like the query string situation, we will also have pages that rely on post data being sent to the page – this applies to pages posting to other pages, or posting back to themselves. A typical example is a search page where the initial page that comes up is simply a textbox and a button to specify search parameters. If we did not specify any post data then we would only be testing that initial view of the page, which would give us an unrealistic view of performance since it would not include the actual searching, which can be performance intensive. As we saw earlier in this chapter, this area will also store all of our view state information that is posted to the page on each postback. So, let's look at how we could add this information to our settings. The Post data tab of the properties page is where we will do this:

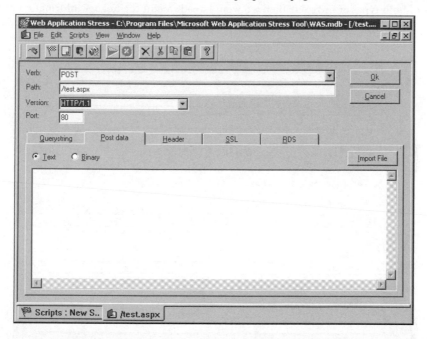

Here we can specify the post data that we want to be used when accessing the page. The fastest and most accurate way to generate this data is to use the Record option when creating your script. Simply go to the pages you want to test, input sample entries in your form fields, and this data will be recorded in the script. Let's take a look at some data that you might find in this field after running a record script on our test applications:

```
__VIEWSTATE=dDwtMTM3NjQ2NjY2NTs7Pu%2Faw0n0KGlHQhK874laI%2Fwt7f2j&tb1=another+test+
string&Button1=Count
```

As we can see in the above data both the view state of the page and the additional post data are recorded on this page. This data will be used to access the page during our test, and the page will act exactly as if we submitted this data manually.

Header

The next tab on the page is the Header tab. This tab shows us the HTTP header information that will be used when the page is accessed. By default, header information is created by the WAS tool to emulate a user with IE 4.0 and Windows 98. If we were testing a page that incorporated controls that were rendered based on the type of browser, then we would want to test our pages using a variety of browser types. Some of the controls that behave this way are the IE Web controls from Microsoft. If the browser is "up-level", meaning IE 4.0+, then they are rendered using DHTML behaviors. If the browser is "down-level" then the controls are rendered without the DHTML behaviors and require more frequent postbacks to accomplish the same usability. If we want to accurately test the behavior of our application with users of both types of browsers then we would need to edit the header information of the pages using those controls. We can add or change the existing entries here to specify specific headers that we want to be sent:

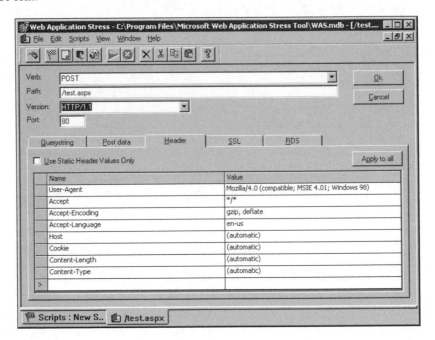

The fields marked (automatic) will be handled by the tool at the time of testing. It's best to keep them on this setting so that, for example, various different cookies can be automatically specified for each user, and the content-type and content-length can also be automatically set when we are using post data. For our example, we would set the value of the User-Agent value field to a value similar to this:

```
Mozilla/4.0 (compatible; MSIE 6.0; Windows NT 5.1; .NET CLR 1.0.3705)
```

This would then tell the pages that we are testing using IE 6.0, and the controls would be rendered in "up-level" mode, thus creating a more accurate test of our pages, since this setup is more typical of that we will be expecting from our users. We would also want to test the pages using the "down-level" browsers so we would create an identical test entry, except we would leave the default IE 4.0 setting.

SSL

The next tab is the SSL tab. This simply allows us to specify whether the request should be using Secure Sockets Layer (SSL) or not:

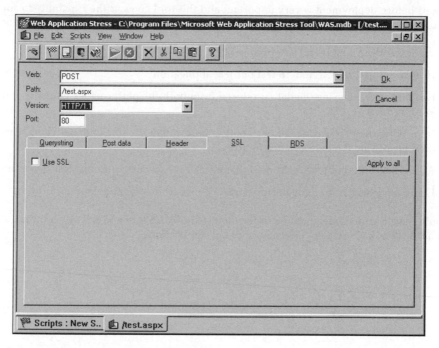

It is important to be sure to enable SSL if the page will be using SSL in production. Using SSL is more performance-intensive and if it were not enabled in testing then we would get an inaccurate view of the resources needed to process these pages.

Security

Even if you will not be using the WAS tool there are some security issues created by its existence that everyone should be concerned about. As you have probably by now realized, there is the opportunity to use this tool to run denial of service attacks on other web sites – anyone could very easily set up a system to send tremendous amounts of traffic to an unsuspecting web server. There is a straightforward security measure that will stop the stress tool from hitting your site. You simply need to add the following line to your robots.txt file like so:

```
Disallow: /
User-Agent: stress-agent
```

If you do not already have a robots.txt for your site then you can simply create a new text file with the above text inside it. If you watch closely the first thing the tool does when starting a test is check for the robots.txt file, and if the file is found and the above line is found in it then the tool will not run.

Summary

The Web Application Stress tool is very valuable to us when testing our applications. Testing our applications before deployment is very important and this tool gives us the capability to simulate a large number of users and examine the performance of our site. In this chapter we have covered:

- ❑ What the WAS tool is and where to get it

- ❑ How to setup the WAS tool to test our test application

- ❑ Reading and analyzing the data produced from both the performance counters and the WAS reports

- ❑ Improving the performance of our application through caching and managing viewstate and then measuring the performance increase

- ❑ Additional settings of the WAS tool that we can use to customize our tests even more

- ❑ Using the `robots.txt` file to stop someone else from stressing your application

You should have a good understanding of how to use the WAS tool and we will continue using it throughout this book to test the performance of our applications.

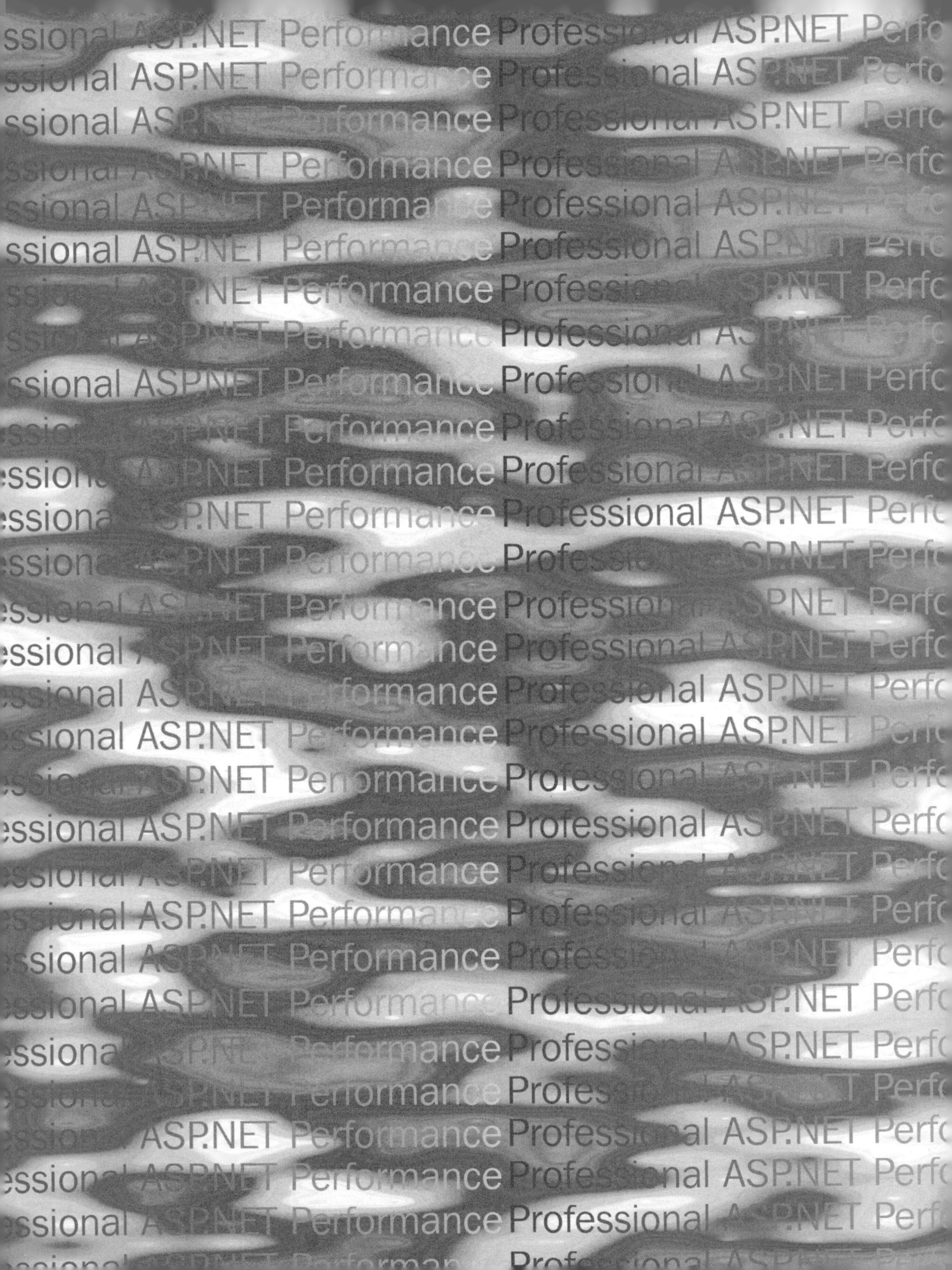
Professional ASP.NET Performance

7

Using Microsoft Application Center Test

Microsoft **Application Center Test** (also known as ACT) is designed to simulate multiple web clients making simultaneous HTTP requests to a web server. This allows you to optimize performance by reproducing the behavior of your application under the expected load of the live data center.

Since the free release of Web Application Stress (WAS) a few years ago on the Microsoft.com web site, (http://www.microsoft.com/technet/itsolutions/intranet/downloads/webstres.asp.) customers have been requesting more features to help test increasingly complex web applications. ACT is not the end-all solution to all of these feature requests, but it is a significant step in the right direction. Unlike WAS, ACT contains a scriptable test object model that can be executed at run time. This allows you to analyze each response and take conditional actions based on either the header or the body of that response. This feature allows you to test more advanced web development projects.

Microsoft originally intended to sell two versions of ACT, one geared to the developer and the other geared more to the operational needs of testing applications deployed to a large cluster. The only version that is shipping at the time of writing, is the one designed for the developer. This product ships in Visual Studio .NET Enterprise Developer and Visual Studio .NET Enterprise Architect. The cost of these software packages is approximately $1,799 US and $2,499 US, respectively. When comparing this price to many other web stress tools on the market, ACT is considerably less expensive, even though Visual Studio .NET contains quite a bit more than just the ACT web stress software.

However, because of the design goals of ACT in Visual Studio .NET, it is not without its limitations for the operations tester. The most significant of these is that it only supports one client machine. This means that the product can only be run on one machine at a time; it cannot execute tests across multiple client machines simultaneously, as WAS can. You can run isolated instances of ACT on several machines, but this is not particularly practical since it requires multiple Visual Studio .NET licenses and would also require that you manually consolidate the report data across these clients when the test completes.

In this chapter, we will cover the following:

- ❑ The differences between ACT and WAS.
- ❑ How to test an ASP.NET application with ACT.
- ❑ Testing Web Services with ACT.
- ❑ What test settings are available in ACT.
- ❑ Working with cookies, authentication, encryption, and other useful ACT hints.

Comparing ACT and WAS

To follow is a table containing the main differences between ACT and WAS so that you can make a decision about which tool is best suited to your testing needs. WAS is geared to the tester that needs to simulate load against multiple web servers. ACT is better suited to the developer running tests against components of a .NET web application. The main limitation of WAS is that it does not have a "dynamic test interface".

FEATURE	DESCRIPTION	WAS	ACT
Script creation			
Browser record	Records browser activity as you navigate your web application	Yes	Yes
Dynamic test interface	A scriptable object model that allows you to execute code as the test is running	No	Yes
Static test grid interface	An easy to understand Excel-like interface for creating tests	Yes	No
Web server log file import	Import IIS supported log file types	Yes	No
Application object model	A scriptable object model that allows you to automate the user interface	Yes	Yes
Integration with Visual Studio .NET	Utilizes features in the Integrated Development Environment (IDE)	No	Yes
Client machines			
Multiple client machine support	The ability to control one or more test machines from one centralized machine and get consolidated reports across these test machines	Yes	No

FEATURE	DESCRIPTION	WAS	ACT
Reporting			
Tabular reports	Report data shown in a table format	Yes	Yes
Graphical reports	Report data shown in a chart format	No	Yes
Collect performance monitor counters	Add and collected counters from the test machine	Yes*	Yes
Show standard deviation	A statistic that illustrates the distance of a point from the mean	No	Yes
Authentication and encryption			
Forms	A method of authentication on web pages using forms	Yes	Yes
Basic	Basic authentication	Yes	Yes
NTLM	Windows authentication scheme	Yes	Yes
Passport	Microsoft authentication scheme for web application and services	No	Yes
Digest	Internet Explorer authentication scheme	Yes	Yes
SSL support	Secure Socket Layer encryption	Yes	Yes
Operating system support			
NT 4.0	Windows NT 4.0 operating system (all service packs)	Yes	No
Windows 2000	Windows 2000 operating system (all service packs)	Yes	Yes
Windows XP	Windows XP operating system (through SP1)	Yes	Yes
Other			
Application tracing	The ability to log all the information sent to and from the web server.	Yes	Yes
Built-in query string editor	An editor that makes it easy to add multiple query string name-value pairs to a web page	Yes	No
Warm-up time	A period of time at the beginning of the test when no report data is collected	Yes	Yes
Request delays	Delays between each request, either static or dynamic	Yes	Yes

Table continued on following page

FEATURE	DESCRIPTION	WAS	ACT
Request multiple domains in one test	The ability to test servers in more than one domain from a single test	No	Yes
Run test for a number of iterations	Iterate through the test for a predefined number (as opposed to running the test for a length of time)	No	Yes
Data storage	The data storage mechanism of test data and reports	Access	XML
Supported by Microsoft support services	Formal support by Microsoft	No	Yes

* Note: WAS does not collect counters on Microsoft Windows XP machines

User Interfaces

ACT has two user interfaces, one that is integrated into the Visual Studio Integrated Development Environment (also known as the IDE) and a standalone user interface. You can access the integrated version by opening the Visual Studio .NET IDE and adding a new project or adding an ACT project to your open solution containing other projects. You then add a new test item by either browser recording, or manually creating your test in JScript or VBScript. We'll be walking through the browser record process later in the chapter. Note that ACT does not support the new .NET languages of Visual Studio .NET, it only supports COM based languages.

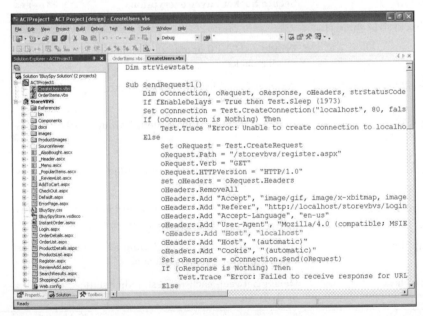

You can also access the standalone environment from the Windows Start menu at Start | Programs | Microsoft Visual Studio .NET | Visual Studio .NET Enterprise Features | Microsoft Application Center Test:

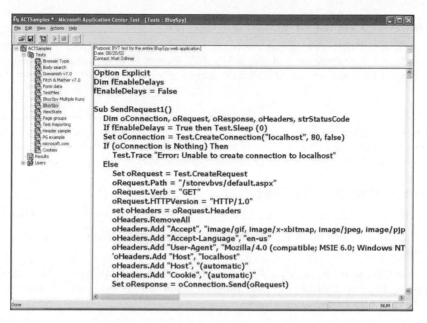

```
Option Explicit
Dim fEnableDelays
fEnableDelays = False

Sub SendRequest1()
    Dim oConnection, oRequest, oResponse, oHeaders, strStatusCode
    If fEnableDelays = True then Test.Sleep (0)
    Set oConnection = Test.CreateConnection("localhost", 80, false)
    If (oConnection is Nothing) Then
        Test.Trace "Error: Unable to create connection to localhost"
    Else
        Set oRequest = Test.CreateRequest
        oRequest.Path = "/storevbvs/default.aspx"
        oRequest.Verb = "GET"
        oRequest.HTTPVersion = "HTTP/1.0"
        set oHeaders = oRequest.Headers
        oHeaders.RemoveAll
        oHeaders.Add "Accept", "image/gif, image/x-xbitmap, image/jpeg, image/pjp
        oHeaders.Add "Accept-Language", "en-us"
        oHeaders.Add "User-Agent", "Mozilla/4.0 (compatible; MSIE 6.0; Windows NT
        'oHeaders.Add "Host", "localhost"
        oHeaders.Add "Host", "(automatic)"
        oHeaders.Add "Cookie", "(automatic)"
        Set oResponse = oConnection.Send(oRequest)
```

Both interfaces allow you to create and run tests. These same tests can be opened in either environment, although a single test cannot be open in both environments at the same time. The stand-alone interface provides more test options such as the ability to create your own users and view graphical reports. The IDE interface has a better-looking test editor by providing some of the features of Visual Studio .NET, such as color coding.

Testing a .NET Web Application with ACT

For the next few pages, we are going to demonstrate ACT's dynamic test object model by creating tests for the IBuySpy sample web application that ships with Visual Studio .NET. IBuySpy is an ideal web application for this because it utilizes many of ASP.NET's new features and shows how ACT's script-ability makes it possible to test this new technology. Some of the things we'll be testing are forms based authentication, ASP.NET viewstate, and web services that require SOAP.

To install the latest version of the IBuySpy sample application, go to http://www.ibuyspy.com (or http://www.asp.net) and download the IBuySpy Store (not IBuySpy portal). You can download either the VB.NET or C# version. Although the IBuySpy application works with either MSDE or SQL server as its database, using MSDE imposes some restrictions such as a connection limit, and therefore is inappropriate for performance testing with multiple connections. The same is true for the Personal edition of SQL Server. You'll get errors if the application is placed under heavy load. Therefore, we recommend using the full-blown SQL server product or some other enterprise database product.

Recording a test in ACT is a fairly simple process. ACT contains an HTTP recorder that enables you to navigate your web application or web service just as a customer would. During this process, a test is being created in ACT. After recording the test, you can then modify any part of the request to simulate multiple customers requesting pages with different parameters.

Creating an ACT Project in Visual Studio .NET

Open Visual Studio .NET, click on File | New | Project, and expand the Other Projects folder. Select Application Center Test Projects, and then select ACT Project from the templates view. Name your new ACT project `IBuySpy Tests`. Once a new project is created, you can start adding tests to that project.

The IBuySpy application requires that all new users register before accessing certain parts of the application. We're going to record this procedure so that we have a test that allows us to create several new users in the customer table of the IBuySpy database. This makes subsequent tests more accurate because we can log in as a new user every time the test executes.

Browser Recording an ACT Test

❑　Right-click on the new `IBuySpy Tests` project and choose Add | Add New Item.

❑　Click Browser Recorded Test (.vbs) in the Templates view, and name the test `RegisterUsers.vbs`.

❑　Select OK and the browser record dialog opens. Click the Start button. Your default browser opens. Type the URL of your local IBuySpy application in the browser's address bar, for example: http://localhost/storevbvs/.

❑　Click the Sign In icon on the top right-hand side of the application, then click the Register option from the bottom of the Sign In page.

❑　Fill in the register page with your full name, email address, and password, then click Submit.

❑　Close your browser and click Stop and OK on the browser record dialog. A new browser recorded test displays in the Visual Studio work area.

> **Keep in mind that ACT records all HTTP traffic on the local machine; if you have a stock-ticker running in the background for example, ACT will record this traffic as well.**

Examining this new test we see that there are approximately 25 different requests in the `main()` subroutine located at the bottom of the test window. ACT records every request for a page and all the elements in the page as a new request subroutine.

> *Tip: If you would like to transpose a test from another tool into an ACT test you can run the test in the other tool while ACT's browser recorder is activated. ACT will record all the HTTP events created by the other test tool.*

For the purpose of creating several new IBuySpy users, we only need the GET and POST requests to the `register.aspx` page. You can locate requests to this page by looking at the `.PATH` property of each request. These requests will be toward the end of the test. The reason we need the GET and the POST is explained when we discuss the .NET view state later in the chapter. Search the test to locate these two subroutines and then you can safely delete all the other subroutines. Rename these two subroutines `SendRequest1()` and `SendRequest2()`, and delete all the other call statements from the `main()` subroutine. Also, go ahead and remove `Option Explicit` from the test as well. You should end up with two request subroutines, a main subroutine that calls these request subroutines, and a main statement outside of all subroutines that calls `main`.

> You can eliminate images in your browser record session by turning off **Show pictures** on the **Advanced** tab of Internet Explorer's **Internet Options**. This can greatly decrease the size of a test but, of course, it can also decrease the accuracy of your test.

Changing the Users

We are now ready to modify the POST request so that it registers a new user with each request. Look at the oRequest.Body statements in the POST subroutine. They should look something like this:

```
oRequest.Body = "__VIEWSTATE=dDwtMTE1NzA2NDE3MTs7bDxSZWdpc3RlckJObj"
oRequest.Body = oRequest.Body + _
                "s%2BPnCGRpbLLjeSGeLG0X4YKsuAb0S7&Name=Matt+Odhner&"
oRequest.Body = oRequest.Body + _
                "Email=mattod@email.com&Password=Password&ConfirmPa"
oRequest.Body = oRequest.Body + "ssword=Password&RegisterBtn.x=29&RegisterBtn.y=9"
```

Replace the reference to your login name with Test.GetCurrentUser.Name. You'll need to concatenate this text into the body using ampersands. Replace all occurrences of your password with Test.GetCurrentUser.Password. This will also need to be concatenated with ampersands. By doing this, ACT replaces every occurrence of Test.GetCurrentUser.Name with the next user in the users node. Since we did not define any users, ACT automatically creates users for us. Each iteration through the test will get a new user. The same is true for Test.GetCurrentUser.Password, except these will be automatically replaced with passwords.

Note that the email name needs to be in the format of an email address in order for the POST to work, so concatenate "@email.com to the end of Test.GetCurrentUser.Name for the email address.

ASP.NET Viewstate

We also need to modify the viewstate in this POST. The viewstate GUID is new with .NET applications and is very useful for tracking information that has already been typed into a form as well as other information about the form elements. In this test, we are going to replace this GUID with a variable. Make sure you remove the entire viewstate and replace it with a variable called strViewState – some of the viewstate may be concatenated to additional lines.

After making these changes, the body of your POST should look something like this:

```
oRequest.Body = "__VIEWSTATE=" & strViewState
oRequest.Body = oRequest.Body + "&Name=" & Test.GetCurrentUser.Name
oRequest.Body = oRequest.Body + "Email=" & Test.GetCurrentUser.Name &
            "@email.com&Password=" & Test.GetCurrentUser.Password & "&ConfirmPa"
oRequest.Body = oRequest.Body + "ssword=" & Test.GetCurrentUser.Password &
                "&RegisterBtn.x=29&RegisterBtn.y=9"
```

At the top of the test, outside all subroutines, dimension the strViewState variable. This makes it a global variable available to all subroutines in the test. This is useful when the test contains more than one request because this variable can be re-used with each occurrence of the viewstate:

```
Dim strViewState
```

Add the following snippet of code to the GET request. Just add the code between the BEGIN and END viewstate parsing comments – we've included some additional code to show you where to add these lines in the GET subroutine. It should be added after the oResponse object has been set:

```
If (oResponse is Nothing) Then
    Test.Trace "Error: Failed to receive response for URL to " +
                        "/StoreVBVS/register.aspx"
Else

    '******** BEGIN VIEWSTATE PARSING

    oRequest.ResponseBufferSize = 20000 ' default is 8192
    If InStr(oResponse.Body, "__VIEWSTATE") Then
      Pos1 = InStr(InStr(oResponse.Body, "__VIEWSTATE"), oResponse.Body, _
                      "value=")
      Pos2 = InStr(Pos1, oResponse.Body, ">")
      strViewstate = Mid(oResponse.Body, Pos1 + 7, Pos2 - Pos1 - 10)
      strViewstate = Replace(strViewstate, "+", "%2B")
      strViewstate = Replace(strViewstate, "=", "%3D")
    End if

    '******** END VIEWSTATE PARSING

    strStatusCode = oResponse.ResultCode
  End If
  oConnection.Close
  End If
End Sub
```

Let's stop here for a moment because this viewstate parsing code deserves some discussion. The first line of this code snippet is increasing the ResponseBufferSize of ACT from its default size of 8,192 bytes. This ensures that the response buffer has enough room to store the entire response from the web server. On occasion, viewstate GUIDs can be rather large so not having a buffer that is big enough will cause the response to be truncated, and some or all of the viewstate will be lost, preventing this routine from parsing the correct value or any value at all. If the viewstate is invalid, your test will get HTTP errors.

The next line is looking for the __VIEWSTATE attribute in the response. This attribute will likely only appear once in the response, so we just need to locate the first occurrence. The rest of the routine does some text manipulation to extract only the viewstate value from the response.

To summarize what we are doing here, it works like this. Web forms generally require a GET request in order to first display the form. A viewstate is returned in the response body of this GET request. This viewstate value is then passed back to the web server with the associated POST to the same form. Within the ACT test, we grab the viewstate in the GET and then pass it back in the POST. This can occur several times in a single test, so each GET for a form that uses viewstate requires this snippet of code. The strViewState global variable is replaced each time this routine executes. As long as the POST occurs after its associated GET, this method works fine.

You also have the option of turning viewstate off on specific controls or forms if you don't need it or don't want to use it, but it is a good idea to test your application the way it will be configured in the data center. In other words, if viewstate is being used on the live site, capture it in your ACT test. It may represent a significant source of bandwidth. If you just leave the viewstate as a static value in your ACT test, the web server returns an error when POSTing to the form that requires a dynamic viewstate.

Running the RegisterUsers Test

You now have an ACT test that can be used to create as many users as you like in the IBuySpy database. Let's run this test so that it creates 200 new users. To do this, right-click the `RegisterUsers.vbs` test in the Solution Explorer and choose **Properties**. Within the test properties view, set the iterations to 200. Switch back to the Solution Explorer, right-click on the test, and choose **Start Test**.

The **Output** window displays the status of the test. This is the extent of the reporting while running tests from within the Visual Studio IDE. Examine the **Final Results** to confirm that the test ran for 200 iterations and that no errors occurred.

If there are script errors, ACT displays an error in the output window. The values in parenthesis in the error are the line number and column number, respectively, where the compilation error occurred in the test.

```
C:\Visual Studio Projects\IBuySpy\RegisterUsers.vbs(41,9) : VBScript compilation
error: Expected 'Sub'(41,9)
```

If you have SQL Server installed, you can use the **Query Analyzer** to view the contents of the `Customers` table within the `Store` database and confirm that 200 new customers have been added after running a successful test, as shown in the screnshot below:

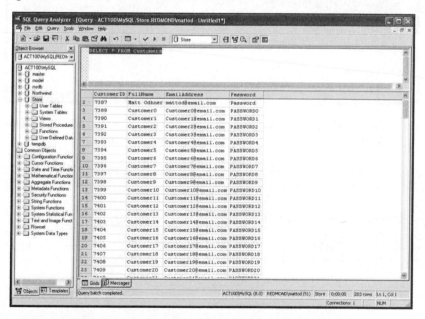

Testing SOAP-Enabled Web Services

The IBuySpy sample application contains some web service methods that are accessed from the **Services** icon in the top right corner of the web application browser display. We're going to use one of these web service methods to add several new orders to the IBuySpy application to see if there is any contention when multiple customers order items simultaneously. ACT does not contain direct support for passing SOAP requests to a web service, so you'll need to modify the body to make this work correctly. This section describes the details of this process.

Click on the **Services** icon (top right corner of the IBuySpy application) and select the **OrderItem** method to view the web service help page. Create a new empty ACT test named `OrderItems.vbs` and copy the SOAP envelope from the `OrderItem` method help page, as shown by the highlighted items in the following screenshot:

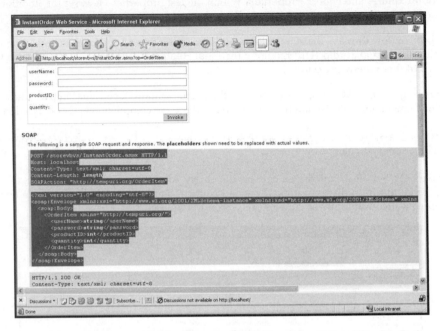

Paste this data using the **Paste as HTML** option on the **Edit** menu of Visual Studio. Reformat the headers that you copied over so that they look similar to the following:

```
Set oConnection = Test.CreateConnection("localhost", 80, false)
Set oRequest = Test.CreateRequest
```

```
oRequest.Path = "/storevbvs/InstantOrder.asmx?op=OrderItem""" ' replace with your
                                                             ' correct path
oRequest.Verb = "POST"
oRequest.HTTPVersion = "HTTP/1.1"
```

```
oRequest.Headers.RemoveAll
oRequest.Headers.Add "Host", "(automatic)"
oRequest.Headers.Add "Content-Type", "text/xml; charset=utf-8"
oRequest.Headers.Add "Content-Length", "(automatic)"
oRequest.Headers.Add "SOAPAction", "http://tempuri.org/OrderItem"
```

Highlight the SOAP envelope, that you pasted in, and choose **Edit | Find and Replace | Replace** from Visual Studio Edit Menu. In the **Find What** edit box, type a double-quote mark ("). In the **Replace** box, type the following:

```
"& chr(34) &"
```

This should include the quotes, ampersands, and spaces on each side. Click Replace All, there should be twelve occurrences in this example.

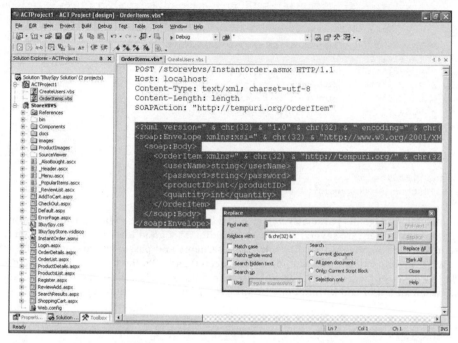

Add Body = " to the first line, and Body = Body & " to all the subsequent lines of the modified SOAP envelope. Also, add a quote at the end of each line. Then add the following lines to the end of the test:

```
oRequest.Body = Body
Set oResponse = oConnection.Send(oRequest)
```

Your ACT web service SOAP request should look like this now:

```
set oConnection = Test.CreateConnection("localhost", 80, false)
set oRequest = Test.CreateRequest

oRequest.Path = """/storevbvs/InstantOrder.asmx?op=OrderItem"
oRequest.Verb = "POST"
oRequest.HTTPVersion = "HTTP/1.1"

oRequest.Headers.RemoveAll
oRequest.Headers.add "Host", "(automatic)"

oRequest.Headers.Add "Content-Type", "text/xml; charset=utf-8"
oRequest.Headers.Add "Content-Length", "(automatic)"
oRequest.Headers.Add "SOAPAction", "http://tempuri.org/OrderItem"
" " " " " " " " " " " "
Body = "<?xml version=" & Chr(34) & "1.0" & Chr(34) & " encoding=" & Chr(34) & _
       "utf-8" & ⌐ Chr(34) & "?>"
Body = Body & "<soap:Envelope xmlns:xsi=" & Chr(34) & _
```

```
            "http://www.w3.org/2001/XMLSchema-instance" & Chr(34) & " xmlns:xsd=" & _
            Chr(34) & "http://www.w3.org/2001/XMLSchema" & Chr(34) & _
            " xmlns:soap=" & Chr(34) & "http://schemas.xmlsoap.org/soap/envelope/" & _
            Chr(34) & ">"
    Body = Body & "   <soap:Body>"
    Body = Body & "      <OrderItem xmlns=" & Chr(34) & "http://tempuri.org/" & _
            Chr(34) & ">"
    Body = Body & "         <userName>string</userName>"
    Body = Body & "         <password>string</password>"
    Body = Body & "         <productID>int</productID>"
    Body = Body & "         <quantity>int</quantity>"
    Body = Body & "      </OrderItem>"
    Body = Body & "   </soap:Body>"
    Body = Body & "</soap:Envelope>"

    oRequest.Body = Body
    Set oResponse = oConnection.Send(oRequest)
```

Now we need to change the parameter values of the SOAP envelope so that it is passing unique values with each request. There are several ways to do this, but it's a good idea to use the random function because it is one of the simplest methods. For the username and password parameter values this is fairly simple. We want to randomly select a number between 0 and 199, the number of users and passwords we added to the customers table earlier with `RegisterUsers.vbs`. A good way to generate a random value between an upper and lower bound in VBScript is to use the following formula:

```
Randomize
Int((upperbound - lowerbound + 1) * Rnd + lowerbound)
```

The following snippet of code generates an `iUserNum` number between the upper and lower limits that we added to the customer database:

```
Randomize
iUserNum = Int((199 - 0 + 1) * Rnd + 0)
```

Adding a quantity parameter is straightforward as well. We'll use random quantities from 1 to 100:

```
Randomize
iQty = Int((100 - 1 + 1) * Rnd + 1)
```

The `ProductID` parameter presents a bit of a problem because the product IDs in the `Products` table are not sequential – some values are missing in the 355 to 406 range of IDs. This is not a particularly uncommon occurrence when creating a test that works with database data. One way to transpose this data into something ACT can use is to employ the export feature of SQL Server Enterprise Manager to export the `ProductID` column to a comma separated text file. After doing this, we create the `ProdNum` array, and then create the statement to select ID elements from within this array randomly:

```
ProdNum = Array(355,356,357,358,359,360,362,363,364,365,367,368,370, _
                371,372,373,374,375,376,377,378,379,382,384,385,386,387, _
                388,389,390,391,393,394,396,397,399,400,401,402,404,406)
```

```
Randomize
id = Int((UBound(ProdNum) - LBound(ProdNum) + 1) * Rnd + LBound(ProdNum))
```

When complete, the web service test looks like the following:

```
set oConnection = Test.CreateConnection("localhost", 80, false)
set oRequest = Test.CreateRequest

oRequest.Path = "/storevbvs/InstantOrder.asmx?op=OrderItem"
oRequest.Verb = "POST"
oRequest.HTTPVersion = "HTTP/1.1"

oRequest.Headers.RemoveAll
oRequest.Headers.add "Host", "(automatic)"
oRequest.Headers.Add "SOAPAction", "http://tempuri.org/OrderItem"
oRequest.Headers.Add "Content-Type", "text/xml; charset=utf-8"
oRequest.Headers.Add "Content-Length", "(automatic)"

Randomize
iUserNum = Int((199 - 1 + 1) * Rnd + 1)

Randomize
iQty = Int((100 - 1 + 1) * Rnd + 1)

ProdNum = Array(355,356,357,358,359,360,362,363,364,365,367,368,370,
                371,372,373,374,375,376,377,378,379,382,384,385,386,387,388, _
                389,390,391,393,394,396,397,399,400,401,402,404,406)

Randomize
id = Int((UBound(ProdNum) - LBound(ProdNum) + 1) * Rnd + LBound(ProdNum))

Body = "<?xml version=" & Chr(34) & "1.0" & Chr(34) & " encoding=" & Chr(34) & _
       "utf-8" & Chr(34) & "?>"
Body = Body & "<soap:Envelope xmlns:xsi=" & Chr(34) & _
       "http://www.w3.org/2001/XMLSchema-instance" & Chr(34) & " xmlns:xsd=" & _
       Chr(34) & "http://www.w3.org/2001/XMLSchema" & Chr(34) & _
       " xmlns:soap=" & chr(34) & "http://schemas.xmlsoap.org/soap/envelope/" & _
       Chr(34) & ">"
Body = Body & "  <soap:Body>"
Body = Body & "    <OrderItem xmlns=" & Chr(34) & "http://tempuri.org/" & _
       Chr(34) & ">"
Body = Body & "      <userName>Customer" & iUserNum & "@email.com</userName>"
Body = Body & "      <password>PASSWORD" & iUserNum & "</password>"
Body = Body & "      <productID>" & ProdNum(id) & "</productID>"
Body = Body & "      <quantity>" & iQty & "</quantity>"
Body = Body & "    </OrderItem>"
Body = Body & "  </soap:Body>"
Body = Body & "</soap:Envelope>"

oRequest.Body = Body
Set oResponse = oConnection.Send(oRequest)
```

Try running this test for 10 iterations at first to make sure everything is working as expected. Watch for HTTP errors in the output window, this would likely mean there is a typo in the test. View the contents of the `Orders` and `OrderDetails` tables using SQL query analyzer to see the results of your test, for example:

```
SELECT * FROM OrderDetails
```

Alternately,

```
SELECT * FROM Orders
```

You can then increase the stress level and test length to test for contention. The stress level is increased by increasing the "Simultaneous browser connections" on the property page for a test. Watch the processor utilization on the client, if it goes above 90% for an extended period of time the test results could be invalid. This happens because the ACT client becomes so saturated trying to run the ACT test that it cannot delegate processor power to collecting the result data, so some data can get lost or skewed.

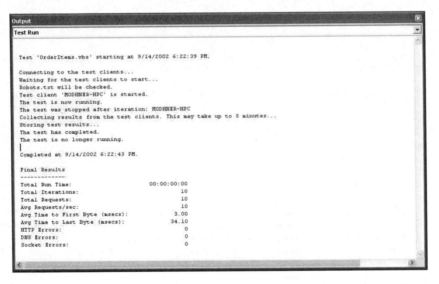

You now have two ACT tests that can be used to determine the performance of the IBuySpy registration page and the `orderItems` web service method.

Test Properties

Now that you have an idea of how to create ACT tests, we are going to delve into some of the test settings that are available. Test properties are available by right-clicking a test in the standalone user interface, or viewing the properties window in the IDE interface. The property page for a test in the stand-alone interface contains three tabs, and a few more options than the Visual Studio properties for a test.

General Test Properties

The General tab is where you define the stress level and the test duration.

Test Load Level

Each increase in the Simultaneous browser connections of the test load level simulates an additional web user requesting pages from your application. If you want to simulate 40 users simultaneously requesting pages from your application, change this value to 40, and so on.

Keep in mind that this is not the same as 40 requests/second. In fact, depending on the complexity of the application being tested, it is probably quite different from 40 requests per second.

One thing to remember when setting the stress level is that ACT contains a much more efficient stress engine than WAS does. Therefore, it requires many fewer simultaneous browser connections to achieve a high stress level. Again, be careful that you do not saturate the processor on the client machine by using too big a value for the stress level. If you cannot achieve web server saturation with one client, you may need to use a more powerful client machine. Start with a small number such as 1 or 2 for the simultaneous browser connections, and increase in increments of 5 or 10.

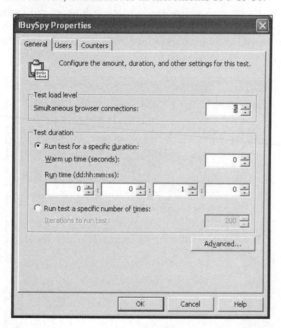

Test Duration

ACT provides the ability to run a test over 999 days, or up to 999,999 iterations. For performance tests on specific pieces of an application, I like to run each test for 10 minutes at increasing stress levels until the web server reaches a point of saturation on some resource. The iterations option is especially useful for commerce applications where you only want to simulate ordering an item a certain number of times.

There is also a warm-up option in the test duration section. This prevents report data from being collected for the length of time that the warm up is set. This is useful for applications that use extensive caching or contain several objects that must be instantiated before the performance test begins. Also, note that ASP.NET applications recompile when the first page is requested from that application after a change in one or more pages. This process, although usually very quick, may take some time with large applications. You can watch the processor on the web server during the recompile phase to see how long this operation takes for your application. Once you determine this, this is what the warm up should be set to.

Advanced button

Selecting the advanced button at the bottom of the general properties tab displays a dialog that allows you to turn on or off the collection of detailed report data. This controls the amount of information generated and saved during a test run. Using the less-detailed reporting option will decrease the amount of time it takes to create a report, especially for tests which request a larger number of unique paths.

If detailed results are used, reports will include information for each page that was requested in the test. If detailed results are not used, average values for the test run will be calculated and saved, but the page-level information will not be stored in the report.

Users Test Properties

By default, when an ACT stress test runs, ACT automatically creates user names and passwords for you. We can utilize these properties directly in your test by adding Test.GetCurrentUser.Name and Test.GetCurrentUser.Password where appropriate, just as we did earlier in the IBuySpy test. ACT automatically creates up to 5,000 users as a test is running, and then starts over again with the first user. The user names and passwords are CustomerX and PASSWORDX, where X is an incrementally increasing value from 0 to 5,000.

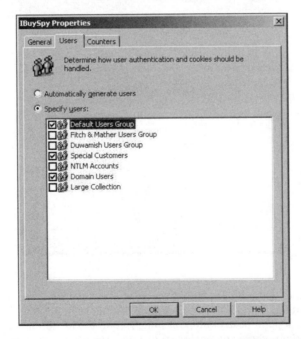

You also have the option of creating your own unique usernames and passwords. This must be accomplished in the standalone ACT user interface. Create your custom user group in the Users node located under the tests in the tree node on the left-hand side of the stand-alone interface.

To create a user group, select the users node, right-click, and choose add. A user group named New User Group is added. You can change the name of this group just as you would change a file name in Windows Explorer – by clicking it and typing a new name. It probably goes without saying that you should give your user groups a name that represents the type of users in that group.

Note that you are not quite done though. Users need to be added to each test that will use them. After creating this user group, right-click on a test, choose **Properties**, select the **Users** tab, and if the **Automatically create users** option is selected, change this to **Specify users**. Any groups you created in the users node will appear in the users property page for all tests. Also, enable the user group that you created by putting a check next to it and deselect any user groups you don't need.

One more thing you should know about ACT users is that they also store cookie data (see the *Working with Cookies and Other Header Data* section later in this chapter for more information), and they can be used to authenticate. When using a browser against an authenticated web application, the browser pops up a dialog asking you to enter your username and password for each request that requires your credentials. ACT does the same thing when an application requires credentials, except it grabs the users from the users list instead of requesting this information from you. It looks for the next available user in your custom list and passes the user name and password (see the *Authentication and Encryption* section later in this chapter for more information).

Counters Test Properties

In short, the purpose of web stress testing is to locate the bottleneck. Locating the bottleneck would be very difficult without performance monitor counters. For this reason, ACT allows you to collect counters as the test is running. Collection stops when the test stops. The counters collected are summarized and shown in the results:

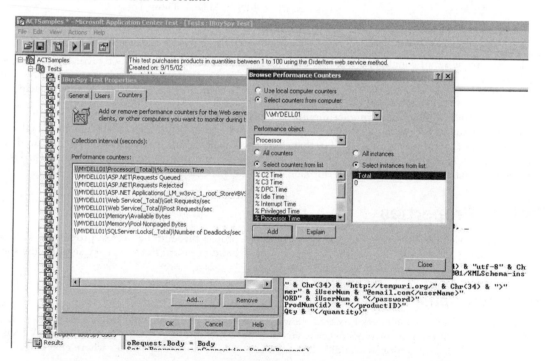

There is an abundance of counters available on Windows servers. To avoid overload, in the number of counters being collected as well as your brain, the trick is to sample only a small number of them to get an idea of where the bottleneck lies, then drill down on this object to find out the cause.

With web applications, bottlenecks will happen in one of the following five areas:

❑ Processor

❑ Memory

❑ Disk

❑ Bandwidth

❑ A resource that the web server utilizes, but is not part of the web server, and is preventing the request rate from increasing. For example, SQL server.

I start with the following general counters for each bottleneck type when stress testing .NET web applications:

Type of Counter	Measures
Processor	Processor, % CPU Utilization
Memory	System, Context Switches/Sec
Network bandwidth	Network interface, Bytes Total/Sec
Disk	Physical Disk, % Disk Time_Total
Backend resource	ASP.NET, Requests Queued

This is a sparse set of counters to start with, and you will probably have your own favorites. It is a good idea to watch the processor on the machine running ACT as well. If the client processor becomes more than 90% saturated, you should decrease the stress level or switch to a more powerful client machine.

Windows also includes a performance monitor tool that allows you to log all the counter samples collected. You can access this tool by typing perfmon in the Start | Run menu. The benefit of collecting performance monitor counters in ACT is that counter collection starts and ends with the test run. If you use Windows Performance monitor, you must start and stop the collection of counters manually. For more information on the Windows Performance monitor, see Chapter 9.

Project Properties

You can access properties that affect all of the tests in a project through the project properties. This two-tabbed dialog contains settings that affect the way ACT handles robots.txt, proxy settings, the socket request time-out, and some debug trace files settings.

Test Server Options

This section provides one check box that allows you to enable or disable checking for robots.txt. This option is different from WAS because you now have the option to disable it, whereas in WAS it is always checked. This option is available because there are certain circumstances where checking robots.txt will break the functionality of the tool.

If enabled, ACT looks for a robots.txt file in the root virtual directory of each unique web server in the test. If the following line is found in that file when the test begins, ACT will not allow you to stress test that server:

```
# Stress Agent is the user-agent string ACT sends when identifying itself
User-agent: Stress-Agent
# / excludes ACT from all parts of the Web site
Disallow: /
```

The purpose of robots checking is to provide web site owners with a way to protect themselves from someone (perhaps inadvertently) stress testing their site. You'll receive the following message if you turn off robots checking in ACT:

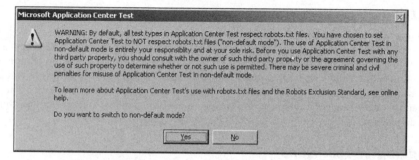

This rather scary message is simply saying that if you turn off checking for robots.txt you are responsible for any harm done to others, such as denial of service attacks. See the Help topic *ACT and the Robots Exclusion Standard* in the Help file of the stand-alone version of ACT for more information about this option:

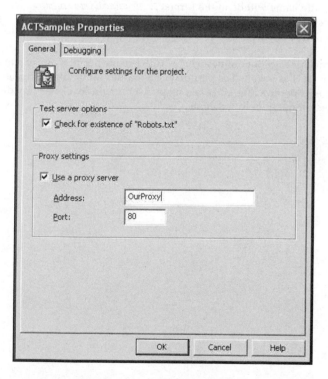

Proxy Settings

The proxy settings allow you to specify the proxy server and port that ACT will use when running a test. This does not have any affect on proxy used when the browser is recording tests; ACT uses the proxy settings of the browser when recording. You'll need to manually set the proxy used when running a test on the project property page if you intend to stress test a site over a proxy server. Testing a web application over a proxy is not recommended, since proxies can distort the load by responding from their cache instead of letting the request go to the web server.

Socket Settings

Socket request timeout is the time that ACT waits for each response from the web server. After a request is sent, ACT expects the web server to respond within the time specified by the socket request timeout. Under special circumstances, such as when a request is performing some complex and time intensive activity, this value can be increased from its default setting of two minutes. You generally would not want a page to take this long if a user will be viewing it, but web services being requested by another machine may require long execution times – and in that scenario the response time may not be as much a concern.

Enable Logging of Test Runs

This feature allows you to enable or disable the logging functionality, control the log file recycle size, and specify what folder the log file should be created in. The log file is called `ACTTrace.log` by default; (see the *Debugging Tests* section later in this chapter for more information) and also by default, it is created in the folder where ACT is installed. If you change the folder where the log file is to be created, the new log file name will be in the format `ACT_<machine name>.log`. Make sure the `ACTUser` has permissions to write to the folder or share specified in this dialog, otherwise no log will be created and no warning is displayed.

The `ACTUser` is a machine account under which ACT gets its permissions to run and save files. This user is created when ACT is installed as part of Visual Studio setup. Since this user is simply a Windows user, you can change its permissions and even make it a domain level user. By default, ACTUser is a member of the Users group on your machine:

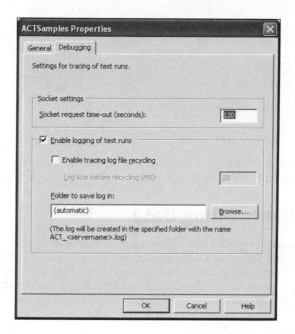

Working with Delays

You'll notice that when you create a test using the browser recorder, ACT adds some script that imposes a delay in the test, based on how long this activity was required when you recorded the test with your browser. This is an attempt to simulate real web user delays. Delays are only needed if you want to accurately simulate the arrival times of real Internet traffic. This is not always as important when performance testing, because in that scenario we are often trying to determine the maximum load of a system.

Nevertheless, delays are an important part of creating an accurate stress test that simulates real web customers. To get a clearer understanding of what delay should be used for each request, analyze the web server logs of the live site (if they are available), to determine the difference between request arrival times from the same IP address.

The delay code that ACT creates is based on the time it took for you to request the pages during the browser record process, for example you waited 23 milliseconds before requesting the next page in the following example:

```
Dim fEnableDelays
fEnableDelays = False
...
If fEnableDelays = True Then Test.Sleep (23)
...
End If
```

If you set fEnableDelays to True, the script calls the Test.Sleep method to cause the current thread to pause for the number of milliseconds specified. This means that each simultaneous browser connection will delay for the exact same amount of time. This is called a static delay. Often it is more realistic to impose a random delay. For example, let's say you want to impose a random delay between 5 and 40 milliseconds. You can do this by modifying the snippet above to read like this:

```
Dim fEnableDelays
fEnableDelays = True
...
Randomize
iDelayTime = Int((40 - 5 + 1) * Rnd + 5)

If fEnableDelays = True Then Test.Sleep (iDelayTime)
   ...
End If
```

Be careful with delays. Too large a delay can bog down the ACT client machine because all of the threads spend too much time in a sleep state, and less load is getting generated.

Working with Query String Data

ACT does not contain a user interface that allows you to define query string name-value pairs like WAS does. This is probably O.K though since the WAS query string editor is so buggy. In any case, with ACT's script-ability, you can create much more flexible query string parameters. For example, if you want to ensure a unique query string value regardless of the number of simultaneous browser connections, you can do something like the following using GlobalIndexes. Note that GlobalIndexes allow you to store your own data in memory as a test is running – it can almost be equated to application state in ASP.NET.

```
Set oConnection = Test.CreateConnection("localhost", 80, false)
Set oRequest = Test.CreateRequest

NUM_CONNECTIONS = 20

If Test.GetGlobalIndex (1) > NUM_CONNECTIONS Then
  Call Test.SetGlobalIndex(1, 0)
  strQueryStringValue = Test.GetGlobalIndex(1)
Else
  Call Test.IncrementGlobalIndex(1, 1)
  strQueryStringValue = Test.GetGlobalIndex(1)
End If

oRequest.Path = "/default.aspx""?QS=" & strQueryStringValue
oRequest.Verb = "GET"
Set oResponse = oConnection.Send(oRequest)
oConnection.Close
```

We have already discussed randomizing data and reading query string values from an array in previous examples in this chapter. One other thing you have the option of doing in ACT is to read the query string values from a text file. For example, the following snippet of code reads one line at a time from the myQueryStrings.txt file, and passes each line as a query string appended to the request for default.aspx.

```
Set oConnection = Test.CreateConnection("localhost", 80, false)
Set oRequest = Test.CreateRequest

strFileName = "c:\myQueryStrings.txt"
```

```
Set oFileSystemObj = CreateObject("Scripting.FileSystemObject")
Set oQSFile = oFileSystemObj.OpenTextFile(strFileName, 1)

Do While (oQSFile.AtEndOfStream <> True)
  strQueryStringValue  = oQSFile.ReadLine
  oRequest.Path = "/default.aspx""?QS=" & strQueryStringValue
  oRequest.Verb = "GET"
  Set oResponse = oConnection.Send(oRequest)
Loop

Call oQSFile.Close()
oConnection.Close
```

Working with Cookies and Other Header Data

Lets start with cookies first. In WAS, you could go to the Users node and view all the cookies associated with each user – as long as they were in the same domain. There were some advantages to this, but for the most part, it was an inconvenience to have to delete all the cookies between each test run. In ACT, cookies are only maintained between tests if they have not expired. For example, an ASP.NET session cookie expires as soon as the test completes, so these cookies cannot be viewed in ACT after the test. Any cookies that have not expired are viewable, by domain, in the Edit Cookies view. To view un-expired cookies, go to the Users view, select a user, and choose Edit Cookies from the Actions menu:

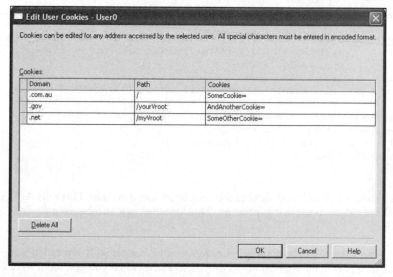

Cookies can be 2,000 bytes in size for the version of ACT that shipped in the first release of Visual Studio .NET. If you have Service Pack 1 of Visual Studio .NET, the cookie size can be 20,480 bytes in size. You can also get this fix from product support services without obtaining Service Pack 1 of Visual Studio .NET.

Default Headers

With regard to other header values, ACT uses a default header if you don't supply one. These header values do not change regardless of the browser type or/and operating system you are running the ACT test on. Since ACT supplies the header for you if you don't specify one, you can create and run a simple test like the following. This by the way, is a perfectly valid test:

```
Test.SendRequest("http://localhost/default.aspx")
```

The default headers that are used are:

```
Host: localhost
User-Agent: Mozilla/4.0 (compatible; MSIE 5.01; Windows NT 5.0)
Accept-Encoding: gzip, deflate
Accept: image/gif, image/x-xbitmap, image/jpeg, image/pjpeg, application/vnd.ms-
powerpoint, application/vnd.ms-excel, application/msword, */*
Accept-Language: en-us
Connection: Keep-Alive
```

If you add headers to this simple test, the headers you add are appended to the default headers. You will commonly want to remove all the default headers, and then add your own custom headers. For example:

```
Sub SendRequest1()
   Set oConnection = Test.CreateConnection("localhost", 80, false)
   Set oRequest = Test.CreateRequest
   oRequest.Path = "/default.aspx"
   oRequest.Verb = "GET"
   oRequest.HTTPVersion = "HTTP/1.0"
   set oHeaders = oRequest.Headers
   oHeaders.RemoveAll  ' this removes the default headers

   oHeaders.Add "Accept", "image/gif, image/x-xbitmap, image/jpeg, image/pjpeg, _
               application/vnd.ms-excel, application/vnd.ms-powerpoint, _
               application/msword, */*"
   oHeaders.Add "Accept-Language", "en-us,ja;q=0.5"
   oHeaders.Add "User-Agent", "Mozilla/4.0 (compatible; MSIE 6.0; " & _
               "Windows NT 5.1; .NET CLR 1.0.3705)"
   oHeaders.Add "Host", "(automatic)"
   oHeaders.Add "Cookie", "(automatic)"
   Set oResponse = oConnection.Send(oRequest)
   oConnection.Close
End Sub
```

Notice the keyword (automatic) next to the host header and cookie. This tells ACT to allow the web server to set these values as the test is running. This keyword can also be used for the Content-Length header.

If you want to see what else can be done with headers, see the sample ACT test called sample-Browser-Type.vbs which is part of the ACTSamples project, available when you first setup ACT on a machine.

Authentication and Encryption

As we said earlier, ACT draws on the Users node for the user names and passwords it uses to authenticate. One important point here is that ACT does not support browser recording authenticated or encrypted web applications, with the exception of basic authentication, only play-back. But, ACT does support play-back of tests against all authentication and encryption types. If your web application is locked down with Windows authentication scheme for example, there are two ways you can get a recording of this web application:

Turn authentication off on the web server temporarily

- ❏ Turn off authentication
- ❏ Record the test
- ❏ Add the appropriate users in the users node, in the format: DOMAIN\username
- ❏ Enable Integrated Windows authentication on the web server
- ❏ Run the ACT test

Change authentication to basic temporarily

- ❏ Change to Basic authentication on the web server
- ❏ Record the test
- ❏ If using NTLM, add the appropriate users in the users node, in the format: DOMAIN\username
- ❏ Enable Integrated Windows authentication on the web server
- ❏ Comment the lines in your recorded test that contain: `oHeaders.Add "Authorization", "Basic..."`
- ❏ Change all HTTPVersion header references to HTTP/1.1 from HTTP/1.0
- ❏ Run the ACT test

When running an ACT test, all of the following authentication schemes are supported:

- ❏ Basic
- ❏ Integrated Windows
- ❏ Digest
- ❏ Passport
- ❏ Forms

In addition, the following encryption types are supported when running an ACT test, but not when recording:

- ❏ Secure Socket Layer 40 bit session encryption key
- ❏ Secure Socket Layer 128 bit session encryption key

If recording encrypted pages, turn off encryption; record the test, then turn encryption back on. Also, change the `CreateConnection` object in ACT to use encryption by setting the last parameter to true and changing the port, for example:

```
Set oConnection = Test.CreateConnection("localhost", 443, true)
```

When testing authenticated web applications using a browser-recorded test, one thing you may run into is the fact that ACT re-authenticates with each request. This is because ACT's browser recorder close the connection after each request, and this may or may not be the behavior you want. If it is not, then change the test to use the same connection throughout. That way, a single user will authenticate only once through one iteration of the test. For example:

```
set oConnection = Test.CreateConnection("servername",80,false)
set oRequest = Test.CreateRequest()
oRequest.path="/default.aspx"
oRequest.HTTPVersion = "HTTP/1.1"
oRequest.headers("Connection") = "Keep-Alive"
call oConnection.Send(oRequest)

set oRequest = Test.CreateRequest()
oRequest.path="/myPage2.aspx"
oRequest.HTTPVersion = "HTTP/1.1"
oRequest.headers("Connection") = "Keep-Alive"
call oConnection.Send(oRequest)
```

The request to /default.aspx and /myPage2.aspx will use the same socket, assuming the web server is set to use keep-alives. Note, you will probably have to change the HTTPVersion header in your browser-recorded test from HTTP/1.0 to HTTP 1.1 to take advantage of keep-alives.

ACT does not support using client certificate authentication of IIS.

Debugging Tests

ACT does not have the full-featured debugging capability of other languages in Visual Studio .NET, but it does have some tools that are very useful for debugging. For example, if you would like to see all of the data being passed between ACT and the web server you can add the following line within one of the subroutines of the test:

```
Test.TraceLevel = -1
```

For more information about this option, search on TraceLevel in the ACT Help file. This property is useful for debugging tests because it writes all the data passed to and from the web server into a file named ACTTrace.log. By default, this file is created in the folder where ACT is installed, which is usually \Program Files\Microsoft ACT. The location of this file can be changed in the ACT project properties though, as discussed earlier.

In addition, you can customize the data that is written to the ACTTrace.log by using something like this:

```
Test.Trace <add your debug information here>
```

For example, if you only wanted to see the result code from one of the requests in a test, you could add the following snippet of code after the oResponse object is set for that request:

```
Test.Trace oResponse.ResultCode
```

You may also write more advanced information to the trace file as a test is executing such as the response time of a page and other data about the test, for example:

```
If oResponse.TTLB > 1000 Then
  Test.Trace "TTLB:" & oResponse.TTLB & _
  ", Customer Number:" & iUserNum & _
  ", Product Number:" & ProdNum(id) & _
  ", Quantity:" & Qty
End if
```

When writing data to the trace file keep in mind that each simultaneous browser connection is iterating through the test, so if the stress level is high the ACTTrace.log file can become large quickly. ACT has a log file recycle option on the debugging property page that can help prevent this from becoming a problem.

Understanding the Results

ACT collects and summarizes all of the response times for each request. The summary of the test is shown in the output window when running tests within Visual Studio .NET. If you are using the standalone user interface, reports are accessed from the Results node. You can also open a test that was run from within the Visual Studio .NET IDE in the standalone interface for further report details. The reports are grouped by the test name, and each test run within a test can be expanded and analyzed.

All report data is stored in XML format. The ACT results node is merely a view of this XML data. You can also use other products that understand XML as your viewer, or you can create a XSL transform to customize your view of this data. See Example of Using ASP and XSL to Create a Custom HTML Report in Help for an example of how this can be accomplished.

Each report contains three major sections:

- **Overview** – Provides summary data of the test and performance monitor counter information.

- **Graphs** – Allow you to graphically view data collected for a test, with the exception of performance monitor counters.

- **Requests** – Displays a summary of all requests, and individual request data.

Here is a sample report with additional information about the various sections:

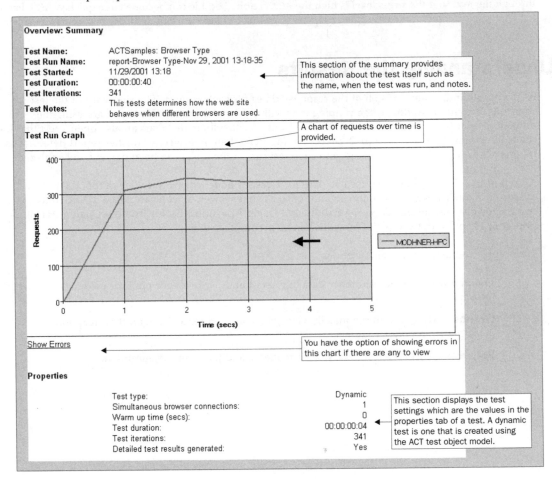

Overview: Summary

Test Name:	ACTSamples: Browser Type
Test Run Name:	report-Browser Type-Nov 29, 2001 13-18-35
Test Started:	11/29/2001 13:18
Test Duration:	00:00:00:40
Test Iterations:	341
Test Notes:	This tests determines how the web site behaves when different browsers are used.

This section of the summary provides information about the test itself such as the name, when the test was run, and notes.

Test Run Graph

A chart of requests over time is provided.

MODHNER-HPC

Show Errors

You have the option of showing errors in this chart if there are any to view

Properties

Test type:	Dynamic
Simultaneous browser connections:	1
Warm up time (secs):	0
Test duration:	00:00:00:04
Test iterations:	341
Detailed test results generated:	Yes

This section displays the test settings which are the values in the properties tab of a test. A dynamic test is one that is created using the ACT test object model.

Summary

Total number of requests:	1,367
Total number of connections:	341
Average requests per second:	341.75
Average time to first byte (msecs):	1.18
Average time to last byte (msecs):	1.38
Average time to last byte per iteration (msecs):	5.55
Number of unique requests made in test:	1
Number of unique response codes:	1

This section displays the summary results of the test run, such as number of request, connections, and the average TTFB/TTLB.

The number of unique requests represent the number of items in the test.

Errors Counts

HTTP:	0
DNS:	0
Socket:	0

This section displays different types of errors that may have occurred during the test run. Socket errors are further broken down in the network statistics section under connection errors.

Additional Network Statistics

Average bandwidth (bytes/sec):	376,785.00
Number of bytes sent (bytes):	321,951
Number of bytes received (bytes):	1,185,189
Average rate of sent bytes (bytes/sec):	80,487.75
Average rate of received bytes (bytes/sec):	296,297.25
Number of connection errors:	0
Number of send errors:	0
Number of receive errors:	0
Number of timeout errors:	0

This section provides information related to how much data was transferred over the network during the test, and how fast.

The connection errors section is a further breakdown of the socket error type. This is useful for determining whether the problem is related to the client, the web server, or the web application itself.

Response Codes

Response Code: 200 - The request completed successfully.

Count:	1,367
Percent (%):	100.00

This section provides a count and a percent for each response code that occured over the course of a test run. These codes are for all pages. To view response codes on an individual page level, see the requests report.

The ACT stand-alone interface also allows you to collect performance monitor counters as the test is running. These counters are averaged and summarized in the ACT results, so if you need more detailed counter information, use the logging feature of the performance monitor tool. To view the collected performance monitor data in ACT select the overview report type, then choose performance counter from the report section window.

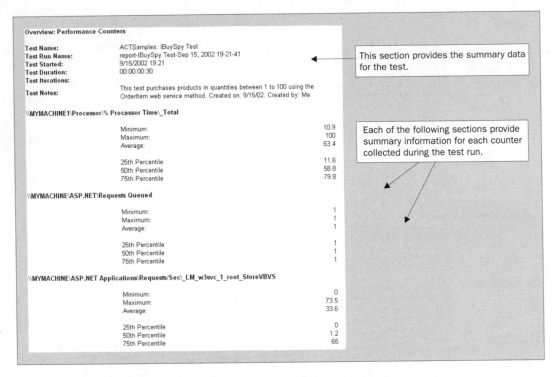

ACT uses **Time to First Byte** (TTFB) and **Time to Last Byte** (TTLB) to accurately represent response time. This is the same metric as WAS uses in its reports. The TTFB is the time from the request until the first byte is received on the client. TTLB is stamped when the last byte of a request is received. Although this does not include browser render time, this provides a key indication as to how long a page takes to display in the user's browser. Look for items with the largest TTLB and drill down on these to determine if performance can be improved.

It is a good idea to define an acceptable TTFB and TTLB for your application prior to running the tests. Many people use 10 seconds as the greatest amount of time a customer should wait for a web page. Once you decide on an acceptable response time, you can determine the amount of load your application can handle before it exceeds acceptable response time.

Reports can also be sorted into percentiles. These provide a good indication of where most response times are clustered over the course of a test. For example, if 99 responses have a TTLB of 500 milliseconds, but just one response in this group took 15 seconds, the average would be skewed to 645 milliseconds. Percentiles alleviate this skew by showing where most of the requests fell. The 50th percentile displays a value in which 50 percent of the requests are greater and 50 percent are less. The values within the 25th and 75th percentiles are the best indication of response time.

Here is a request summary report with some additional information called-out for the various sections:

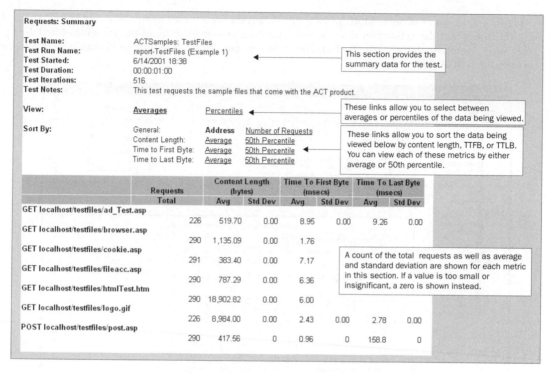

Each test run report can be viewed against another test run from either the same test, or a different test altogether, by selecting the appropriate checkboxes in front of each run in the Test Runs view.

A common goal of performance testing is to view test runs where the browser connections are increased incrementally until a bottleneck occurs. Bottlenecks are generally easy to spot because they show up as decreasing requests per second, despite the fact that the browser connections are increasing, or increasing HTTP and/or socket connect errors. The cause of a bottleneck, however, takes more research. With web applications, the bottleneck will occur in one of five resources: memory, processor, bandwidth, disk, or a backend resource – such as your database server, as discussed earlier.

Graphs can sometimes make a bottleneck easier to locate. For example, here are the steps to create a chart that illustrates a bottleneck:

❑ Run a series of tests against one page of a web application, increasing the simultaneous browser connections with each run.

❑ Select all the test runs for a particular test in the Results node of the stand-alone user interface.

❑ Select Graphs from the report type drop-down.

❑ Select Requests/sec (avg), Total HTTP errors, and Time to Last Byte – TTLB (avg) from the Source(y-axis) selection list.

❑ Select Test runs or Browser connections from the Measured against(x-axis) drop-down.

Using this chart, you can determine, for example, when the web server begins to throw HTTP errors. It is at this point that the web server has reached saturation on one or more of the resources listed previously. Compare this with the performance counters collected while the test is running and you can surmise the bottlenecked resource:

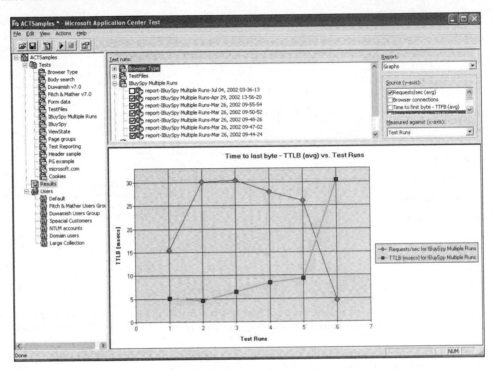

Watch the resources on the client machine carefully. Socket errors can occur when the client machine is saturated – but this does not necessarily mean that the web server has reached a bottleneck. If the client becomes saturated before the web server you can either use a more powerful client machine, or decrease the simultaneous browser connections and extrapolate the bottleneck.

You can view the latest results of a test by selecting the report of interest and choosing View Latest Results on the Action menu:

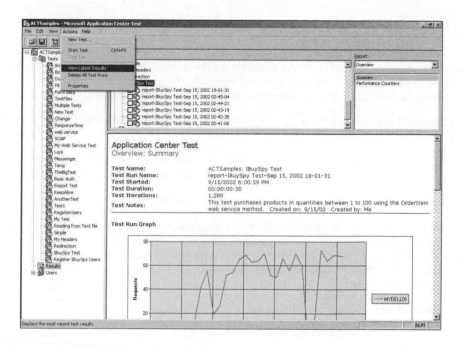

Common ACT Questions

This section contains answers to common questions that people have about the ACT product.

Q. Can I use ACT to test web servers other than Internet Information Server, for example Unix and Linux web servers?

A. Yes. You can use ACT to stress test any web server that adheres to the HTTP protocol specification.

Q. Will ACT ever be able to test protocols other than HTTP?

A. Perhaps, but not likely. Microsoft originally considered creating a transaction engine that other protocols could then easily plug into, however, the future appears to be just HTTP at this time. Various Windows Resource Kits contain tools for stress testing other technologies such as LDAP and SQL.

Q. When will the operations edition be available?

A. No date has been set for this version of the product. It is known that features slated for this version (such as bandwidth throttling and multiple client support) are important to many customers outside the development market. As of the time of writing this book, it is not clear what Microsoft is going to do in this space.

Q. Can ACT execute client-side code?

A. No, not directly. The tool is designed to gather performance of server-side script execution only. However, complex client-side code can be executed from within the ACT scripting object model so that the client script accurately tests more client-code intensive web applications.

Q. Is ACT the new version of Web Application Stress (also known as Homer)?

A. No. ACT is a completely re-architectured and supported product. Microsoft learned a lot about what the customer needs are by making WAS available on the web for free and they heavily utilized this information when designing ACT. For example, one of the biggest feature requests for WAS was the ability to have code execute as the test is running. ACT contains this feature.

Q. Can I import my current Web Application Stress scripts or tests from other web stress tools into ACT?

A. Yes, by running the other tool's test on the same machine that the ACT browser recorder is running. This will create an ACT dynamic and scriptable test from the static WAS test or other products test.

Q. Can I run multiple ACT tests simultaneously on one client?

A. No, only one test can be executed at a time on one client machine. You can, however, run multiple tests on multiple client machines or use scripting to create one test that runs multiple subroutines. Customers often desire to run multiple tests simultaneously so that it simulates the activity of different types of "users" concurrently. This can usually be accomplished with IF and CASE statements in the script of a single ACT test.

Q. Can I record SSL (Secure Socket Layer) enabled web pages?

A. No, turn off SLL encryption on the web server, record the test, turn it on again and change the ACT test to use HTTPS by changing the connection object, as discussed earlier in this chapter. Also, the only supported authentication type for recording is Basic.

Q. How does ACT compare, feature-wise, to other stress tools available?

A. The Visual Studio .NET edition of ACT is designed with the developer in mind and really should not be compared feature for feature to other stress tools. The operations edition, if this product ever becomes available to the public, is more feature-full and can be compared feature for feature against the competition.

Q. What operating systems does ACT require?

A. ACT is supported on Windows 2000 and Windows XP operating systems.

Summary

Web stress testing is not an easy thing to do because it often requires in-depth knowledge of the application being tested, the web server configuration options, and the HTTP protocol. Keep in mind that web stress testing is an iterative process. It is a good idea to start with a low number of concurrent connections and then increase them in equal increments until the web server becomes saturated, or you reach the desired request rate. It is recommended that you use this approach at several intervals throughout the web development cycle to ensure that the product is always meeting your performance objectives.

In this chapter, we have discussed a good deal of the functionality available in Microsoft Application Center Test. We hope this makes the product a bit easier to use. ACT does not contain a lot of fancy user interface, but the good news is that ACT contains a flexible object model that lets you test even the most complex web applications.

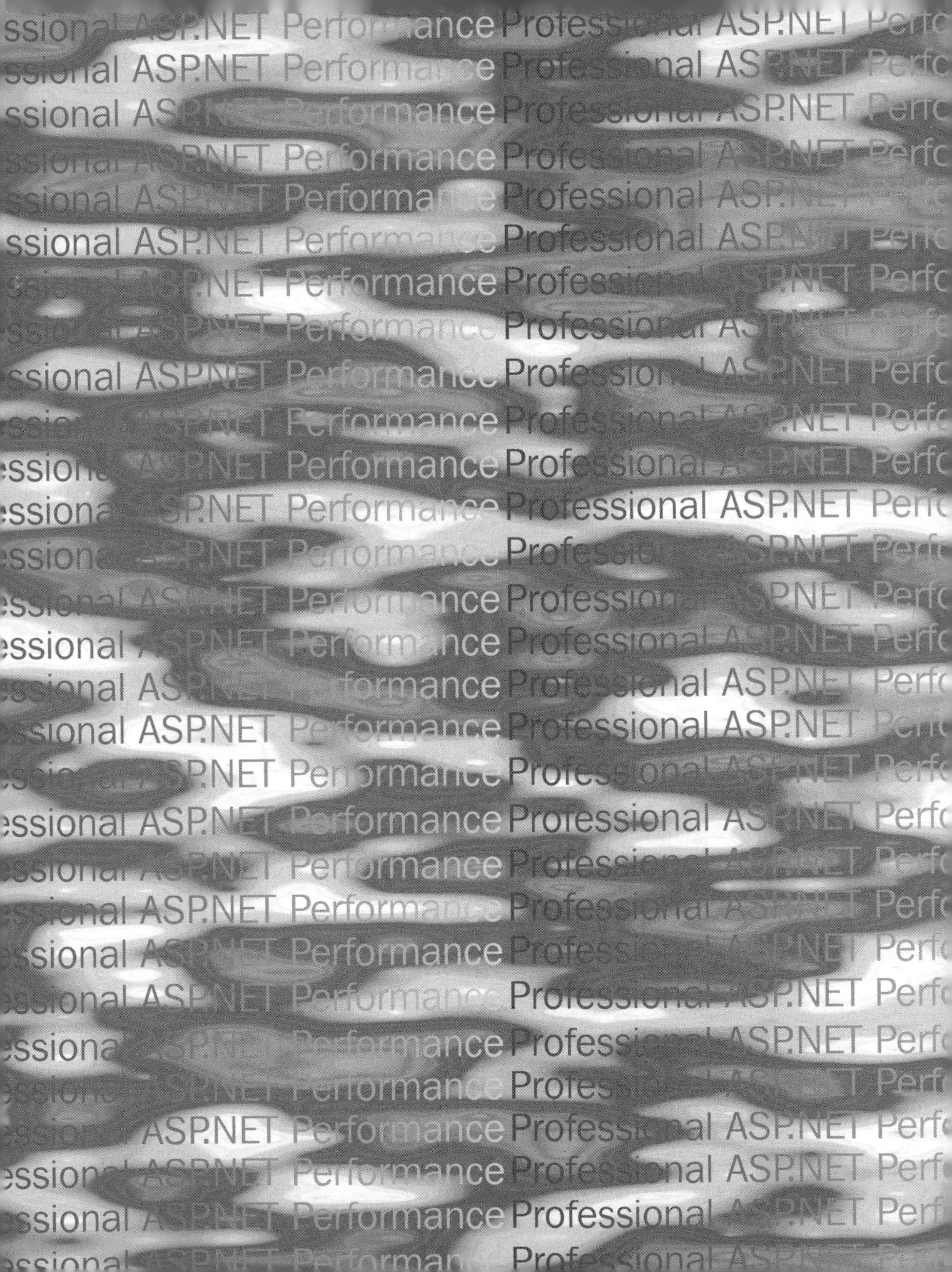
Professional ASP.NET Performance

8

Performance Tuning

If it is found that an application is performing unacceptably, then one of the most cost-effective solutions may be to find optimizations that can be made in the source code. The tuning and re-writing of the segments that are used most frequently, or take the longest to execute, can make the difference between a system that's fit for purpose and one that is unacceptable, removing the need to purchase more expensive hardware to run the application on.

However, there are no quick and simple ways of improving the performance across-the-board on an application that has not been designed efficiently. Improving performance via code-tuning can be a slow, iterative process, and major changes shouldn't be made unless it has been identified that there is definitely a need to increase the performance of that particular part of the application, and that the changes to be made will yield a perceptible improvement.

Poor performance regularly comes from poor application design. This is exacerbated by the use of RAD (Rapid Application Development) methodologies, where there is little opportunity to do sufficient research and design into the most efficient solution architecture up-front. Unfortunately, once an application has been developed, it is very difficult to go back and re-work the underlying architecture.

This chapter covers common areas that cause performance issues in applications that have already been written – but written without taking into consideration all of the best-practices given throughout the book, and it also demonstrates ways of improving them. Many of these items are things that could have been implemented from the start, and we'll see things that were mentioned in previous chapters – however, at this point in the book we have the means to effectively measure the performance costs of our applications, and so we are able to compare and contrast different approaches to the same problem.

Performance comparisons and timings are given throughout the chapter – these were carried out on a machine with the following specification; and will obviously differ in the actual timings, if not the ratios, from other machines.

❑   Dell Inspiron 8100

❑   Pentium III-850 CPU

❑   512MB RAM

❑   Microsoft Windows XP Professional (Service Pack 1)

❑   Internet Explorer v6.0 (Service Pack 1)

❑   .NET Framework (Service Pack 2)

Finding Areas for Optimization

Within any given application, it is very unlikely that every piece of code can be optimized cost-effectively, or that it is already truly optimal. There are always ways of increasing the performance; the difficulty is in finding which ones will have the most noticeable impacts on the system for the least investment.

This section details both ways of determining which areas should be considered for attention, and what considerations should be made when implementing changes.

Identifying bottlenecks

In previous chapters, the measuring of performance has been covered in detail. The results that have been retrieved from the tests, such as details of the individual page execution times and the maximum number of concurrent page requests, can be used to identify areas of the system that should be examined for potential improvements. We saw the page performance calculcation in Chapter 6, a metric that is commonly used to determine such areas. This formula considers both the number of times a piece of code has been executed, and the amount of time an individual call takes to execute.

Once a general area of a system, such as a page, has been identified as making use of more resources than seems appropriate, using tools such as Application Center Test and the Web Application Stress Tool, more fine-grained techniques can be employed to determine the exact subroutines that are causing the inefficiencies. This is where performance counters, traces, and custom techniques such as hand-written timers and stepping through code become the best ways of pinpointing areas for improvement.

Monitoring Performance

As discussed earlier in the book, Trace features are an invaluable tool for determining which portions of a page are using the most resources. The time-stamp for each line of information given, and the display of the memory being used by controls are the key indicators in this, but custom information such as the length of a string being built up can be equally valuable.

Determining where to insert Trace statements is not always immediately obvious. A good place to start is at the entry and exit point of major procedures. Once the procedures that are taking unacceptable periods of time to execute have been identified, more statements can be inserted to track down exactly where the problems are occurring. Stepping through the code in Debug mode is another possibility at this point – however, there is the following caveat:

> It should be remembered that the more in-depth the tracking of performance, the more that the performance is actually altered by performing such tracking.

A further consideration is that the load on the system should be consistent with a production environment when retrieving Trace information, otherwise there may appear to be no performance issues in the system when observing it.

Setting Priorities for Tuning

When performing optimizations, priorities must be set for the type of changes to be made, and where in the application they should be introduced, as benefits to one aspect of a system may be detrimental to another. These should be derived from both the current state of the application and its usages, and expected future developments to the system. Consideration should be given to the topics that are covered below:

- ❑ The aspect of the optimization
- ❑ The nature of the application
- ❑ The required flexibility of the system
- ❑ Physical vs. perceived performance

Depending on the individual application, there may be other considerations that should be used when setting priorities, such as the need for a certain piece of functionality to be reused on a future project.

Optimization Aspects

Although closely linked, there are two separate scenarios for which an application's performance can be optimized – either for individual performance, or for maximum system load.

- ❑ Optimize for individual performance –the easier of the two to improve is usually the speed at which a given task can execute in an isolated environment. Finding more efficient data-structures, developing algorithms that are optimized for the task in hand, and making better use of caching can all greatly decrease the execution time of a code segment in a specific area of a system.

- ❑ Optimize for system load – if individual requests to the application perform well, but the response time or resource usage of the system degrades unacceptably when multiple concurrent requests are made, then a solution is usually harder to find, as it means that there is inefficient usage of resources in one or more parts of the system – potentially not just in a localized area.

Usually an improvement in either one of these two areas will benefit the other but there are certain occasions when improvements in one cause problems in others. These occasions generally arise either from memory usage, or from the locking of limited resources. Such a problem could arise when a routine requires much information retrieving from a database. To improve the performance, this may either be cached locally in a DataSet, or the connection to the database may be kept open whilst the routine is executing, allowing a Command to be sent without acquiring and releasing resources each time. If either of these techniques were implemented, then the resources required while processing would increase, making for a system that drains resources quicker when many requests are being processed at once.

One of the key factors in deciding whether such debatable optimizations should be made lies in whether or not the decrease in the time taken to execute the code allows for the throughput of more requests, even though less may be processed at any given time.

Nature of the application

The types of optimizations that can be made to an application depend largely on its nature, and how it has been fundamentally created. For instance, if a simple data-driven online encyclopedia is taken as an example, then output caching entire pages would vastly improve the performance of the system, removing the need for almost all processing from the most commonly accessed pages. If the same site had the look and feel of each page customized based upon the time of day, or some other highly dynamic feature, then such caching would not provide any real benefit, and an alternative area for optimization would need to be found.

Speed vs. Flexibility

Throughout this chapter, the trade-off of speed vs. flexibility will be prevalent – it is one of the key topics when analyzing and tuning the performance of an application. Whenever an application is optimized towards a particular task, there is generally a removal of some of the flexibility in the system, usually in one of the following areas:

- ❑ The types/structure of the data that can be processed.

- ❑ The ability of the system to detect and act on errors when processing.

- ❑ The reusability of the code.

- ❑ The readability/maintainability of the code. This is generally the case when algorithms are changed from following the real-world business processes they are implementing to a more esoteric, yet logically equivalent form.

Where possible, the performance optimizations described below avoid producing code that suffers from any of the above issues, and in some cases improve on the original situation. There are examples in which one of these must be compromised in order to obtain greater performance, unfortunately.

A good example of this would be sorting a list. If it were known that the list only ever contained integers, then creating a data-structure and sorting algorithm based upon this would be more efficient than having a generalized method that supported strings, dates, and so on.

Whenever the choice has to be made between speed and flexibility, consideration should be given as to whether the code being edited is, or ever will be, used by other parts of any applications. Whether the overhead of shoe-horning data into different formats, detecting errors under certain circumstances when there is no intrinsic error-handling strategy, and other such issues that could potentially lead to the optimizations eventually slowing the system down should also be considered.

Perceived Performance

As mentioned earlier in the book, performance can be measured in two ways:

- ❑ Objectively – The physical time that a page takes to process, render, etc. as measured using some fixed unit such as milliseconds.

- ❑ Subjectively – The perceived performance of the application from the point of view of the end user.

From a developer's point of view, the first of these two aspects is the most approachable, as empirical results can be obtained and acted upon. The subjective aspect is far more difficult to address – rather than simply performing analytical tests and acting on their results, peoples' opinions and the way that they think must be taken into consideration. There are also many more variables that cannot be tested by the tools regularly used to perform objective analysis, such as the time a page takes to finish displaying on a client once the browser has received all of the data.

A good example of how difficult perceived performance can be to measure is given in a fact documented by usability gurus, including the likes of Schneiderman (see "Designing the User Interface", Addison-Wesley, ISBN 0-201-69497-2 for example); if an application responds too quickly to what is perceived as a complex task, the user regularly does not believe that the task has been carried out successfully. So, in some situations, having a highly efficient application is not desirable from every point of view. Having said that, the faster an application runs, the more satisfied all parties involved will be, on the whole.

Working with Controls

Web Server Controls have been introduced with ASP.NET as a new way of creating a bridge between traditional Windows development techniques and HTML when creating user interfaces. They provide a powerful method of building web pages, and dealing with the data and events that are related to them, while dramatically reducing the amount of time required to develop code by having support for state-maintenance. They also support rendering to browsers on different machines, making it far easier to produce cross-platform applications. To provide such rich functionality they perform a lot of processing behind the scenes that uses up many different resources, such as CPU cycles, memory, or network bandwidth.

Pruning the control tree

Due to the breadth of their functionality, and the manner in which they can adapt themselves to different browsers, server controls require a relatively large amount of processing time when compared to simple HTML tags. For this reason, in order to maximize performance, their use on pages should be minimized.

For each control that is added to a web page, a cost is incurred in the time taken to process the code-path of the page. The overhead of this is directly proportional to the number of controls created, with a linear slowdown of processing. **Composite controls** – those that are created by making use of several other controls, generally have a greater overhead associated with them.

If unchanging content is to be rendered to the page, or a simpler method of providing information and retrieving changes made to it on a form is possible, then the controls to do this should be removed and replaced with lighter-weight alternatives. An example of this would be the usage of a Label control for the output of static text or a server-side table for the alignment of other controls, when standard HTML code would have sufficed. Of course, if controls are removed then this should be documented to stop other developers from programming against the controls, in either the current page or others that inherit from it.

> *By enabling Trace functionality, the control tree for a page can be viewed. Examining this, and the execution time of the various methods that populate and render controls should determine whether there is a need for re-working such pages.*

Choosing Controls

Picking the control that is most suited to the task in hand is also an important consideration when trying to improve the performance of a system. The `DataGrid` control is the most flexible of the data-bound controls, allowing for complicated information to be rendered to the client with a great deal of control over its presentation. The overhead involved in using this control when compared to simpler data-bound controls, such as the `CheckBoxList`, or just outputting raw HTML cannot be overstated, especially as the `DataGrid` is regularly used on very common pages – such as those containing search results. Switching to controls that provide no more functionality than required, or even to hand-rendered HTML, should be done wherever possible.

Using standard HTML controls with a `RunAt` attribute set to `Server` rather than true ASP.NET controls whenever event-handlers are required, and values needing to be assigned dynamically is another way of improving performance by altering the controls used. Possibly the best example of this is the `LinkButton` control. If no server-side processing is required, and the control is only being used to dynamically alter the page linked to, then replacing it with a `<a />` tag is more efficient as it navigates the user straight to the target page, unlike the `LinkButton` which first posts back to the current page before redirecting the user.

If certain functionality is common across multiple pages, then implement such functionality as a template page that is inherited and extended by the individual pages; the effort that is put into ensuring these are high performance doesn't necessarily come at the expense of a productivity loss.

AutoEventWireUp

Using `AutoEventWireup` allows methods to be implicitly linked to events raised by pages and controls through their names. For instance, the `Page_Load` method will automatically handle the `Load` event of the page. Whenever this functionality is used, a `CreateDelegate` function call is made behind the scenes to link the method to the event. Rather than leaving this to the system to handle, to improve performance, `AutoEventWireup` should be disabled (by setting the page-directive `AutoEventWireup="false"`), and the `OnLoad` method should be overridden by hand.

```
Public Class WireupTest
   Inherits System.Web.UI.Page

   Private Sub Page_Load(ByVal sender As System.Object, _
          ByVal e As System.EventArgs)
     'Perform processing
   End Sub
End Class
```

```
Public Class NonWireupTest
   Inherits System.Web.UI.Page

   Protected Overrides Sub OnLoad(ByVal e As System.EventArgs)
     'Perform processing
   End Sub
End Class
```

The example above shows how the `Load` event of the page should be rewritten to override the default event handler, rather than requiring a delegate to be created. Note how the method has had its access level changed from `Private` to `Protected`, and its parameters altered so that it matches the required signature of the event-handler.

Repeated control population

When moving from a traditional ASP development approach to the event-driven model of ASP.NET, a fairly common issue arises where developers aren't sure under what conditions, and in what order, events fire. Because of this, controls such as drop-down lists, labels displaying error messages, etc. may be assigned to data multiple times before the page is finally rendered to the client. This situation can also occur where an original implementation of a page was developed, then extra events were implemented later that needed to override earlier values.

> *Finding occurrences of this within an application can usually be done by looking for repeated calls to the same methods on business objects, or to the same database queries.*

There is no quick-fix to overcome this problem; although checking the `IsPostBack` method can remove the most common occurrences of this – it is often the case that controls are populated and then overridden as processing of the page is carried out, and more details of the user's action are known. The best technique is generally to code a single method that sets values for all of the controls that are to be rendered to the client. This method should be called at the end of each event handler, or in the `Page_Load` routine, if the page is not a `PostBack`. The example below shows the conversion of a typical ASP.NET page to one where the setting of values is more structured, and requires less processing:

```
Public Class ControlTest : Inherits System.Web.UI.Page
   Protected WithEvents lstMyList  As DropDownList
   Protected WithEvents cmdSubmit  As Button

   Private Sub Page_Load(ByVal sender As System.Object, _
         ByVal e As System.EventArgs)
     With lstMyList.Items
       .Clear
       .Add(New ListItem("-Select-", ""))
       .Add(New ListItem("First Item", "1"))
       .Add(New ListItem("Second Item", "2"))
     End With
   End Sub

   Private Sub cmdSubmit_Click(ByVal sender As System.Object, _
         ByVal e As System.EventArgs)
     With lstMyList.Items
       .Clear
       .Add(New ListItem("First Item", "1"))
       .Add(New ListItem("Second Item", "2"))
     End With
   End Sub
End Class
```

```
Public Class ControlTest : Inherits System.Web.UI.Page
   Protected WithEvents lstMyList  As DropDownList
   Protected WithEvents cmdSubmit  As Button

   Private Sub Page_Load(ByVal sender As System.Object, _
         ByVal e As System.EventArgs)
     If Not IsPostBack Then RenderLists(True)
   End Sub
```

```
    Private Sub cmdSubmit_Click(ByVal sender As System.Object, _
            ByVal e As System.EventArgs)
      RenderLists(False)
    End Sub

    Private Sub RenderLists(ByVal RenderDefault)
      With lstMyList.Items
        .Clear
        If RenderDefault Then .Add(New ListItem("-Select-", ""))
        .Add(New ListItem("First Item", "1"))
        .Add(New ListItem("Second Item", "2"))
      End With
    End Sub
End Class
```

The code above could be optimized further to make use of view-state so that the list does not need to be generated each time – we discussed the use of the view-state (and its overuse!) in Chapter 2.

If is it not possible to convert code to such a format as above, then any results that are being returned for populating lists should be cached the first time they are retrieved, to minimize the impact of such inefficiencies on other areas of the system.

Data Retrieval

As discussed earlier in the book, wherever possible, it should be ensured that only the amount of data required for the application is retrieved and rendered to the client. An example of this would be the check-out of an online store. If it is not known whether the user is going to pay by cash, cheque, credit-card, or has an existing account that orders can be charged to, then displaying drop-down lists of the available credit-card types, the expiry date, and the issue number may not be required in the majority of cases. The retrieval of such redundant data should be weighed up against the cost of posting a page back to the server and requesting the next page.

If such a page is causing performance issues, then either splitting it up into a linear process of separate pages, or having pop-ups to deal with such variable types of input will remove the initial load on the system, allowing data to be retrieved and rendered only when required.

The criteria used for deciding whether this is necessary or not are largely down to the individual situation, but the higher the frequency that the page is called, the lower the amount of data that should be retrieved (and hence processing performed).

Data Validation

If there are many opportunities for errors on the page, then as many validation controls as possible should have client-side implementations developed for them (obviously server-side checks will still be needed, as not all browsers will support the execution of such code). This will not only improve the perceived performance of the application to the end-user by removing the need for round-trip requests, but will also lower the load on the server, as it will not have to process as many requests.

Validating input at the user-interface layer, rather than once it has been passed deeper into the system also provides the benefit of not having to perform costly operations such as rolling back transactions. For this reason, initial validation shouldn't just be a cursory check to ensure fields haven't been left blank, but that date-ranges entered are valid, credit card numbers adhere to such checks as the MOD-10 algorithm, and so on.

Database Tuning

As the majority of systems are data-driven, there is usually a database at the core of most ASP.NET applications. Depending on the type of system, this may be a typical RDBMS (such as SQL Server), a flat-file mechanism, an object-based store (such as Active Directory), or one of several other types. There are a few performance tips that are common between all – caching frequently-used data, keeping data as close to the client as possible, making sure data is ordered/indexed so that it can be searched and retrieved quickly, etc.

> *Detecting when it is the database that is causing the performance issues is usually a fairly easy task – having* Trace *lines around database calls can quickly determine if they are taking up the majority of processing time. Similarly, looking at CPU usage graphs on the Database server compared to front-end servers will show the load on each. If the application is being executed entirely on one server, then the* **Task Manager** *figures for the total CPU time of each process could be checked. If, given the amount/complexity of data-access that is being carried out, these figures seem inordinately high, then looking more closely at the methods of data access that are being used and can bring large performance gains.*

Stored Procedures

If, after investigation, it is found that performance issues are present in the execution of SQL queries, then the introduction of **stored procedures** should be considered. Other than an appropriate database design, the introduction of these to perform data access is one of the most common methods of improving database performance with SQL Server. Stored procedures are compiled SQL statements that reside in the database, and can be called from business logic making use of ADO.NET (or earlier data-access technologies such as ADO).

The reasons that such a sizeable gain can be made are:

❑ Pre-parsing of SQL – whenever a stored procedure is created, it is checked for syntactic correctness immediately. If it does not constitute a valid SQL statement (or set of statements) then it is rejected from the system. This reduces the number of errors in the system that require extra code to deal with them, lowers the load on the database server as this check only has to be performed once, and increases responsiveness to the call of each procedure.

❑ Singular creation of execution plan – when a SQL statement is executed, whether it is dynamic SQL or a stored procedure, SQL Server has to create an execution plan. This plan is its way of knowing what order to retrieve certain items in, what indexes to use, and so on. If stored procedures are used, then the execution plan that is calculated the first time that the procedure is run is stored for use during subsequent calls (unless specifically told to do otherwise). As dynamic SQL statements are "disposable", there is no such caching of the plan, requiring it to be recreated during each call. In large queries that have many joins, great deals of data, or other complexities, creating the execution plan can take a great percentage of the overall operation time; an overhead that is not desirable.

❑ Reduced network latency – as stored procedures simply consist of a name such as sp_DoStuff and a set of parameters, the amount of data that must be sent to SQL Server to instruct it on the operation to perform is far lower than if the entire set of SQL statements had to be transmitted with each call. As before, the more complex the query, the greater the penalty for using dynamic SQL.

Naming

Care should be taken when picking the names of stored procedures.

> **Don't prefix the name of your stored procedures with sp_**

System stored procedures in SQL Server begin with sp_. If your stored procedures also begin with the same three letters as the system defined ones, then rather than being found in the portion of the database allocated to user-defined procedures, and executed immediately, the system will first look through all of the system-defined ones (such as sp_addarticle) to see if it exists. This will cause a very minor slowdown, but as it is done on every single table-access there is no need to suffer this overhead for the sake of a slight modification to naming conventions. As a further benefit, using a different naming convention will also help developers distinguish between custom functionality for the application being developed, and standard functionality provided by the underlying system.

Retrofitting stored procedures

If a system has been developed with all of the SQL statements stored in the business or presentation tiers of the system mixed in and among application logic, then converting the implementation to use stored-procedures is no trivial task.

The first step is to identify the most important pieces of functionality to convert – those that are used most commonly, and those that are the most complex. Subsequently, other procedures that are used infrequently, and atomic operations that are harder to optimize, can be improved.

When a piece of SQL is executed, there is a set of zero or more input variables, and a set of output results/result sets. The identification of these should not be difficult as they are generally the parameters and return values to the function making the database call.

When values are being returned from stored-procedures, there is a more efficient and flexible mechanism available than is the case with standard dynamic SQL statements that just return rows of data. With such dynamic statements, the only real options are to either perform an ExecuteScalar (which internally retrieves the first row of data to the client before selecting and returning the value of the first column), or to return a complete result set using a data reader or DataAdapter, and retrieve the desired values programmatically from the correct rows and columns.

If stored procedures are used, then there is a further option – the use of **parameters**. These both improve the maintainability of code and increases performance by using functionality that was specifically designed for the task of managing individual values, rather than large amounts of tabular data. Parameters for stored procedures are similar to those in VB.NET and C# - they can both pass values into a method or return values, and can be any one of the standard SQL data-types.

As an example, if a stored procedure were written to retrieve details on the most recent entry created in the Suppliers table of the Northwind database, it would look like one of the following depending on whether parameters were used or not:

```
-- No parameters
CREATE PROCEDURE [dbo].[usp_GetData_NoParams] AS
SELECT TOP 1     [SupplierID], [CompanyName]
FROM            [Suppliers]
ORDER BY        [SupplierID] DESC
```

```
-- With Parameters
CREATE PROCEDURE [dbo].[usp_GetData_WithParams]
   @SupplierID    INT OUTPUT,
   @CompanyName   NVARCHAR(40) OUTPUT
AS
SELECT TOP 1
   @SupplierID    = [SupplierID],
   @CompanyName   = [CompanyName]
FROM     [Suppliers]
ORDER BY  [SupplierID] DESC
```

The VB.NET code required to retrieve the values if parameters weren't used would be as shown below. Obviously, if only one value was required, rather than both, then the `ExecuteScalar` method could have been run instead, making for a noticeable performance boost.

```
objCommand    = New SqlCommand("usp_GetData_NoParams", objConnection)
objCommand.CommandType = CommandType.StoredProcedure
Dim objDataTable    As DataTable     = New DataTable()
Dim objDataAdapter  As SqlDataAdapter = New SqlDataAdapter(objCommand)
objDataAdapter.Fill(objDataTable)

Dim objRow As DataRow  = objDataTable.Rows(0)
Dim intSupplierID   As Integer = objRow("SupplierID")
Dim strCompanyName  As String  = objRow("CompanyName")
```

The equivalent code to access the version of the stored procedure that uses parameters would be:

```
objCommand   = New SqlCommand("usp_GetData_WithParams", objConnection)
With objCommand
   .CommandType = CommandType.StoredProcedure
   .Parameters.Add("@SupplierID", SqlDbType.Int, 4)
   .Parameters(0).Direction = ParameterDirection.Output
   .Parameters.Add("@CompanyName", sqlDbType.NVarChar, 40)
   .Parameters(1).Direction = ParameterDirection.Output

   .ExecuteNonQuery()
   Dim intSupplierID   As Integer = .Parameters("@SupplierID").Value
   Dim strCompanyName As String  = .Parameters("@CompanyName").Value
End With
```

If the above code is executed 1,000 times, then the performance gains are clear – without using parameters the execution time is 1.2 seconds, compared to 0.8 seconds when they are used; a difference of 50%. As an aside, the execution time for retrieving one value via a parameter is almost identical to retrieving it through a call to `ExecuteScalar`, as long as only the required column is brought back in the SELECT statement.

If it is found that the code being executed cannot be written as-is in SQL without making use of inefficient mechanisms, such as cursors, then it is often possible to make use of dynamic T-SQL instead, where a SQL statement is built up in the stored procedure itself, and called using the EXEC function. The string handling provided by T-SQL may not outperform that of the CLR, but it will still make for a decrease in the bandwidth consumed, and provide more readable code.

Indexing

If you feel satisfied that the queries being performed against the database server are well-crafted, and you are already making use of stored-procedures, but you are still experiencing poor performance on tables that contain large amounts of data, then the problem may be down to **Indexing**. One of the easiest ways of spotting this problem is if the system performance degrades over time, as the amount of data stored is increasing.

Indexing can provide one of the greatest increases in the performance, but there is a caveat – selecting the appropriate columns to add indexes to, and what type of indexes to create is far more complex than the act of creating them!

Indexes allow records to be located far quicker, by creating an ordered lookup of values on the selected columns. There are trade-offs to consider in their creation though– they may require substantial storage space on sizeable tables, are only effective if the data stored in the indexed columns meets certain criteria, and can adversely effect other operations being performed on the tables involved.

Single Column Indexes

The simplest view of index selection is that they should be added to every column. If this were an optimal solution then SQL Server would, no doubt, do this by default. If you add too many indexes to a table then performance actually degrades – every time a record is INSERTed, DELETEd or UPDATEd, SQL Server has to make amendments to its index lists. While the overhead for one or two columns isn't great, when half a dozen or more are indexed, this overhead can become a large percentage of overall execution time. Hence, as a general rule, indexes should only be added to the individual columns of a table, or the sets of columns (for composite indexes) that searches are to be regularly run against, such as primary keys and product codes.

The type of application being developed also affects how indexes should be chosen – if it involves relatively static data where the majority of operations are SELECT statements returning result-sets, then having many indexes may not impede performance. This is especially true in situations where complex user-defined queries can be entered into the system. If on the other hand, an application (or even a single table) is used mainly for updating information, such as a table storing users' session information, then indexing several columns will probably have a detrimental effect on performance, as the type of queries – along the lines of "*retrieve all items for user X*" – will be known as the application is being designed and developed.

One further complication is in whether or not SQL Server actually uses the indexes that are present. When a query is executed, the Query Optimizer decides how best to find the data that is required. On certain columns, this may not be to use an index if one exists. If, this is the case, then the index should be deleted to remove the overhead associated with its maintenance. The Query Optimizer's logic in deciding how best to locate data is necessarily complex, but it basically comes down to whether or not the overhead of using a reference-based structure such as an index is more efficient than performing a brute-force search. Two reasons for this are that:

❑ The table may not contain sufficient rows to overcome the overhead of using an index.

❑ The data in the table may not be sufficiently unique (as a rule, it must be 95% unique to be used by SQL Server). If many rows contain the same value, then simply finding the location in the index doesn't mean finding the item itself – there may be a further search through many matching items to be performed.

Clustered Indexes

A clustered index is one where the data stored in the table is actually ordered by the column selected for the index. Obviously, the data can only be primarily ordered by one column – meaning that only one clustered index can be created per table. As this is the case, great care should be taken over choosing which column is to be used.

Clustered Indexes perform well for the following operations:

❑   They perform well where large numbers of rows are returned, as these do not have to be de-referenced from a standard index.

❑   They are good for queries that make use of JOIN clauses.

❑   Although they perform well for columns that only store a few values, they should not be used for fields with highly limited values – such as a BIT field. Such fields should not be indexed at all, as a large search may still have to be performed through all values matching the specified values.

❑   They are ideal for queries that need to return results that are sorted (using clauses such as ORDER BY), or results that contain a particular range of values (using such commands as BETWEEN). This is due to the data being pre-sorted according to the index.

❑   They are good for queries that search for a record based on a unique value, and when large portions of this record need returning (such as a singleton SELECT statement that returns many columns).

If no column is selected to be a clustered index, but there is a primary key on the table, then SQL Server automatically makes this column the clustered index. If several columns seem to be ideal candidates for the clustered index, then the SQL Indexing Wizard could well shed some light on which is the better choice by running regularly called stored-procedures against the database to find the most efficient use of indexing. If another column is selected as the clustered index, then SQL Server will remove the one that already exists.

Non-Clustered Indexes

Once a clustered-index has been chosen for a table (or has been left set to the default), selecting non-clustered indexes is a far easier task, as there is no real limit to the number that can be created. As mentioned before, they shouldn't be added to all columns though. Instead, the following should be taken into consideration when deciding on columns:

❑   Non-clustered indexes perform best on queries that only return a few records, and the index is largely unique.

❑   SQL Server's Query Optimizer will most likely not use an index if the values stored in the field aren't at least 95% unique, as mentioned above. For this reason, columns of data-types such as BIT, and CHAR(1) are not often good choices for indexed columns.

❑   When creating indexes across multiple columns, select the minimum number of columns possible, otherwise the size of the index can become large, and will take many more Read operations to retrieve data from the index.

❑   Indexes on columns of integer types are more efficient than those of character types, as there is less overhead involved.

❑　If a table has its data retrieved mainly by one query, then a **covering index**– one that contains all of the columns referenced by the query – should be considered for the table. If this is done, then the index will contain all of the data that will be used for the query, reducing the amount of I/O required. Care should be taken that this index does not become too large – either from having too many rows or too many columns, and that the entire table hasn't been blanket-indexed.

Full Text Indexes

Full text indexing is an important feature in SQL Server as it provides a simple mechanism for performing types of queries that are regularly desired by users, but loathed by developers due to their complexity. Due to the way that full text indexing works, there can potentially be performance issues with it; rather than being an integral part of SQL Server, it is a separate component that in turn makes use of the Microsoft Search Service.

The performance issues arise when the query has both criteria on the full text index, and standard columns. As the Search Service is external, its search is performed separately from that of restricting on the internal criteria. When a query is executed, the Search Service returns all of the records it finds to the Query Optimizer, which then combines these with those it has found. The problem with this is when the internal query returns a small number of records compared to the full text search, as far more rows are being handled than necessary.

There is no single solution that guarantees optimal performance for all examples of this situation, there are only workarounds that can be implemented to try and give the Search Service a hint. The most common of these is to include extra information in the text to replicate some of the data being stored in other fields that are likely to be searched on. If this is done, then these internal criteria can also be applied to the textual search, hopefully greatly reducing the number of rows returned.

Data Types

Detecting when the usage of data types is causing inefficiencies in an application is difficult, as it can manifest itself in seemingly minor slow downs, but in a number of areas. These are largely concerned with the amount of data that is passed as parameters to and from method calls, the amount of data returned in result-sets, and the speed that a SELECT statement can execute at.

Data types and sizes should always be the smallest one, that allows for all conceivable valid values to be stored. For instance, if you're storing a number between 1 and 8, then a TINYINT is more appropriate than an INT. Similarly, if you're storing a telephone number, then a VARCHAR(50) allows for many extra (unused) characters. By picking such small data-types, you gain two advantages:

❑　The smallest amount of data possible is transferred to the client, minimizing communication times.

❑　The maximum amount of data can be stored in a **Page** in SQL Server. Pages are of a fixed size, and it is these that limit the size of a record to 8 kilobytes. Storing more rows in a page reduces the amount of I/O that is necessary to search through the database.

The same applies when picking the basic type of a field – if only integers are to be stored, then a textual field type should not be chosen; not only does it require far more storage space, it also makes performing searches and calculations on such columns far less efficient.

Due to the plethora of available data types, textual fields offer some of the greatest opportunities for optimizations:

❑ If the data in a textual field may vary greatly in length – such as a product description, then a VARCHAR should be used. If the length is relatively static, then a CHAR is the better choice. This is due to the fact that although VARCHARs require slightly more processing, they can potentially require far less storage space, allowing more records per page.

❑ When picking textual data types, use CHAR and VARCHAR instead of NCHAR and NVARCHAR unless absolutely necessary. The first two types store data in ASCII format, the last two in Unicode format – requiring twice the storage space (16 bits rather than 8) and transmission overhead.

❑ TEXT data types should be avoided unless more than 8000 characters are to be stored. A VARCHAR offers greater performance than a TEXT field, as it must be de-referenced to retrieve the actual values that are stored elsewhere. Performing SELECT statements that have criteria based upon the data contained in a TEXT field is also inefficient.

Archiving

If, as described above, a system that was once performing adequately has now degraded to unacceptable levels, this is most likely down to the amount of data in the system. Although adding indexes can greatly improve the speed of data-access, the sheer quantity will eventually cause slow-downs, no matter how well constructed the indexes. To stop this from occurring, subsets of the data stored by the system could be archived.

Many systems contain tables that regularly have rows added, but are never read from during the routine operation of the system (examples of this include transaction logs and audit trails). Even those that do have records retrieved are regularly only concerned with data that was inserted recently (such as customer orders). When either of these is the case, the need for all of the data to remain online in a single system should be examined. Data that is not used regularly could be archived in one of several different ways:

❑ It could be moved to a different table in the same database, keeping all data in the same system, but making searches across more recent data much quicker.

❑ It could be moved to a different database (either on the same database server, or on a second machine). Searches would be more disparate, but benefits such as smaller backups of the core system would be received.

❑ It could be backed up and taken offline entirely, requiring a restore operation if it's ever needed.

Selecting one of these operations is obviously largely dependent on the specific system and the needs of the users accessing it, requiring a discussion that is beyond the scope of this book.

Atomic vs. Bulk Operations

When small operations are being performed against a database server, such as deleting single rows, retrieving the details of one particular user, then the time taken to perform such operations is clearly very small. In such situations, it makes sense to have a **blocking operation** – one where the code waits for a reply from the server before continuing processing. If the task being performed is more complicated – such as the generation of a report of all activity across an enterprise over the last year, then the task may take several minutes or longer to perform.

If such time-consuming tasks are performed by the system, then an alternative strategy should be considered. This is especially true if the end-user initiated the operation and is expecting a response. The two main options that can be chosen from are **asynchronous communication** and **delayed processing** (scheduled tasks).

Detecting whether the introduction of either of these techniques is viable is fairly simple – if the system suffers from slow downs only when specific operations are performed, or specific tasks cause the user to have to wait unacceptable times for a response.

Asynchronous Communication

If an operation doesn't require any set of data to be returned to the user, the task to be performed requires a large amount of processing, and the system is never subjected to an overwhelming load, then performing a task asynchronously is a simple way of improving the perceived performance to the user. Once initialized, a call to an asynchronous operation will return control to the program, allowing a response to be sent to the user almost immediately. The main drawback with this type of operation is that providing the user with details of the success/failure of the operation is very difficult via a web-page interface. Instead, options such as e-mails have to be looked at.

Delayed Processing

Delayed processing can be carried out in a system through the use of scheduled tasks, regularly implemented using Windows Services. Historically, it was only possible using either C++ or custom written wrappers around code in other languages such as Visual Basic. With the introduction of .NET, their development has become far easier due to the simplified process involved, and the inclusion of such classes in the Framework as System.Timer. This allows for the more feasible creation of applications that run unattended for extended periods of time, performing processing based on a schedule.

Creating a system such as this allows routine maintenance tasks to be performed outside the general operational hours of a system – early in the morning if the system isn't in continual usage, or potentially whenever the system load drops below a certain level. Although this doesn't reduce the amount of work that the system has to perform, or the time that is required to do it, the perceived performance of the system will increase due to the more even distribution of processing over time.

Producing services is still a more difficult task than writing standard applications mainly due to the lack of a user interface, and the inability to reference it from any test-harness projects that are created. The extra time that is involved in debugging services should be taken into consideration before functionality is transferred to such a system. The advantages are regularly worth the effort, however, especially if the functionality has already been tested in a user-interaction driven application.

Transactions (keeping to a minimum)

Whenever there is the possibility of one or more tasks failing in a series of operations, using transactions provides an automatic way of restoring the database to the point it was at before the transaction began. This in itself can greatly aid performance, as a transaction can either be rolled back or committed from any tier of an application (although logically this should usually be the business tier), removing the need for an intricate message-passing system. This means that there is no need for code that is remote from the database to deal with storing the changes being made, and retracting them should an error occur. Instead, the database handles this automatically, and in an efficient manner. Even if the transaction involved several databases, then through the DTC (**Distributed Transaction Coordinator**) each database can rollback the changes internally.

Although necessary on occasion, transactions should be kept to a minimum as they do require large amounts of server resources to maintain. They can also prove to be a bottleneck in a system, as the details are stored for all transactions in one location.

Detecting when this has become the case can be a fairly involved operation, as the number of transactions being processing simultaneously, how these are distributed across machines, and what other processing is being carried out at the same time are all factors that affect the execution time. If Trace calls are placed around the execution of large transactions in a live version of the system (or a simulation of a live environment), then it should be possible to see if involved processes such as debiting a credit card or creating a new account are causing problems.

If it has been found that a specific transactional operation is causing performance issues, then it should be examined to determine whether the entire operation needs to be transactional, or just a sub-set of the functions it performs. The shorter a transaction can be made – both in terms of the amount of time it lasts, and the number of database calls it makes, the greater the performance.

A further performance gain related to transactions can be achieved when using the SQL managed provider. Automatic transaction enlistment is enabled by default, requiring extra processing to be performed. This can be disabled application-wide very simply by adding the Enlist=false name-value pair to the connection-string used for accessing the database, as shown below:

```
// Transaction-enlisted connection string
string strConnString = "Data Source=localhost;User Id=sa;Password=;Initial
Catalog=Northwind;";
```

```
// Non transaction-enlisted connection string
string strConnString = "Data Source=localhost;User Id=sa;Password=;Initial
Catalog=Northwind;Enlist=false;";
```

Triggers

The usage of triggers allows certain types of functionality to be added to systems far more easily than would otherwise be the case, with tasks being performed implicitly, rather than explicitly from other tiers, under certain conditions (on specific INSERT, UPDATE, or DELETE operations). As these triggers fire every time the specified operation occurs, they can add a substantial overhead to the processing time, so should be used cautiously.

Detecting such problems is straightforward – if a database call is taking an unexpectedly long amount of time and there are triggers present on tables involved, then their need/functionality should be examined.

One of the biggest performance impacts in SQL Server is when transactions are rolled back. Having a trigger that detects an error in an operation and causes the rollback of a transaction is an inefficient use of resources – if this is the case, then code should be added where possible to detect the error before the trigger is fired.

Triggers should also not be used to manually perform tasks that can be handled by other areas of the system in a more efficient manner. For instance, if they are being used for referential integrity checks in the database, then these should be handled using constraints, which execute far quicker than writing T-SQL to validate the operations by hand.

Cursors

Cursors are T-SQL's method of allowing individual records to be processed serially from within stored procedures (and other code). Although cursors are necessary for certain functionality, such as the data reader in ADO.NET, they consume resources, and can be fairly slow, especially when used from within stored procedures, and compared to the bulk-operations available in SQL, such as UPDATE.

If possible, server-side cursors should be removed, and an alternative method for implementing the same functionality/an alternative location to perform the processing should be found. For instance, the data could be returned to the components, and have operations performed there. The rationale behind this is that it's fairly easy to add more application servers to an application to improve responsiveness/throughput, but clustering database servers incurs a sizeable overhead.

Determining whether cursors are causing a problem can be achieved simply by searching for their usage in any SQL statements (either dynamic SQL or stored procedures) that are performing badly. The number of cursors that are in use at once can also cause an issue in terms of resource usage; any database calls that are performed regularly should avoid them.

Sometimes cursors are the only option though. If this is the case, then there are several ways of optimizing the processing being performed:

❑ Only retrieve those records required – the fewer records that are returned, the fewer resources will be required by the cursor.

❑ Select the most appropriate type of cursor – SQL Server offers several types of cursor, allowing for different access methods, and read/write permissions. The most efficient of these is that used by the data reader – the forward-only, read-only cursor.

❑ Dispose of cursors properly within stored procedures – once processing has been completed, CLOSE the cursor. Following this, it should be DEALLOCATEd. This informs SQL Server to reclaim the resources used by the cursor immediately, rather than waiting until the procedure has finished execution.

Chunky Calls

When making database calls, a large portion of the time involved is regularly in the creation of a connection and command, population of parameters, network latency, and so on. These are overheads that are incurred with every call. Rather than making many atomic calls to retrieve data items, where possible, associated calls should be combined into one larger one. A typical example of this is shown below, where the properties of a class are being set:

```
Sub PopulateClass(ByVal PersonID As Integer, _
                ByRef InputClass As PersonClass)
    InputClass.Name   = GetProperty(PersonID, "Name")
    InputClass.Age    = GetProperty(PersonID, "Age")
    InputClass.Gender = GetProperty(PersonID, "Gender")
End Sub

Function GetProperty(ByVal PersonID As Integer, _
                    ByVal ColumnName As String) As String
    Dim objCommand As SqlCommand = New SqlCommand(m_objConn)
    With objCommand
        .Open()
        .CommandType = CommandType.StoredProcedure
        .CommandText = "usp_GetProperty"
        .Parameters.Add("@PersonID",   Int,      4).Direction = Input
        .Parameters.Add("@ColumnName", VarChar, 50).Direction = Input
        .Parameters.Add("@Value",      VarChar, 255).Direction = Output
```

```
        .ExecuteNonQuery()
        .Close()

        Return .Parameters.Item("@Value").Value.
    End With
End Function
```

In this code, even though a single connection is used, there is still a lot of repeated work being performed to retrieve three values. The work is not just being repeated in the VB.NET code, either. The stored procedure that this code interacts with must also be executed three times, with the row specified by PersonID having to be located each time. Such a method of retrieving data would also cause any audit-logs to grow far quicker.

If analysis is performed on code that is not performing well enough and it is detected that numerous database calls are being made from it, then writing custom SQL statements to retrieve the data that is required for the entire method in one operation can provide a sizeable performance gain. Bearing this in mind, an alternative implementation is given below:

```
Sub PopulateClass(ByVal PersonID As Integer, _
                  ByRef InputClass As PersonClass)
    Dim objCommand As SqlCommand = New SqlCommand(m_objConn)
    With objCommand
        .Open()
        .CommandType = CommandType.StoredProcedure
        .CommandText = "usp_GetProperty"
        .Parameters.Add("@PersonID", Int,      4).Direction  = Input
        .Parameters.Add("@Name",     VarChar, 255).Direction = Output
        .Parameters.Add("@Age",      Int,      4).Direction  = Output
        .Parameters.Add("@Gender",   Char,     1).Direction  = Output

        .Parameters("@PersonID").Value = PersonID
        .ExecuteNonQuery()
        .Close()

        InputClass.Name   = .Parameters.Item("@Name").Value
        InputClass.Age    = .Parameters.Item("@Age").Value
        InputClass.Gender = .Parameters.Item("@Gender").Value
    End With
End Function
```

The implementation of this method provides other fringe benefits, such as the likelihood of an improved query-plan in SQL Server, as the original example would probably have required dynamic-SQL within the stored procedure. Even with such performance benefits, a price has been paid; this is another example of a situation where flexibility has been compromised for the sake of performance. If an extra property of Position became necessary, the first example would only require one extra line of code to populate it. In the second version, there would need to be two more lines in the VB.NET code, along with an update to the stored-procedure being called.

XML

Although XML can be used for communication between many different systems, the verbosity, complexity of data formats, and need to validate documents imposes severe overheads. As a general rule, when performance is a major concern, XML should only be used either for external interfaces to a system, or where a portion of a system will need to accept changing data-formats (optimizations in such areas will never be long-standing). Where XML has been used throughout a system, and is not going to be replaced with more efficient techniques, there are several ways of optimizing its usage:

❏ Selecting between XmlReader and XmlDocument.

❏ Optimizing schemas.

❏ The method of creating, querying, and updating documents.

❏ The way in which documents are passed between routines.

The different factors involved in determining when each of these optimizations should be applied to code are described in detail below. It should be fairly easy to determine whether the use of XML is causing tangible performance issues, within an application simply by measuring the amount of CPU time and memory processing involving XML is taking.

Readers and Documents

Where large quantities of data that aren't to be cached locally (due to the infrequency of its usage), such as transaction logs, entire product catalogues, and so on are being processed, only the minimum amount should be loaded into memory at any given time. Not only does the loading of an entire document guarantee the usage of large amounts of memory being required, but the parsing of a substantial document also requires many CPU cycles.

Instead of retrieving a large XML document, and passing it into a LoadXml method in order to access it, an XmlReader instance can be created instead. Then, rather than looping round the ChildNodes collection and retrieving values, the Read method can be called. This advances the XmlReader each time it is called, moving on to the next element of the document. As only one element is accessible at a time, such a technique can only be used where values are being accessed serially. It is also far more difficult to use when the document structure has many levels, as rather than retrieving all of the child-nodes of one element, the entire document tree will be returned one item at a time. When the document is suitable for being returned via an XmlReader, the performance can be hundreds of times better, depending on the size of the document.

The code below shows a conversion of a code fragment from reading an XmlDocument in its entirety, then looping round the child-nodes one at a time to retrieve an attribute, to an implementation that uses an XmlReader to perform the same operation.

```
Dim objXmlDoc      As XmlDocument  = New XmlDocument()
Dim strXML         As String       = GetSomeXml()
Dim intCount       As Integer      = 0

objXmlDoc.LoadXml(strXML)
With objXmlDoc.DocumentElement.ChildNodes
    For intCount = 0 To .Count - 1
        Dim strValue As String = _
```

```
                .Item(intCount).Attributes("SomeValue").Value
    Next
End With
objXmlDoc = Nothing
```

```
Dim objXmlReader    As XmlReader    = GetXmlReader()
While objXmlReader.Read()
    Dim strValue As String = objXmlReader.GetAttribute("SomeValue")
End While

objXmlReader.Close()
objXmlReader = Nothing
```

If the code above is executed with an XML document containing 20,000 rows of data, the XmlReader version executes 88 times faster than the XmlDocument version, taking 0.46 seconds rather than 40.62. The larger the document is, the greater this gain becomes. This is due to the slow-down using an XmlReader being linear, whilst the usage of an XmlDocument appears to give a geometric slow-down.

Optimizing Schemas for Performance

As well as the method of retrieving the data out of the document in the most efficient manner, the format of the document itself can be optimized for performance. Obviously, once an application has been developed it is often not possible to redefine the XML documents. If it is possible, then the following changes can be made to increase efficiency:

❑   Minimal amount of data – rather than having one XML document that specifies the data for an entire system, consider documents that are tailored to specific cases, and only contain the data that is required for such circumstances.

❑   Short yet descriptive element and attribute names – there is no need to replicate parent item names in child items. For instance, a child item of an order-line could be named price rather than orderline_price, thus reducing the data overhead further.

❑   Remove redundant data – if certain information is redundant, or can be rapidly derived, then it should be considered for removal. For instance, if we know that (either system-wide, or through some extra definitions in the XML) VAT (a tax) of 17.5% is to be applied to all order-lines, then there's no need to store the amount of this tax at both the line level and the order level, unless both sets of values are to be used for further operations.

❑   Ease of querying – if XPath querying is to be used, rather than XSLT processing, the ease with which elements and attributes can be reached is important. If a regularly required item is found far down the XML tree, then locating this using a query will be far more time-consuming that finding items nearer the root.

As an example of this, compare the fragment of the first XML document below with the second, both provide the exact same information, but the second is far terser (allowing for more rapid data-transfer), and can be loaded and validated more quickly, with the other values being calculated from those given, if required.

```
<customerorder>
  <customerorder_orderlines>
    <customerorder_orderline>
```

```
        <orderline_itemcode>311079</orderline_itemcode>
        <orderline_descriptivename>
          Special offer item #1
        </orderline_descriptivename>
        <orderline_price>10.00</orderline_price>
        <orderline_vat>1.75</orderline_vat>
        <orderline_total>11.75</orderline_total>
     </customerorder_orderline>
     <customerorder_orderline>
        <orderline_itemcode>311080</orderline_itemcode>
        <orderline_descriptivename>
          Special offer item #2
        </orderline_descriptivename>
        <orderline_price>1.00</orderline_price>
        <orderline_vat>0.175</orderline_vat>
        <orderline_total>1.175</orderline_total>
     </customerorder_orderline>
   </customerorder_orderlines>
   <customerorder_total>
     <total_price>11.00</total_price>
     <total_vat>1.925</total_vat>
     <total_total>12.925</total_total>
   </customerorder_total>
</customerorder>
```

If we take it as a given that our VAT is set at 17.5%, then the value of the two orderline_vat tags above could be calculated by a multiplication if required. Each orderline_total value could then be worked out by adding these two together. If these values and the totals aren't required, then the following XML document would suffice:

```
<order>
  <orderline itemcode="311079" descriptivename="Special offer item #1"
price="10.00" />
  <orderline itemcode="311080" descriptivename="Special offer item #2"
price="1.00" />
</order>
```

Obviously, if the VAT values and totals are to be used regularly, then transmitting extra text could be a lower overhead than performing multiple operations on the data. From this, it should be clear that schemas should not only be designed to represent the data that they contain, but also the purposes that such data is required for.

Querying, Updating, and Other Operations.

When dealing with XML documents, there are regularly occasions when operations such as searches for specific elements of data, or updates to represent new information, are made. Performing these in the most efficient manner can afford considerable performance gains, as XML's inefficiencies are a notorious side-effect of its power and flexibility.

Searching Documents

When multiple attributes or child elements of a given node are required, rather than querying from the root each time, such nodes should be cached in a local variable, and methods such as `SelectNodes`, `SelectSingleNode`, etc. should be performed from this node. This removes the need to search through large portions of the document each time, saving CPU time. An example of how this conversion could be performed is given below:

```
Dim docXml As New XmlDocument()
docXml.LoadXml(strSomeXml)
Dim strValue1 As String =
docXml.SelectSingleNode("/root/node1[@attrib=something]/node2").Attributes( _
                        "attrib").Value
Dim strValue1 As String =
docXml.SelectSingleNode("/root/node1[@attrib=something]/node3").Attributes(" _
                        "attrib").Value
```

```
Dim docXml As New XmlDocument()
docXml.LoadXml(strSomeXml)
Dim objNode As XmlNode = docXml.SelectSingleNode("/root/node1[@attrib=something]")
Dim strValue1 As String = objNode.SelectSingleNode("/node2").Attributes( _
                        "attrib").Value
Dim strValue1 As String = docXml.SelectSingleNode("/node3").Attributes( _
                        "attrib").Value
```

Transforming XML Documents

When an XML document is to be converted, whether it's to another XML document, or to an HTML page, relying on XSLT is not the most efficient method. In fact, it is possibly the least efficient means possible. XSLT is basically an interpreted language, with each transformation definition having to be parsed for correctness and converted into code each time it is executed. Furthermore, as it is a generic solution, it doesn't know when to make use of caching on certain nodes, ignoring others, and so on. If it is found that a large amount of the processor's time is spent performing XSLT transformations, the possibility of changing these to using the DOM and manually manipulating the data should be seriously considered.

Creating XML Documents

When XML documents are being created by business logic rather than being retrieved from the database, it is far more efficient to do this as a string rather than instancing an `XmlDocument`. If this string is to be passed straight to a database (such as SQL Server) for processing, then this method is clearly more efficient. Even if it requires further processing by other areas of the system in `XmlDocument` format, this method is still noticeably faster.

As a secondary advantage, producing the documents using `String` or `StringBuilder` can sometimes give more readable code. The main drawbacks to this are that it removes the possibility of readily editing and validating the document, as this would require it to be first loaded into an `XmlDocument` object.

Passing around

When passing XML between methods, the format in which it is transferred should be considered. Both XmlDocument and String are reference-types; pointers to each will be passed to methods, rather than the values of each being transferred on the stack. This means that neither will impose serious overheads in terms of memory usage, or time taken for method-calls. Under certain circumstances, performance does suffer when they are passed around as strings, though, as this may mean making further calls to LoadXml on an XmlDocument object from within methods. If the XML is to be processed within the application (as opposed to in the database server), then once it has been created as a string, loading it into an XML document and using that from then on is potentially a worthwhile amendment to an application. This also then provides a stricter interface for programming against, ensuring that valid documents are being passed between methods, rather than arbitrary strings.

COM Interop

Almost anywhere that COM Interop is being used within an application there is potential for performance issues, and improvements. This section looks at the two major causes of these issues – call overhead and threading, describing the best-practices for improving performance in these areas. We hinted at these problems in Chapter 4.

Call overhead

Every time a method is called that is encapsulated within an Interop wrapper, extra processing has to be performed. The majority of the work that is carried out is to do with converting between the data types that are being passed in as parameters, and those that are being expected by the COM based method. The size of the penalty that is imposed depends upon which category each parameter falls into– whether it is a **Blittable** or a **Non-Blittable** type, and whether it is passed ByVal or ByRef. A similar overhead is imposed when methods exit, and the return values have to be passed back.

Blittable Types

Blittable types are the easiest to deal with, as they incur almost no overhead in the transitions to and from unmanaged code. This is due to the similarity in the format of the data in both environments. Such data-types include:

- ❑ Integer numbers – all standard integer types, including Bytes, Integers, Long Integers, in both signed and un-signed formats can be used with next to no overhead (note that the names may change between languages – an Integer in VB.Net is a Long in Visual Basic).

- ❑ Floating point numbers – these include Single and Double precision numbers, and follow the same rules as Integers.

If these data types are being used for Interop calls, there is little that can be done to improve performance.

Non-Blittable Types

Non-blittable types are far more difficult and time-consuming to deal with, as there is a need to perform marshaling on the data contained within a variable of such types every time it is passed between managed and un-managed code. Non-blittable types include:

- ❑ Booleans – although it would appear that these should be a blittable type, COM actually allows a Boolean value of True to be represented by either 1 or -1, which is not the case in managed code.

❑ Strings – these are all stored in Unicode format in managed code, and must be converted to their ASCII equivalents (this is one of the most costly conversions).

❑ Dates – although the information stored is almost identical, the format of this storage has changed with the introduction of the CLR.

❑ Objects – depending on the specific type of object, these are either converted to Variants, or to Interfaces. The performance issues involved in this depend on what operations are performed, the number of interfaces, and so on.

If any variables of these types are being used, then they should, where possible, be converted to blittable types. If such conversions cannot be made, then their usage via Interop should be kept to a minimum. In the case of passing objects out of the managed world of the .NET runtime, rewriting the Interop code in a .NET language is an option worth investigating if such calls are being made on a regular basis.

Threading Models

In addition to having an overhead imposed during method calls, a more fundamental issue is raised by the usage of existing COM components – the threading model that they run under. A large number of components developed for classic ASP, including all those developed in Visual Basic, ran as STA (Single Threaded Apartment), whereas the managed world of .NET is Free Threaded. The performance issues stem from the fact that STA COM relies on a messaging system to serialize thread requests. What this means is that unmanaged threads essentially share a single thread for Interop – allowing only one request to be processed at once. The overhead that this imposes cannot be overstated, and the choice to use such components in large-scale systems should not be taken without serious consideration. Imported components that support MTA COM do not have these overheads.

> *If an application that uses Interop is performing acceptably on a per-request level, but is not scaling well, this is often the source of the problem.*

Improving Interop Performance

Converting a working knowledge of the underlying techniques involved in Interop into real-world performance gains depends on the amount of time available. In the perfect world, all legacy code would be rewritten to run in a managed environment, removing all potential bottle-necks. As this is usually not possible due to time constraints and the usage of third party components that do not come with source-code, priorities should be assigned to the conversion of methods, with the most important candidates for optimization being given below:

Chunky Calls

As with database calls, chunky calls through Interop – those which perform large amounts of processing, are more efficient than multiple smaller ones. If an imported class has a lot of light-weight methods that are called regularly, then these should either be rewritten in a managed environment, or, more feasibly, should be wrapped up in an extra method in the COM component, or in a separate COM component that is imported (if the original source code is unavailable). This is demonstrated below, where an order is being placed through legacy code.

```
Sub SubmitOrder()
    Dim objClass As New ImportedClass()
```

```
      objClass.UserID = Session("UserID")
      objClass.AddItemsToOrder(Session("OrderLines"))
      objClass.SubmitOrder()
      Dim intCode As Integer = objClass.ReturnCode
      Dim intOrderID As Integer = objClass.OrderID
      Dim strMessage As String = objClass.GetMessageForCode(intCode)

      objClass = Nothing
      Response.Write(("Order ID '" + intOrderID + "' returned the result of: '" + _
                  strMessage + "'"))
   End Sub
```

If the separate properties and methods specified above were wrapped up into a single method, as shown below, then the overhead of switching between managed and unmanaged code would be reduced from six calls to just one. This also makes sense as it would help in the creation of a stateless component, which would further improve performance through object pooling in COM+.

```
Sub SubmitOrder()
   Dim objClass As New ImportedClass()
   Dim intCode As Integer = 0
   Dim intOrderID As Integer = 0
   Dim strMessage As String = ""

   objClass.SubmitOrder(Session("UserID"), Session("OrderLines"), _
                     intOrderID, intCode, strMessage)
   objClass = Nothing
   Response.Write(("Order ID '" + intOrderID + "' returned the result of: '" + _
               strMessage + "'"))
End Sub
```

Use AspCompat Attribute

If particular ASP.NET pages that make use of Interop are found to be running slowly, there is a likelihood that this is due to the threading model that is being used to execute the imported COM component.

By default, ASP.NET doesn't allow any STA COM components to be run within a page. If any imported components run as STA, then the AspCompat attribute of a page must be set to True in order to function properly. When this is done, the thread pool that is used for the execution of the page is switched to an STA thread pool. The context and other objects provided by the page are still available to the COM object, and it also provides a performance benefit, in that it avoids any marshalling of calls from MTA (Multiple Threaded Apartment) to STA threads.

Once this is done, the biggest related performance issue occurs when the STA component is created during the construction of the page. This can be demonstrated by the following ASP.NET page:

```
<%@ Page Language="VB" AspCompat="True" %>
<script runat="server">
   Dim objImportedComponent = new STAComponent()

   Public Sub Page_Load()
      lblUserName = objImportedComponent.UserName(Session.Item("UserID"))
   End Sub
```

```
    </script>

    <html>
      <body>
        <asp:label runat="server" id="lblUserName" /><br />
      </body>
    </html>
```

Although at first glance this page appears not to create any problems, if we consider how the objImportedComponent variable is being dealt with, then it can be seen that there is a huge penalty to pay. When a class is instanced during construction of the page, as it is in the case above, the variable would be created from an MTA thread, rather than the STA one that will be created by the runtime to actually execute the page. The result of this is that marshaling between MTA and STA threads will have to be done to construct the page.

Instead, the assignment of an instance of the STAComponent class should be left until the Page_Load() method is called, at which point the STA thread that will run the page has been entered, as shown below:

```
    <%@ Page Language="VB" ASPCompat="True" %>
    <script runat="server">
      Dim objImportedComponent As STAComponent = Nothing

      Public Sub Page_Load()
          objImportedComponent = New STAComponent()
          lblUserName = objImportedComponent.UserName(Session.Item("UserID"))
      End Sub
    </script>

    <html>
      <body>
        <asp:label runat="server" id="lblUserName" /><br />
      </body>
    </html>
```

Shared Resources

A further optimization can be made by removing any STA COM components that are being stored in a shared resource that allows access from multiple threads (multiple pages being rendered). The most common example of this is when an instance of such a component is cached in the Application object. Such shared resources include the cache and session state. The reasoning behind this is that only the thread that constructed the component can actually service a request to one of its methods. This means that all calls would have to be marshaled to and from the creator thread, and if this thread is in use then the calls would block until the thread was free. This produces not only a performance issue, but concerns over scalability if many calls all have to rely on a single thread.

Summary

In this chapter, we've looked again at some areas of application development that can lead to performance problems, and discussed how to identify the symptoms.

As we mentioned at the outset of this chapter, improving performance via code-tuning can be quite a painful process, but hopefully, we have given you some ideas of when to spot possible problems, and what the cause of these problems may be.

Professional ASP.NET Performance Professional ASP.NET Perfo
Professional ASP.NET Perfo
Professional ASP.NET Perfo
Professional ASP.NET Perfo
Professional ASP.NET Perfo
Professional ASP.NET Perfo
Professional ASP.NET Perfo
Professional ASP.NET Perfo
Professional ASP.NET Perfo
Professional ASP.NET Perfo
Professional ASP.NET Perfo
Professional ASP.NET Perfo
Professional ASP.NET Perfo
Professional ASP.NET Perfo
Professional ASP.NET Perfo
Professional ASP.NET Perfo
Professional ASP.NET Perfo
Professional ASP.NET Perfc
Professional ASP.NET Perf
Professional ASP.NET Perf
Professional ASP.NET Perf
Professional ASP.NET Perf
Professional ASP.NET Perf
Professional ASP.NET Perf

9

Monitoring Performance

Monitoring the performance of our applications is a very important step toward ensuring a good user experience. There are two parts to monitoring the performance of our applications. The first part is to test our application before it is ever deployed, to ensure that it can perform as required under the expected load. We covered this testing in Chapter 6, but some of what we'll learn in this chapter can be used in a pre-deployment application too.

The second part is to continue to monitor the "performance" of our servers and applications after their deployment while they are in production. "Performance" here is a catch-all term meaning how optimally our application is running, whether it's the processor load or the number of failed requests, or whatever we're interested in. Most of us are not going to be using our applications ourselves every day, and so we will not be aware of changes in performance that may greatly affect our users. We need some way to keep track of our application's performance. Two tools that are available to monitor and diagnose our applications are the Performance Monitor and performance counters. We will mostly be using performance counters in conjunction with the Performance Monitor – it's very easy to use, so you should be able to just pick it up as we go along. We'll also be looking at how we can use counters *outside* of the Performance Monitor.

What we are going to do in this chapter is cover the tools and the knowledge that are needed to accurately monitor and diagnose both ASP.NET applications, and the system as a whole. It is then up to us as developers or system administrators (or both!) to monitor and fix our applications.

In this chapter, we are going to cover:

❑ How to use the default ASP.NET performance counters to monitor and improve the performance of our ASP.NET applications.

❑ Creating custom performance counters to monitor and report on our applications.

❑ Comparing custom performance counters to system default performance counters.

❑ How to access and use performance counters directly in our ASP.NET applications.

Monitoring Plan

Before we take a look at the performance counters available to us, let's take a second to talk about how we should plan the monitoring of our applications. An important step before monitoring any application, whether in production or still in development, is to carefully plan how you will be monitoring the application. This is essential to maintaining consistent readings and gathering useful, relevant information.

The first item to decide is what statistics you will be monitoring; this will determine what counters you'll use, which is the main topic of this chapter. We want to be sure to monitor the same kind of data each time we monitor our application, so that when we are doing comparisons to past data, we are comparing like with like. This is especially important when you are actively trying to make improvements to performance, because if you do not use the same data you will not be able to determine if there is an actual improvement in performance or not.

The next item in our monitoring plan is *when* we will monitor our application. This is not relevant when dealing with applications in development, but can be critical when dealing with live applications. We need to be sure to get a good sampling of the performance of our site. If we only measured the performance of the site on certain days or times we would not have a good representation of what our performance is. Performing a 24 hour log on a selection of different days is the best way to monitor live applications. For example, we would want to include a weekday, weekend day, and another random day. We'll also need to consider times when the content of your site will create extra traffic and impact performance. For example, a site that posts football scores would generate large traffic on the weekends or Monday night, so it would be worthless if we only monitored performance on Tuesdays.

The last item in our plan is how the data will be used and stored. There are various options in the performance monitor on how we can preserve the data for future use, and we will be looking at those techniques a little bit later. The main goal here is that we want to record our data each time in the same way so that we can easily compare it to the other data we already have.

A good monitoring plan is essential to accurately monitoring and improving the performance of our applications, and we will be covering many different topics in this chapter that will help us build the best plan possible.

Let's get on with the show and start looking at performance counters and how we can use them to monitor the performance of our applications.

Understanding Performance Counters

Performance counters are the chosen method of collecting and displaying real-time performance information in the Windows environment. Performance counters gather information and report it through the Performance Monitor, which can be found on any Windows NT, 2000, or XP system. You can access the Performance Monitor through Start | Settings | Control Panel | Administrative Tools | Performance, or you can simply go to Start | Run, type perfmon, and then hit *Enter*.

> Performance counters do not *store* performance data like an event log, or an entry in a database. A performance counter will only retain data for as long as there is a reference to the counter. When the last reference to a counter ends, whether it is from our code or from the Performance Monitor, the counter is reset to 0.While we can use logging and trend analysis to get a good idea of performance over a period of time, a performance counter is designed to record only while active, and we need to remember this while using and coding these counters, and explicitly save our results if required.

Categories, Counters, and Instances

There are three objects related to the concept of performance counters that we need to talk about:

❑ **Categories** – Performance Counter Categories are collections of different counters and instances which are related to each other. Some of the categories you will find are ASP.NET Applications, Processor, and Memory.

❑ **Counters** – Counters collect and report data on a single aspect of your system. There are many different types of counters, and we'll talk about a number of them throughout this chapter. There are counters for everything from processor usage to the number of active ASP.NET sessions, and you can create your own to monitor other things, such as total sales, or ad clickthroughs per second. Later on, we'll see how you do this.

❑ **Instances** – Instances represent applications that will access the counters. For example, you may be running two applications and want to know the failed cache lookups individually for each application. Instances are grouped by category, and not by counter. There are also instances that show the sum of all the applications, usually called __Total__.

The easiest way to get a grasp on these three different objects is to simply look in the Performance Monitor. Take a look at the next screenshot to see what the monitor looks like:

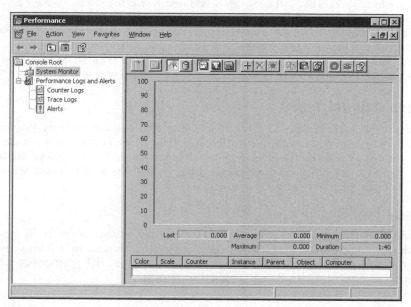

As you can see in the previous screenshot, we have the System Monitor selected on the left and a blank canvas to the right. When we add counters to the monitor, the status of those counters will be represented on that canvas. We can also access different settings to display our data in different ways, or record our data to a database. You will also see on the left the different logs and alerts that we can configure to run on our servers, and we will talk about these a little bit later. First, let's take a look at the screen used to add counters, which we can access by clicking the plus button:

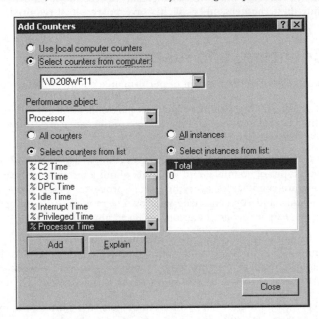

As you can see in this screenshot, when we go to add counters to the monitor we see a drop-down of counter categories to choose from. Each category is a grouping of similar counters, such as ASP.NET Applications or Processor. After we have selected a category, we see the listing of counters and instances populated. The next thing we choose is an instance of that counter. A counter can have many different instances, one for each separate application or object that it monitors. We are going to walk through creating and using each one of these objects in the following pages.

Performance Counter Types

There are many different types of counter to choose from. Different types of counters monitor and display different types of data in different ways. While there are more types than just the selection we'll cover here, we will try and examine the ones you will use the most. For a complete list, take a look at the `PerformanceCounterType` enumeration in the `System.Diagnostics` namespace, which is the namespace that performance counters reside in.

Number of Items

The first type of counter we are going to look at is the Number of Items counters. These counters are used to maintain a simple count of an object. These counters perform no calculations and only represent the most recent total of an item. An example of this type is the ASP.NET counter Application Restarts which is simply incremented each time an application restarts.

This group includes the types `NumberofItems32` and `NumbersofItems64`. You should only use the `NumbersofItems64` type if you need to store a very large number. Also available are the hex counters `NumbersofItemsHEX32` and `NumbersofItemsHEX64`, which simply use a hexadecimal value to display the most recent value. Most of the time we will not need anything more than `NumberofItems32`, and that is what we will use in our examples here.

Average Per Second

The Average Per Second counters keep track of the average occurrence of an event for each second in the sample interval. These counters perform a calculation which creates an average of how often an event is occurring every second. An example of this would be the ASP.NET counter **Requests/Sec** which takes the number of requests and averages it over the time frame of the sample. We'd use this type of counter to monitor events that occur frequently enough to warrant being measured by the second.

This group includes the type `RateOfCountsPerSecond32` and `RateOfCountsPerSecond64`, with `RateOfCountsPerSecond64` only being used if the value will be very large.

Average Per Operation

The third group of counter types we are going to cover actually includes three different counter types, but they are all used to gather the same type of data. The goal of these counters is to display the number of times something has happened, or the amount of time that has passed, during the operation.

Let's look at the three counter types:

❑ **AverageBase** – this counter type stores the base or denominator that is used by the other 2 counters below. This counter would hold the number of operations that have been performed during the sample period.

❑ **AverageCount64** – this counter uses the value of the `AverageBase` counter, and calculates the number of items processed during a particular operation. For instance we could track the average number of bytes that are processed for each request.

❑ **AverageTimer32** – this counter is similar to the `AverageCount64` counter except that it measures the amount of time for each operation. Using the `AverageBase` counter, it calculates the amount of time that passes during each operation. For instance, we could track the average amount of time that passes for each request to the system.

Default ASP.NET Performance Counters

The quickest way to get into performance monitoring is to use the performance counters that are installed with the .NET Framework. We can use these counters to monitor everything from application restarts to the cache hit ratio of an individual application. These counters are found in the ASP.NET and ASP.NET Applications categories in the performance tool.

The .NET Framework includes two types of ASP.NET performance counters:

❑ Application-based

❑ System-based

Application-based counters represent information about a single ASP.NET application running on the web server. This includes counters like Cache Hit Ratio, which calculates the ratio of hits to misses when trying to pull from the cache. Application-based counters are used to monitor and optimize individual applications.

On the other hand, **system-based** counters represent the entire web server, with such counters as Application Restarts, which counts the number of times applications have been restarted during the server's lifetime. System-based counters monitor the entire web server and entire ASP.NET process, instead of focusing on one single application.

We will also be using the Web Application Stress Tool that we met in Chapter 6. We will be using the tool to simulate a large number of users hitting our site, so that we can test the performance of our site *before* we promote it and let our users start using it. The other reason for using WAS is that we don't have a live site that we can monitor, so simulated users are going to have to do.

We are going to cover many of the available counters here in detail, but for full coverage you should refer to Appendix A.

Application-Based Performance Counters

Application-based counters are just that, performance counters that collect data based on our applications. You can select a single application by selecting its instance, or you can select the __Total__ instance which represents all the applications running on the server. Application counters can be found under the ASP.NET Application category in the Performance Monitor.

Cache Counters

Caching is one of the tools that we can use to squeeze better performance out of our applications. When we cache pages, we save the processor from having to process that page again. Cache-based counters track the effectiveness of caching in our application, or applications. There are three sets of cache-based counters: one is based on the total effectiveness of the cache, one singles out caching accessed through exposed APIs, and the last set is based on output caching, or page-level caching. We will only be going over the counters based on the total cache here, as they all behave in exactly the same way, except for the above stated differences.

Cache Total Entries	This counter tracks the total number of entries in the cache. This is a count of every object that is currently being stored in the cache.
Cache Total Hits	Cache Total Hits counts the number of times that the server requests an object from the cache and the object is available. This shows the effectiveness of your caching policy, in other words which objects you choose to cache and the amount of time you cache them for.
Cache Total Misses	The opposite of hits, cache misses are when the server requests an object from the cache and the object has expired and is not found.
Cache Total Hit Ratio	This counter represents the ratio of hits to misses of the cache. Obviously, you want to have more hits than misses, and this counter can be very effective in telling us if we are utilizing caching to its full capabilities.

Cache Total Turnover Rate	This is the number of additions and removals of objects to the cache per second. This shows us how effectively the cache is being used, as a high turnover rate indicates that too many objects are being added that might not need to be cached, and that the high-traffic objects are not being cached for long enough.

Error Counters

Error counters provide us with a method of tracking the frequency of errors in our applications. There are a number of counters provided to track errors, but we are only going to look at the most important ones. While the counters do provide a nice method of tracking errors, it would be prudent to also track the errors in a database, or even send yourself an e-mail on each error.

Errors Total	This counter is the sum of a number of counters that we will not be covering here. It represents all the errors that have occurred during the execution of HTTP requests on our application. This includes any parser, compilation, or run-time errors. This counter should give us a good idea if we are having problems with our applications or not. Any number larger than zero here means that we need to check our code and include better error handling techniques.
Errors Total/Sec	This counter is similar to the Errors Total counter but on a per-second basis. If we are at the point where we can measure the errors of our applications by the second, then we are really in trouble. Hopefully this is not a counter that we will need. It would be more useful to people hosting a large number of ASP.NET applications, such as a hosting company or ISP.
Errors Unhandled During Execution	This counter tracks the number of errors that occur in our code, and **are not** trapped by our code. These will be errors that have slipped through any error-catching code that we may have and are instead handled by the internal ASP.NET error handling, usually resulting in an ugly error message being presented to our users. This is the type of error that we definitely want to avoid, since it will have a direct result on the usability of our application.

Request Counters

Request counters provide us with a method of measuring the number of requests to a particular application. This includes the current number of requests, requests that time out, requests that fail, and more. We will use these counters to help us ensure that a large number of requests are not failing, and to get an idea of the number of requests each of our applications is receiving.

Requests Executing	This counter represents the number of requests that are currently executing. It is not much use to us other than giving us a view of the current level of traffic for our application.
Requests Not Found	This counter tracks the number of requests that have failed because the resource was not found, resulting in either a 404 or 414 error code. This counter is excellent for showing us how many files are not being found in our applications. Note that this counter will only record 'not found' data for files with .NET extensions, like .aspx, not failed requests for .htm or .asp files.

Table continued on following page

Requests Failed	This counter tracks the total number of failed requests for an application. This counter is a total of the Request Not Found, Requests Not Authorized and Requests Timed Out counters. Please note that this counter will not track the requests that are rejected, because the rejecting is done by IIS (when the queue is full), and not by the ASP.NET process.
Requests Timed Out	This counter tracks the number of requests that have timed out. This is a good counter to track because if there are a large number of requests timing out then we definitely need to take action. Requests will time out when they reach the time limit set on the server for a request to execute. This could be due to the server not having the resources to complete the request, or it could be a very large search or report being run. We should first monitor our server and be sure that it does have adequate resources to process the request, then either try and break our search or report down into smaller sections, or increase the timeout limit on our server.
Requests/Sec	This counter displays the total number of requests executed each second. This counter is useful because it is a fairly good representation of the traffic that our application is receiving, and we can then take this value and compare it to our system counters to track what kind of traffic we can handle on our server.

Session Counters

These counters track the in-memory sessions that are maintained, as opposed to the session counters we will talk about in the *System-based Performance Counters* section, which tracked sessions maintained through the state server. We will use these counters to get an idea of the number of users that we are supporting with our application. A session is assigned to a user when they first hit the site, and it will (by default) normally stay "alive" for 20 minutes. So, while monitoring sessions will not tell us how many users we have had for a large period of time, it will give us a good idea of the number of users the site is presently supporting.

Sessions Active	This counter tracks the current number of active sessions for our application. We can use this counter to track the current number of users using our application, and compare it to the system resources and requests that are being used. By doing this, we can get an idea of the hardware needed to support the number of users that we are anticipating.
Sessions Total	This counter represents the total number of sessions since the application was started. This counter will give us a rough idea of the number of users that we have supported since the application was last started.

Transaction Counters

The last type of application-based counters we are going to talk about is transaction counters. We are going to use these counters to track the behavior of transactions in our application. They are only useful if you are actually using transactions in your business logic. We are only going to cover a couple of the counters here, but you can see the rest in Appendix A.

Transactions Aborted	This counter tracks the number of transactions that have been aborted or rolled back by the application. We want to track this counter because we can then compare this number to the number of transactions total, and then get an idea of the success rate of our transactions. A high rate of failure would mean that we'd need to examine and optimize our business logic.
Transactions Total	This counter represents the total number of transactions since the application was started. We can use this counter to compare against the Transactions Aborted and get an idea of the percentage of transactions that are failing.
Transactions/Sec	This counter shows us the number of transactions starting each second. It is useful because it is an excellent indicator of the transaction traffic we are handling. We can also compare this counter to our system counters and see the impact a larger number of transactions per second has on our system resources.

System-Based Performance Counters

System-based performance counters can be found under the ASP.NET category in the Performance Monitor. They consist of counters that apply to all applications running on the web server. An example is Applications Running, which is a count of the number of applications currently running on the server. These counters are not application specific.

Application Counters

Application counters are used to keep track of the applications that are running on our web server. These counters will be most beneficial to system administrators or ISP and hosting companies, but will also be useful for making sure that your server is not overburdened with its total application load.

> *Note that these application counters are not the same as **application-based** counters, but are actually system-based counters that collect information about **all** of the applications running on the server, and present them as a total across all applications.*

Application Restarts	The Application Restarts counter tracks the number of times that an application has restarted. The value of this counter is reset each time IIS or the web server is reset, and is incremented each time the `Application_OnEnd` event is triggered. It is a good idea to monitor this counter because a high number of application restarts can cause problems for your users, considering that it takes time for the application to start again, and also because all application and session state information is flushed on a restart. If you notice a large number of application restarts on your server, then the application is probably being updated too often, as most changes to the application will cause a restart, including changes to the config files or any file in the bin directory of the application. This can also be caused by anti-virus programs that write back to the files after they scan them. We would expect this counter to be higher on a development or pre-production system than on a production system.
Application Running	This counter simply records the number of applications that are currently running on the web server – a great help for a system administrator who wants to keep track of how many different applications are available at any given time.

Request Counters

The following counters keep track of the HTTP requests that our web server is handling. They do not represent the time that it takes for a page to load, but they can measure the amount of time that the request is waiting to be serviced. If the request performance is not optimal then we have two choices: either upgrade our server hardware, or optimize our applications to free up more system resources.

Requests Disconnected	This counter keeps track of the number of requests that have been disconnected due to a communications issue. While there will always be some communications problems, a high number of disconnects is definitely an issue, and it should be brought to the attention of the network provider.
Requests Queued	This counter records the number of requests waiting to be processed in the queue. Obviously, you want this number to be very low, as requests waiting in the queue means users are waiting. This leads us to the next counter.
Request Wait Time	This counter records the amount of time in milliseconds that the most recent request waited to be processed in the queue. This is the number we really want to keep an eye on as it directly corresponds to our users waiting for the page to come up, which is effectively our perceived performance.
Requests Rejected	This counter records the number of requests that are rejected because the server is too busy. These requests return a 503 HTTP status code to the user telling them that the server is too busy. We want to avoid requests being rejected at any cost, and as soon as this counter starts moving then we need to take action and either upgrade our the server or optimize our applications.

Using Performance Counters

Now that we have covered some of the system- and application-based counters provided by the .NET Framework, let's take a look at how we can read and use this counter data. There should be two different times that we measure the performance of our applications. The first should be before the application is ever deployed, and the second is when the application is running in production. To test the application while it is still in development, we are going to be using the Web Application Stress Tool which was covered in depth in Chapter 6. The importance of testing the application before it is deployed cannot be stressed too much. It's much easier to find problem areas and make changes while the application is in development than when it is already in production and you are getting complaints from your users.

For this little exercise, we have created a couple of test files (which you can find in the code download under the `test1` directory) and set up our WAS tool to hit the application pretty hard. Here are the counters we'll use in this example:

- ❑ ASP.NET Applications – Requests/Sec
- ❑ ASP.NET Applications – Output Cache Hit Ratio
- ❑ Processor – % Processor Time
- ❑ Memory – Pages/sec

❑ Physical Disk – Avg. Disk Queue Length

❑ Network Interface – Current Bandwidth

We didn't cover all of these above, but descriptions can be found in Appendix A, and they should be fairly straightforward to understand. We'll now add the above counters to the Performance Monitor and then set up the WAS tool to hit our application.

First let's take a look at the Performance Monitor setup:

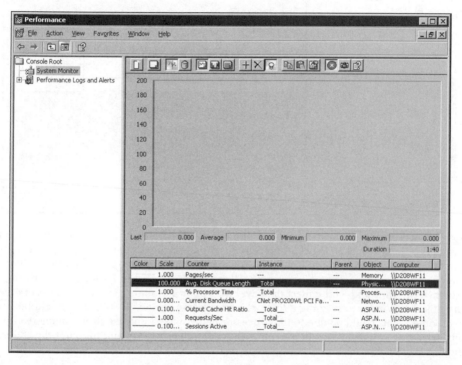

In the above screenshot, we have our counters added to the performance monitor and we are ready to start testing our application. We have also increased the scale of the monitor from the default 0-100 up to 0-200, because we are including Requests/sec which could be higher than 100. To change the scale of the monitor, simply right-click and select **Properties**, then under the **Graph** tab change the vertical scale settings. First, we are just going to look at the current performance, and then we will look at saving our data to a log. Next, let's look at a screenshot of the WAS setup:

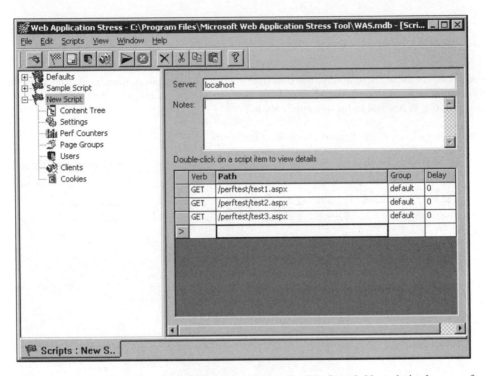

In the above screenshot, we have added our three files to the WAS tool. Next, let's change a few settings. Set the stress level and sockets level to 1 and the maximum delay to 3, to provide a small random delay. We are going to do a short test since we are testing an application that is in development, so set the test to 5 minutes. When monitoring a live server, it is best to create a log using the Performance Monitor and let it collect data over a 24-hour period, to get the best idea of how the server is being utilized. What we are going to be looking for is any period where a user might be experiencing long wait times. This could be due to the processor being maxed out, the drives being overused, or even the network being clogged. We will use our ASP.NET counters to try and pinpoint the action that is causing this bottleneck.

Let's take a look at our performance monitor after running the test:

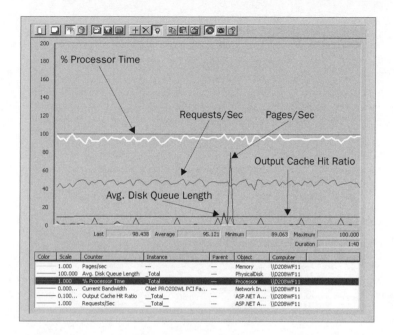

In the screenshot above, we see that the processor usage is very high, hovering in the high 90s and hitting 100% usages at times. This is not acceptable for our server, and we need to use some of the other data from our other counters to see how we can get this percentage lower. We can see that the memory and drives do not seem to be a problem though, as both of those counters have stayed mostly at very low levels of stress.

Looking at the Requests/Sec counter, we can see that we are getting around 40-50 requests handled by our server a second. While this is a decent amount of requests, we should be able to handle more than this with almost 100% usage. We can also see that our Output Cache Hit Ratio counter is around 90, which is pretty good, but this is where we are going to look for improvement. The other reason we are going to look to caching to improve our performance is because currently we have a very high processor cost per request. On our site only a single page is implementing page-level caching, and the timeout for that page is very low. We are going to increase the timeout of the page already using caching, and then add caching to two other pages (the modified files are included in the download). We simply need to add the following line to all of our pages, replacing the line that existed before in page1.aspx:

```
<%@ outputcache duration="70" varybyparam="none" %>
```

Doing so adds cache to two pages that did not have it, and increases the timeout of the caching already implemented on the first page.

Let's run the exact same test using the WAS tool, and take a look at the screenshot:

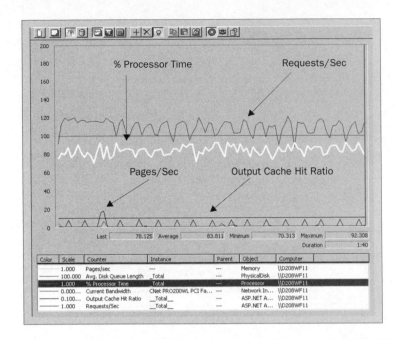

This time our processor is slightly less used, averaging around 80% instead of 95%. However the major difference is that we are now handling many more requests per second, averaging around 110. So even though we saw a small *decrease* in processor usage, we are handling almost 100% more requests per second. In this example, we only really used the Output Cache Hit Ratio counter to look for areas of improvement, but you could use any of the counters that we talked about earlier. For instance, if we were using a transaction-heavy application then we would have included those counters here as well. This is the type of monitoring and diagnosis that we should be doing on a regular basis with our applications and servers. So, let's take a quick look at the logging features of the performance monitor and how we can use them to run this same test on our live applications.

Using the Log

We are going to be running the same test as above, but this time we will run the test for longer and record the results in a log. We will also be tweaking our WAS tool settings to try and better simulate what a live production site would act like. First, let's take a look at how we are going to create our log. The first step is to add a log entry to the Counter Log section of the Performance Monitor. We do this by right-clicking and selecting New Log Settings. Next, we specify a name for our log and are presented with the settings for our log:

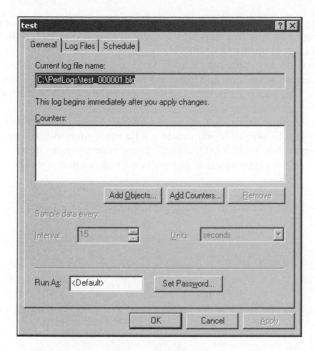

We can then add the counters that we used in the above test to this log:

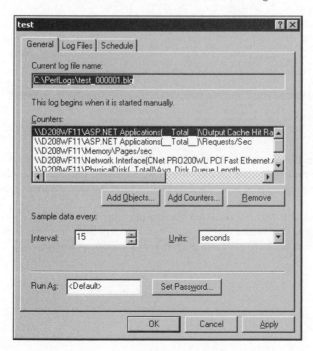

The only other settings change we are going to make is changing the startup time under Schedule. We will change the first setting to Manual so that we can be sure our log does not start until we are ready. After we hit OK, we will see the log in our list of available logs. Before we can start the log, we need to set up the WAS tool. Again, normally we would not be using WAS as we would be working on a live production site. However, for this example, we will try and tweak the WAS tool to act more like we would expect a live production site to act. This means more sporadic use. Let's take a look at our adjusted settings:

We'll set the stress level (threads) to 75, run the test for 20 minutes, and include a random 0 to 1000 millisecond delay. This is by way of trying to add a little more unpredictability to the traffic. It is not as good as a real live server, but it will work for our logging example here. First, we will start our log, and then start the WAS test. Let's take a look at our log results in the performance monitor:

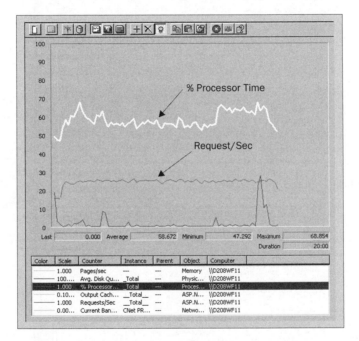

As you can see, it is rather similar to the test above, but this time the time frame is larger. You will also see that the readings are more consistent, even though we increased our random delay in the WAS tool. This is because when using the logging tool, the data is only sampled every 15 seconds instead of every second.

Logging is a very valuable feature when we are dealing with live production sites, or in our case a "simulated" production site. When logging performance data for a live site, it is best to log over a 24-hour period so you can see how your site performs at all times of the day.

Custom Performance Counters

In this section, we are going to cover creating and using custom performance counters. We will go over how to create a custom category, creating counters and instances, and how we can actually use the data we collect. Custom counters can be a very valuable tool by enabling us to track the business logic of our applications, along with the system performance and ASP.NET application performance counters. For instance, we could track the number of reports that are run on our system and see the direct and immediate influence that running those reports has on the performance of our server. This is invaluable information when it comes to server hardware planning and diagnosis performance issues. Before we get started, let's take a look at the namespace that we will be using to perform these operations.

System.Diagnostics Namespace

The `System.Diagnostics` namespace contains the classes we will be using: all the tools to work with the event log, Windows process, debugging and tracing, and performance counters. In this section we will only be taking a look at the performance counter classes of the namespace.

PerformanceCounter Class

The performance counter class represents a single Windows performance counter. This class contains methods to increment and decrement the counter value, as well as various methods of retrieving the value of the counter including raw, calculated, and sampled data. We will be using this class in both of the next sections, and we will get into the various methods and their usage in much more depth.

PerformanceCounterCategory Class

The performance counter category class represents a counter category. These are the categories that you see in the performance monitor when we add a new counter. This class contains methods for us to check and see if a counter exists, as well as methods to retrieve lists of counters and categories. Also contained in this class are the methods to create new categories and counters.

PerformanceCounterType Enum

The performance counter type enumeration includes a complete list of the different counter types available to use in the .NET Framework. We covered some of the more often-used counter types in the last section, and you can see the other types here.

Security Issues

Before we can get started working with custom counters, there are some security issues to address. The default ASP.NET process model runs under the restricted `ASPNET` user account. This account is restricted in what it can do on our server, and helps prevent any major damage from being done if a security hole is found in ASP.NET allowing a hacker to run malicious code on our machine. Using this account does make our life a little more difficult, but it is well worth the price. Let's take a look at some of the account's permissions and how they apply to us:

❑ This account cannot create custom performance counters. This does not present too much of a problem since we can create our counters either in a secure area, such as an area that uses impersonation, or run the code from a console application.

❏   This account cannot read from performance counters. This is more of a hassle to us, since reading from performance counters could actually help us in our ASP.NET applications. We will have to relegate to only reading values from secure areas where we can implement impersonation.

❏   This account **can** write to custom performance counters, so we will be able to write to our custom performance counters with no problem.

There are a couple of security solutions that we are going to cover briefly. We will not need to make any changes to write to custom performance counters, but changes will need to be made to be able to create and delete custom counters, as well as to read values from any type of counter. We have basically two options available to us.

Setting the User to "system" instead of "machine"

This action is highly discouraged on a production machine as it can create a serious security hole if someone could gain access to our system. It might be an option if you are running on an intranet, or you are just working on a development system, but it's still not advisable. To change the setting, you need to edit a line in the `machine.config` of your web server. You should find this file in `Winnt\Microsoft.Net\Framework\ (version) \Config`. Open the file using either VS.NET or a simple text editor and change the following line:

```
<processModel enable="true" timeout="Infinite" idleTimeout="Infinite"
            shutdownTimeout="0:00:05" requestLimit="Infinite"
            requestQueueLimit="5000" restartQueueLimit="10" memoryLimit="60"
            webGarden="false" cpuMask="0xffffffff" userName="machine"
            ... .../>
```

The line we will change is `username="machine"`, and all we need to do is change this to `username="system"`. While this is an easy solution, we should remember never to do this on a production machine, or anywhere else where security is important.

Implement Impersonation

The second, and more secure option, is to implement impersonation on the site that you want to use to either view performance counter data or create custom counters. By implementing impersonation you will be asking for a Windows login when users hit the site, and then if that user has admin access on the web server or the web server's domain, then they will be able to perform the desired functions. Obviously, this solution is geared more towards an admin page or special users section. It is fairly easy to implement impersonation on either a single application or the entire system, but for our purposes we'll implement it for a single application. First, we need to add the following line anywhere in between the `<system.web>` tags in our `web.config` of our application:

```
<identity impersonate="true"></identity>
```

The next step is modifying the security options of our virtual directory in the IIS manager. We simply uncheck the checkbox for anonymous access and users will be forced to log in with a domain account to access our application. The username and login that they use will then be used by the application to access performance counter data or create custom counters. If they are not administrators of the domain or server, they will receive errors when trying to perform these functions, but for the administrators everything should work perfectly.

Please keep these issues in mind while reading the next two sections, and be sure to implement one or the other before trying examples that create, read, or delete performance counters.

Creating Performance Counters

There are two ways to create our own performance counters. The first way is to create them directly in our code, and the second uses Visual Studio .NET. We will examine both of these methods in turn.

Creating Counters in Code

First, let's actually create a custom performance counter in code. The first thing that we need to do is to create the new category and counter. This will add both the category and counter to the Performance Monitor, and it will also make it possible for us to create instances of these counters later on in our code and use them to represent the performance of our applications by incrementing and decrementing the counter. When you add a category and counters, you are adding the information to the OS, and the categories and counters will persist through restarts and will not be removed until you specifically delete them. You only need to create the counter once, either in the Application_Start method of our Global.asax, or in a separate admin page or utility. As we discussed earlier, using a separate page or utility presents less of a security risk.

Let's move along and get started on creating our custom counter. We can't just create a category by itself; instead we need to create a category and add all of the counters we want at the same time. Nor will we be able to add counters to an existing category later. What we will do is add each of the counters to a collection and then create the category using that collection. All of the following code can be found in the code download in the file named customcounters.aspx.

We need to be sure to first import the System.Diagnostics namespace:

```
<%@ import Namespace="System.Diagnostics" %>
```

The next thing that we need to do is make sure that the category we want to add does not already exist:

```
If Not PerformanceCounterCategory.Exists("Wrox Counters") Then
'...we'll add our new counters here...
End If
```

By calling the Exists method of the PerformanceCounterCategory and passing it the name of our category we will have a Boolean value returned to us letting us know if the category exists or not. You can also provide a machine name along with the category name if you are working with categories on another system. If you are trying to perform these operations to another system on the network, the same code would look something like this:

```
If Not PerformanceCounterCategory.Exists("Wrox Counters", "MySystem") Then
'...add new counters...
End If
```

Inside this If statement, we are going to add the code that will create our category and counters.

Creating a Collection

The first thing that we are going to do is create a `CounterCreationDataCollection` object. This object will hold the various `CounterCreationData` objects that we are going to create. Each `CounterCreationData` object contains the information to create an individual counter, including its name, help text, and the type of the counter. When we create our various `CounterCreationData` objects, we are going to add them to our collection. First, though, let's create the collection:

```
If Not PerformanceCounterCategory.Exists("Wrox Counters") Then

    Dim CounterDataGroup As CounterCreationDataCollection
    CounterDataGroup = New CounterCreationDataCollection()

    End If
```

The above code simply creates a `CounterCreationDataCollection` instance, which we name `CounterDataGroup`.

Our next step is going to be to start defining the counters that we are going to add. Again, the only way that we can add counters to a category is when we first create the category. We cannot create counters in existing categories, either system categories or categories we may have already created. Trying to do so will raise an exception. If we needed to add a counter to a current category, we would need to delete the category and then recreate the category including all of the counters. It is for this reason that we will first work on collecting our counter data and then on adding it when we create our category, even though it does seem backwards.

Creating the Counters

Let's create our first counter, which we are going to call **Orders per Second**. We are going to use this counter to track the number of orders per second for our e-commerce site. While we do collect this information in our database, we want to have a real-time indicator of the number of orders coming in, without having to run performance-costly reports on the database.

The first thing we will need to do is create an instance of the `CounterCreationData` object which we will call `CounterData`. You can find the code for this example in `customcounters.aspx` in the code download for this chapter:

```
Dim CounterData As CounterCreationData
CounterData = New CounterCreationData()
```

Using this variable, we will specify the various options that we have when creating a counter. The first two that we will assign are the `Name` and the `Help` text of the counter:

```
CounterData.CounterName = "Orders per Second"
CounterData.CounterHelp = "The number of orders per second"
```

The `CounterName` property sets the name of the counter that will appear in the Performance Monitor, and we will use that later on to increment the counter value. The `CounterHelp` property is the text that will be displayed when a user presses the **Explain** button in the Performance Monitor. We will also reference this text in the next section when we create an online performance monitor.

The last property that we need to set is the `CounterType` property which defines the type of counter that we want to create:

```
CounterData.CounterType = PerformanceCounterType.RateOfCountsPerSecond32
```

For this counter, we are going to use the `RateOfCountsPerSecond32` type, so we specify that by using the corresponding value in the `PerformanceCounterType` enumeration. Since this is the last piece of data needed for this counter, we are now going to add it to the `CounterDataGroup` collection that we declared earlier. This will not create the counter, but simply add it to the collection which we will later use when we create our category.

```
CounterDataGroup.Add(CounterData)
```

Now that we have our first counter completed, we can move on to the second counter. Since we have already gone through this once, it'll be easier just to show the code that we will use. The only things that change are the values we are specifying.

```
Dim CounterData2 As CounterCreationData
CounterData2 = New CounterCreationData()
CounterData2.CounterName = "Orders Total"
CounterData2.CounterHelp = "The total number of orders"
CounterData2.CounterType = PerformanceCounterType.NumberOfItems32
CounterDataGroup.Add(CounterData2)
```

Again, we create a `CounterCreationData` object and specify the `Name`, `Help`, and `Type` of the counter. Please take note that this time we used the `NumberOfItems32` type, so that we would be able to keep track of the total number of orders that have been processed. Again, we add the counter data to the collection that we created earlier. We now have two counters in the collection. Let's take a look at what our code looks like before we go on to create our category:

```
If Not PerformanceCounterCategory.Exists("Wrox Counters") Then

  Dim CounterDataGroup As CounterCreationDataCollection
  CounterDataGroup = New CounterCreationDataCollection()


  Dim CounterData As CounterCreationData
  CounterData = New CounterCreationData()
  CounterData.CounterName = "Orders per Second"
  CounterData.CounterHelp = "The number of orders per second"
  CounterData.CounterType = PerformanceCounterType.RateOfCountsPerSecond32

  CounterDataGroup.Add(CounterData)

  Dim CounterData2 As CounterCreationData
  CounterData2 = New CounterCreationData()
  CounterData2.CounterName = "Orders Total"
  CounterData2.CounterHelp = "The total number of orders"
  CounterData2.CounterType = PerformanceCounterType.NumberOfItems32
  CounterDataGroup.Add(CounterData2)

End If
```

Creating the Category

Finally, we are ready to create the category and add the counters with this line of code which we insert into our `If` statement:

```
PerformanceCounterCategory.Create("Wrox Counters", _
        "Counters for Wrox's ASP.NET Performance Book", CounterDataGroup)
```

We create our category and add our counters using the `PerformanceCounterCategory`'s `Create` method. The first thing that we need to specify is the name of our category, `Wrox Counters`, and then add some text that will be used to describe our category. This is the text that appears when the Explain button is clicked in the Performance Monitor Add Counters window. Lastly, we add our counters using the collection that we created. This will add our category, counters, and descriptions to the local system. To see the results, take a look at the image below:

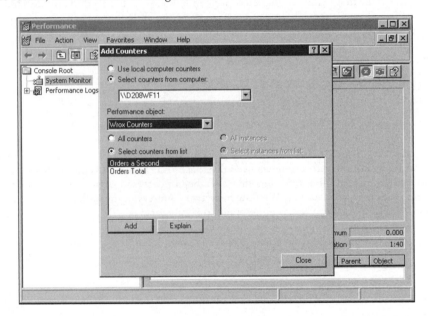

In the screenshot above, you can see our category and the two counters that we created. Now that we have created our category and counters, we can move on to incrementing and manipulating the data of the counters, but first let's take a look at an alternative way of creating counters: using Visual Studio .NET and the Server Explorer.

Creating a Custom Counter with VS.NET

We'll now go through the process of creating custom counters using Visual Studio .NET. Creating new categories and counters is made much easier with the use of the Server Explorer. The Server Explorer is only available with the multi-language versions of VS.NET, not with the single-language versions. To pull up the Server Explorer, select it from the View menu or press *Ctrl + Alt + S*. Once inside the Server Explorer, right-click on the Performance Counters listing and choose Create New Category.

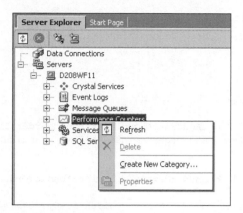

When you choose **Create New Category,** you will be asked to specify a **Category Name** and **Description,** then we can start adding counters:

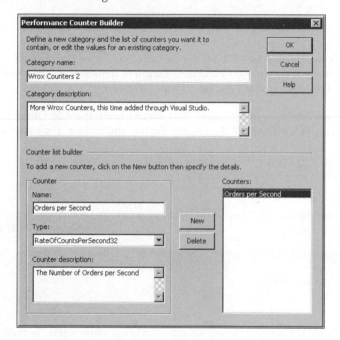

After pressing **OK,** the category and counter are added to the system. As you can see, the Server Explorer and VS.NET make it very easy to add custom categories and counters.

Incrementing and Manipulating Counter Data

Now that we have created our two counters, we need to start using them to track data. To demonstrate using these counters, we will create a quick little page with a button to place an order, then we will increment both counters accordingly. We will also go through being able to decrement and modify the raw values held by the counters. But first, let's take a look at the page we will use to "place an order". You will find the following code in the addcounters.aspx file in the code download.

```
<%@ Page Language="VB" %>
<%@ import Namespace="System.Diagnostics" %>
<html>
<head>
</head>
<body>
  <form runat="server">
    <p>
      <asp:Button id="btnAddOrder" onclick="btnAddOrder_Click" runat="server"
                  Text="Add Order" Width="136px"></asp:Button>
    </p>
    <p>
      <asp:Button id="btnAddOrders20" onclick="btnAddOrders20_Click"
runat="server"
                  Text="Add 20 Orders" Width="136px"></asp:Button>
    </p>
    <!-- Insert content here -->
  </form>
</body>
</html>
```

All we have here is two quick ASP.NET button controls, one for adding a single order and the other for adding 20 orders. We will use the **Add 20 Orders** button to demonstrate the per-second order counter. Notice how we also need to import System.Diagnostics.

The next thing we need to do is to increment the counters when the **Add Order** button is pressed. We will also be creating a new instance of the counter for our application. Let's take a look at the code:

```
Sub btnAddOrder_Click(sender As Object, e As EventArgs)
  Dim pcCounter as PerformanceCounter
  Dim pcCounter2 as PerformanceCounter

  If (PerformanceCounterCategory.CounterExists("Orders Total", _
                                               "Wrox Counters")) Then

    pcCounter = New PerformanceCounter("Wrox Counters", "Orders Total","App1", _
                                       False)
    pcCounter.Increment()

  End If

  If (PerformanceCounterCategory.CounterExists("Orders per Second", _
                                               "Wrox Counters")) Then

    pcCounter2 = New PerformanceCounter("Wrox Counters", "Orders per Second", _
                                        "App1", False)
    pcCounter2.Increment()

  End If

End Sub
```

The first thing we did was create two `PerformanceCounter` variables, one for each of the two counters that we created earlier. Then we used the `PerformanceCounterCategory` method `CounterExists` to be sure that the counter that we want actually exists. If we tried to assign our variable to a nonexistent counter, an exception would be generated.

The next step is to assign the first variable to our first counter. To do that, we create a new `PerformanceCounter` object and specify the category, counter, and instance it refers to, and whether the counter is read-only or not. Let's take a close look at it:

```
pcCounter = New PerformanceCounter("Wrox Counters", "Orders Total", _
                                   "App1", False)
```

First we specify `"Wrox Counters"`, our category. Next, we specify `"Orders Total"`, which is the counter that we want to use and increment. The next string is the name of the instance that we would like to use; in this case the instance will be created, since it did not exist before. The last parameter that we specify is the Boolean value `False` which tells the counter that we wish to be able to modify the performance counter (in other words, it is not read-only).

The next line of code is where we then increment the counter by one:

```
pcCounter.Increment()
```

The `Increment` method simply adds one to the current value of the performance counter. Next, we do the same thing for our second counter `"Orders per Second"`, checking to be sure the counter exists, creating a performance counter and then calling the `Increment` method.

Now we want to wire up the events for the **Add 20 Orders** button:

```
Sub btnAddOrders20_Click(sender As Object, e As EventArgs)
   Dim pcCounter as PerformanceCounter
   Dim pcCounter2 as PerformanceCounter

   If (PerformanceCounterCategory.CounterExists("Orders Total", _
                                              "Wrox Counters")) Then

     pcCounter = New PerformanceCounter("Wrox Counters", "Orders Total", _
                                      "App1", False)
     pcCounter.IncrementBy(20)

   End If

   If (PerformanceCounterCategory.CounterExists("Orders per Second", _
                                              "Wrox Counters")) Then

     pcCounter2 = New PerformanceCounter("Wrox Counters", "Orders per Second", _
                                      "App1", False)
     pcCounter2.IncrementBy(20)

   End If

End Sub
```

Everything here is very similar to the previous code, except that instead of using the
PerformanceCounter Increment method, we use the IncrementBy method. The IncrementBy
method simply accepts an integer and then increases the counter by the amount specified. In our case,
the counter will be incremented by twenty.

Let's test out our application by opening the Performance Monitor and selecting our counters. Once we
have the counters recording, we can then run the ASP.NET application, press some buttons, and see the
results in the performance monitor. Take a look at this screenshot to see some sample results:

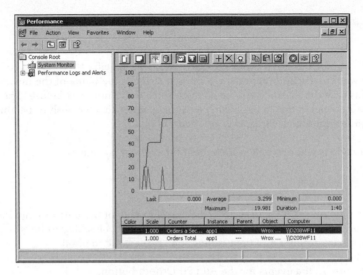

As you can see in the screenshot, when we press the buttons our counters react accordingly, creating for
us a real-time method of keeping track of both the total number of orders and the numbers of orders per
second. Remember that this type of data collection is not a replacement for good database logging and
reporting, though – it should only be used to give us a feeling for the immediate performance of the site.

Decreasing a Counter Value

In our test situation, we also want to be able to represent when an order is cancelled, so we will need to
create a way to subtract from both of our counters. This code is included in the addorders.aspx file
in the code download.

First, let's add a button to our page to subtract from the counters:

```
<html>
<head>
</head>
<body>
  <form runat="server">
    <p>
      <asp:Button id="btnAddOrder" onclick="btnAddOrder_Click" runat="server"
                  Width="136px" Text="Add Order"></asp:Button>
```

```
    </p>
    <p>
      <asp:Button id="btnAddOrders20" onclick="btnAddOrders20_Click"
runat="server"
                  Width="136px" Text="Add 20 Orders"></asp:Button>
    </p>
    <p>
      <asp:Button id="btnDeleteOrder" onclick="btnDeleteOrder_Click"
runat="server"
                  Width="136px" Text="Delete Order"></asp:Button>
    </p>
  </form>
</body>
</html>
```

Now that we have a button, let's add the event that will do the decrementing of our counter value. We will be using the `Decrement` method of the `PerformanceCounter` class to decrease our counter by one:

```
Sub btnDeleteOrder_Click(sender As Object, e As EventArgs)

  Dim pcCounter As PerformanceCounter
  Dim pcCounter2 As PerformanceCounter

  If (PerformanceCounterCategory.CounterExists("Orders Total", _
                                     "Wrox Counters")) Then

    pcCounter = New PerformanceCounter("Wrox Counters", "Orders Total", _
                                 "App1", False)
    pcCounter.Decrement()

  End If
  If (PerformanceCounterCategory.CounterExists("Orders per Second", _
                                     "Wrox Counters")) Then

    pcCounter2 = New PerformanceCounter("Wrox Counters", "Orders per Second", _
                                 "App1", False)
    pcCounter2.Decrement()
  End If

End Sub
```

Clicking our **Delete Order** button will now decrease both of our counters by one. There is no `DecrementBy()` method, so to decrease our counter by a large value we would need to perform a loop and call `Decrement()` each time. If you take a look at the following screenshot, you will see that when we press the **Delete Order** button a couple of times, the **Orders Total** counter decreases by one each time. We also see that the **Orders per Second** counter drops off the chart as the value turns negative, since a negative number of orders is being processed each second.

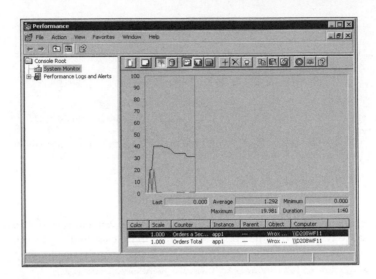

Resetting a Counter Value

The next operation that we are going to perform is to reset the value of a counter. Using our current example of tracking orders, we'll want to reset the counter every day to make sure we're only seeing the total orders for today. Since this does not apply to the per-second counter we will only be working on resetting the value of the **Orders Total** counter. The first thing we are going to do is add yet another button to our page to reset the value of our counter:

```
<html>
<head>
</head>
<body>
  <form runat="server">
    <p>
      <asp:Button id="btnAddOrder" onclick="btnAddOrder_Click" runat="server"
                Width="136px" Text="Add Order"></asp:Button>
    </p>
    <p>
      <asp:Button id="btnAddOrders20" onclick="btnAddOrders20_Click"
runat="server"
                Width="136px" Text="Add 20 Orders"></asp:Button>
    </p>
    <p>
      <asp:Button id="btnDeleteOrder" onclick="btnDeleteOrder_Click"
runat="server"
                Width="136px" Text="Delete Order"></asp:Button>
    </p>
    <p>
     <asp:Button id="btnResetTotal" onclick="btnResetTotal_Click" runat="server"
                Width="138px" Text="Reset Total"></asp:Button>
    </p>
  </form>
</body>
</html>
```

Here is the code that will reset our counter back to zero:

```
Sub btnResetTotal_Click(sender As Object, e As EventArgs)

  Dim pcCounter as PerformanceCounter

  If (PerformanceCounterCategory.CounterExists("Orders Total", _
                                    "Wrox Counters")) Then

    pcCounter = New PerformanceCounter("Wrox Counters", "Orders Total", _
                          "App1", False)
    pcCounter.RawValue = 0

  End If
End Sub
```

We simply need to set the RawValue property of the counter to 0, which essentially resets our performance counter. (We'll look into raw values, along with the other kinds of values held by counters, later in the chapter.) You could also use this method to set the value of this counter to another number, but it is usually better to use the Increment and Decrement methods of the counter.

Accessing Counters with Visual Studio .NET

We saw earlier how adding categories and counters is made easier by using Visual Studio .NET and the Server Explorer, and accessing and incrementing the data is made easier as well. Let's again pull up the Server Explorer and find the counters that we want to access under the Performance Counters listing:

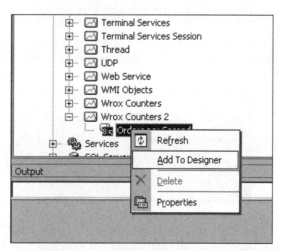

Right-click on the counter you wish to work with and choose **Add to Designer**. The counter will be added to the last page we used and will appear at the bottom of your page. As we will see in the next image, we will be able to access the properties of the counter that we previously needed to specify in code:

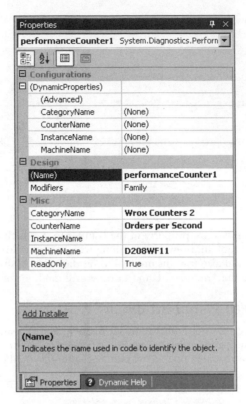

Once you have the counter added to your page, you will be able to access the same methods as we used above to increment and decrement the counter. When the counter is added to the page, it appears at the bottom of the page like this:

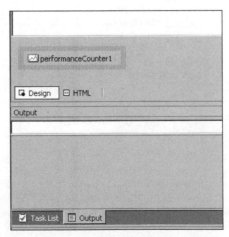

Visual Studio .NET also adds the following line to our code-behind:

```
Protected WithEvents PerformanceCounter1 As System.Diagnostics.PerformanceCounter
```

We can then access the `PerformanceCounter1` object anywhere in our code, and it acts the same as if we had created the counter ourself. As you can see, Visual Studio .NET has once again made our lives easier when dealing with counters.

Deleting Counters and Categories

The last thing we are going to cover in this section is deleting the counter category and all the counters contained within it. Remember that when we delete these counters we are actually deleting them from the operating system and they will not show up again unless we go through the process of recreating them.

> **There is no need to delete instances as they will die when the application that created them ends.**

To delete our category and counters, we would again use the `PerformanceCounterCategory` class:

```
If PerformanceCounterCategory.Exists("Wrox Counters") Then
    PerformanceCounterCategory.Delete("Wrox Counters")
End If
```

First, we call the `Exists` method of the `PerformanceCounterCategory` class to be sure that the category that we want to delete actually exists. If we tried to delete a category that does not exist, an exception would be thrown. Then, we simply need to call the `Delete` method, specifying the name of the category we wish to delete, and it is deleted. We can only delete user-created performance categories using this method. If you try to delete a system category, then again an exception will be generated.

Deleting Performance Counters and Categories using Visual Studio .NET

Once again Visual Studio .NET makes our job easier by providing a quick and easy way for us to delete our categories. Simply return to the Server Explorer and right-click on the name of the category you with to delete and you will see a menu like this:

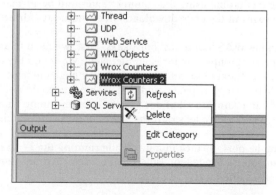

Click the **Delete** option and the category, including all the counters, will be deleted.

Using Custom Counters with Default Counters

In the previous examples, we used the idea of tracking orders for an online store using Performance Counters, but there are many other ways that custom performance counters can be used to help us monitor the performance of our ASP.NET applications.

One of the best applications of custom performance counters is being able to display business logic side-by-side with system performance data. Let's say we have an order entry web application that allows a user to enter orders, search on the orders, and run reports on the orders. This application has been live for a couple of weeks and we have started to get complaints from our customers that the application is running very slowly. The first thing we do is to check our system performance counters, and we see that the processor is at 90% a large amount of the time. Now, a couple of different things could be contributing to the processor being maxed out. We can first check the ASP.NET system-based application counters for things like Requests/Sec, Transactions/Sec, and so on. Assuming that we do not find the problem there then we know that the problem is somewhere in our code or business logic, but we really don't know where to start. This is where Custom Counters come into play.

The first thing we should do is create three custom per-second counters:

❑ **Orders per Second**– the number of orders entered per second from our applications.

❑ **Searches per Second** – the number of searches performed every second.

❑ **Reports per Second** – the number of reports generated each second.

Using these counters, we will be able to try and find a correspondence between our processor usage and the particular use of a certain function in our application. (Use the addcounters.aspx file in the test2 directory of the code download to create these counters.)

To demonstrate this, let's look at three separate files (report.aspx, search.aspx, and order.aspx), which are included in the code download, one for each of the counters above. Each page increments the counter by 5, and one of the pages also does a five hundred thousand count Response.Write loop (which actually does not take as long as one might think). This page is the culprit of our performance issues and we need to figure that out using the counter values and performance monitor information. (You can also find these pages in the code download under the test2 directory.)

The next step is to set up the WAS tool to test our pages. First, we need to add our three pages to the tool and create three separate groups, one for each file. Next, we set up the tool to hit the search page the most, the reports page the next most, and the order entry page the least. The reason for this to best simulate how users would be using the pages, and that each page would not be used evenly. Now, let's start the Performance Monitor and add all of our custom counters along with the % Processor Time counter. With everything ready to go, let's start the WAS tool test and watch the performance counter.

Here are the results from the performance monitor while running the WAS tool test and monitoring our three custom counters and the % Processor Time counter. This first image has the Orders per Second counter highlighted (the bold line):

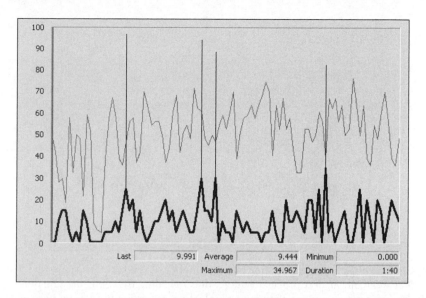

| Last | 9.991 | Average | 9.444 | Minimum | 0.000 |
| Maximum | | | 34.967 | Duration | 1:40 |

What we are looking for is a correlation between high traffic times for the orders (the thick line) and the high processor times (the top line). The four vertical lines on the image were added to show the highest order traffic times, and you can see that these do not correspond with the times where usage of our processor was highest. So, we know that the adding of orders is not our system hog. Next, let's check out the graph with the search counter highlighted (remember, we're comparing it to the top line, the processor usage):

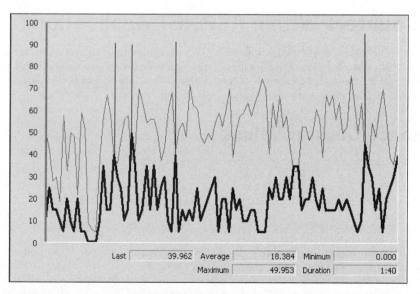

| Last | 39.962 | Average | 18.384 | Minimum | 0.000 |
| Maximum | | | 49.953 | Duration | 1:40 |

I have once again drawn four lines, and again there does not seem to be a correlation between the number of searches and our peak processor usage times. Even though we set up the search page to be the most frequently hit, it is still not our culprit. So, let's take a look at the reports counter:

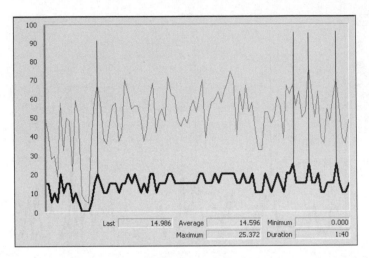

This time, the four lines that represent our highest number of reports per second directly match up to the points that show our highest processor usage, thus revealing the reporting function as the processor hog. With this information, we can then take a look at the reporting process and better optimize the business logic surrounding it. While this example is somewhat simplified, hopefully it demonstrates the power of custom performance counters in diagnosing performance issues. This is just one of the many uses for custom performance counters, and hopefully you will find many more in your ASP.NET applications.

Using Counters Within ASP.NET Applications

In this section, we are going to discuss how to view and make use performance counter data collected from our ASP.NET applications. First, we are going to go over the different values that a performance counter has, and how we can access each of these values. Then, we will walk through creating a complete performance monitor to demonstrate using this information.

Performance Counter Values

Performance counters have a number of different types of value that we can use:

- **Raw Value** – the raw value of a counter is the current value of the counter at that exact instance in time, and no calculations have been performed on it. The raw value of the counter is, as you can imagine, very inconsistent and a single reading of this value will not give you a very good idea of the overall performance state of the object you are measuring.

- **Calculated Value** – this value is calculated by taking multiple raw data points and returning a single, more relevant value. The value will also have any counter-specific calculations performed on it. This value is fairly accurate for the exact time that you call it. It is still not a good representation of overall performance for an object, but it is a step in the right direction.

- **Sampled Data Value** – sampled data is a sampling of the performance counter data. This type allows us to grab multiple samples and then use the built-in `Calculate` method to get a single value that best represents the performance of the object over the time period.

In the following sections we will go over retrieving all three types of performance data.

Retrieving Raw Data

The first type of data, which we have actually seen before, is the raw data type. Retrieving the raw data of a counter is very quick because no calculations need to be done to the data. Using the raw data value is most useful when dealing with counters that represent a running total of an object, since this value will not fluctuate like a "per second" counter will. To retrieve the raw data of a counter, all we'd have to do is to create an instance of the `PerformanceCounter` object, set the category, counter, and instance names, then read the raw value of the counter. Be sure to import the `System.Diagnostics` namespace before running this code.

```
Dim pcCounter As New PerformanceCounter()
Dim rawvalue As Integer
pcCounter.CategoryName = "ASP.NET Applications"
pcCounter.CounterName = "Errors Total"
pcCounter.InstanceName = "__Total__"
rawvalue = pcCounter.RawValue
```

This code will set the integer `rawvalue` to the total number of ASP.NET errors that have occurred for all applications running on our server. We can then either display this value or use it to send off a notification email, or other action, based on this value. Please note that when dealing with counters that are calculated as a percentage of the whole, or a per/second counter, that the raw data of the counter will not be very useful because these calculations have not been performed on the data. You will see this later in the performance monitor example.

Retrieving Calculated Data

The second type of data is the calculated value. We can retrieve this value in much the same way as the raw value. We create an instance of the `PerformanceCounter` and then set the category, counter, and instance names just like we do when retrieving the raw data value. Instead of reading the `RawValue` property, we need to call the `NextValue` method of the counter. Again, make sure to import the `System.Diagnostics` namespace before running this code.

```
Dim pcCounter As New PerformanceCounter()
Dim calcvalue As Int64
pcCounter.CategoryName = "ASP.NET Applications"
pcCounter.CounterName = "Requests/Sec"
pcCounter.InstanceName = "__Total__"
calcvalue = pcCounter.NextValue()   'Will return 0
calcvalue = pcCounter.NextValue()
```

The `NextValue` method will calculate the value of the counter at the exact instant that you call the method. Sometimes, the raw value is not in any format that you could use, for example if you're trying to measure a percentage. The calculated value would return a percentage, whereas the raw value would return a relatively meaningless number. This is much better than the raw value, but it's not as complete as sampled data. Also, the first time we call the method it will return 0, so we will need to call it twice to get the calculated value that we want.

Retrieving Sampled Data

The third and last type of data we can retrieve is the sampled data value. This value is based on a sampling of the counter data, and for many counters represents the most accurate view of the data, because it uses multiple readings to generate a more relevant average reading. Unlike the other two data types, the way to do this is to retrieve two separate sampled data values and then use the Calculate method to give us the sample value. As always, import the System.Diagnostics namespace before running this code.

First we create our variables:

```
Dim sample1 As CounterSample
Dim sample2 As CounterSample
Dim sampvalue As Single
```

Then, we create our PerformanceCounter object and set the category, counter, and instance names just like when we retrieved the raw and calculated data values:

```
Dim pcCounter As New PerformanceCounter()
pcCounter.CategoryName = "ASP.NET Applications"
pcCounter.CounterName = "Request/Sec"
pcCounter.InstanceName = "__Total__"
```

Next, we retrieve a sample value and assign it to one of our variables:

```
sample1 = pcCounter.NextSample()
```

Then, we pause our application for 1 second using the Thread.Sleep method:

```
System.Threading.Thread.Sleep(1000)
```

Then, we set our second sample value with a new sample from the performance counter:

```
sample2 = pcCounter.NextSample()
```

Now that we have both of our samples, we need to use the Calculate method to create our final data value:

```
Sampvalue = CounterSample.Calculate(sample1, sample2)
```

This method of performance data retrieval is the slowest of all the methods, but it provides the most realistic and accurate look at the performance counter data.

Creating a Performance Monitor

Now that we know how to retrieve the various types of data from a performance counter, let's walk through creating an online real-time performance monitor. This application will demonstrate how to retrieve a list of categories, counters for those categories, and instances for those counters, as well as a demonstration of the different values associated with a performance counter. The following code is all available in the code download in the file called perfmonvb.aspx.

First, let's take a look at the HTML and web controls that we will be using:

```
<%@ Page language="VB.NET" %>
<%@ import Namespace="System.Diagnostics" %>
<!DOCTYPE HTML PUBLIC "-//W3C//DTD HTML 4.0 Transitional//EN" >
<html>
  <head>
    <title>Performance Monitor</title>
  </head>
  <body>
    <form id="Form1" method="post" runat="server">
      <P>Category:
      <asp:dropdownlist id="ddlCategories" runat="server"
                        AutoPostBack="True" Width="208px"></asp:dropdownlist></P>
      <P>Counter:  
      <asp:dropdownlist id="ddlCounters" runat="server"
                        Width="207px"></asp:dropdownlist></P>
      <P>Instance: 
      <asp:dropdownlist id="ddlInstances" runat="server"
                        Width="208px"></asp:dropdownlist></P>
      <P>
      <asp:button id="btnAddOrder" runat="server" Width="48px"
                  Text="Read"></asp:button></P>
      <P>Raw Data:
      <asp:Label id="lblRaw" runat="server"></asp:Label></P>
      <P>Calculated:
      <asp:Label id="lblCalc" runat="server"></asp:Label></P>
      <P>Sampled:
      <asp:label id="lblSample" runat="server" Width="78px"></asp:label></P>
    </form>
  </body>
</html>
```

First, you will see that we are importing the `System.Diagnostics` namespace, as this namespace contains all of the performance counter classes that we will be using. We will be using three drop-down lists to contain our categories, counters, and instances. We have named these controls respectively: `ddlCategories`, `ddlCounters`, and `ddlInstances`. Please note that we have set `AutoPostBack="true"` on `ddlCategories` so that when we select the category the page will postback and we can populate the counter and instance drop-down lists. We have then added a simple button control to initiate the reading of the performance data. Next, you will see that we have added three label controls to hold the values of the three types of counter data: Raw, Calculated, and Sampled Data.

What we are going to do is first populate the `ddlCategories` drop-down list with all of the available categories on the host system. When the user selects the category that they want to view data about, the page will post back and the counters and instances drop-down lists will be populated with the counters and instances for that category. When the user has selected the counter and instance that they want to see data for and clicks the **Read** button, we will populate the three labels with the appropriate pieces of data from that counter.

Let's take a look at the `Page_Load` event, where we will be loading our categories.

```
Sub Page_Load(sender As Object, e As EventArgs)
  If Not Page.IsPostBack
    ddlCategories.DataTextField = "CategoryName"
    ddlCategories.DataSource = PerformanceCounterCategory.GetCategories()
    ddlCategories.DataBind()
    Dim liItem As ListItem
    liItem = New ListItem("Select", "000")
    ddlCategories.Items.Insert(0, liItem)
  End If
End Sub
```

First, we are checking to make sure that it is not a postback, since we only need to load the list of categories on the first load of the page. After we are sure that it is not a postback, we set the `DateTextField` property of the `ddlCategories` drop-down list to `CategoryName`. Once we have this value set, we are going to set the `DataSource` of the drop-down list to the list of categories on the system. We do that with this line of code:

```
ddlCategories.DataSource = PerformanceCounterCategory.GetCategories()
```

The `GetCategories` method of the `PerformanceCounterCategory` class returns us an array of all the categories available on the system, which we can then databind to and populate our drop-down list. Next we create a new `ListItem` and assign it the string values of `"select"` and `"000"`, then add the list item to our drop-down list. If you pulled the page up at this point, you would see all the counter categories available on your web server populated in the drop-down list.

The next step will be populating the other two drop-down lists based on the selection of the categories list. To do that, we are going to create a `SelectedIndexChanged` event for the `ddlCategories` drop-down list:

```
Sub ddlCategories_SelectedIndexChanged(sender As Object, e As EventArgs)
  Dim sCat As String
  Dim pcCats As PerformanceCounterCategory
  sCat = ddlCategories.SelectedItem.Value.ToString()
  pcCats = New PerformanceCounterCategory(sCat)
  ddlCounters.DataTextField = "CounterName"
  ddlCounters.DataSource = pcCats.GetCounters("")
  ddlCounters.DataBind()

  ddlInstances.DataSource = pcCats.GetInstanceNames()
  ddlInstances.DataBind()

  Dim liItem As ListItem
  liItem = New ListItem("Select", "000")
  ddlCounters.Items.Insert(0, liItem)
  ddlInstances.Items.Insert(0, liItem)
End Sub
```

Let's look at this code a little closer:

```
Dim sCat As String
Dim pcCats As PerformanceCounterCategory
sCat = ddlCategories.SelectedItem.Value.ToString()
pcCats = New PerformanceCounterCategory(sCat)
```

The first thing we do is create the two variables we are going to use. A string to hold the category name, and a `PerformanceCounterCategory` to generate our counters and instances lists for our drop-downs. Then we assign the name of the category selected in the drop-down list to the `sCat` variable. Using that string, we assign `pcCats` to a new `PerformanceCounterCategory`.

Our next step is binding the counters to the `ddlCounters` drop-down list, which we do with these lines of code:

```
ddlCounters.DataTextField = "CounterName"
ddlCounters.DataSource = pcCats.GetCounters("")
ddlCounters.DataBind()
```

We use the `GetCounters` method of the `PerformanceCounterCategory` class which creates an array of counters for us to databind to. Take note that we must provide a blank string to get all of the counters; you could optionally leave this blank (with no string at all, rather than with a blank string) if you only wanted counters which have no instances attached to them. You could also add the name of an instance like `GetCounters("_total_")` to receive only counters that have that instance attached to them. We are going to leave this blank as we want all the counters for that category, regardless of what instances the counter has.

Next we will need to get the instances available for that category:

```
ddlInstances.DataSource = pcCats.GetInstanceNames()
ddlInstances.DataBind()
```

We again use a method of the `PerformanceCounterCategory` class, but this time we use the `GetInstanceNames` method to return us a list of the instances available within this category. The last lines of code simply add extra items to the counters to provide starting places for the drop-down lists, as otherwise they would default to the first item. If you run this code you will find that when you select the category, the counters drop-down list and the instances drop-down list are fully populated with the correct counters and instances.

Our next step will be to wire up the **Read** button and read from our performance counter. First, we will start by creating our subroutine and declaring some variables:

```
Sub btnAddOrder_Click(sender As Object, e As EventArgs)

    Dim sCat As String
    Dim sCount As String
    Dim sInstance As String
    Dim pcCounter As PerformanceCounter
    Dim sample1 As CounterSample
    Dim sample2 As CounterSample
```

Our next step will be to assign our string variables to the selected values of their respective drop-down lists:

```
sCat = ddlCategories.SelectedItem.Value.ToString()
sCount = ddlCounters.SelectedItem.Value.ToString()
sInstance = ddlInstances.SelectedItem.Value.ToString()
```

Since some categories don't use instances we need to check and see if an instance has been selected or not. To do that we simply check whether the string is equal to "000" (the value of the items that we added to be the default selection for our drop downs).

```
If sInstance <> "000" Then
    pcCounter = New PerformanceCounter(sCat, sCount, sInstance)
Else
    pcCounter = New PerformanceCounter(sCat, sCount)
End If
```

We check to see if the value is not "000" and if not then we assign a new `PerformanceCounter` to our variable using the category, counter, and instance names. If the value is "000", then we assign a `PerformanceCounter` just using the category and counter names.

Next, we will start assigning values to our label controls:

```
lblRaw.Text = pcCounter.RawValue.ToString()
```

First, we assign the `Raw` value of the counter to the `1Raw` label. Next, we will assign the calculated value:

```
pcCounter.NextValue()
lblCalc.Text = pcCounter.NextValue().ToString()
```

Here we call the `NextValue` method of the `PerformanceCounter` class, then we call it again and assign that value to the `1Calc` label. Lastly, we need to assign the sample value:

```
sample1 = pcCounter.NextSample()
System.Threading.Thread.Sleep(1000)
sample2 = pcCounter.NextSample()
lblSample.Text = CounterSample.Calculate(sample1, Sample2)
End Sub
```

Here we call the `NextSample` method and assign the value to the first variable. Then we pause the thread for one second (1000 milliseconds), and then call the `NextSample` method again. Using the `CounterSample.Calculate` method, we then generate the sampled data value and assign it to our `1Sample` label.

When the user presses the **Read** button, all three labels will be populated with the correct performance counter data, as you can see in the following screenshot.

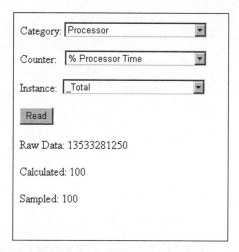

As you can see in the figure, the different data types can sometimes return very different results. In this case, the raw value for the processor seems to be a very large number, before it's been manipulated and calculated to be shown as a percentage. It is not until we view the calculated and sampled data that we can see that the processor was at 100% usage. We could not get this information from the raw data alone without performing our own calculations.

The last thing we will do with this example is add some helpful descriptions to the application. Both the category and counter classes have help strings attached to them that we are going to show to the user. The first thing we need to do is edit our HTML to add two label controls:

```
<form id="Form1" method="post" runat="server">
  <p>
  Category:
  <asp:dropdownlist id="ddlCategories" runat="server" Width="208px"
                    AutoPostBack="True"
                    OnSelectedIndexChanged="ddlCategories_SelectedIndexChanged">
  </asp:dropdownlist>
  </p>
  <p>
  <asp:Label id="lblHelp" runat="server" Width="348px">Label</asp:Label>
  </p>
  <p>
  Counter:  
  <asp:dropdownlist id="ddlCounters" runat="server"
                    Width="207px"></asp:dropdownlist>
  </p>
  <p>
  Instance: 
  <asp:dropdownlist id="ddlInstances" runat="server"
                    Width="208px"></asp:dropdownlist>
  </p>
  <p>
  <asp:button id="btnAddOrder" onclick="btnAddOrder_Click" runat="server"
              Width="48px" Text="Read"></asp:button>
  </p>
```

```
        <p>
        <asp:Label id="lblHelp2" runat="server" Width="346px">Label</asp:Label>
        </p>
        <p>
        Raw Data:
        <asp:Label id="lblRaw" runat="server"></asp:Label>
        </p>
        <p>
        Calculated:
        <asp:Label id="lblCalc" runat="server"></asp:Label>
        </p>
        <p>
        Sampled:
        <asp:label id="lblSample" runat="server" Width="78px"></asp:label>
        </p>
    </form>
```

Now that we have the controls that will be holding this information, all we need to do is add a couple of lines to our existing code. The first thing we will change is the categories DropDownList's SelectedIndexChanged event:

```
Sub ddlCategories_SelectedIndexChanged(sender As Object, e As EventArgs)

  ...

  Dim liItem As ListItem
  liItem = New ListItem("Select", "000")
  ddlCounters.Items.Insert(0, liItem)
  ddlInstances.Items.Insert(0, liItem)
  lblHelp.Text = pcCats.CategoryHelp
End Sub
```

The line we added will take the CategoryHelp value and assign it to our label. Next, we will need to do the same for the counter value. This time, we will populate the label when the user clicks the **Read** button, so we will be editing the **Read** button's click event:

```
Sub btnAddOrder_Click(sender As Object, e As EventArgs)

   ...

  sample1 = pcCounter.NextSample()
  System.Threading.Thread.Sleep(1000)
  sample2 = pcCounter.NextSample()
  lblSample.Text = CounterSample.Calculate(sample1, Sample2)
  lblHelp2.Text = pcCounter.CounterHelp
End Sub
```

Again, we only need one line to populate the label with the CounterHelp information. When the user selects the category, they will see the help appear for them, and when they click the **Read** button they will see the help for the counter appear. To see our results take a look at this figure:

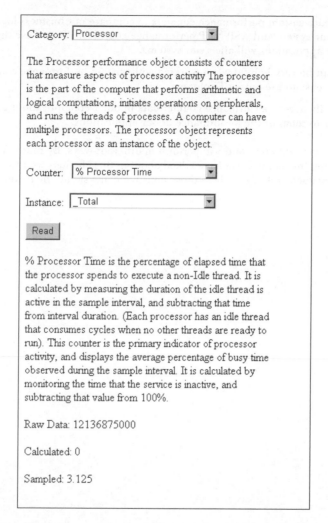

If you wanted, you could go on to use `System.Drawing` or one of the charting and graphing components available to make this a fully operational Performance Monitor, but that is out of the scope of this book.

Summary

Monitoring the performance of our applications is essential to providing a good user experience. Throughout this chapter, we have looked at various methods of monitoring the performance of our applications. Let's take a quick look at what we have discovered:

❑   There are a large number of counters installed with ASP.NET and the .NET Framework that we can use to monitor both the performance of our application and server.

❑　We can create custom performance counters to compare our business logic metrics side by side with our system and ASP.NET performance counters. We can use this to get a better idea of how our applications will affect our systems.

❑　VS.NET can be very helpful when working with custom performance counters by providing us with the easy-to-use Server Explorer.

❑　We can easily access performance counter data in our web applications and use them to create better ways to monitor the performance of our applications.

Every application is very different and will perform in different ways. By monitoring the performance of our applications using the methods we have talked about in this chapter, we can determine if improvements are needed and, if so, where those improvements should be made.

Performance Counters

When ASP.NET is installed on a server it also installs a number of very helpful performance counters. We can use these counters to monitor and tweak the performance of both our applications and servers. Performance counters are essentially objects of the moment, as they do not keep a history or store lots of data. They simply store the last bit of data for the object they are tracking. We can overcome this by using the logging and database features of the performance monitor to track the values of performance counters, and with this data we can monitor and optimize our applications.

System-Based Performance Counters

System-based counters can be found under the ASP.NET category. These are counters that track global metrics, as opposed to counters that track application-specific numbers.

Application Restarts

This counter is incremented each time the Application_OnEnd event is fired. This value will be reset when the web server, or the IIS service, is restarted. This counter represents the total number of application restarts while the service has been running.

Application Running

This is the total number of applications currently running on the web server. This counter will be most useful to shared hosting administrators.

Requests Disconnected

This represents the number of requests that have been disconnected. It is useful to monitor this value because these are requests that are disconnected due to some sort of communications failure, or the user terminating the connection.

Requests Queued

This is the number of requests waiting to be executed on the server.

Requests Rejected

This represents the number of requests that have been rejected, resulting in 503 HTTP errors being returned. A 503 error code is returned when the server is too busy to process the request.

Request Wait Time

This is the amount of time in milliseconds that the most recent request waited to be processed.

State Server Counters

These counters are only available when the `aspnet_state` service is running on your web server. If you are not sure if this service is running, then simply open the Services console from Administration Tools and check the status of the service. These counters represent the sessions that are being handled by ASP.NET, not the total sessions of your web service.

State Server Sessions Abandoned

This is the number of sessions that have been abandoned by the user, meaning that the user explicitly closed the browser or navigated to another site.

State Server Sessions Active

This represents the number of current active sessions on your server. This number is a good measurement of the number of current users you have on your site at any given time.

State Server Sessions Timed Out

This is the number of sessions that have timed out due to user inactivity.

State Server Sessions Total

This is the total number of sessions that have been created in the lifetime of the process. This value should equal the sum of the abandoned, active, and timed out values.

Worker Process Restarts

This is the number of times the worker process has restarted on the server. The worker process is the process that handles all of the ASP.NET requests, and you will see it running on your system as the `aspnet_wp.exe` file.

Worker Process Running

This is the number of worker processes running on the server.

Application Based Performance Counters

The application-based performance counters can be found under the ASP.NET Applications category. These counters track more application-specific objects.

Anonymous Requests

This is the total number of ASP.NET requests that are using anonymous authentication.

Anonymous Request/Sec

This represents the number of ASP.NET requests per second that are using anonymous authentication.

Cache Total Entries

This is the combined total of cache entries for both internal caching done by ASP.NET, and caching exposed through external APIs.

Cache Total Hits

This is the combined total of cache hits for both internal caching done by ASP.NET and caching exposed through external APIs. A hit is when an object is looked for and found in the cache.

Cache Total Misses

This represents the combined total of cache misses for both internal caching done by ASP.NET, and caching exposed through external APIs. A miss is when an object is searched for and not found in the cache.

Cache Total Hit Ratio

This represents the hit to miss ratio of cache access for both internal caching done by ASP.NET, and caching exposed through external APIs.

Cache Total Turnover Rate

This value represents the total number of additions and subtractions from the cache per second. If items are frequently being added and removed, then the cache is not being used efficiently.

Cache API Entries

This is the total number of cache entries in the application cache.

Cache API Hits

This is the total number of cache hits accessed through the external cache APIs. This does not include items cached internally by ASP.NET.

Cache API Misses

This represents the total number of cache misses accessed through the external cache APIs. This does not include items cached internally by ASP.NET.

Cache API Hit Ratio

This is the ratio of cache hits to misses accessed through the external cache APIs. This does not include items cached internally by ASP.NET.

Cache API Turnover Rate

This represents the number of additions and subtractions to the cache each second when it is being used through the external cache APIs. This does not include items cached internally by ASP.NET.

Compilations Total

This counter shows the total number of compilations that have taken place in the current lifetime of the web server process. Compilation takes place the first time an `.aspx`, `.asmx`, `.ascx`, `.ashx`, or code-behind file is accessed and the application is dynamically compiled.

Debugging Requests

This is the total number of debugging requests that have occurred.

Errors During Preprocessing

This is the total number of errors that have occurred during parsing and configuration.

Errors During Compilation

This represents the total number of errors that have occurred during the compilation of ASP.NET pages or controls.

Errors During Execution

This is the total number of errors that have occurred during the execution of the request.

Errors Unhandled during Execution

This represents the total number of errors during execution that were unhandled by our code. This does not include errors that are not shown to the user and handled by a custom error, or when an error page is enabled. Errors that are cleared, or result in the user being redirected, are also not included.

Errors Unhandled During Execution/Sec

This is similar to the counter above, except recorded as a per second value.

Errors Total

This is the total number of errors that have occurred. This counter is the sum of the Preprocessing, Compilation, and Execution error counters.

Errors Total/Sec

This is similar to the counter above, except recorded as a per second value.

Output Cache Entries

This is the current number of entries in the output cache.

Output Cache Hits

This is the number of cache hits for items in the output cache.

Output Cache Misses

This is the number of cache misses for items in the output cache.

Output Cache Hit Ratio

This is the ration of hits to requests for the output cache.

Output Cache Turnover Rate

This is the number of additions and subtractions from the output cache per second.

Pipeline Instance Count

This is the total number of active pipeline instances. A pipeline instance represents a single concurrent connection to the application.

Request Bytes in Total

This is the total size of all requests.

Request Bytes out Total

This is the total size of all responses to the users, not including the standard http header responses.

Request Executing

This is the total number of requests that are currently executing.

Requests Failed

This is the total number of failed requests. It does not include requests that are rejected, as that is done by IIS and cannot be recorded by ASP.NET

Requests Not Found

This is the number of requests that failed due to the page or resource not being found. Results in a 404 or 414 error being returned to the user.

Requests Not Authorized

This is the number of requests that failed due to lack of authorization, resulting in a 401 error being returned to the user.

Requests Succeeded

This is the number of requests that have been successfully executed.

Requests Timed Out

This is the number of requests that have timed out.

Requests Total

This is the total number of requests that have been processed since the start of the service.

Requests/Sec

This is similar to the above counter, except reported as a per second value.

Sessions Active

This is the current number of sessions active on the server.

Sessions Abandoned

This is the number of sessions that have been explicitly abandoned.

Sessions Timed Out

This is the number of sessions that have timed out.

Sessions Total

This is the total number of sessions since the application was started.

Transactions Aborted

This is the number of aborted transactions.

Transactions Committed

This is the total number of committed transactions.

Transactions Pending

This is the total number of transactions currently pending.

Transactions Total

This is the total number of transactions since the server was started.

Transactions/Sec

This is the total number of transactions started per second.

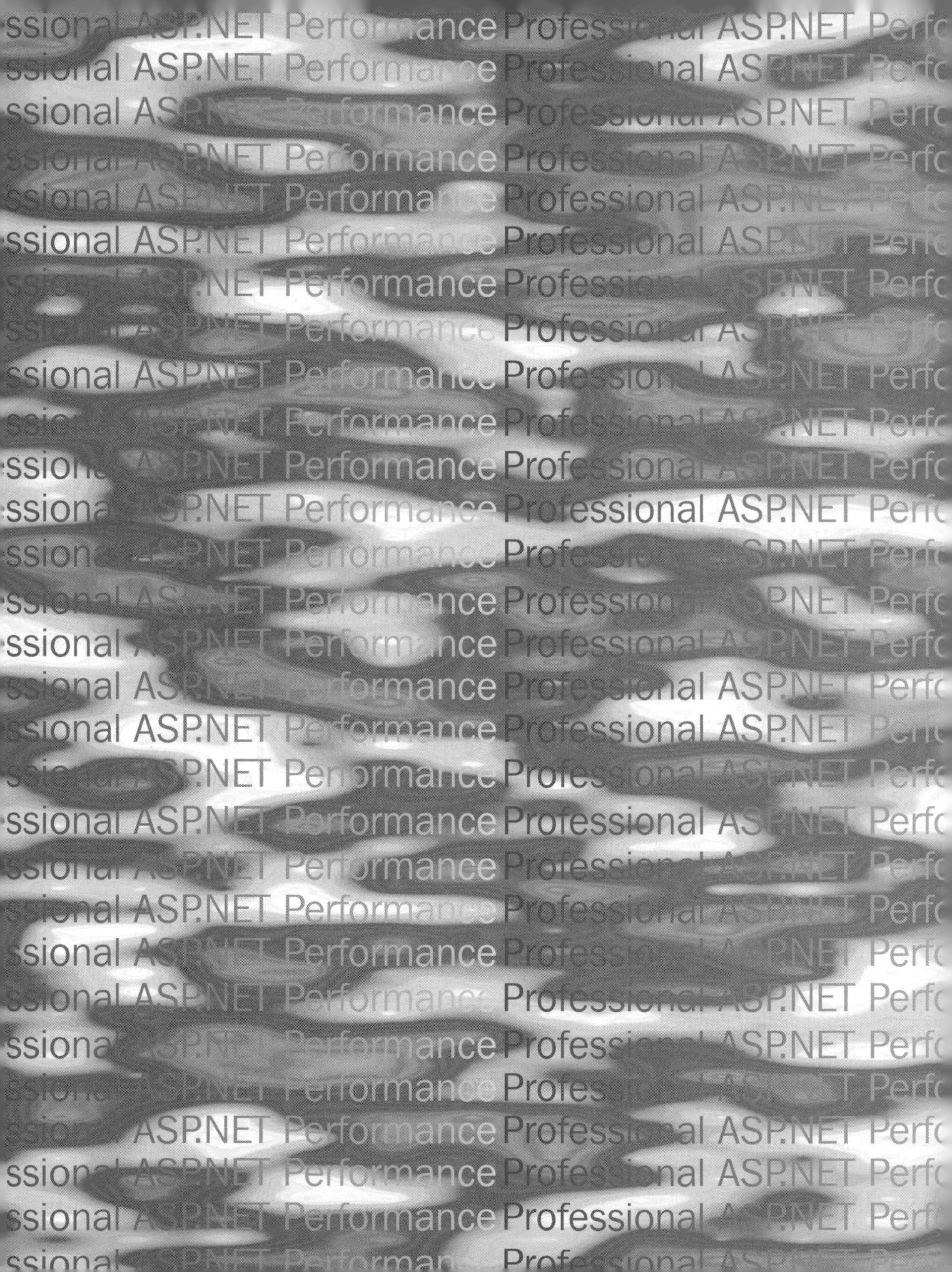
Professional ASP.NET Performance

Index

A Guide to the Index

The index is arranged hierarchically, in alphabetical order, with symbols preceding the letter A. Most second-level entries and many third-level entries also occur as first-level entries. This is to ensure that users will find the information they require however they choose to search for it.

T

Notes

Notes

Notes

Notes

ASP Today

The daily knowledge site for professional ASP programmer

ASPToday brings the essence of the Wrox Programmer to Programmer philosophy to you through the web. Every working day, www.asptoday.com delivers a new, original article by ASP pr grammers for ASP programmers.

Want to know about Classic ASP, ASP.NET, Performance, Data Access, Site Design, SQL Server, and more? Then visit us. You can make sure that you don't miss a thing by subscribing to our free daily e-mail updates featuring ASPToday highlights and tips.

By bringing you daily articles written by real programmers, ASPToday is an indispensable resource for quickly finding out exactly what you need. ASPToday is THE daily knowledge site f professional ASP programmers.

In addition to our free weekly and monthly articles, ASPToday also includes a premier subscription service. You can now join the growing number of ASPToday subscribers who benefit from access to:

- Daily in-depth articles
- Code-heavy demonstrations of real applications
- Access to the ASPToday Living Book, our collection of past articles
- ASP reference material
- Fully searchable index and advanced search engine
- Tips and tricks for professionals

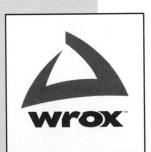

Visit ASPToday at: www.asptoday.cor

C# Today

The daily knowledge site for professional C# programmers

C#Today provides you with a weekly in-depth case study, giving you solutions to real-world problems that are relevant to your career. Each one is written by a leading professional, meaning that you benefit from their expertise and get the skills that you need to thrive in the C# world. As well as a weekly case study, we also offer you access to our huge archive of quality articles, which cover every aspect of the C# language. www.csharptoday.com

C#Today has built up an archive of over 170 articles, in which top authors like Kaushal Sanghavi, Matthew Reynolds and Richard Conway have tackled topics ranging from thread pooling and .Net serialization to multi-threaded search engines, UDDI, and advanced techniques for inter-thread communication.

By joining the growing number of C#Today subscribers, you get access to:

- a weekly in-depth case study
- code heavy demonstration of real world applications
- access to an archive of over 170 articles
- C# reference material
- a fully searchable index

wrox

Visit C#Today at: www.csharptoday.com

p2p.wrox.com
The programmer's resource centre

A unique free service from Wrox Pres
With the aim of helping programmers to help each oth

Wrox Press aims to provide timely and practical information to today's programmer. P2
is a list server offering a host of targeted mailing lists where you can share knowledg
with four fellow programmers and find solutions to your problems. Whatever the level
your programming knowledge, and whatever technology you use P2P can provide you
the information you need.

ASP
Support for beginners and professionals, including a resource page with hundreds of links,
and a popular ASP.NET mailing list.

DATABASES
For database programmers, offering support on SQL Server, mySQL, and Oracle.

MOBILE
Software development for the mobile market is growing rapidly. We provide lists for
the several current standards, including WAP, Windows CE, and Symbian.

JAVA
A complete set of Java lists, covering beginners, professionals, and server-side programme
(including JSP, servlets and EJBs)

.NET
Microsoft's new OS platform, covering topics such as ASP.NET, C#, and general
.NET discussion.

VISUAL BASIC
Covers all aspects of VB programming, from programming Office macros to creating
components for the .NET platform.

WEB DESIGN
As web page requirements become more complex, programmer's are taking a more import
role in creating web sites. For these programmers, we offer lists covering technologies suc
Flash, Coldfusion, and JavaScript.

XML
Covering all aspects of XML, including XSLT and schemas.

OPEN SOURCE
Many Open Source topics covered including PHP, Apache, Perl, Linux, Python and more.

FOREIGN LANGUAGE
Several lists dedicated to Spanish and German speaking programmers, categories include
NET, Java, XML, PHP and XML

How to subscribe:
Simply visit the P2P site, at http://p2p.wrox.com

Got more Wrox books than you can carry around?

Wroxbase is the new online service from Wrox Press. Dedicated to providing online access to books published by Wrox Press, helping you and your team find solutions and guidance for all your programming needs.

The key features of this service will be:

- Different libraries based on technologies that you use everyday (ASP 3.0, XML, SQL 2000, etc.). The initial set of libraries will be focused on Microsoft-related technologies.
- You can subscribe to as few or as many libraries as you require, and access all books within those libraries as and when you need to.
- You can add notes (either just for yourself or for anyone to view) and your own bookmarks that will all be stored within your account online, and so will be accessible from any computer.
- You can download the code of any book in your library directly from Wroxbase

Visit the site at: www.wroxbase.com

Register your book on Wrox.com!

When you download this book's code from wrox.com, you will have the option to register.

What are the benefits of registering?

- You will receive updates about your book
- You will be informed of new editions, and will be able to benefit from special offers
- You became a member of the "Wrox Developer Community", giving you exclusive access to free documents from Wrox Press
- You can select from various newsletters you may want to receive

Registration is easy and only needs to be done once. After that, when you download code books after logging in, you will be registered automatically.

Just go to www.wrox.com

wrox

Programmer to Programmer™

Registration Code: 75580V7L0DR4W701

Wrox writes books for you. Any suggestions, or ideas about how you want information given in your ideal book will be studied by our team. Your comments are always valued at Wrox.

Free phone in USA 800-USE-WROX
Fax (312) 893 8001

UK Tel.: (0121) 687 4100   Fax: (0121) 687 4101

Professional ASP .NET Performance – Registration Card

Name _____

Address _____

_____

_____

City _____ State/Region _____

Country _____ Postcode/Zip _____

E-Mail _____

Occupation _____

How did you hear about this book?

❑ Book review (name) _____

❑ Advertisement (name) _____

❑ Recommendation _____

❑ Catalog _____

❑ Other _____

Where did you buy this book?

❑ Bookstore (name) _____ City _____

❑ Computer store (name) _____

❑ Mail order _____

❑ Other _____

What influenced you in the purchase of this book?

❑ Cover Design ❑ Contents ❑ Other (please specify):

_____

How did you rate the overall content of this book?

❑ Excellent ❑ Good ❑ Average ❑ Poor

What did you find most useful about this book? _____

_____

What did you find least useful about this book? _____

_____

Please add any additional comments. _____

_____

What other subjects will you buy a computer book on soon?

_____

What is the best computer book you have used this year?

_____

Note: This information will only be used to keep you updated about new Wrox Press titles and will not be used for any other purpose or passed to any other third party.

wrox

Programmer to Programmer™

Note: If you post the bounce back card below in the UK, please send it to:

Wrox Press Limited, Arden House, 1102 Warwick Road,
Acocks Green, Birmingham B27 6HB. UK.

Computer Book Publishers

NO POSTAGE
NECESSARY
IF MAILED
IN THE
UNITED STATES

BUSINESS REPLY MAIL

FIRST CLASS MAIL   PERMIT#64   CHICAGO, IL

POSTAGE WILL BE PAID BY ADDRESSEE

WROX PRESS INC.,
29 S. LA SALLE ST.,
SUITE 520
CHICAGO IL 60603-USA